FUNDAMENTALS *of* E-BUSINESS

CUSTOM EDITION

Taken from:
Foundations of E-Commerce
Effy Oz

D1451278

Taken from:

Foundations of E-Commerce, Fourth Edition
by Effy Oz
Copyright © 2002 by Pearson Education, Inc.
Published by Prentice Hall
Upper Saddle River, New Jersey 07458

This special edition published in cooperation with Pearson Custom Publishing.

Printed in the United States of America

10 9 8 7 6 5 4

ISBN 0-536-81383-3

2005160671

AP

Please visit our web site at *www.pearsoncustom.com*

PEARSON CUSTOM PUBLISHING
75 Arlington Street, Suite 300, Boston, MA 02116
A Pearson Education Company

ABOUT THE AUTHOR

Effy Oz received a Bachelor of Arts degree in economics and statistics and a Master of Business Administration from the Hebrew University of Jerusalem, then received a doctorate in Management Information Systems from Boston University. For 11 years Dr. Oz served as an executive for a large aerospace corporation and as the controller of a small company. His practical experience includes financial management, project management, cost accounting, inventory planning, contract administration and negotiation, development of information systems, and strategic planning.

Dr. Oz has served on the faculties of Boston University, Boston College, Wayne State University, and Pennsylvania State University, where he now serves as an associate professor of management science and information systems. He is the author of five books and numerous articles in academic and professional journals, including *MIS Quarterly, Communications of the ACM, Decision Sciences, Information & Management, Omega, Journal of Systems Management, Journal of Business Ethics, Journal of Computer Information Systems,* and *Journal of Global Information Management.* Dr. Oz has been on the editorial boards of two academic journals and on the *Encyclopedia of Information Systems.* His opinions on systems integration and computer ethics have been quoted by print and television media. Dr. Oz is a frequent speaker before corporate and professional groups.

In 1997, the Information Systems Section of the American Accounting Association awarded Dr. Oz the Notable Contribution to the Information Systems Literature Award. In 2000, his campus colleagues awarded him the Distinguished Research Award.

In April 2000, Dr. Oz co-founded 2ce, Inc., a software company that specializes in development of three-dimensional Web browsers. Until February 2001 he served as the company's CIO and CFO.

Dr. Oz is married and has four children. His favorite leisure activities include racquetball, in-line skating, and numismatics.

BRIEF CONTENTS

CONTENTS

3 THE THREE LEVELS OF WEB SITES   38

4 WEB SOFTWARE   55

5 ESTABLISHING A WEB SITE   78

6 EDI AND THE INTERNET   106

7 BUSINESS-TO-BUSINESS: A VARIETY OF MODELS   120

8 BUSINESS-TO-CONSUMER E-COMMERCE   144

MARKETING ON THE WEB   178

10   SECURITY AND PRIVACY ISSUES   209

11   LEGAL ISSUES   240

12 E-MONEY 266

13

PREFACE

The goal of *Foundations of E-Commerce* is to provide a real-world understanding of electronic commerce: its infrastructure, business models, challenges, and promises. The book was written for business and computer science students. Observations from the past decade or so indicate that e-commerce will eventually pervade the entire global economy. Thus, the book provides students with a firm foundation of the principles of building online businesses and/or online arms of traditional businesses. The book is intended to help build successful careers—no matter what type of business students enter.

The World Wide Web has spawned tremendous changes in the economies of many nations. While stock markets may fare better or worse, the facts are simple: our economy is increasingly reliant on information systems in general, and on e-commerce in particular. Web browsers are the most popular type of software application ever. They are free, easy to use and, therefore, ubiquitous. Their universality has accelerated the rush of both consumers and businesses to the Web. Regardless of how well online businesses do on stock markets, a growing amount of the national GDP (Gross Domestic Product) of nations is passing through computer networks, mainly the Internet.

Foundations of E-Commerce takes a fresh case approach to reinforcing e-commerce principles. Each part of the book opens with a brief case or telling statistics relevant to the discussion in the chapter. In addition, at the end of each chapter, there is a case with a set of critical-thinking questions.

Foundations of E-Commerce provides students with the proper balance of technical information and real-world applications. No matter what field they undertake, students will enter the business world knowing how to harness the Internet to work for them. If they are interested in enrolling in an e-commerce program, or only in taking an e-commerce course, this book will help them understand the necessary principles of the relevant technology, business processes, and marketing.

ORGANIZATION AND APPROACH

Foundations of E-Commerce is organized into thirteen chapters, followed by a glossary, a table of measurement units, and an index. The book starts with both historical and future perspectives on the Internet, telecommunications, and basic types of Web use for commercial activities. It then proceeds with thorough discussions of Web software and the mechanics of establishing and operating a Web site. Once the student has a good grasp of what a business can do with the Web's capabilities, the book provides thorough discussions of business-to-business, business-to-consumer, and government online business. Special emphasis is given to establishment of Web sites, marketing on the Web, online payment methods, security, privacy, and legal issues. The book ends with a look into future Internet technologies and e-commerce.

Chapter 1, *The Internet: Past and Present,* provides a historical perspective of the world's largest computer network. The student can follow the development of the network as well as the organizations that constantly improve it with new standards and controls. We cover the latest initiatives, such as Internet2 and the Next Generation Internet, to prepare the student for what lies ahead.

Chapter 2, *Essentials of Telecommunications,* is a primer in telecommunications technology. Students who wish to learn about electronic commerce must have a basic understanding of the infrastructure used for online activities. The chapter introduces various network topologies, explains the TCP/IP set of protocols used on the Internet, discusses various physical communications media, clarifies the notion of Internet addresses, and concludes with business considerations in choosing telecommunications alternatives.

Chapter 3, *The Three Levels of Web Sites,* describes the three major levels of business activities on the Web: passive Web presence, mechanisms of improving offline activities, and pure play businesses that interact with clients only through the Web. The chapter provides extensive illumination of one of the most important aspects of electronic commerce, Web advertising, and explains the methods used to measure the effectiveness of such advertising. It also explains phenomena that are unique to the Web, such as cross-linking. This chapter is placed at the beginning of the book to give the student an overarching understanding of the degree to which businesses in different industries have adopted the Web. The student can then see how the Web provides much value to some companies and less value to others.

Chapter 4, *Web Software,* discusses all the current applications that make up the software infrastructure of the World Wide Web. It introduces SGML, the overarching standard for Web programming languages. The chapter explains the purpose and capabilities of HTML, XML, and Java. It covers software that allows one to interact with organizational databases through the Web as well as software for tracking Web browsing, which is important for understanding ideas discussed in subsequent chapters, such as consumer profiling. The chapter concludes with a brief discussion of the newest types of Web browsers: three-dimensional browsers.

Chapter 5, *Establishing a Web Site,* takes the student through the stages of establishing a commercial Web site, different alternatives for establishing such enterprises, relationships with Internet service providers, scalability of hardware and software of a Web site, and detailed advice for building an effective commercial site. At the end of this chapter we take a glimpse into legal challenges, which are discussed extensively in Chapter 11.

Chapter 6, *EDI and the Internet,* lays the technical ground for the most important element of online business-to-business activities: electronic data interchange. The student is made aware that electronic commerce is not a new phenomenon; it has been around for at least two decades in the form of proprietary EDI. This chapter explains how VAN EDI works and the benefits and challenges of transferring EDI onto the Web.

Chapter 7, *Business-to-Business: A Variety of Models,* is a long chapter covering a variety of business models between and among businesses. It also covers the growing presence of online business between governments and businesses and between governments and citizens. In addition to numerous examples, the chapter provides analyses of successful and unsuccessful B2B business ideas. This chapter is located before the chapter on business-to-consumer issues because despite its lower visibility, B2B has a significantly stronger impact on the economy than B2C; about eighty percent of all e-commerce is between businesses.

Chapter 8, *Business-to-Consumer E-Commerce*, emphasizes online retailing in all its forms and shapes. It extensively discusses the important elements for successful online retailing, such as branding, as well as the challenges, such as the delivery challenge and channel conflicts.

Chapter 9, *Marketing on the Web*, provides a comprehensive analysis of methods and approaches for attracting new online shoppers, turning them into buyers, then keeping them as repeat customers. There are numerous examples of how to construct effective Web pages, with an emphasis on cultural differences. The chapter also explains various affiliate marketing models, cross-linking and cross-luring, targeted marketing on the Web and through e-mail, and the metrics for measuring online marketing success. This long chapter covers a large number of topics—topics that often are the subjects of entire books.

Chapter 10, *Security and Privacy Issues*, is dedicated to two important elements of doing business on the Web: protecting Web sites against security breaches and protecting the privacy of consumers. Both have become major concerns.

Chapter 11, *Legal Issues*, explains the legal challenges posed by a commerce medium that has no political boundaries. The discussion addresses the major concerns of the digital age in general and Internet-based commerce in particular: electronic signatures, protection of intellectual property, free speech, legal restrictions on e-commerce, and legislation for privacy.

Chapter 12, *E-Money*, discusses a variety of methods for making payments through the Internet. The discussion addresses current popular means of payments such as credit, debit, and charge cards and the increasingly popular online person-to-person transfers. The chapter explains the challenges of micropayments. It emphasizes how acceptable solutions to this challenge can give e-commerce a great boost. It also discusses electronic cash and points—a method that practically creates a new form of money—and explains why the latter may have a serious impact on money markets.

Chapter 13, *The Future of E-Commerce*, takes a look into the future of e-commerce and discusses what we may expect to see five to ten years from now in terms of new Internet technologies, customer-centric manufacturing, and buying patterns.

EMPHASIS ON REALITY

This is the only e-commerce book committed to portraying the world as it is, not as we wish it to be. *Foundations of E-Commerce* does not only marvel at the Internet, but also describes and analyzes failures. Many of these failures cost investors millions of dollars. These cases provide an important educational tool.

ILLUSTRATION BY EXAMPLES

The chapters are laced with current cases of success and failure of business models on the Web. At the end of each chapter the reader finds a recent case describing technology, business models, or events relevant to the chapter's discussion. These in-chapter and end-of-chapter examples bring to life the principles discussed in each chapter. All of the examples and cases are from the year 2000 and onward.

EMPHASIS ON ETHICAL CONSIDERATION

The book puts a great emphasis on some of the questionable and controversial uses of the Internet in general and of online commerce in particular. Students are required to weigh the positive and negative impacts of the Internet and to convincingly argue their own positions on important issues such as privacy and free speech. Many questions at the end of chapters solicit the students' ethical thought and argumentation.

CURRENT REAL-WORLD CASES

Real-world cases are given as examples throughout the book. The end-of-chapter case study is included to illustrate the chapter's discussion. The case is followed by several questions designed to invoke the student's critical thinking. The questions ask not only what happened but also what the student would do differently or would do in addition to what was done.

EMPHASIS ON BUSINESS MODELS

A sound business model is imperative for the success of any business. This is doubly so on the Web, the technologies of which are, for the most part, available to all and therefore can be emulated. The text analyzes and explains what has worked and what has not worked in a variety of business models, both in business-to-business and business-to-consumer activities.

FEATURES

There are several features both in the text and at the end of each chapter:

LEARNING OBJECTIVES

Each chapter opens with the chapter's learning objectives phrased as actions that students are able to perform after reading the chapter. These objectives help students focus on the chapter's overarching issues. The instructor can measure the extent to which the students have accomplished the objectives through the Review Questions and Discussion Questions provided at the end of the chapter. The learning objectives are followed by an illustrative brief story or by statistics that should pique the student's curiosity about the chapter.

INTERESTING...

Each chapter is peppered with *Interesting...*, boxed short vignettes of anecdotes and statistics that punctuate the subject matter covered in the chapter. These information capsules may be used to illustrate a phenomenon or give a realistic perspective to a topic discussed in the chapter.

END-OF-CHAPTER MATERIAL

Each chapter ends with features to help the student review and internalize the learned material:

Summary

The summary highlights the most important points of each chapter. It is presented in a bulleted list for easy review.

Key Terms

The summary is followed by a list of key terms. These are usually the terms bold-faced in the chapter. The list helps refresh the student's memory about the most important terms and concepts of the chapter.

Review Questions

Review questions test the student's knowledge of the material discussed in the chapter. While some simply enforce the understanding of the concepts and issues, others require that the student apply this understanding to situations somewhat different from those mentioned in the chapter.

Discussion Questions

Discussion questions help students determine if they have absorbed the material in the chapter and can be used by professors to initiate discussions in the classroom. Most of these questions do not directly address the concepts and terminology detailed in the chapter, but require that the student use the knowledge gained from the material and by applying his or her own judgment to technical, business, and ethical issues.

Assignments

Learning by doing is an important element in the teaching of any subject. The assignments require students to further research a topic, critique, analyze, and make a proper presentation. Many of these assignments send students to Web sites so they can observe and analyze a real business or concept.

END-OF-BOOK MATERIAL

At the end of the book you will find the following items:

Glossary

Often an instructor or a student may run into a term and not be sure of its meaning. The glossary at the end of the book is an alphabetical list of all the terms mentioned throughout the book and their meanings.

Measurement Units

Several measurement units are used both in telecommunications and electronic commerce. Both instructors and students can turn to this list at the end of the book for help with measurement conventions.

INSTRUCTOR'S PACKAGE

Foundations of E-Commerce includes teaching tools to support professors in the classroom. These supplements are designed to enhance the accessibility, versatility, and teachability of the text material.

Instructor's Resource CD-ROM (0130969745)

The Instructor's Resource CD-ROM includes the Instructor's Manual, Test Item File, PowerPoint slides, and Test Manager.

The Instructor's Manual

This supplement, prepared by the text's author, is available on the Instructor's Resource CD-ROM and for download from the password-protected instructor's section of *www.prenhall.com/oz*. The purpose of this manual is to provide materials to help instructors make their classes not only informative but also interesting and thought-provoking. The manual offers several approaches to teaching the material, with a sample syllabus and comments on different components. For each chapter, the manual includes a chapter outline, learning objectives, lecture notes (including discussion topics), teaching tips, and solutions to Review Questions and Discussion Questions, as well as the questions following each case study.

The Test Item File and Test Manager

The test item file contains multiple-choice, true-false, and essay questions. The questions are rated by difficulty level, and answers are referenced by section. For instructor convenience, the Test Item File and Prentice-Hall Test Manager are included on the Instructor's Resource CD-ROM.

PowerPoint Presentations

Prepared by Dr. Irina Newman of the New Jersey Institute of Technology, the slides illuminate and build upon key concepts in the text. They are available to both students and instructors for download from *www.prenhall.com/oz*. They are also found on the Instructor's Resource CD-ROM.

MyPHLIP/Companion Website

There is a dedicated Web site for the text, located at *www.prenhall.com/oz*, that provides a dynamic ongoing complement and update to the book. The site includes an Interactive Study Guide for students, access to the Instructor's Manual, PowerPoint slides, and Internet links. Features of this new site include real-time news headlines and the ability to customize your home page.

Prentice Hall's Guide to E-Commerce and E-Business

This useful guide to e-business and e-commerce introduces students to many aspects of e-business and the Internet. It allows students to discover the role the Internet can play in continuing their education, distance learning, and looking for jobs. This guide is free when packaged with the Oz text.

Web Strategy Pro

Prentice Hall is pleased to offer this powerful educational version of Web Strategy Pro software. This Windows-based, easy-to-use program allows you to bring the entire process of planning an Internet strategy alive in your classroom in seven easy steps. Web Strategy Pro is not available as a stand-alone item but can be packaged with the Oz text at an additional charge. Contact your local Prentice Hall representative for more details.

Online Courses

BlackBoard *www.prenhall.com/blackboard*

Prentice Hall's on-line content, combined with BlackBoard's popular tools and interface, result in robust Web-based courses that are easy to implement, manage, and use, taking your courses to new heights in student interaction and learning.

CourseCompass *www.prenhall.com/coursecompass*

CourseCompass is a dynamic, interactive on-line course management tool powered exclusively for Pearson Education by BlackBoard. This exciting product allows you to teach market-leading Pearson Education content in an easy-to-use customizable format.

ACKNOWLEDGMENTS

Any book of this magnitude is the result of the hard work of several people, not only the author. I would first like to thank my colleagues in the IS area whose ideas and opinions over many years have helped me understand the real educational needs of our students in a new and fast changing field. I thank David Alexander for his initial interest in this project and Bob Horan, who took over and helped me complete it. My developmental editor, Trish Nealon, did a great job with both content and style suggestions.

Many thanks to Kyle Hannon for her prompt help and assistance with the text and supplements. Kyle made sure there were no loose ends in this project. Sharon Turkovich keenly captured the topical and pedagogical gist of this book for her marketing effort. Joan Waxman has done a great job in managing the media project for this book. Gail Savage provided excellent copy-editing. I appreciate her extra effort to ensure the accuracy and currency of this text, which is about a topic that is akin to a moving target. Vanessa Nuttry ensured smooth production; I thank her for her prompt help. Visual appeal and accuracy are important elements in this type of book. My thanks to Karen Quigley for the superb interior design, and Joseph DePinho for the great cover design, as well as to Proof Positive/ Farrowlyne Associates, Inc. for the highly professional graphic composition.

Reviewers are the most important resource for any writer, let alone one who prepares a textbook for college students. I would like to thank the following reviewers for their candid and constructive suggestions:

Bob August, Our Lady of the Lake University
Phillip Gordon, University of California, Berkley
James I. Gray, Florida Atlantic University
Jim Henson, Barry University
Jane Mackay, Texas Christian University
Rick Mull, Fort Lewis College
Ken Petersen, University of Oregon
Dan Sarel, University of Miami
Bindiganavale Vijayaraman, University of Akron
J. Michael Weber, Barry University
Ken Williamson, James Madison University

Lastly, I would like to thank the members of my family. Narda, my wife of 27 years, kept encouraging me while making and ensuring a comfortable environment in which I could pursue this project. My children, Sahar, Adi, Noam, and Ron, accepted my long hours typing this book rather than spending more time with them. I thank them for their patience and their belief in me.

THE INTERNET: PAST AND PRESENT

LEARNING OBJECTIVES

WHEN YOU FINISH THIS CHAPTER YOU WILL BE ABLE TO:

- Discuss the business opportunities the Internet presents
- Explain the roots of the Internet
- Compare the capabilities of today's Internet with those of tomorrow's
- List the goals of Internet organizations
- Identify the world regions where Internet use is growing

When was the Internet born? There is no date officially recognized, but rather a series of events leading to its birth. If we agree that the Internet was born when one computer talked to another for the first time, then the date is October 26, 1969. Weeks earlier, however, on September 2, 1969, a computer had communicated to a router, or a switch. Charlie Kline, a UCLA graduate student, was the first person to use a computer to log in to a remote computer. It was in 1971 that an ARPANET engineer named Ray Tomlison sent the first e-mail message. Its content: "Testing, one, two, three." (Adapted from *Infoworld*, October 4, 1999, p. 40.)

INTRODUCING THE INTERNET

The history of a technology may help put its story into realistic perspective. If you know the roots of the Internet, you will have a better idea of its promises, as well as its limitations. You will discover first, that electronic commerce is not as new a concept as many people believe, and second, that much electronic commerce has been carried out without relying on the Internet. Some of these commercial activities have been gradually integrated into the Internet.

Electronic commerce, or e-commerce, as it is popularly called, is not a new phenomenon. It has been around for at least three decades. The forerunners of today's Internet-based e-commerce were electronic fund transfer (EFT) and electronic data interchange (EDI). Banks have used their own telecommunications networks or leased communications lines since the early 1960s to transfer funds electronically from one branch to another and from one bank to another. This may be regarded as the earliest use of commerce executed by means of electronic data transferred through communication lines.

Soon other industries started using computers to transfer data between business partners through communication lines. The predominant players outside the financial services sector were the three big automakers in the United States: General Motors, Ford, and Chrysler (now DaimlerChrysler). Through an organization called the Automotive Industry Action Group (AIAG), the major players in this industry coordinated standards for hardware and software as well as procedures for electronic commerce between parts suppliers and the three automakers, affecting practices such as price lists, shipping lists, and invoices.

The reason e-commerce became so visible in the second half of the 1990s was the commercial aspect of the Internet. Once the Internet was opened to commercial activity, this worldwide network became the major carrier of business-to-business electronic data interchange. Indeed, a growing number of companies that once operated proprietary EDI software over private or leased communication lines have shifted EDI to the Internet. Furthermore, a great opportunity for business-to-consumer commerce opened up. Interestingly, business-to-consumer commerce receives more attention both from the media and from individuals despite the fact that about 80 percent of e-commerce takes place between businesses. The reasons are simple: Most individuals simply are not aware of or do not fully understand the economic activities taking place between businesses online, and, as reflected in the media, people are probably just more fascinated by business-to-consumer activities.

To understand e-commerce one must understand both the technologies that serve as the infrastructure and the business models taking advantage of the technologies. Both the technologies and business models currently used are innovative and fascinating. However, we must realize that within several years almost all commerce will be e-commerce to some extent. No one considers doing business via telephone or fax as *t-commerce* or *f-commerce*. It is only a matter of time before we realize that there is no reason to call business that is executed digitally via the Internet or other networks "e-commerce." To get to that point, we must create professionals who will make both the technologies and business practices easy to use. This book will help you understand both the technologies and the business models involved in digital online commerce.

IF WE ARE NUKED: ARPANET

Amid the hoopla of surfing the Net and shopping online, it is easy to forget the modest beginnings of "the mother of all networks." The Internet was not created for online shopping and real-time chatting; it was created to enable Americans to cope with a nuclear attack by the former Soviet Union. In the 1950s and 1960s, all communications systems were centralized. In centralized systems, all communication is routed through a single hub. Military communications systems depended on communications centers, as did mass media such as radio and television. Destroy the communications center, and you eliminate the ability of much of the country to communicate. Thus, the U.S. Department of Defense decided to develop a means of communication that did not depend on any single center: If one node were destroyed, the rest of the network would still function. The result was ARPANET, so called after the Advanced Research Projects Agency, the arm of the Pentagon that funded the research and development of that network. ARPANET connected Pentagon offices, research institutions, and universities to support research and development efforts. Figure 1.1 provides a timeline of the major events in the history of the Internet.

In 1961, several research teams started developing what is now known as TCP/IP (Transmission Control Protocol/Internet Protocol), which is the set of rules governing the transfer of information through the Internet. By 1968, the hardware that could support the protocol was available. In 1969, tests were conducted by the University of California at Los Angeles and Stanford University to prove the validity of the concept. The term *Internet* emerged publicly in 1973 at the Internet Computer Communication Conference. The higher education system in the United States eagerly adopted the new network and established its own branch of the network called *BITNET*.

BITNET

BITNET (*Because It's Time NET* or *Because It's There NET,* depending on whom you ask) was once the world's largest wide-area network, connecting thousands of universities and research institutions throughout the world. It was established in 1981 to serve institutions of higher education and research. The network was the first to use LISTSERV software for managing electronic mailing lists. The Internet gradually supplanted BITNET.

FIGURE

1.1 A TIMELINE OF THE INTERNET

1962–	John Licklider, a scientist at MIT, publishes a memo describing a globally interconnected set of computers that would provide access to data and computer programs from anywhere.
1968–	The first packet-switched networks are developed.
1969–	ARPANET is established.
1971–	The first e-mail message is sent from one computer to another.
1977–	ARPANET has 100 host computers.
1983–	The term *Internet* is coined, and TCP/IP becomes its standard network protocol.
1987–	The Internet has 10,000 hosts.
1988–	The Internet has 60,000 hosts. On a Friday afternoon, 6,000 of the hosts are disabled by the first computer virus (*worm*) to hit the Internet.
1989–	The Internet has 100,000 hosts.
1990–	Tim Berners-Lee develops hypertext markup language (HTML) and the World Wide Web. ARPANET folds. The network is now known only as the Internet, with 300,000 hosts.
1991–	The National Science Foundation lifts the ban on commercial traffic on the Internet. Electronic commerce on the Internet begins.
1992–	The Internet has 1,000,000 hosts; 50 of them use HTML to form Web sites. Jean Armour Polly coins the term *surfing the Internet*.
1993–	The Internet has 10 million hosts. Internet2 project is announced.
1997–	The Internet has 19.5 million hosts; 1.2 million of them are Web sites.
1998–	The Internet has 36.8 million hosts; 4.2 million of them are Web sites.
1999–	Retail sales on the Internet are estimated at $7.8 billion.

Source: Infoworld, October 4, 1999, pp. 34–36.

For a decade or so, thousands of academics used electronic mail (e-mail) before commercial organizations and individuals even knew what it was. Students, too, were allowed to use BITNET, which helped educate millions of young people about how to use e-mail. Perhaps the system's greatest contribution was educating a whole generation of young people that they could use electronic means to communicate ideas. In the 1980s and early 1990s, BITNET was the only means by which college students could experience e-mail. We no longer distinguish between BITNET and the Internet as a whole, but BITNET is still a very large branch of the Internet. We are made aware of its existence every time we see the .edu extension of an e-mail or Web address.

BASICS OF THE INTERNET

BITNET was an extension of the much larger network that we now simply call the Internet. For several years, the Internet connected only research and higher education institutions. The administration of the network was in the hands of the National Science Foundation (NSF), an agency of the U.S. government. In the 1980s, NSF was put in charge of administering the Internet features that required management, such as assigning domain names, and incorporating them in databases.

The **Internet** is a loose association of thousands of networks. Each of these networks is made up of at least one computer, called a **server** or **host,** that is connected directly to the Internet's backbone, and of several computers that are connected to that server.

The Internet's **backbone** is physically made up of its main communication lines, which carry the bulk of traffic. It is the result of connecting the networks of major Internet service providers (ISPs), such as those of GTE, WorldCom, Sprint, UUNet, and America Online (AOL). You may think of the backbone as a system of transportation highways, such as the interstate highways in the United States or the autobahns and autostradas in Europe. Each locality can connect its own smaller roads to the backbone at a certain point. The backbone's lines are mainly made of optical fibers but also rely on other technologies such as microwave, including satellite microwave.

In the United States, the networks have several major centers (which are like airline hub cities) called Network Access Points or metropolitan access exchanges. Figure 1.2 depicts the centers and major links of the U.S. Internet backbone as of 1997. Large telecommunications corporations operate these hubs: Ameritech, Sprint, MFS Communications, Inc., and Pacific Bell. In other countries, local communications companies operate other segments of the Internet backbone. The backbone provides many different combinations of segments for the transfer of information from one point to another.

A combination of segments, or legs, from one point to another is called a **communication path**. The existence of multiple paths is called **redundancy**. If one path carries heavy traffic, special devices called **routers** route the messages to alternative paths to minimize delays. Where there is a high degree of redundancy, such as in the United States, delays are not as common or as severe as in countries whose shares of the Internet backbone are sparse. However, telecommunications companies worldwide continue to augment the backbone.

New lines of communication use technologies that provide greater and greater bandwidth. **Bandwidth** is communication-line capacity (or, more simply, speed). The greater the number of bits per second the line can support, the

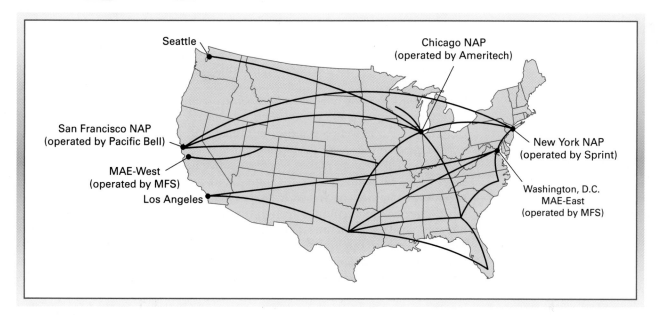

greater the bandwidth. Bandwidth is determined by the medium itself and by the technology of the devices that determine how the signal is communicated through the medium. For example, optical fibers are capable of transmitting millions of bits per second. However, the laser switches that create the light signals representing bits can only operate at speeds about 1,000 times slower than the lines can accommodate.

Communications companies are working to develop faster switches. In January 2000, WorldCom announced that it successfully tested a hair-thin strand of optical fiber that carried one terabit of information per second. (That is one thousand billion bits per second.) Thus, the fiber can support one million one-megabit-per-second multimedia connections.

Think of bandwidth whenever you sit at your computer waiting for a Web page to download to your screen. Experts expect the Internet's bandwidth to grow manifold in the near future.

The Internet is a seemingly chaotic network because anyone can establish a link to the backbone and hook up additional computers—and therefore users—to the network. Despite the loose control, however, the Internet is working very well. We will discuss the issue of Internet control, which includes more than just the physical shape of networks, later in this chapter and later in this book.

INTERNET APPLICATIONS

The Internet enables us to communicate in ways that would not be possible otherwise. The following are the main applications that make the network such an important asset in business, education, and government services. Note that in the 1980s and 1990s there were other applications on the Web, such as Gopher, WAIS,

Veronica, and Telnet. Many of these applications are no longer in use, are embedded in Web browsers, or used infrequently. It is unlikely that you will have to deal with them directly. Thus, we do not discuss them here.

E-MAIL

By far the most popular Internet application is e-mail. E-mail may be regarded as a combination of telephone and traditional mail (called *snail mail* by some people). You have to use a unique address for the recipient, but you do not use paper or stamps or have to allow a few days for delivery. As with telephoning you can communicate relatively instantly, but unlike with telephoning the communication is asynchronous—i.e., the parties do not have to exchange information at the same time. This feature makes e-mail so convenient. You can retrieve your messages whenever you want. On the other hand, for timely communication e-mail requires that parties check their messages frequently.

E-mail facilitates communication within and between organizations. It saves busy employees a lot of time. The ability to attach documents to e-mail messages saves the need to copy and mail or fax documents, even if they are more than simple text. E-mail has replaced regular mail for many marketing firms: They pay significantly less for e-mail address lists than for physical address lists, then pay virtually nothing for broadcasting their message to millions of potential customers.

Many e-mail applications are given away free of charge, which means that anyone with access to the Internet can use e-mail without paying for the software. Over time, several companies (such as Juno Communications and NetZero) started to offer free or low-fee connection to the Internet as well as free e-mail addresses, which made e-mail even more available to anyone with a telephone connection and a computer. Some sociologists consider e-mail a great equalizer: the rich and not-so-rich, the bright and not-so-bright, the conservative and the liberal—anyone from any walk of life can communicate ideas throughout the world. Note, however, that this is true only of people who have access to the Internet and can use e-mail. True "equalizing" will occur only when a substantial number of the world's citizens have access to the Internet. We present some profiles of Internet users later in this chapter.

FILE TRANSFER PROTOCOL

File transfer protocol (FTP) is a communications standard that lets e-mail users transfer whole files to others through the Internet. In the past, one had to know the special commands of FTP to send and receive files. Now, FTP is part of e-mail applications. FTP is also invoked automatically when downloading files from Web sites. In fact, many people download files without even knowing that they are using FTP; it is transparent to them.

FTP is extremely important in electronic commerce. It enables businesses to sell or give away any intellectual creation that can be digitized (and what intellectual creation cannot be digitized?) through a Web site or by e-mail. This includes catalogs, research documents, music, software, movies, and presentations.

THE WEB

While the Internet is the physical network of networks, the World Wide Web, or simply the Web, is a manner in which we use the network. The Web is enabled by an Internet protocol called **HTTP** (HyperText Transport Protocol), which allows the transmission and reception of information in different forms, such as text, pictures, animation, and sound. Think of the Internet as the infrastructure and the Web as the way we use the infrastructure, like a highway and a series of places to visit along the highway.

Tim Berners-Lee, a scientist at CERN (Conseil Européen pour la Recherche Nucleaire) in Geneva, Switzerland, came up with the idea for the Web. He proposed a network for better communication of hypertext and pictures among scientists who worked at several different sites. The result of his effort was **HTML** (hypertext markup language), which instructs an application called a Web **browser** how to display elements in Web pages. The *hyper* in hypertext refers to the ability to link elements, such as text and pictures, within and among pages in a visual and active manner, so that by clicking on an element, another element or page is displayed.

In September 1990, after he published an article on the idea, Berners-Lee started developing the first browser using a NeXT computer that his boss allowed him to purchase. He called the project "World Wide Web," or WWW. Several people joined the project to improve the browser, and work continued until 1993. By January of that year there were 50 servers (computers connected directly to the network) that used HTTP, the communication standard of the Web. The entire World Wide Web in 1993 was only 50 servers! In March of that year, a mere 0.1 percent of the traffic on the Internet was in the form of Web pages.

In 1993, a team headed by Marc Andreessen of the National Center for Supercomputing Applications (NCSA) developed the first Web browser with a graphical interface. They called the browser Mosaic. In 1994, Andreessen cofounded Netscape, the company that developed and marketed the first commercial Web browser, Navigator. In May 1994, the First International WWW Conference was organized at CERN in Geneva. Over 800 people subscribed, but only 400 attendees were admitted to what became known as the Woodstock of the Web. By June of that year, the Web increased to 1,500 servers.

Over the next few years several other browsers were developed, but by 2001 only two major commercial browsers were used by 99.5 percent of Web users: Microsoft's Internet Explorer and Netscape's Navigator. Web browsers are the "killer application" of the Web and are what made the Web so popular. People who know little about computers find browsers easy to use. Web browsers are the world's most widely used type of software application.

INTERNET RELAY CHAT AND AUDIOVISUAL APPLICATIONS

Internet Relay Chat (IRC) provides a service that is similar to CB radio used on the highway, except that instead of speaking, users type with a keyboard and employ a mouse. Many people can join a conversation, and there is no limit to the number of participants. Participants can be active or just view the text exchanged among other people. IRCs provide features that can limit discussions to a one-on-one basis or to a small group by use of passwords. The most popular IRCs are AOL's Instant Messenger, ICQ (I Seek You), Microsoft's Instant Messenger, and Yahoo!'s Messenger. Current IRCs let users compose a list of people with whom they would like to communicate. They can find who of the people on the list is currently online anywhere in the world. Sometimes an IRC is integrated into an online videoconferencing application and an Internet phone (voice) system, which can turn the session into an audiovisual one. The most popular of these applications are Microsoft's NetMeeting and Intel's Video Phone. Both can be obtained free of charge.

NetMeeting lets you decide which part of the application you want to use: synchronous chat, video, or turning your entire computer into a shared resource. The latter is a powerful tool that can transform the session into a remote collaborative effort—several users from different places in the world can work on the same text document, drawing, or other type of file, with equal measure of control.

Both text-only and audiovisual applications can be used as serious business conference tools. Voice over the Internet has not yet reached the quality of traditional telephones, and video on the Internet is still jittery, especially if the communication line is not of high capacity. However, as the bandwidth of these lines increases, the quality of both voice and video will improve.

THE INTERNET OPENS FOR BUSINESS

By the time the Web was invented, administration of the fast-growing Internet was transferred from the U.S. Department of Defense to a civilian agency of the U.S. government, the National Science Foundation (NSF). Administration mainly included the assignment of Internet Protocol numbers (IP numbers) and domain names. In 1991, NSF made it possible for nonacademic and non-U.S. government organizations to connect to the Internet. This move opened the Internet for business, literally. Private businesses from anywhere in the world could now exploit the network for commercial purposes. Because no one government or organization owns the Internet, it provides a free and democratic environment for business.

Note that *democratic* in this context means that the size and financial strength of organizations have little impact on their ability to establish commercial Web sites, so that both big, successful organizations and small, cash-poor startups are on nearly equal footing on the Web. However, we do not mean that the Internet environment is democratic in any political manner; governments can still control communications companies and the ability of individuals and organizations to establish a link to the Internet. Some countries, such as Syria, Libya, and Iran, have governments that tightly control the establishment of Web sites and their content. China's government, too, controls the spread of the Internet and its use for the dissemination of information and commercial activities.

GROWTH OF THE INTERNET

An Internet domain server, or host, is defined in this book as any server connected to the Internet with its own **uniform resource locator (URL),** which is also called a **domain name**. As Figure 1.3 indicates, the number of domain servers increased from zero in 1991 to 45 million in 1999 to almost 120 million in January 2001.

To fathom the power of the Internet in general and the Web in particular, you should follow the statistics and demographic profiles of the groups who use the technologies. Businesses in particular must know the audience for whom they set up Web sites. Changes in Web demographics spur modifications of Web site features and the use of various technologies to best accommodate Web users.

Figure 1.4 shows the online population of the Internet by country and the respective percentage in each country's total population. Note that the table lists only the top 15 online populations in absolute numbers. As you can see, the number of users in some countries is large in absolute terms, such as in China and Brazil, but "onliners" make up a relatively small fraction of the total population.

1.3 THE NUMBER OF INTERNET DOMAIN SERVERS CONTINUES TO GROW
Source: Internet Software Consortium

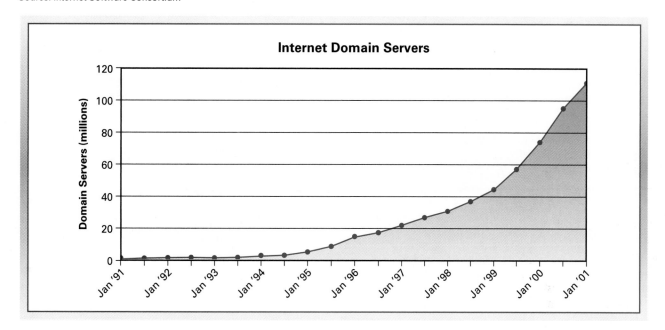

Some small countries have significantly higher percentages of Internet users. These include Finland and Israel, each with a population of no more than six million people but with over a quarter of their populations online.

F I G U R E

1.4 INTERNET USAGE IN DIFFERENT COUNTRIES

Nation	Online Population in 1999 (millions)	Total Population in July 1999 (millions)	Ratio of Online to Total Population (%)
United States	110.8	273	40.6
Japan	18.2	126	14.4
United Kingdom	13.9	59	23.6
Canada	13.3	31	42.9
Germany	12.3	82	15.0
Australia	6.8	19	35.8
Brazil	6.8	172	4.0
China	6.3	1,247	0.5
France	5.7	59	9.7
South Korea	5.7	47	12.1
Taiwan	4.8	22	21.8
Italy	4.7	57	8.4
Sweden	3.9	9	43.3
Netherlands	2.9	16	18.1
Spain	2.9	39	7.4

Source: Computer Industry Almanac, U.S. Central Intelligence Bureau

1.5 INTERNET USER PROPORTIONS BY REGION

Source: Computer Industry Almanac, 2000

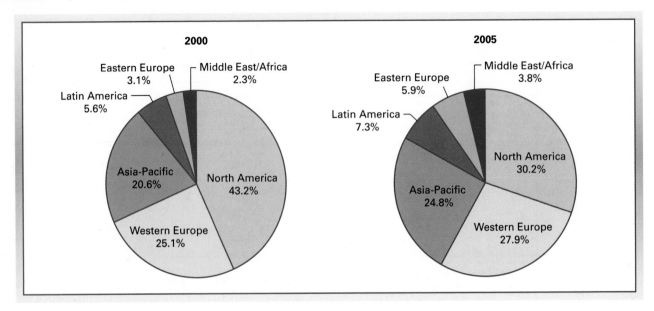

While North America still has the largest capacity in terms of network nodes and high-speed communication lines, it is gradually losing its quantitative dominance as other countries develop their branches of the Internet. In 2000, North America for the first time had less than half of the worldwide online population (43 percent), and by 2005 the proportion is expected to fall to 30 percent. As Figure 1.5 shows, the Asia-Pacific region will have about one quarter of the world's online population at that time. Other regions that are expected to see growth in their online populations are Eastern Europe, Latin America, the Middle East, and Africa.

As the Internet is growing faster in regions outside North America, the English language is becoming less and less dominant, although it is still considered the language of the Internet. In 1999, 57 percent of Internet users spoke English. The other 43 percent spoke the languages outlined in Figure 1.6, with Japanese being the most frequent. Note that this distribution may not be a good indicator of the

I N T E R E S T I N G . . .

ONE FOR THE ROAD

Nokia, the Finnish cellular phone maker, predicts that by 2005 every new car will be equipped with at least one Internet address. The company introduced its first wireless system for automobiles in 2000, offering GPS (Global Positioning System) services such as traffic updates and other location-based information. Nokia calls its wireless automobile equipment "telematics systems."

Source: Adapted from *Investor's Business Daily*, February 28, 2000, p. A2

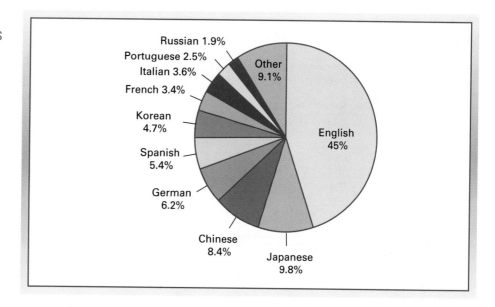

number of English and non-English Web sites, because many sites maintained by residents of non-English-speaking countries are maintained in English or in multilingual "mirrors," whereby the same Web pages are presented in more than one language for the users' convenience. English is typically one of those languages.

WEB DEMOGRAPHICS

In its early days, the Internet was the land of young men from developed countries who were technically savvy. Since then, the demographic profile of the Internet, and especially of the Web, has changed in some respects and remained unchanged in others. The most reliable demographics (and statistics in general) are collected from the U.S. Web population. Statistics generated by the firm Mediamark Research and published in *The Industry Standard* are telling. Consider Figure 1.7.

F I G U R E

1.7 U.S. WEB SURFER PROFILE
Source: Mediamark Research, published in *The Industry Standard,* March 8, 2000

Web Population Profile–1996 to 1998			
	1996	**1997**	**1998**
Total	27.0 million	37.6 million	55.9 million
Male Female	58% 42	55% 45	52% 48
Age 18–34 Age 35 or older	48 52	43 57	42 58
Income $75,000+ Income less than $75,000	38 62	40 60	39 61
College graduate Did not graduate college	49 51	48 52	44 56
White-collar jobs Other job, not employed	57 43	59 41	54 46
White Nonwhite	89 11	87 13	88 12

1.8 DEMOGRAPHICS OF U.S. WEB USERS IN 1998

Demographic	All U.S. Adults 196.4 Million (%)	Web Users 55.9 Million (%)	Index (Web Users to All U.S. Adults)
Gender			
Male	48	52	109
Female	52	48	92
Age			
18–24	13	16	126
25–34	21	26	125
35–44	22	28	124
45–54	17	21	125
55–64	11	6	61
65+	16	3	17
Household Income			
$150,000 or more	3	7	217
$100,000–$149,999	8	15	207
$75,000–$99,999	10	17	173
$50,000–$74,999	21	29	137
$35,000–$49,999	17	16	90
$20,000–$34,999	20	11	56
Less than $20,000	21	5	24
Education			
Postgraduate	7	16	228
Bachelor's Degree	15	28	190
Attended Some College	26	35	135
High School Graduate	33	18	53
Did Not Graduate High School	19	3	18
Occupation			
Professional, Managerial	20	40	205
Technical, Clerical, Sales	19	28	148
Craft, Precision Production	7	5	70
Other	19	13	64
Not Employed, Retired	35	14	41
Race			
White	84	88	104
Black	12	7	57
Asian	2	4	149
Other	2	2	132
Speaks Spanish at Home	10	8	74
Marital Status			
Single	23	28	121
Married	57	62	108
Divorced, Other	20	10	51

Source: Mediamark Research, published in *The Industry Standard*, March 8, 2000

While the number of U.S. Web surfers more than doubled from 1996 to 1998, some aspects of the demographic profile of this growing population did not change significantly. This is true of income, occupation, and race. However, the gender and education gaps did become narrower, and the number of older Web surfers grew. Older Americans are catching up with teenagers and college students.

Figure 1.8 provides even more statistics for 1998. You can compare the proportion of each demographic on the Web with its equivalent proportion in the total adult population. The index in the right column is the ratio of Web users to all U.S. adults; this indicates how close the two proportions are. A number of 100 points means that they are identical; a number larger than 100 means that the group's proportion on the Web is larger than in the general population, and vice versa.

Between 1996 and 1998, the number of Web surfers neared 60 million. When comparing 1998 figures with those from 1996, which was when people began to truly flock to the Web, the educational, age, and gender profile of U.S. Web surfers came closer to that of the general population. However, there has not been a significant change in terms of income groups. In 1998, Web surfers were likely to be college-educated professionals or managers with a high income. The percentages of young, single, and Asian users were also significantly higher than in the general population.

BUSINESSES ON THE WEB

Commercial organizations the world over are looking to the Internet to take advantage of the great potential of the Web as a channel for doing business. However, even in the United States, the country that is making the greatest commercial use of the Web, the majority of businesses are still not present there. As Figure 1.9 shows, only 36 percent of U.S. businesses in 1998 had a Web site, and only 6 percent of those that did use their site for transactions. Not to worry, though—the pace of businesses joining the Web is increasing. The number of U.S. businesses expected to have a Web presence by 2003 is a whopping 80 percent, 32 percent of which are projected to actively use the Web for transactions.

WHO CONTROLS THE INTERNET?

No one fully controls the Internet or has the power to do so, but several nonprofit organizations tend to the development, improvement, and smooth running of the Internet in various ways. The following is a list of these bodies and their main functions.

INTERNET CORPORATION FOR ASSIGNED NAMES AND NUMBERS (ICANN)

Since 1999, ICANN has been the organization in charge of overseeing the assignment of Internet Protocol (IP) numbers and domain names to those applying for Web sites. (The organization succeeded the Internet Assigned Numbers Authority.) An IP number is a unique code made up of four blocks of numbers, where each block may be any number between zero and 255. Thus, an IP number can be anything from 0.0.0.0 to 255.255.255.255. The number identifies an Internet server or a group of servers owned by an organization.

ICANN does not directly assign IP numbers and domain names. Rather, it delegates this task to several private businesses that have access to the registration

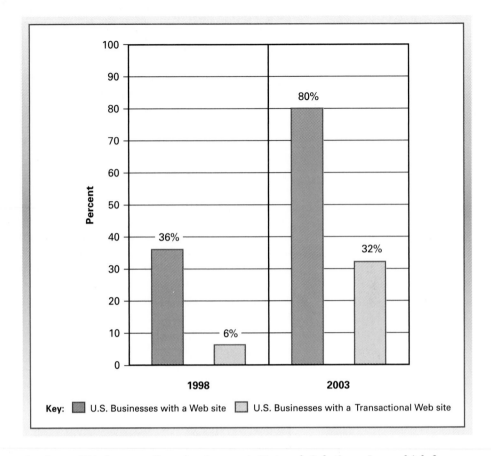

Key: ▉ U.S. Businesses with a Web site ▢ U.S. Businesses with a Transactional Web site

database. Chief among these businesses is Network Solutions, Inc., which for several years had owned the sole right to sell this service. Registration of most domain names cost $15–$35 per year. Individuals and organizations may register domain names with .com, .org, and .net suffixes, plus other suffixes as approved by ICANN from time to time. These suffixes are often called *top level domains*, because they are the most general part of an address.

To make the address of a Web site easy to remember, or to communicate the name or purpose of the organization that operates it, those applying for an IP number usually also apply for a domain name, such as *www.wonderfulsite.com*. However, anyone can apply to one of the domain-name registrars and receive a domain name that has not been reserved by someone else. Once the owner of a domain name establishes a link between an IP-numbered server and the Internet, the owner can apply the domain name to that IP number. From that moment on, there is a unique relationship between the domain name and the IP number. If you know the IP number of a Web site, you may use it instead of the domain name. Either one may serve as the site's address following the *http://* prompt. Thus, either *www.cookexpress.com* or *167.160.226.126* will take you to the same site. The IP number or the domain name that follows the *http://* prompt is called a URL (uniform resource locator) because it uniquely identifies the resource—namely, the server—in the Internet universe.

ICANN took over the overseeing of domain registration from Network Solutions, which itself had been granted the sole right of registration by InterNIC (Internet Network Information Center). As of 1999, though, any organization authorized by ICANN may offer registration services. There are more than 100 registrars in the United States and around the world. Although the number of domain-name registrars is growing, none suffers from a lack of customers. In 1995, there were only 100,000 registered domain names; in 1997, one million domain names had been registered; and by 1998, that number had doubled. By early 2000, there were 10 million registered domain names, and ICANN expects the number to reach 140 million by 2003.

Note that you can register a domain name but choose not to use it. It remains reserved for you as long as you pay the registration fee. If you neglect to pay the annual fee, you may lose the domain name, and it may be assigned to someone else.

WORLD WIDE WEB CONSORTIUM (W3C)

W3C sets the standards for HTML and other specifics of the Web. The organization was founded in October 1994 "to lead the World Wide Web to its full potential by developing common protocols that promote its evolution and ensure its interoperability." It makes recommendations for HTML standards and publishes online statements on recommended standards. The organization's director in 2000 was Tim Berners-Lee, the creator of the Web. The organization is a nonprofit international consortium relying on support from the Massachusetts Institute of Technology in the United States, the Institute National de Recherche en Informatique et en Automatique in Europe, and Keio University in Japan. It provides

1. a repository of information about the Web for software developers and users
2. reference codes for the promotion of standards
3. prototype and sample applications to demonstrate the use of new technology

The W3C team includes 57 engineers from more than 10 different countries. All of the specifications and software that the organization develops is made available to everyone free of charge. W3C is not open to individual membership, but it is open to any organization that is willing to sign the membership agreement. In 2000, the consortium had 401 member organizations from all over the world, including hardware and software companies, television networks, telecommunications companies, brokerage houses, government agencies, and electronics manufacturers. Specifically among the members you will find Microsoft, IBM, Compaq, the Massachusetts Institute of Technology, NASA, ARPA, Merrill Lynch, Motorola, Intel, France Telecom, Fujitsu, the European Broadcasting Union, the British Broadcasting Corporation, and the China Times Interactive Company.

THE INTERNET ENGINEERING TASK FORCE (IETF)

IETF, "a large international community of network designers, operators, vendors, and researchers," is concerned with the evolution of the Internet's architecture with a specific emphasis on keeping the Internet running smoothly as a whole. It regards itself as "the protocol engineering and development arm of the Internet." The technical areas of the organization are handled by the following three working groups.

- The Internet Engineering Steering Group (IESG) is responsible for the technical management of IETF activities and the Internet standards process.
- The Internet Architecture Board (IAB) is responsible for defining the overall architecture of the Internet (the backbone and all the networks attached to it) and providing guidance and broad direction to IETF.

- The Internet Society (ISOC) is a supervisory organization made up of experts who comment on policies and practices. The experts represent corporations, nonprofit organizations, and government agencies from the Internet community. The society oversees a number of other boards and task forces—including IESG and IAB—that deal with Internet policy issues.

INTERNET2 AND THE NEXT GENERATION INTERNET

A consortium of more than 175 universities, corporations, and nonprofit organizations called the University Corporation for Advanced Internet Development (UCAID) is working to advance networking in higher education. While the purpose of this research effort is to advance communication among educational institutions, the results may serve all Internet users. One project of the consortium is Internet2, a slew of innovative Internet applications. UCAID's other project, the Abilene Project, is an effort to develop a nationwide advanced backbone network to support the Internet2 applications. One of the consortium's goals is to "rapidly transfer new network services and applications to all levels of educational use and to the broader Internet community, both nationally and internationally."

In 1996, the U.S. government initiated the Next Generation Internet (NGI) effort. Then-President Clinton's administration earmarked funds for research and development across federal agencies. Efforts are expected to result in better and faster applications in the areas of quality of services; security and robustness; network management, including the allocation and sharing of bandwidth; systems engineering and operations, including definitions and tools for service architectures, metrics, measurement, statistics, and analysis; new or modified protocols for routing, switching, multicasting, reliable transport, security, and mobility; computer operating systems, including new requirements generated by advanced computer architectures; and collaborative and distributed application environments.

SUMMARY

- The Internet is a communication network that grew out of a need to survive a nuclear attack. Its lack of a central transmission and reception point is one of its greatest assets, allowing this loose network of networks to continue to grow. It also makes communication more efficient, because a message, or even parts of the same message, can be routed through any of numerous paths (depending on network congestion) to reduce delays.
- The Internet's backbone, the equivalent of a highway system, continues to grow. In the United States, GTE, WorldCom, Sprint, UUNet, and America Online (AOL) maintain the lion's share of the backbone. Other telecommunications companies own and maintain other countries' part of the backbone.
- Institutions of higher education were among the first to adopt Internet technology. They created the largest of the Internet networks, called BITNET. While the Internet is still used for research and military purposes, the fastest-growing developments in recent years have been for commercial purposes. Although created by the U.S. government, the Internet is neither owned by anyone nor managed by any single organization to the extent that it can control the Internet's growth or use.

- While the Internet is the infrastructure, the Web is the manner in which the infrastructure is used. HTML is used in Web browsers to allow us to receive information not only in text form, but also in the form of pictures, animation, and sound. Web browsers are now the most widely used type of software in the world.
- With the opening of the Internet for commercial activities in 1991, thousands of businesses the world over have hooked up and started doing business online, from establishing a mere presence to using their sites for transactions. Because browsers are easy to use, they provide even the least knowledgeable person with a simple way to use the Web.
- While no organization controls the Internet, several nonprofit organizations oversee essential elements of its use and ongoing development. Chief among them are the Internet Corporation for Assigned Names and Numbers (ICANN), the World Wide Web Consortium (W3C), and the Internet Engineering Task Force (IETF). ICANN makes policies on domain names and licenses private organizations to register domain names for fees. IETF is generally concerned with the evolution of the Internet's architecture and has a specific concern to keep it running smoothly. IETF also has several suborganizations that deal with specific issues of the Internet.
- The Internet continues to develop not only the number of its communications paths, but also better technology. A consortium of 175 universities, corporations, and nonprofit organizations created the University Corporation for Advanced Internet Development (UCAID) to advance networking in higher education. UCAID is developing Internet2, a faster higher-education alternative to the Internet. In 1996, the U.S. government initiated the Next Generation Internet (NGI) effort, for which it has allocated funds aimed at researching advanced technologies.

KEY TERMS

BITNET	bandwidth
Internet	file transfer protocol
server	HTTP
host	HTML
backbone	browser
communication path	IRC
redundancy	URL
router	domain name

REVIEW QUESTIONS

1. In what sense is the Internet different from other communication networks such as telephone, radio, and television?
2. The Internet is a U.S. creation. Can the U.S. government control the Internet? If not, why? If the government can control it, in what sense and how?
3. What is meant by the Internet's *backbone*? Who owns the backbone?
4. Who owns the networks that make up the Internet? Can these organizations exert any control over traffic on the Internet? Explain.

5. A person who has never logged on to the Internet asks you, "What is the difference between the Internet and the Web?" What is your answer?
6. What is the purpose of ICANN?
7. You are planning to open an online retail business. You plan well and want to target audiences not only in the immediate future, but also three to five years from now. Other than North America, which world region would you target? Why?
8. Web browsers are the "killer application" of the Internet. What is a killer application, and why are browsers so popular throughout the world?
9. What is the purpose of W3C? Could the Web exist without this organization? If it could, then what is the contribution of this organization?

DISCUSSION QUESTIONS

1. Would the Internet have become a reality had the U.S. government, or any other government, not allotted millions of dollars to its development and construction? Why or why not?
2. Could a business initiative achieve what is now the Web? Why or why not?
3. Sociologists have equated the Internet to other communications media such as radio, television, mail, and telephone. In what sense does the Internet resemble each of these media? In what sense is it different from these media?
4. What about the Web annoys you? How would you improve the Web to alleviate the problem?
5. In terms of communicating with friends, discuss the pros and cons of using the phone versus e-mail. Which do you prefer for communication with coworkers? Your boss? Family members? Explain.
6. Examine Figure 1.8. Several indexes are greater than 200 points. What may be the reasons for the high index values of these demographic characteristics?
7. What are the advantages of the fact that no single body fully controls the Internet? What are the disadvantages?

ASSIGNMENTS

1. Search the Web to find the following statistics: (1) the number of servers (host computers) connected to the backbone; (2) the estimated number of users who logged on to the Internet over the past week; and (3) the total number of domain names that have been assigned. E-mail the statistics to your professor.

2. Use PowerPoint or another presentation application to make a five-minute presentation about Internet2. Identify what the purpose of it is, who the participants of this project are, how it is funded, what has been accomplished, and what is planned for the future.

3. Is there any need for Internet organizations other than ICANN? Log on to the W3C site, research some projects, and prepare a five-minute presentation (using PowerPoint or similar software) about one contribution that the organization has made or is about to make.

4. Search the Web for Internet history. Pick the 10 most important events. Prepare a two-page report outlining the events and explaining how each contributed to the development of the Internet.

5. Do you expect the demographic profile of Web surfers the world over to change in the next five years? Which aspects of the profile do you expect will change? Why?

Oracle: A Taste of Its Own Medicine

Oracle Corporation of Redwood Shores, California, is the world's largest developer and seller of database technology and the world's second largest developer of software. For years, company managers had tried to convince potential customers that Oracle's database applications could streamline their business processes and save them money. "Install and link our database servers in your company's sites," company salespeople touted, "and you'll save your company millions of dollars." However, Oracle itself was not exactly a paragon of efficiency.

For a long time the company had used at its own facilities the concept it promoted: the client/server architecture, which linked employee PCs by department to a server containing databases and applications. Like the client companies that had implemented the concept, Oracle ended up with a multitude of clusters of local systems that could not talk to each other. An employee from one department could not obtain information that resided on another department's server.

The problem was not only the inability to move data quickly from one organizational unit to another. Each client/server cluster needed a dedicated maintenance team. For example, financial planning and analysis data were stored in 60 different databases running on 32 different servers around the world. If Oracle wanted to change a financial model, programmers had to make the changes on each individual server. Consider also that the company's internal e-mail system employed more than 120 databases accessed through 95 servers worldwide.

The decentralization problem was even worse when employees from remote sites tried to collaborate on projects. Employees in the United States had to wait until a late hour to catch, by phone, an employee in Asia. To communicate written information, employees had to use fax machines and express-delivery services. Employees experienced long waiting times, confusion, and inaccuracies. Staff requirements to support these systems were enormous: Oracle had 1,500 technicians maintaining the database systems at a cost of $600 million per year, and the company employed 60 technicians to maintain the e-mail system.

In 1999, the software giant embarked on a major overhaul. Management decided to link all of its 43,800 employees in more than 100 countries so that they could easily access all the data they needed and collaborate on projects in real time. Information-system professionals put all of Oracle's software on a small number of servers.

Now, all employees have access to the servers through a single network: the Internet. Employees use their Web browsers to access corporate applications and databases. A salesperson in Mumbai, India, can get the same information as a salesperson in Tokyo, Japan, or one in San Francisco.

The company also shut down 38 data centers in various locations around the world and placed all of its databases in two data centers in Redwood Shores. Instead of a multitude of servers, today the company employs just a few powerful ones. All of Oracle's business software for each business process, from sales management to inventory tracking, is available from those few powerful servers running Oracle database management systems. The centralization of large amounts of organizational data enables all employees to receive the same information through a Web browser from anywhere in the world at any time.

Recall the example of the financial services data. Now the company is running all of its financial data on two servers and five databases, and the e-mail system is maintained on two servers supported by only 12 technicians. At a time when the company's overall personnel increased by several thousand people, the technical staff shrunk by 120 people.

The customer service cycle is shorter now, too. Salespeople use a form that they download from the Web. They fill out the form with customer requirements and post it back on a site that can be accessed by other salespeople from any Oracle office.

Between June 1999 and May 2000, Oracle saved $1 billion dollars. The power of the Internet is that great.

Source: Kang, C., "Oracle Corp. takes its own advice," *The Philadelphia Inquirer*, May 21, 2000, Q7

Thinking About E-Commerce at Work

1. Some observers claim that using the Internet brought companies back to the time when all computing was centralized. In terms of information resources and communications, which resources are centralized at Oracle, and which are not?
2. What kind of virtual network has the company created by linking resources through the Internet?
3. Some intercompany communication must still be executed using telephone and fax. Research the Web. Can you use telephone and fax systems on the Internet? Explain your answer.

- Compare and contrast network topologies
- Explain the basic functions of the TCP/IP protocols
- Evaluate the limitations of the various classes of Internet addresses
- Select the best Internet link service according to organizational or individual needs

Japanese government figures released in June of 2000 show that just over 27 million people, or one in five of the total Japanese population, now have Internet access. Around 40 percent of Japanese people own mobile phones, and eight percent, or 10 million people, go online through mobile connections, according to the Ministry of Posts and Telecommunications (MPT). Further growth is expected in mobile Internet connection, and MPT estimates that the number of mobile users will reach 80 million by 2005, while the number of Internet users will have tripled to 76.7 million. Mobile connection to the Internet is not limited to Japan. As the Internet backbone is growing, so is wireless communication in general and wireless use of the Internet in particular. Soon, most of us will probably talk to our favorite Web sites via small, handheld devices rather than type into wired computers. (Source: Japan's Ministry of Posts and Telecommunications)

NETWORK TOPOLOGIES

To understand the technical side of e-commerce, one must understand the fundamentals of intra- and interorganizational networks. To do so, you might be advised to take a course or read a textbook on computer networks. Business managers need not know every technical detail related to e-commerce, but they should keep abreast of what technology enables their companies to do. The following sections provide a succinct review of the most essential elements of computer networks.

A computer network is composed of computers and other devices, such as special communication equipment, printers, and other peripheral pieces. For the sake of simplicity, we will use the word *computer* for all the devices. A network comprises *nodes*, which are connection points in the form of computers that are capable of recognizing and processing or of forwarding transmissions to other nodes. Communication devices often are not used for computing per se but rather for communication purposes such as routing or amplifying signals. At least one of the devices in a network must be able to perform communication tasks.

Again, a network is made up of nodes and the communication lines that connect the computers. The physical layout of a network is called **topology** (from the Greek *topos*, meaning "place"). As Figure 2.1 illustrates, in a **star topology** all the computers are connected to a single computer that performs the tasks of accepting messages and routing them to their respective destinations. In a **ring topology** every computer is connected to two other computers. No single device has full control over the network. In a **bus topology** all computers are connected to a single cable called a *bus* or a *backbone*. Unlike in a star topology, in a bus topology each computer relies on its neighbor to relay a message. Only computers actually addressed by a signal pay attention to the signal and pick it up. The others ignore the signal.

Note that few networks form a pure star, ring, or bus topology. For example, many networks are made up of a high-capacity bus to which lower-capacity stars are connected.

Networks can generally be classified as **peer-to-peer networks** or **client-server networks.** In a peer-to-peer network, each computer has equal capabilities and responsibilities. In a client-server arrangement, some computers are dedicated to serving the other computers. These servers are usually more powerful than the other computers. Client-server systems are predominant on the Internet, where many computers are linked to a single server that is linked to the Internet backbone.

FIGURE

2.1 NETWORK TOPOLOGIES

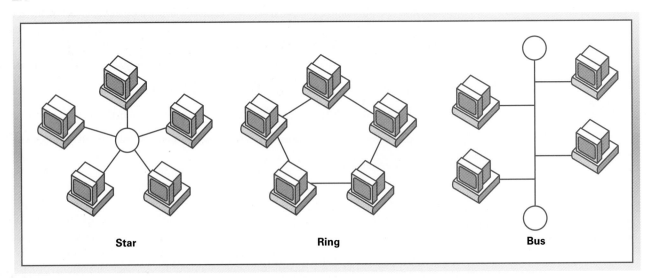

Star   Ring   Bus

SWITCHING TECHNIQUES

Special devices called *switches* must be present in any communication network. Switches direct the flow of electrical or optical signals and route communication traffic in networks.

In **circuit switching,** the entire path of the communication between two devices is reserved for those devices for the duration of the communication session between them. This is the type of switching that takes place in telephoning, both analog and digital. Whether the line is actually used or not, all the segments of a certain path in the network are reserved for those devices until one disconnects. This ensures a high quality of voice communication. However, this also means that the path is occupied even during times when no information is communicated—or, as engineers like to say, when silence is communicated. Thus, there is some waste of resources when digital transmission uses circuit switching.

In **packet switching,** the digitized form of the communication, be it data, sound, or pictures, is divided into groups of several bytes. Each group is called a *packet*. Each packet may be sent through a different path in the network. When all packets reach the destination device, they are arranged in the correct order, and the party at the receiving end receives a coherent message. Packet switching is more efficient than circuit switching, because the packets are optimally routed through the paths that have the least amount of traffic at any given moment. Thus, the overall amount of information that can be transmitted at the same time from multiple users is higher, and there is less waste of network time when there is silence. As you will soon read, the Internet uses packet switching.

NETWORK PROTOCOLS

Nodes in communication networks must be able to recognize, process, and forward information that flows through the network. To this end, network protocols have been established. A **network protocol** is a set of rules that governs the flow and processing of information in a network. Protocols include such rules as the type of error checking used, the method of data compression, how the sending device indicates that it has completed sending a message, and how the receiving device indicates that it has received the message.

As mentioned in Chapter 1, **TCP/IP** (Transmission Control Protocol/Internet Protocol) is a set of protocols developed by the U.S. Department of Defense in the 1960s and 1970s as part of the general effort to develop the Internet. The two best-known protocols in the set are TCP and IP. TCP/IP was designed to be robust—that is, to withstand errors via automatic recovery without central management. On the Internet and in organizational intranets and extranets (discussed in Chapter 6), the TCP and IP protocols are used.

IP is a packet-switching protocol. IP handles addressing to ensure proper routing, fragmentation of the message into packets, reassembly of the packets at the destination, and *multiplexing*, which is a method of transmitting several streams of messages through the same communication line.

The IP protocol of the TCP/IP protocols set handles the transmission of data packets between host computers—that is, from one node to another. It operates on hosts that move data from the departmental host within the organizational network to the organization's host, from that host to the region's host, and from there to anywhere in the world. The next generation of IP, IPv6 (IP version 6, popularly called IP next generation, or IPng), is now under development. It will replace the current version, IPv4. IPv6 will support Internet traffic for many years into the future, providing enhanced capabilities relative to the existing IPv4. IPv6 will allow the transmission of larger packets than the current 64 KB, include additional addressing schemes, and provide better data security measures.

TCP verifies the correct delivery of data from client to server. It detects transmission errors and executes retransmission if a packet of data is not received by the destination host, until all packets are correctly and completely received.

LANS AND WANS

Any of the topologies we have discussed can be used both in local area networks and wide area networks. A local area network (**LAN**) is a network serving a building or a campus of several adjacent buildings. Usually, the entire LAN is owned and operated by an organization for internal purposes. However, nowadays most LANs are linked to the Internet to enable communication with other organizations and to provide access to sources of information.

A wide area network (**WAN**) is a network spread over large regions, often national or international territory. Telephone networks and the networks that make up the Internet are examples of WANs. To link nodes, WANs usually employ more than one type of physical medium, such as copper wires, optical fibers, TV cable, microwave transceivers (receivers-transmitters), and communication satellites.

An important factor in accelerating e-commerce is the ability of organizations to maintain their own LANs for daily operations while connecting them to the outside world, especially to the Internet. Organizations can use LANs for their internal business processes and then transmit information about products, shipping and receiving, bids in auctions, and the like to business partners and consumers over the Internet.

Many organizations have connected their LANs to the Internet. They have done so not only to enable their employees to utilize this vast resource for information gathering, but also to share a network with their suppliers and clients. In Internet terminology, we speak of intranets and extranets. An **intranet** is a LAN or a network of such LANs that use the TCP/IP protocols for internal purposes. When an organization operates from multiple sites, the disparate LANs can be linked through the Internet so that employees in many different locations can use the intranet.

Similarly, organizations often give suppliers and clients access to their internal networks. The purposes of granting access vary from mere information tapping to transactions such as placing orders and making payments. In this situation, all supplier and client organizations use their own LANs to access another organization's LAN via the Internet. This arrangement creates an **extranet**: LANs of two or more business partners linked through the Internet. Because in both multisite intranets and extranets part of the communicated information passes through the public lines of the Internet, these arrangements pose a serious challenge: how to guarantee that only authorized people have access to a private network.

There are no absolute guarantees that intruders will never gain access to computers that are connected to a public network. However, there are means for minimizing the possibility that uninvited guests will gain access. In Chapter 10 we will discuss measures routinely taken to block access to networked information systems. When these measures are implemented, the LANs at the various sites and the Internet lines connecting them become a **virtual private net-**

work (VPN). A VPN is in reality partially private and partially public, but users experience the network as if it were totally private. Note that at the same time you are using a VPN, people who may not even know about "your" VPN are using some of the Internet lines that you are using—hence the word *virtual* in virtual private network.

INTERNET ADDRESSING

When registering an Internet server, an organization receives an IP number made up of four bytes that are called *blocks*, each representing a number (see Chapter 1). Each device connected to the Internet must be assigned a unique **IP number** (also called *Internet address* or *IP address*), at least for the duration of the link. Each block addresses another level in the hierarchy of Internet addresses: a device (usually a computer) in a department, a department of the organization, the organization, and the region in which the organization is located.

The IP registrar allows the organization to allot the lowest level number, or the two lower levels, to its own devices. For example, if your organization were assigned the number 2.32.104.xxx, the network manager of the organization decides which numbers between 1 and 255 will stand in lieu of the *xxx* and assigns them to particular devices. The organization may assign numbers as *static* IP numbers, which means that devices have their numbers permanently, or have the system assign a *dynamic* IP number to a computer whenever that computer is linked to the Internet via the organization's server. For example, an organization may own all these IP numbers and allocate them internally: 134.108.133.81, 134.108.133.82, 134.108.133.83, and 134.108.133.84.

An IP address consists of two parts, one identifying the network and the other identifying the node. Remember that a block is made up of a binary number. Thus, when an organization is assigned a set of addresses from this class, it can internally assign a maximal number of 256 (2^8) valid addresses. However, two of these addresses are never assigned to any particular node, which leaves the maximal internally assigned number at 254.

The reason we subtract two from the maximal number of nodes is this: When the node part is set to all zeros, such as in 152.219.0.0, this IP number identifies the entire organizational network and is assigned to the server itself.

INTERESTING . . .

RUNNING OUT OF NUMBERS

Telephone companies used to assign the area code 800 for all toll-free lines in America. Then, when the companies ran out of 800 numbers, they started to assign numbers with the area code 888 for toll-free lines, and 887 followed after another shortage occurred. Now, the Internet is running out of IP numbers for addressing networks and their nodes. The current numbering method, part of IPv4, allows a potential of 4.3 billion unique addresses. ICANN and IETF are working to implement IPv6 to ensure that we do not run out of IP numbers as thousands of new sub-nets are linked to the Internet. The new standard augments the potential to a number of 38 digits, which is more addresses than the world will ever need.

When the node section is set to all binary 1s (the decimal equivalent being 255), such as 152.219.255.255, it specifies a broadcast transmitted to all hosts on the network.

If the number of nodes is determined by the last two blocks, up to 65,534 ($2^{16}-2$) nodes can be supported. Therefore, large organizations are interested in an IP number set that can support such a large network of nodes.

As Figure 2.2 shows, there are five network classes that IP numbers can support and are available to ICANN for assignment. The first block of the IP number determines the network class. Class A addresses are for very large networks, such as MILNET (the military network). Therefore, Class A addresses are not available to individual commercial organizations. A Class B network supports up to 65,534 nodes. There are 16,000 Class B addresses, most of which are no longer available. A Class C network can support 254 nodes but is too small for most organizational networks. IETF and ICANN are working on methods to allow additional address numbers.

Figure 2.3 presents the top 10 top-level domain suffixes in terms of the number of Internet servers. Note that many top-level domain names can be registered to anyone regardless of the country where the server resides. For example, businesses from many countries own .com and .net domain names. In 2001, ICANN added more top-level domains to the existing ones, among which were .inc and .corp. There has been strong opposition to augmenting the pool of top-level domain names. We discuss the issue fully in Chapter 11.

FIGURE

2.2 INTERNET ADDRESSING

Class of Network	First Block Is in the Range . . .	Number of Nodes Supported
A	1–126	16,777,214
B	128–191	65,534
C	192–223	254
D	224–239	Reserved; not assigned
E	240–255	Reserved for future use

Note: Numbers with a first block of 127 are not assigned.

FIGURE

2.3 THE TOP 10 DOMAIN SUFFIXES

Top-Level Domain Suffixes	Number of Net Hosts
.com	12,140,747
.net	8,856,687
.edu	5,022,815
.jp (Japan)	1,687,534
.us (United States)	1,562,391
.mil (U.S. Military)	1,510,440
.uk (United Kingdom)	1,423,804
.de (Germany)	1,316,893
.ca (Canada)	1,119,172
.au (Australia)	792,351

Source: Network Wizards, January 2000

DOMAIN NAMES FOR DOCTORS

Countries are given sole permission to register domain names with their own top-level domain suffix. Remember that the physical location of the server whose IP number is associated with a domain name is irrelevant. Moldova, a former Soviet Union republic in Eastern Europe, has the suffix *.md*. Domain Names Trust is the firm that acquired the sole rights to registering that country's domain names and charges $299 per year for the registration. Most of the applicants are doctors and medical organizations. Television stations may be interested in the *.tv* suffix, which, as it happens, has been granted to Tuvalu, a small nation of nine islands in the western Pacific Ocean. A firm called .TV Corporation holds the exclusive rights to register *.tv* domain names, for which it charges a cool $1,000 per year. Interestingly, Tuvalu itself has only one Internet host with its own domain name.

BANDWIDTH, BANDWIDTH, AND MORE BANDWIDTH

Both businesses and individuals wishing to be online must consider the speed of communication—*bandwidth*, as discussed in Chapter 1—they need. This applies both to using the Net to serve others and to using it as a surfer and online shopper. Currently, telecommunications companies, called *telcos*, offer several services, as Figure 2.4 illustrates. Some services are not available everywhere. Most large businesses opt to hook up their servers via the fast T1 or T3 lines. Where available, a faster connection using the ATM (Asynchronous Transfer Mode) standard can be established. Small businesses often opt to pay lower monthly fees for digital subscriber services (DSL). (DSL and ATM will be discussed in detail soon). As development companies find faster ways to transmit digital information through optical fibers and satellites, the optional bandwidth offered to subscribers will grow.

INTEGRATED SERVICES DIGITAL NETWORK

Integrated Services Digital Network (**ISDN**) is an international telecommunications standard for transmitting voice, video, and data via digital lines at a speed of 64 Kbps (thousand bits per second). It is possible to combine (*bond*, in professional jargon) several such lines to reach a greater speed. Combining two ISDN lines to reach a capacity of 128 Kbps is common and widely available, both in North America and Western Europe. The service is available from telephone companies. They charge several tens of dollars per month for a subscription to these lines. Subscribers can use the lines the same way they use regular telephone lines, both for voice communication and as dial-up lines for Internet communication. The standard was first announced in the early 1980s and was expected to provide all the capacity needed so that a single line could support voice, data, and video transmission at the same time. It took a decade for the service to become widely available, and by that time the capacity proved to be quite modest in terms of current speed requirements.

2.4 SERVICES OFFERED BY TELECOMMUNICATIONS COMPANIES

Line	Speed (Downstream/Upstream)	Availability	Pros	Cons
Regular telephone line dial-up	56 Kbps/33.6 Kbps	Universal	Inexpensive and easy to install	Slow
ISDN	128 Kbps/128 Kbps	Widespread	Faster than regular telephone line	Relatively slow for the service fee
Satellite	400 Kbps/33.6 Kbps	Widespread	Available to anyone with a clear view of the U.S. southern sky	Complex installation
Cable (with modem)	1–5 Mbps	Limited	Continuous connection (no need to dial up)	Unlike households, most businesses are not connected to a TV cable line; nodes are shared by many subscribers, causing security problems and a slowing down of speed
DSL of all types	144 Kbps–8 Mbps / 144 Kbps–8 Mbps	Limited	Turns a regular telephone line into a continuous fast connection	Costly and usually requires installation by a technician
T1	64 Kbps–1.544 Mbps / 56 Kbps–1.5 Mbps	Widespread	Guaranteed high speed and quick repair service; continuous connection	Very costly; requires installation by a technician
T3	64 Kbps–44.736 Mbps / 64 Kbps–43 Mbps	Widespread	Guaranteed high speed and quick repair service; continuous connection	Very costly; requires installation by a technician
ATM	1.5 Mbps–2.5 Gbps / 1.5 Mbps–2.5 Gbps	Very limited	Highest speed offered and high reliability; continuous connection	Very costly; requires installation by a technician

Parts adapted from McCracken, H., "Bandwidth on Demand," *PC World*, March 1999, p. 110

SATELLITE SERVICE

Satellite communication service is also widely available in the United States, but it is practically limited to subscribers in the southern part of the country. Due to this fact, as well as the complex installation involved, the service is not popular among individual subscribers.

CABLE MODEM

Cable television companies allow many of their subscribers to connect to the Internet via the same cable they already have for their television sets. As Figure 2.5 illustrates, a device called a splitter is used to to direct one end of the line into the television set and the other into a **cable modem** that is connected to the computer. The computer is then permanently linked to the Internet, so there is no

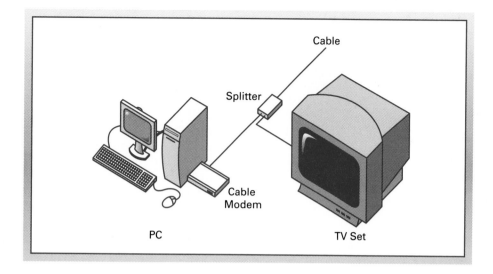

need to dial up. Cable modems link the computer using a network access method called **Ethernet**. Ethernet turns the cable to which all subscribers are connected in a defined area into a shared resource. Therefore, although the overall communication speed of the cable modem is relatively high, the speed varies depending on the number of subscribers using the Internet simultaneously; the more subscribers using it, the lower the speed. There has been fear that this type of shared network may allow one subscriber to invade another subscriber's computer. It is not known if such an "invasion" is possible, nor any reports that it has ever happened. Since most businesses do not subscribe to cable television service, this type of service is more suitable for households.

Note that cable modem service is not the same as cable Internet service or WebTV service. Cable Internet service delivers Internet access to a television set through an enhanced set-top cable box. WebTV delivers Internet access to a television set using an analog modem via a telephone line. The telephone line is connected to the WebTV box, and the WebTV box is connected to the television set. The television set can also be connected to a normal cable for cable television reception.

DIGITAL SUBSCRIBER LINE

Digital Subscriber Line (**DSL**) is a service that telephone companies currently offer in large metropolitan areas of the United States and in some regions of other countries. Over the years, much of the older copper-wire telephone network has been replaced with optical fibers and other media that accommodate high-speed transmission of digital data. However, the few miles of connection from telephone jacks to the telephone exchange office are still made of twisted pairs of copper wires whose transmission speed is "chocked" to accommodate slow speed analog transmission. This is because our telephones are designed for this type of voice transmission. For about two decades, telephone companies have had the equipment to allow high-speed digital streams of bits (which can represent voice, data, and video transmissions) to flow not only between any two telephone exchanges, but also from a telephone exchange to subscribers' telephone jacks at home or in the office. As cable companies started to offer their high bandwidth services, telephone companies started to compete by offering DSL services.

There are several standards and technologies for delivering DSL. Some require a special splitter installed at the subscriber's end to separate voice from the higher-speed data transmission, and some do not. Either type of service requires a special modem connected to the subscriber's computer. However, all standards turn a regular telephone line into a high-speed line whose bit rate reaches that of an expensive T1 line (described below). Unlike ISDN, which is also digital but travels through circuit-switched telephone lines, DSL circumvents circuit switching and provides a continuous, always-on connection to the Internet. The bit rate of a DSL line deteriorates as the distance to a subscriber's premises increases. Therefore, the service is usually offered only to subscribers whose premises are within a few miles of a telephone exchange.

Since downloading information from the Internet is more frequent than uploading information to the Internet, most DSL services are deliberately asymmetrical; they provide a greater download bandwidth than upload bandwidth to better utilize the line. Thus, DSL is usually Asymmetric DSL, or simply ADSL.

T1 AND T3 LINES

T1 lines are 1.544 Mbps (million bits per second) point-to-point dedicated digital lines. *Point-to-point* means that the line is not switched but is always at the service of the subscriber. *Dedicated digital* means that the lines are installed only for digital communication. As such, they provide a continuous connection to the Internet or another network. A T1 line is made up of two wires, one for transmission and one for reception. T1 lines have been in use since the 1960s but have been offered to commercial organizations only since 1983. Monthly subscription fees are usually determined by distance.

A T2 line is a combination of four T1 lines to accomplish a 6.312 Mbps speed. A **T3 line** is a combination of 28 T1 lines. Note that as T1 lines can be combined to provide a larger bandwidth line, they can also be broken up to maintain several communication channels through the same line. T1 and T3 lines are widely used by organizations to form private networks and to connect them to the Internet.

ASYNCHRONOUS TRANSMISSION MODE

Asynchronous Transmission Mode (**ATM**) is a standard that was adopted in the 1980s by the International Telecommunications Union, a United Nations standards organization for telecommunications and high-speed networks. (Do not worry about the meaning of *asynchronous,* because it is a misnomer anyway.) ATM lines are often made of optical fibers to allow speeds of 1.5, 25, 100, 155, 622, and 2,488 Mbps. Note that the lion's share of the Internet backbone supports speeds no greater than 45 Mbps. ATM networks establish a circuit between two devices, but unlike with telephone switching, idle time on the circuit can be appropriated for a different use. For instance, idle time in teleconferencing can be used to transmit textual data.

Bits are transmitted in fixed-length groups of 53 bytes each. The groups are called *cells;* thus, ATM is often referred to as a cell-switching method. Each cell includes a five-byte header and 48 data bytes. The header contains information about the source and destination of the information transmitted. The fixed number of small packets in ATM makes it possible to guarantee limited transmission delays so that cells will not get stuck behind an unusually large packet. Therefore, the same line can be used for both data and high-quality, real-time voice or video communication. Unlike in TCP/IP protocols, in ATM every cell with the same source and destination travels over the same route. When an ATM network is connected to the Internet backbone, special routers ensure that the two standards work well together.

ATM is a standard for both LANs and WANs, and as such it can support transmission from end to end regardless of where the transmission takes place, the LAN portion or the WAN portion. Yet, in the early 1990s organizations shunned ATM because of its perceived complexity and the high cost of ATM equipment, such as switches and routers. In addition, the development of high-speed technology for LANs—such as Gigabit Ethernet, which was cheaper to implement than ATM technology—kept organizations away from ATM. The technology was pronounced dead by many telecommunications pundits. Nevertheless, it has enjoyed a huge revival in the late 1990s and continues to be the choice of telecommunications companies for high-speed lines. The majority of new segments added to the Internet backbone use ATM technology with optical fibers.

WIRELESS COMMUNICATION

One of the most exciting developments in telecommunications is the spread of wireless communication, in which radio and infrared waves are used to carry signals. Wireless technologies have been used in a range of environments, from homes to global connections to the Internet. In homes and small businesses, computers can be linked using simple devices that cost about $100. The computers then form a LAN. The flexibility in using such LANs is great, because computers can be relocated without rewiring, as long as they are placed within a maximal range to keep the signal strong.

An even more exciting development is the use of wireless devices that allow connection to the Internet while on the road. Handheld personal digital assistants

INTERESTING . . .

MIRROR, MIRROR ON THE SWITCH

Of all the media for telecommunications—copper wires, cable, radio, and optical fiber—the latter provides the greatest bandwidth. The major constraints to achieving greater transmission speeds are not the optical fibers themselves, but the devices (the switches) that create and route the bursts of light signals. Whenever light pulses must be transferred, or "switched," from one hub of the network to another, the pulses must first be converted to electrical pulses. The conversion of energy from light to electricity and back to light slows down the transmission.

There is good news, though. A device developed by Xros, Inc., a start-up company in California, uses thousands of small, densely packed mirrors to reflect light beams through the switch. About 1,152 pairs of mirrors are packed on a surface as small as a fingernail. Two large telecommunications companies, AT&T and WorldCom, may use the new switches in their branches of the Internet backbone.

Source: "Mirror Magic for Optical Networks," *Business Week,* March 13, 2000, p. 93

(PDAs) can be used to log on to the Internet. This gives business people (such as salespeople) great mobility: they can log on to their company's intranet or extranet, peruse online catalogs, record transactions, and do anything else they would otherwise have to do from a wired computer. Investors can check stock prices from anywhere using a small PDA that they pull out of their shirt pocket.

Several companies have developed mobile applications for the Internet. In June 2000, IBM declared its plan to develop voice recognition technologies for wireless Web transactions. The company aims to combine three elements: the ease of use of natural speech, the convenience of mobile Internet access, and the low transaction cost of the Web. The company developed a special server application called WebSphere Voice Server. It allows the delivery of voice applications based on a standard called VoiceXML, making Web and call center technologies more effective for e-business. VoiceXML works with Wireless Application Protocol (WAP), the most commonly used mobile Internet protocol.

According to the research firm Cahners-In-Stat Group, worldwide wireless subscribers will reach one billion by the end of 2002, and over the next five years the number of subscribers is expected to grow at a compounded annual rate of 34.5 percent. In 2000, there were about 550 million desktop PC users. Furthermore, Cahners predicts that by 2004 wireless devices will be the most popular means of accessing the Internet.

Interestingly, some analysts say that the small size of such devices will make navigation using a screen and buttons or keys more difficult for older users because of vision and dexterity challenges. This is another reason why IBM and other companies are developing voice technologies for handheld, wireless Internet devices.

BUSINESS CONSIDERATIONS IN TELECOMMUNICATIONS

Organizations must consider several factors when deciding on the type of telecommunications services they want to adopt: bandwidth, cost, security, and ease of maintenance. Often, the ratio that organizations consider is dollars per Mbps, where dollars are the monthly fee they pay. However, if the business depends heavily on fast communication, it should consider the absolute communication speed.

For example, if a business intends to use a Web site for transactions, it must establish a high-speed link. This is also true for companies that perform much of their purchasing online, and for the growing number of companies that use the services of application service providers (discussed in Chapter 7). While a large majority of businesses currently subscribe to T1 and T3 lines, many others that are going online now adopt ATM. The choice makes sense in light of the fact that the ATM standard applies both to WANs and LANs.

While bandwidth is an important issue, the ability to augment a network, especially a LAN, is important as well. Such ability is often called **scalability**. In general, the scalability of wireless networks is less expensive and easier than the scalability of wire-based networks. Adding links is relatively easy. Wireless networks also require less expertise in maintenance.

There are three types of costs involved in telecommunications: the onetime capital investment in the installed lines, both the LANs and the link to a WAN, such as the Internet backbone; the monthly fee, if the line is leased from a telecommunications company, which is often the case; and the ongoing cost of maintenance, which is mainly the salaries of the telecommunications staff. The latter cost depends on the expertise required for different types of technologies and the size and complexities of the LANs and outside links.

Security refers to the degree to which the information that an organization transmits and receives can be intercepted. By and large, guided links such as copper wires, cable, and optical fibers are more secure than unguided links such as satellite and terrestrial microwave links, because the latter can be intercepted remotely without connecting any devices to a physical line. As much as managers consider bandwidth vis-à-vis cost, they also must consider the degree of security that can accommodate different technologies and standards under cost constraints. It would make no sense to spend several million dollars on security measures that might prevent damages estimated in the tens of thousands of dollars or that protect against occurrences whose probability is very small. Chapter 10 presents a complete discussion of such business decisions.

SUMMARY

- To understand the technical side of e-commerce, one must understand the fundamentals of telecommunications and computer networks. Networks generally follow one of several topologies, the geometric layout of the network.
- In a star topology, all computers are connected to each other through a central computer. All communication must pass through that computer. In a ring topology, every computer is connected to two other computers. In a bus topology, computers are linked to the same communication line. In ring and bus topologies, no single computer has more control over the network than any other computer.
- Networks can be classified as peer-to-peer, in which each computer has equal capabilities and responsibilities, or as client-server, in which a relatively powerful computer in terms of processing speed and memory is dedicated to serving the other computers. Client-server is the predominant arrangement on the Internet.
- Many organizations have connected their LANs (local area networks) to a WAN (wide area network) such as the Internet. Any type of network must use a protocol, which is the set of rules that govern transmission, reception, and proper interpretation of received messages.
- On the Internet and on intranets and extranets, a set of protocols called TCP/IP (Transmission Control Protocol and Internet Protocol) is used. IP is a packet-switching protocol. In packet switching, a message is decomposed into several parts, and each of the parts may travel to their final destination through a different path. Intranets and extranets create *virtual private networks*, whereby the paths of communication span both private and public networks but thanks to security measures give the user the feeling of an all-private network.
- Each server that is connected to the Internet backbone is assigned an IP number, also called IP address or Internet address, made up of four blocks of binary numbers. In fact, every device connected to the Internet is assigned such a number, at least for the duration the device is logged on to the Internet. As the number of available IP addresses is fast decreasing, ICANN has considered new schemes to make available more addresses to the public.
- Both organizations and households now have a variety of options to connect to the Internet, in addition to the traditional telephone dial-up connection. ISDN is a widely available service in North America and parts of Europe. Television cable companies offer cable modem connection to the Internet at a high speed. Telephone companies offer DSL service to subscribers located

close enough to regional telephone exchanges. T1 and T3 lines have been used by many organizations for more than a decade, and like cable modem and DSL they provide a continuous connection to the Internet. ATM is the technology used for almost all new extensions of the Internet backbone and is being adopted by a growing number of organizations to obtain the highest communication speeds available.

■ Wireless networks are growing in popularity because they are highly scalable, relatively easy to install and maintain, and less expensive than wire-based networks. Their popularity is growing as the technology supports a growing bandwidth.

■ One of the most exciting developments in telecommunications is the use of wireless links to the Internet. People can use handheld computers to log on to the Internet from any region in the world where support for such technology exists. We are now moving toward a growing mode of mobile connection to the Internet for business and other purposes.

■ When considering implementation of LANs and links to the Internet, several issues should be weighed: the bandwidth that the links provide, their security, their scalability, and their cost. The decision to adopt a certain type of network or link to the Internet should optimize a "package" of all these factors.

KEY TERMS

topology	virtual private network
star topology	IP number
ring topology	ISDN
bus topology	cable modem
peer-to-peer networks	Ethernet
client-server networks	DSL
circuit switching	T1 line
packet switching	T3 line
network protocol	ATM
TCP/IP	scalability
LAN	security
WAN	
intranet	
extranet	

REVIEW QUESTIONS

1. What is bandwidth and how does it affect communications?
2. How many total Internet addresses could be used if they were all available? Explain your calculation.
3. How many internal IP addresses can an organization allocate to its departments if its host's IP number starts with 132? How many can it allocate if its IP number starts with 201?
4. On the Internet, data are transmitted using packet switching. What does packet switching mean, and how does it differ from circuit switching?
5. Explain the difference between an IP number and an Internet domain name.
6. You have a digital picture that you are going to e-mail to a friend. Its size is 2 Mb. Ignoring the geographic distance, how long will it take the picture to

reach your friend's computer if you use a regular telephone dial-up connection? How long would it take if the entire path from your computer to your friend's were the fastest ATM line? Show your calculations.

7. In what sense does the ATM standard resemble using the telephone?

DISCUSSION QUESTIONS

1. When you surf the Web you often witness the lack of enough bandwidth. Give an example. Is there a good reason why some people jokingly interpret WWW as World Wide Wait?

2. Some companies use the TCP/IP protocols for their LANs. They assign addresses to the different nodes without asking for IP numbers from ICANN. Explain how this is possible. Can the computers of these LANs access the Internet? Explain.

3. The sole right of assigning top-level country domain suffixes is given to national governments. The governments can license the right to assign the country's suffix for a fee to commercial organizations. Do you agree with this policy? Why or why not?

4. You are the chief information officer for a large organization with numerous offices in several buildings. Your organization is not yet connected to the Internet. Someone suggests that you establish a connection using cable. Should you accept the suggestion? Why or why not?

5. You are about to start an information business from your home. The information you provide on the Web to subscribers is not available from any other source and will be in high demand by college students. Consider Figure 2.4. To which type of communication service would you subscribe? Consider the cost and quality of service, and explain your choice.

ASSIGNMENTS

1. Several Web sites provide a feature that lets you figure out the IP number of your computer while you are logged on to the Internet. Find out your computer's IP number. Also, find out the class of IP numbers assigned to your school. How many of your school's nodes can be supported? Report all this information in an e-mail to your professor.

2. Outline the LANs of your school (not the entire university, only the college or school in which you are enrolled). On the bottom of your chart, write which topologies you have found and which protocol is used in each topology.

E-COMMERCE AT WORK

Down with the Pigeons

The city of Walnut Creek, California, needed to interconnect the LANs of its various departments. Since the LANs were dispersed throughout downtown, connecting the LANs using any type of physical wires would be prohibitively expensive. It would also require drilling and tearing apart walls. The solution was wireless equipment. Gary Lech, the city's Information Systems manager, figured that a wireless solution of any kind would be easy to implement because the LANs were not far from each other. Many were just across the street. By using wireless equipment, Lech could save the local government a lot of money that would otherwise be spent on leased lines from a telecommunications company.

Lech chose wireless equipment based on infrared technology. Proper devices were installed atop city hall and the city attorney's office across the street. The equipment shot a beam from one rooftop to the other, establishing a 1.5 Mbps connection between the two networks already installed in the buildings. Soon, however, Lech realized that the solution was a bad one. The wireless LAN connection was riddled with problems.

An infrared link can be maintained only when the communicating devices are aligned within a certain angle. The system was so sensitive that trucks passing between the two buildings could throw off the alignment of the infrared equipment, breaking the connection between the two networks. Heavy fog and wildlife also disrupted the connection. "Pigeons would walk by the equipment [on the roof] and the beam would go out," Lech says. "It was a comedy of errors."

The infrared system was down about 80 percent of the time, requiring the city's IS staff to call in a telecommunications company. The city ordered a combination of 56 Kbps and T1 (1.5 Mbps) lines from Pacific Bell. A star topology connected the buildings' various LANs to the network hub and Internet gateway in city hall.

This solution was technically solid, but the cost of leased lines quickly began to mount. What Lech needed was a network link that lowered operating costs and did not require him to tear up downtown streets to lay cable, so he revisited the idea of wireless LANs. He contacted a local firm and agreed to test RadioLAN Inc.'s CampusLAN wireless equipment.

Like the infrared-based equipment, the CampusLAN device established line-of-sight LAN interconnections. Buildings on the campus could be as far as 1,000 feet apart and be connected at 10 Mbps. But unlike the infrared-based equipment that had caused such a disaster, the CampusLAN device carried data over radio waves, which are not disrupted by local traffic, weather conditions, or birds.

Since the 56 Kbps and TI leased lines had already replaced the infrared connection between city hall and the city attorney's office, Lech decided to use CampusLAN devices to interconnect LANs at city hall and the Regional Center of the Arts, one block away. Antennae were attached to the roofs of the two buildings, and holes were drilled into the ceilings for the equipment's conduits. Then the CampusLAN devices were connected to each building's Ethernet LAN. The arts center depends on the connection for Internet connectivity, e-mail, and access to financial and Web-development software on servers at city hall.

Lech estimates a return on investment on the wireless equipment in little more than a year. Each node cost about $3,000 to connect. By comparison, a local T1 circuit costs $180 per month, in addition to installation charges and $2,000 to $5,000 for the routers.

In addition to the cost savings, Lech found the radio-based infrastructure far more reliable than the infrared equipment. "There has been no unexpected downtime whatsoever" after three months of continuous use, he says. Moreover, maintenance of the CampusLAN hardware is effortless, according to Lech. "There is no maintenance required. It is unlike a PC or even a router in that regard—it's completely plug-and-play. Once it is configured you can simply forget about it," he says.

Lech does not recommend outfitting entire organizations with radio wireless networks, though. A standard wire network using Ethernet technology provides greater bandwidth. Standards-based wireless equipment can only operate at 1 Mbps to 2 Mbps speeds; the proprietary RadioLAN technology operates at 10 Mbps. For speeds of 100 Mbps and 1 Gbps, wire-based systems were the best choice when Lech had the equipment installed.

However, this is changing. The next generation of RadioLAN wireless LAN hardware can operate at fast Ethernet speeds. Although it may not be able to match the speeds of the fastest wire equipment, wireless LAN equipment is proving to be an acceptable alternative to slow and expensive leased lines in an extended campus environment.

Source: Stone-Collonge, L., "A wireless LAN unfettered by pigeons," *Internet Week*, October 26, 1998

Thinking About E-Commerce at Work

1. Although the distances for which the city needed the links were short, the alternative to wireless links would be WAN links. Explain why. Who would provide these links?
2. What is plug-and-play? How does plug-and-play equipment make maintenance of hardware almost unnecessary?
3. Wireless communication is said to be more scalable than wire-based communication. What does *scalable* mean in this context? Explain the claim.

THE THREE LEVELS OF WEB SITES

LEARNING OBJECTIVES

WHEN YOU FINISH THIS CHAPTER YOU WILL BE ABLE TO:

- Use a framework for determining the extent to which the Internet can play a role in business
- Classify companies in different categories by their Internet-related activities
- Explain how companies incrementally develop business activities on the Web

What's wrong with these statistics? In 1997, only 47 percent of U.S. small businesses had Internet access. This number rose to 57 percent in 1998, and about 28 percent of small businesses had their own Web site in that year. However, according to a 2000 survey by the financial research firm Dunn & Bradstreet, the percentage of companies that sold or marketed goods online dropped from 29 percent in 1998 to 26 percent in 1999, while revenues from online sales as a percentage of total sales dropped from 12 percent to 8 percent. There are other surprising findings. A 2000 study by McKinsey & Co. and Salomon Smith Barney reached an interesting conclusion: Most offline businesses will find the Internet a profitable sales channel, but few online-only retailers are expected to have long-term success without an offline partner. (Adapted from Mowrey, M. A., "Pure Play: A Losing Model?" *The Industry Standard,* June 19, 2000, online)

Organizations that are considering involving the Internet in their business can learn from the experiences of other organizations by observing what techniques were tried and to what extent the organizations succeeded. By examining what has happened in the e-commerce arena so far, we can create a useful framework within which typical options can be analyzed.

There are several ways to analyze Web-based business activity. One is to look at the amount of activity that the firm intends to have on its Web site, the quantity usually being closely related to the complexity of the site, and, therefore, also to the sums of money spent on the development and maintenance of the site. As illustrated in Figure 3.1, Web sites can be built to do three things:

1. Be passive
2. Improve and enhance existing operations
3. Function as a stand-alone transaction site

Note that in this discussion we do not distinguish between business-to-business and business-to-consumer models. We devote full chapters to these models in Chapters 7 and 8, respectively.

PASSIVE WEB PRESENCE

Creating a passive Web site is often the first step that an organization takes when its managers decide it needs to be present on the Web. At the very least, a Web site provides one or several pages of information about the organization: its purpose, its history, its mission, its location, profiles of top executives, its products and/or services, and other general information. This is akin to having a big sign at a public place announcing: "This is who we are, and this is what we offer."

A passive site often only explains the existence of the business and its purpose. You may find numerous Web sites that consist of a single page, the

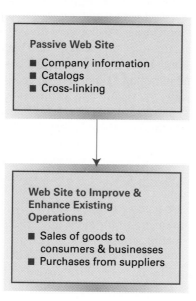

FIGURE 3.1 A WEB-BASED BUSINESS FRAMEWORK

Passive Web Site
- Company information
- Catalogs
- Cross-linking

Web Site to Improve & Enhance Existing Operations
- Sales of goods to consumers & businesses
- Purchases from suppliers

Stand-Alone Web Business

Transactions:
- Sales of physical goods
- Sales of digital goods
- Auctions
- Reverse auctions

Portal:
- Advertisements and tabs
- Business-to-consumer transaction fees

Hubs:
- Business-to-business transaction fees

homepage, which is the first Web page one encounters when logging on to a Web site. This page usually shows the company name and logo, a list of products and/or services, and a mission statement. Some businesses add more layers to their sites, providing clickable links to other pages that offer more detailed information. Yet the site only conveys information; it does not let customers purchase goods or services online.

The second step many companies take is the inclusion of a catalog of their products and pictures of all or some of the products. This is a modest step in helping increase sales. Interested parties, either individuals or other businesses, can get product and price information at any time without telephoning or writing the organization. Often a catalog is later developed into a full transaction site that lets customers order an item from the catalog by clicking an icon.

Some organizations never go beyond passive presence, because they cannot benefit much from an interactive site. This is especially true of nonprofit organizations. For example, the Red Cross advertises blood drives and other activities, but it does not need to provide any transaction-enabling mechanisms on its site. Many government agencies provide online information and the capability of downloading forms, but they have no need to develop their sites into interactive, transaction-enabled sites.

ADVERTISING ON THE WEB

Many companies recognize that they cannot simply hope that people will look for their site. To fully appreciate the effectiveness of this strategy, they must publicize their site at heavily trafficked sites of other businesses. Consider the findings of a study by the marketing research firm Cyber Dialogue. IMS Health Inc. reported that in the first six months of 2000, pharmaceutical companies spent an estimated $833 million on TV consumer advertising, $460 million on print campaigns, and $47 million on Web marketing. Using these figures along with sales information from the pharmaceutical industry, the Cyber Dialogue calculated the following average expenditure per single drug request during that period: $54 per single specific drug request driven by Web advertising, $152 per single specific drug request driven by television advertising, and $318 per single specific drug request driven by print advertising. The conclusion is simple: During this period, advertising on the Internet was the most effective method for generating interest in pharmaceutical products. This demonstrates the power of the Web in stimulating business.

If a firm wants to utilize the power of the Web as an advertising tool, the firm usually cannot count on the limited traffic that its own site generates. **Traffic** is the number of visitors per unit of time. The advertising power of a Web site is similar to that of real estate, television, and radio. Times Square in New York City is an appealing place to place outdoor advertising banners because of the huge amount of people who pass through there; a popular television show attracts advertisers because of the millions of people who watch the commercials; and a popular radio program attracts advertisers because of the millions of people who listen to it (perhaps while commuting or being stuck in traffic jams). Similarly, high-traffic Web sites provide effective advertising opportunities. There are many companies whose own sites are passive that spend heavily on Web advertising. AOL, Yahoo!, Excite, and Mamma maintain sites that millions of visitors log on to daily. Amazon.com, Buy.com, eBay.com, and Priceline.com attract thousands of customers and therefore enjoy heavy traffic. Hence, many companies elect to pay these organizations to place graphical, usually clickable, mentions that lure visitors to the advertisers' sites.

An Advertising Example   Consider the power of advertising on the Web. Amazon.com is the world's largest Web store, with 16 million registered customers. Amazon uses this asset to draw dollars from online businesses seeking attention. In January 2000, it struck a deal with the online car retailer Greenlight.com. Amazon promised to direct customers to the site via ad banners. Greenlight.com agreed to pay $82.5 million over five years. Three days later Amazon signed a contract with Drugstore.com, a company partly owned by Amazon, to rent it a tab on Amazon's site. A *tab* is a graphical icon that many online sites use as a link to categories of a catalog; it looks like a binder tab. The deal's size: $105 million for three years. Is the money worth the publicity? Drugstore.com's CEO believed it was, noting that about one third of his company's customers came from Amazon's customer pool.

HomeGrocer.com, an online grocery service in fierce competition with some 10 other such services, signed a five-year deal in February 2000 to have AOL publicize HomeGrocer at AOL's site and on four other portals controlled by AOL. (A **portal** is a site that provides links to a wide range of information.) The minimum number of people who would be exposed to the advertisement at the time of the deal was 25 million, AOL's captive audience of fee-paying subscribers.

How many Net surfers actually click the advertisement banners and explore the sites they tout? Media experts usually estimate the proportion at two percent. This is not much proportionately, but two percent of several million prospective customers is quite a commercial potential. We will address advertising on the Web again in Chapter 9.

Traffic Ratings for Web Sites   Advertisers always want to know how many people will be exposed to their messages, and for how long. The more the exposure, the greater the potential effect of the ads. Thus, advertisers use information gathered by rating agencies. In the television arena, Americans are familiar with the Nielsen Company, which measures the number of viewers of various television programs. In the Web arena, there are several agencies that provide a similar service. These companies include a Nielsen subsidiary, called Nielsen/NetRatings, as well as MediaMetrix and PC Data. All use a large sample of Web users to measure site-visiting and Web-shopping habits. For example, PC Data uses a sample of 120,000 participants who use their computers at home, work, or school.

I N T E R E S T I N G . . .

PARLEZ VOUS WEB?

English is the predominant language of the Internet, a fact that irritates some governments. The French Finance Ministry is trying to convince the French to stop calling new Web companies *les start-ups* and instead use the term *jeunes pousses d'entreprises* ("young sprouts of companies"). If it were up to the ministry, stock options would become *options sur titre* ("options on a share") and marketing managers would be *directeurs de la mercatique,* according to a ministry list released in March 2000. For e-mail, the Ministry has eschewed *courriel*—which apparently upsets the French—for the longer *message electronique.*

Source: Reuters, March 2, 2000

Nielsen/NetRatings relies on a sample, or *panel*, of 65,000 people who log on from home (57,000) or work (8,000).

Figure 3.2 is a partial report from PC Data's site. It shows the firm's ranking of popular sites by the number of unique visitors who visited the sites in February 2000. Note that the numbers indicate "unique visitors." Ratings specialists have figured out how to count every visitor during the given period only once, even if certain visitors visited a site more than once. **Reach percentage** is calculated by dividing the number of unique visitors by the total estimated population using the Web during the reported time period. In other words, it is an estimate of how many of all Web surfers the site "reached" during the reported period.

There are a number of ways to identify visitors for the purpose of determining unique visitors; one is by checking the cookie of the visitor, which holds unique personal information. (We discuss cookies in Chapter 4.) The other method is to identify the IP number of the computer from which the visitor visited the site. The latter is not an accurate measure, however, because a visitor may use different computers with different IP numbers to surf the Net and visit the same site.

Web rating firms also provide subscribers with figures on the distribution of visitors between home and work. A firm may use this information to target different audiences because it is clear that some people visit predominantly from home, such as school-age children and teenagers, people who work at home, and senior citizens. For additional fees, rating companies can measure the amount of time that visitors spend at a site, and even read the visitor's click stream. A **click stream** is the user's sequence of clicking links at a site. The click stream allows the rating company to figure out what information (and, therefore, what products or services) is of greater or lesser interest to the visitors. Click stream measurement software is often employed by Web sites without involving ratings firms.

FIGURE

3.2 THE MOST TRAFFICKED WEB SITES AS RANKED BY PC DATA IN FEBRUARY 2000

Rank	Site*	Reach (%)	Unique Visitors (thousands)
1	Yahoo Sites	69.6	46,722
2	Microsoft Sites	66.2	44,448
3	AOL Sites	65.2	43,791
4	Lycos	50.2	33,704
5	Excite Network	41.8	28,052
6	Go Network	35.2	23,673
7	NBC Internet	29.6	19,906
8	Time Warner Online	27.4	18,428
9	Amazon.com	23.4	15,701
10	About.com	23.3	15,656
11	AltaVista Network	22.3	14,946
12	eBay.com	21.1	14,159
13	Ask Jeeves Inc.	17.8	11,967
14	AllAdventure.com	17.8	11,904
15	Go2Net Network	17.2	11,523

Source: PC Data, March 2000

* All the sites maintained by the organization

CROSS-LINKING

Cross-linking is another passive feature of the Web that can be effectively used by both passive and transactional sites. Companies that offer related products and services often collaborate to each other's benefit: Company A posts company B's banner at its site, and company B posts company A's banner at its own site. For example, a company that sells music compact discs may create a link to the site of an electronics retailer that sells compact disc players in return for the electronics retailer's hosting of a link to the compact disc seller. Cross-linking is a form of advertising that is unique to the Web. We rarely see it in other media. Its effectiveness lies in the nature of the online hyperlink: With one click one can go from site to site.

WEB SITES TO IMPROVE AND ENHANCE EXISTING OPERATIONS

Sometimes the establishment of a passive site is only the first phase toward developing it into an active one. For example, Hershey Food Corporation established its presence on the Web in 1994 with no more than a few pages telling Web users about the company and showing pictures of its major products. At that time management had determined that people would not buy sweets via the Web. Therefore, there was no point in investing much money in the site. The company did not even hire professional Web page developers. It allowed a few employees to devote some time to developing the pages. Obviously, there was no point in hiring a Web master, either, because the site was quite static in terms of content and posed no technical challenge. By 1998, management had reconsidered its decision. Other companies' experience had shown that consumers were ready to purchase food over the Web, especially when the food was in the form of beautifully wrapped gift packages. Hershey turned its passive site into an active one that improved and enhanced its regular operations: In addition to selling through normal distribution channels, such as large retail food chains and regional distributors, Hershey started selling directly to consumers. With just a few clicks, consumers could use a local search engine, browse through attractive pictures of food baskets, order shipments, and pay.

Often the purpose of using a Web site is not to change the products and services sold but the way in which they are sold. Commercial Web sites provide online catalogs to save paper and telephone time. They provide hyper media information for after-the-sale support of their products so clients have access to such information at all times. Such sites also feature transaction software that lets clients purchase items and pay for them on the Web.

The enhancement of existing operations through the Web is especially promising in industries where the product or service itself does not change and probably cannot change. Consider retail chains, such as office supply superstores. OfficeMax, Staples, and Office Depot are the largest American retailers in this market. All of them have online catalogs and transaction software. The sites have not changed how these chains operate at all. The stores still exist and sell the same items as before. However, many consumers now prefer to order items via the Web and have them shipped directly to their offices or homes. The Web sites only improve an existing operation.

Traditional department store chains have struggled with the notion of Web use. They have felt that they must join the rush to the Web but have been unsure about what to do. Many of them have settled on the following simple model: continue to do businesses in the stores but invite shoppers to buy the same items, or most of these items, through a single company Web site. Customers can then choose their own mode of shopping, either physically in a store or online. The combination of brick-and-mortar stores and online purchasing has led observers to call these chains **click-and-mortar** businesses. Click-and-mortar is the nickname for organizations that combine traditional commerce from bricks-and-mortar buildings with Web commerce. Consumers have a new advantage with click-and-mortars: They can order an item online but return it to any of the chain's stores for a refund if they are dissatisfied with the purchase. For example, Sears extended its "Satisfaction guaranteed or your money back" policy to the Web; online buyers can return items to any of the company's 858 stores. This new convenience may attract shoppers to the company's Web site.

Similarly, companies that deliver goods and services directly to consumers can enhance and improve their operations by moving from mail and phone communication to the Internet. Dell, the giant personal computer maker, built its reputation and fortune by letting individuals configure their own computer systems when ordering them directly from the company (see Figure 3.3). In its early days, clients had to use the telephone to engage employees, but Dell swiftly moved its ordering operations to the Web. Consumers log on to the site, select a basic computer from a long list, add and delete peripheral equipment, and immediately see the impact of configuration changes on the total price they will have to pay. The service saves Dell millions of dollars that it used to pay to employees who took orders over the phone. In addition, the information entered by the customers is immediately in electronic form, so it does not have to be re-keyed into the company's order system.

Another enhancement to Dell's operations is the availability of online conferences with information technology executives of corporate clients. The company is using Web-based teleconferencing tools for this purpose, thus helping Dell's executives learn about customer concerns and maintain loyal customers.

The Internet has allowed some companies to move much of their business to online transactions. Cisco is a classic example. The world's largest company in market valuation terms, this maker of telecommunications routers has gradually shifted from receiving orders by mail and telephone to conducting 85 percent of them (totaling over $17 billion in 1999) online. It also recruits almost all of its new employees via the Internet.

Interestingly, some companies have decided to move fully from brick-and-mortar locations to Web operations only. One such company is Egghead. In the 1980s and early 1990s, Egghead operated a nationwide chain of software stores in the United States. The stores also sold peripheral computer equipment. In 1997, management decided to eliminate all operations in physical stores. Egghead reemerged as a Web-only company named Egghead.com, which sells hardware and software from its Web site. Egghead.com later acquired an Internet company named OnSale.com to utilize that company's expertise in sales and auctions on the Web. (The company later declared bankruptcy.)

Some companies have found ways to provide information on their Web sites and significantly cut their costs. Instead of limiting customer support to 9 A.M. to 5 P.M., the traditional time slot for employing support personnel to answer phone inquiries, information is simply placed on the Web and updated whenever needed, a process that does not involve much expensive human labor. In addition, some information can be communicated better through multimedia, which is so convenient on the Web. Obviously, many customers are more comfortable with a human helper, but many others find it easier to receive at least some information through

3.3 FROM DELL COMPUTER'S WEB SITE

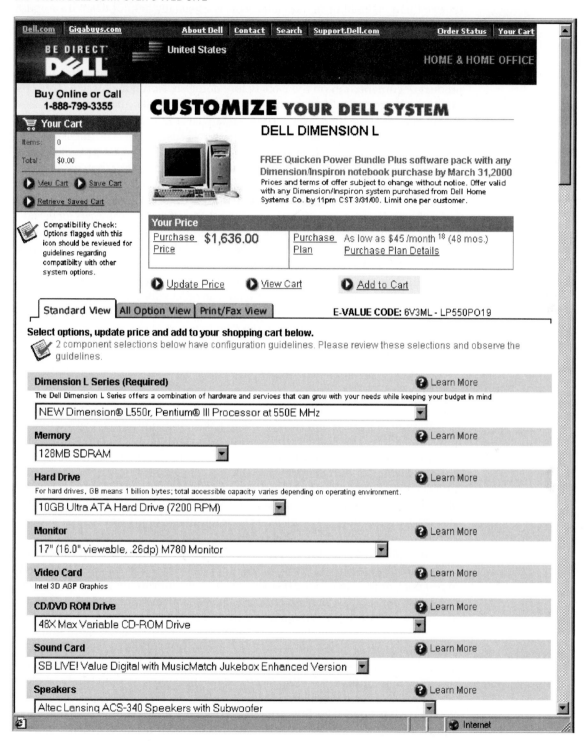

the Web. For example, a Web-site posting of product and maintenance manuals makes customer access to them immediate; otherwise people could not expect to receive them via mail until days later. This is especially helpful when a company has international clients.

One company that uses the Web to enhance customer service is Nashville, Tennessee–based Nortel Networks Corporation, a leader in the design and manufacture of network switches and related products. The company posted all of its product documentation on the Web. Before doing so, Nortel had used a large customer service organization to respond to customer queries and complaints. Now customers can serve themselves. The company also translated its documentation into the diverse languages of its many international customers. (The translation was performed by commercially available software.) Printed manuals were eliminated and with them the high cost of printing and shipping them. Users can easily download manuals at their convenience. The company cut its customer service costs by 50 percent while providing a better service in eight different languages.

In the retail sector, some features that have been offered to customers for decades in stores are now offered on the Web. Moving features to the Web makes a company global, regardless of store locations. J. C. Penney was the first department store chain to offer a gift registry: soon-to-wed couples, bar-mitzvah boys and bat-mitzvah girls, and parents of newborns may designate the chain (that is the entire chain, not a single store) as the place where relatives and friends can order gifts. The relatives and friends use an online table that indicates which items from a list have not yet been ordered and can order those items at the Web site. Within months, almost every other retailer adopted the feature, which some sites now call a "wish list."

STAND-ALONE TRANSACTION SITES

By **stand-alone transaction site**, we mean a business that was conceived to work only through the Web. Many companies started as pure Internet companies. They are often referred to as **pure play** companies. They did not exist before the Internet was opened to commercial ventures, obviously, but further they would not have been established had the Web not provided the opportunity to sustain a whole business online. Many of these companies immediately established a Web site with a transaction mechanism, as their reason for being was to offer a means for buying, selling, or both via their Web sites.

Some pure play companies have become household names. Amazon.com was originally established to sell books online and proclaimed itself the world's largest bookstore, much to the dismay of brick-and-mortar bookstore chains such as Barnes and Noble (which, nonetheless, quickly followed suit and established its own online bookstore). It did not take long before Amazon.com became an online department store selling almost any imaginable nonperishable item. Similarly, CDNow.com, a huge seller of music CDs, could offer a larger selection than any bricks-and-mortar store only because it was Web-based. Online sellers do not have to maintain physical retail stores where the items actually sit on shelves. Other online stores have opened their doors, selling anything from electronics to men's clothing. Some, like Buy.com, try to sell almost everything to anyone, constantly adding item categories; others specialize in a narrow niche, such as Perfumania.com (you guessed it: They sell perfumes) and the Chicago Wine Company.

Some Internet companies would not be possible off the Web. These are the firms that run auction, exchange, and reverse auction sites. They may be called *commerce hubs*, because they take advantage of the ability of sellers and buyers to meet in a virtual place (practically, they all meet at one of the site's servers) and conduct business involving any imaginable item, from rare collectibles to airline tickets to scrap metal. We will discuss these types of Web sites in Chapters 7 and 8. Commerce hubs may offer the greatest contribution in making any market more efficient. Their contribution to the world economy is huge and continues to grow because they provide two important elements in creating efficient markets:

1. They enable information to reach any player in the market almost instantly, so everyone is informed equally.
2. They bring together millions of sellers and buyers (see Figure 3.4).

One of the earliest auction sites was eBay. Catering to individual clients, it is one of the predominant players in this market. Other heavily trafficked sites, such as Amazon.com, followed suit and opened their own auction operations, probably because the commerce hub business model is highly profitable. Unlike online retail, a commerce hub does not require purchasing, warehousing, and shipping goods, nor does it require arrangements with any manufacturers.

Priceline.com invented *reverse auctions*, in which companies compete for a customer's business after the customer has named a price for a product or service. A multitude of organizations have established sites that specialize in getting sellers and buyers of narrowly defined products on the Web. By and large, they facilitate business-to-business activities.

Large purchasers are interested in commerce hubs so they can lower the prices they pay. In 2000, the three biggest American automakers, General Motors, Ford, and DaimlerChrysler, agreed to collaborate in an effort to establish a Web site called Covisint for the sole purpose of making parts manufacturers compete on every order. While the site may not operate as a stand-alone, for-profit business, it is certainly a venture that would not be possible without the Internet. The automakers, who order parts for $240 billion annually, intend to move all of the purchasing activity to this hub.

Another type of business that would be impossible without the Web is the **Application Service Provider** (ASP). This is a company that specializes in renting the use of software applications through communication lines. An ASP maintains the applications such as Microsoft Office and various accounting systems and possibly

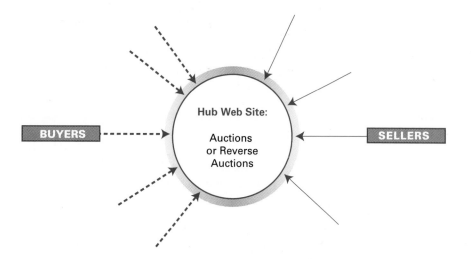

INTERESTING . . .

OLD WORLD WOES

Online business in Europe is significantly more challenging than in North America. Several factors account for the difficulties of Web businesses in Europe. Italians and Germans are not crazy about credit cards: Only one in seven people hold one. To get any attention, a business targeting Europeans must translate anything it communicates into at least five languages. Most Europeans still have to pay for every minute of access to the Internet; retailers lose consumers' impulse shopping when consumers must pay just for being online. Some European companies are adamant about doing business only with businesspeople from their own country; for instance, Milan's businesspeople are notorious for doing business solely with other Italians. Do we, then, really have a worldwide electronic market? Perhaps Europeans will first engage in continent-wide business on the Web.

Source: The Industry Standard, March 13, 2000, p. 137

data files, on its own hardware. The clients' employees then access the applications (and other files) as needed. While some long-standing companies such as IBM and Oracle established units that act as ASPs, several new companies, such as USInterconnect, were established for the sole purpose of providing the service.

Some Web sites that started as simple transactional sites for selling products or services have evolved into sites that generate revenue from additional activities. Many electronic retailers began their journey selling a single type of product and have evolved into selling hundreds of different categories of products. As mentioned earlier, Amazon.com started out selling only books but is now involved in selling compact discs, electronics, household goods, and many other types of products online. WebMD started out as a site that provided medical advice and generated revenue by selling ad space, but it moved on to become the premier integrator of online medical services by linking doctors, medical insurance companies, and drugstores.

Sites that offered search engines with little advertisement potential, such as Yahoo!, Excite, and Mamma, became portals with millions of dollars in revenue from advertisements and also evolved into hubs for business-to-business and business-to-consumer transactions (see Figure 3.5). For instance, Yahoo! and Excite developed

FIGURE

3.5 THE EVOLVEMENT OF SEARCH ENGINES INTO MAJOR E-COMMERCE HUBS

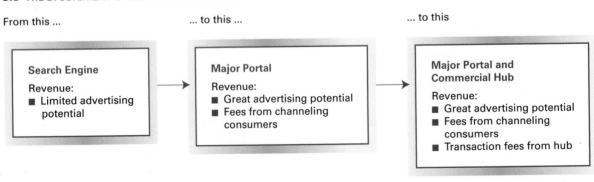

From this ...

Search Engine

Revenue:
- Limited advertising potential

... to this ...

Major Portal

Revenue:
- Great advertising potential
- Fees from channeling consumers

... to this

Major Portal and Commercial Hub

Revenue:
- Great advertising potential
- Fees from channeling consumers
- Transaction fees from hub

into sites that provide personalized information and then became focal points for online retailers. In the latter scheme, the sites host banners and tabs for the retailers and collect from organizations a percentage of any transaction that results from visitors clicking on the banner or tab. Special software tracks visitors' clicking and moving from one site to another to establish a fee-bearing transaction.

SHAPING AND RESHAPING ONLINE BUSINESS

It would be wrong to include all businesses with a Web presence in only one category. To return to Amazon.com as an example, it started as a bookseller and as such could be categorized as a pure transaction site. But it also developed its online business incrementally to sell a much larger variety of items and to include other revenue-generating methods, such as sales of ad banners and tabs. It now also provides an auction site. Sensing it may miss the boat, competitor Barnes and Noble, the largest traditional bookseller, established its own online bookstore. While this venture may look like an extension of the main business, it is practically an independent business that works exactly like its Web-only competitor.

Similarly, it would not be easy to classify publications that have extended their operations onto the Web. *Business Week*, the *Wall Street Journal, The New York Times*, and numerous other newspapers, weeklies, and monthlies have established Web sites. Some allow their regular print subscribers to receive the same information online as they would from the paper issues; some supplement the paper issues with online stories and analysis; and some, like the *Wall Street Journal*, sell subscriptions to the online newspaper separately from the print subscription. The class or category of a Web business or a Web extension of a business is not important in terms of the chances of such a business to survive and profit. The difference between a pure transactional Web business and a Web extension of an existing business is that a Web extension may be terminated while the original business is still viable, whereas if the stand-alone Web business cannot survive, there is nothing on which management can fall back.

The fundamental manner in which Web businesses are developed and earn revenues continues to evolve. Human ingenuity and the great expansion of the Internet, and therefore the Web, have made this bound to happen. Gradually, the Web will become the predominant marketplace for business-to-business commerce and a major marketplace for business-to-consumer commerce worldwide. Few people were willing to shop and purchase online in the mid-1990s. Millions do so now. Few people were willing to pay for online **content**, that is, information. Thousands of people now pay for online content. Thus, as the Web evolves, so will business ideas and models. We will continue to explore these ideas and models throughout the book.

SUMMARY

■ In general, organizations that use the Web for business can be placed in one of three classes: those with a passive presence, those that use the Web to improve and enhance existing operations, and those that create new, stand-alone transaction sites as their main or only business. In the first class we find companies that operated for many years before the advent of the Internet and that basically continue to sell their products and services as they have for years. These companies establish Web sites to have a presence in a new medium of communication. Such Web sites present information about the company and its products, product catalogs, and any other information that the company wants to communicate to existing and prospective clients.

■ Some of these companies pay firms that maintain heavily trafficked sites for advertising. Usually, the advertising is in the form of a clickable graphic that takes the user to the company's site. Some use cross-linking, whereby companies that offer complimentary or otherwise related items place each others' graphical links on their sites.

■ Passive presence can take the form of advertising only. Advertising on the Web has been shown to be more efficient than television and print advertising. For a smaller expense, a company can attract the same or a larger audience to its products. To evaluate how attractive a site is to Web users, rating firms can be hired. They track unique visits per a time frame and the reach of popular sites. Advertisers can use this information to decide how much to spend on advertising at a given site.

■ A growing number of companies, especially large retail chains, have augmented their existing businesses with transaction sites. They sell through their Web sites the same or all of the items that they sell at their stores. This has turned such companies from brick-and-mortar businesses to click-and-mortar businesses. These businesses offer consumers extra convenience: the consumer can purchase items through the Web site and return unwanted items to a local store for a refund. Manufacturers and distributors have established Web sites through which they sell their parts or finished goods to other businesses. In some cases, brick-and-mortar businesses have reinvented themselves completely as Web-only businesses.

■ Some companies have incrementally reshaped themselves from traditional brick-and-mortars into pure play Web companies. Others decided to become a combination of brick-and-mortar stores and an online operation. As business strategies on the Web change, so do business models.

KEY TERMS

homepage
traffic
portal
reach percentage
click stream
cross-linking

click-and-mortar
stand-alone transaction site
pure play
Application Service Provider (ASP)
content

REVIEW QUESTIONS

1. What is a passive Web site? Why is it called passive?
2. Businesses that use the Web instead of publishing catalogs can save costs. What types of costs can they save?
3. In the early days of Web commerce, businesses measured the popularity of their Web sites by the number of hits per day or per week. Why is this an inappropriate measure of site traffic? What measures do Web sites use now?
4. In measuring Web site traffic, what does *reach* mean? How is it computed?
5. What is a click-and-mortar business? Do these businesses have an advantage over brick-and-mortar businesses? If so, what is the advantage? Do these businesses have an advantage over Web-only sites? If so, what is the advantage?

6. How does the growth of the Internet affect the decisions of commercial organizations about the level of their Web site involvement?
7. In the past, people tended to be reluctant to pay for some types of information on the Web. Mention at least one such type and explain why you think many people now agree to pay for this service.
8. How can a large purchaser of certain items save costs by creating a Web site through which all of its suppliers must access purchase bids?
9. This chapter gives some examples of how organizations have enhanced and improved their operations by using the Web. How have banks used the Web to provide better service and save costs? Explain.

DISCUSSION QUESTIONS

1. Are there types of businesses that could not use a transaction mechanism at their Web sites because these mechanisms could not support the business? In other words, are there types of businesses whose Web sites should remain passive? Explain.
2. How does an efficient market differ from an inefficient one? How does the Web help make markets more efficient?
3. You are the chief executive officer of a large youth-apparel retail chain. You are considering advertising the chain at heavily trafficked sites. Can you tell from Figure 3.2 which sites would be best for this strategy? If not, what further information do you need from the ratings firm?
4. Egghead's management decided to completely shut down its chain of stores and become a Web-only retailer of hardware and software. Would you make the same decision? Why or why not? Which other types of retail businesses should make the same move, and why?
5. Dell, the giant computer maker, has gradually moved from serving customers over the phone to serving them over the Internet. What other types of businesses could make the same move?

ASSIGNMENTS

1. Surf the Web and find three sites that are passive. Write a one-page report that explains (1) why you consider the sites passive, and (2) what you would recommend to the executives of these firms to better utilize the Web and increase customer awareness and sales. If there is nothing more that the firms can do on the Web, explain why.
2. Many Web-based businesses have failed. Search the Web, identify such a business, and prepare a 5-to-10-minute software-based presentation (such as PowerPoint) explaining what happened. In your presentation, answer the following questions: (1) Was the business concept bad? (2) Was the failure a result of too few Web surfers at the time the business was launched? (3) Was the failure related to security issues? In your conclusion, tell if you think the same business concept would work today (because of the larger number of Web surfers and/or the greater enthusiasm of businesses and consumers for doing business online).

From Idea to the Web in Nine Months

One day in December 1998, Sue Levin met with Steve Hochman in a beer microbrewery in Portland, Oregon. Levin was the head of the women's-brand division at Nike. Hochman was a senior product manager at Intel. They worked not far from each other. Levin and Hochman's wife, Juliet, were friends. For some time, Hochman had been asking Levin to meet with him. Now, he popped the question. He wanted her to leave Nike and be the president of his yet-to-be-formed start-up company.

Hochman's wife was a workout enthusiast and kept complaining about the difficulty of buying workout clothes. The variety of women's sportswear was limited in stores and practically nonexistent on the Web. Hochman wanted to establish the first women's-only online sportswear store, but he needed someone with the proper professional background and expertise to help him.

Levin had helped promote the U.S. women's basketball and soccer teams before their gold medal–winning performances in the 1996 Summer Olympics, when the teams wore Nike's apparel. She had also signed several prominent athletes—Mia Hamm, Picabo Street, and Sheryl Swoopes, namely—to represent Nike. Hochman needed Levin for the new venture. Would she be interested? At this time she was not. However, she promised to think about it further and get back to him. Two weeks later, Levin told him she was in. A month later, both quit their jobs to devote all their time to the new business.

In 1999, women's basketball and soccer received growing attention in the media. The total sporting-goods market was estimated at $77 billion, and women purchased more in this market than men. Hochman and Levin knew that if they were aware of the fact that the selection of women's sportswear online was close to nothing, so were other people. This meant that to succeed they would have to move fast. Furthermore, since others were bound to follow, they had to find ways to distinguish themselves from their potential competitors.

Hochman and Levin decided to offer a mix of sportswear and fashion. They planned to buy ads in women's sports publications and fashion magazines. However, the first thing they needed was cash. They contacted everyone who could help them with referrals to venture capital firms. Levin's husband had attended Stanford University with a man whose father, Jim Gaither, Sr., was a partner at Cooley Godward, a Silicon Valley law firm that specialized in helping Internet start-ups. Impressed with their business plan, Gaither, Sr., agreed to represent the new company and to introduce the two entrepreneurs to some friends who were venture capital executives. In April 1998, Hochman and Levin went to Silicon Valley.

Apparently, Hochman and Levin approached the right people at the right time. In 1999, venture capital dollars invested in Internet start-ups reached a record high of $10.8 billion, five times more than the previous year. Hochman and Levin were introduced to Bill Younger, a partner at Sutter Hill Ventures in Palo Alto, which had made several successful investments in Internet start-ups. Younger liked the business plan. He liked the enthusiasm and knowledge of the two entrepreneurs. He became totally convinced to make the investment when they all toured the shopping center at Stanford, and he saw how poor the selection of women's sportswear really was. Younger brought onboard another venture capital firm, Foundation Capital. In late May, the two firms agreed to invest $4.5 million.

Usually, venture capital firms do not fund ventures at such an early stage of their lives. They want to see an existing and operating organization that has proven its concept. Therefore, Levin was surprised at how fast they received the money. She later realized that the venture capitalist knew there was no time for proof of concept; it was a waste of time. By the time they had proven the concept, they would have been well behind their competitors.

Indeed, they did have competition. In summer 1998, Athleta and Title 9 Sports were online. These two small, mail-order companies that sold women's sportswear started selling through their new Web sites. However, neither made the kind of splash that Hochman and Levin had in mind. Now, with cash in the bank and a law firm to advise them, they had to establish an organization. Their plan was ambitious: launch the site by October, just five months away. The two spent May and June hiring people. They hired Bill Johnson as engineering vice president, Bonnie Choruby as merchandising vice president, Vicky Reed as marketing director, and Katy Tisch as creative director. Most of them were Levin's acquaintances from Nike or the sports industry in general. The rest were hired through headhunters (the nickname for firms specializing in executive placement).

The next executive they felt they needed to hire was someone who could make deals with major portals to bring their own Web site to the attention of millions of consumers. Levin contacted an old friend, Kate Delhagen. In the early 1990s, Delhagen and Levin had worked together as journalists covering women's sports. Now Delhagen headed the online retail research unit at Forrester Research, a research and consulting firm. She specialized in sites catering to women. Her expertise was so valuable that she was receiving several job offers from companies every week. Delhagen agreed to join.

The company contracted with an apparel maker, Norm Thompson Outfitters, Inc. Norm Thompson owned the physical warehouse in West Virginia from which the new Web site would ship products to its online clients. The company also operated warehouse and inventory control software that Hochman and Levin liked.

Yet not all went without problems. Hochman and Levin hired two companies to implement the information systems and telecommunications for the site, Organic Online and Q Strategies. Organic provided the e-commerce software. Such software includes several components, including those for ordering and payment. As it turned out, Organic's e-commerce software did not include a component to connect the online store's cash-register function with Norm Thompson's warehouse-inventory control application. Hochman and Levin decided to give almost all the work, including the development and integration of the software, to a single firm, Q Strategies. The old software was dumped, and Q Strategies used its own platform, which included the missing component. Organic was still kept to work on the online store's Web pages' appearance.

As the development of the site went on, one thing was missing. The site had no name. Hochman and Levin considered many options: E-Motion, SkipJump, SeeJaneGo, HailMary, Zazi, Junie, PinkGrapefruit, Amezzo, Citrus, and many other fruit names. Eventually they settled on the name of a dog that Delhagen once owned: Lucy. The domain name happened to be registered to an Organic employee, who after some negotiations, agreed to give it to them.

By late July, the company had 15 employees. Sutter Hill and Foundation, the two venture capital firms, invested another $3 million, and the company moved to a new office in Portland. The entrepreneurs hired an advertising agency, a public relations firm, and an e-mail marketer. They also had verbal agreements with close to 40 apparel makers, some of which agreed to make the clothes with a Lucy logo.

The site's launch was postponed to mid-November. Hochman and Levin decided to launch it without much advertising at first, to test whether all was working well. In the meantime, they had not concluded the contract they had been negotiating with AOL. Delhagen explained that AOL attracted to its site the kind of consumers that Lucy.com targeted and that the site could gain a lot from advertising with this giant. However, Hochman and Levin felt that AOL demanded too much money for its service.

In October, the company had 35 employees. Engineers were finishing networking the site's servers, located hundreds of miles south of Portland, in San Jose, California. The site was managed by a telecommunications company called AboveNet. The servers were connected to the Internet via high-speed lines. AboveNet provided 24-hours-per-day, seven-days-per-week maintenance and security crews.

Two weeks before the official launch, the managers opened the site to a limited number of family members and friends, as a test. All that could go wrong went wrong, as Hochman said later. The engineers and programmers fixed the problems. In the meantime, Levin and Delhagen conducted a two-week cross-country publicity tour. While in New York City, they featured Jackie Joyner-Kersee, the Olympic gold medalist, as their first Lucy.com celebrity endorser.

On November 15, 1999, at 4 P.M., Lucy.com was online and open for business. For 30 minutes nothing happened. Then, a woman from San Francisco bought apparel worth $52. The site was live, but it needed much more cash for promotion. In January 2000, Hochman and Levin signed deals with two new venture capital firms. The original firms and the two new ones collectively invested another $28 million. The money was earmarked for advertising in print and online. Billboard advertising also was in the works.

In February 2000, overall sales were still small, but the average sale was 25 to 50 percent greater than the entrepreneurs had forecast. The AOL deal was closed, but it would take time to figure out how many people clicked through from AOL to Lucy.com. In March 2000, the company had 55 employees and planned to hire an additional 20 people. Unfortunately, time did tell, and the message was not good. On February 2001 the site was shut down.

Adapted from Rafter, M. V., "Lucy.com; Diary of a start-up," *The Industry Standard*, March 13, 2000, pp. 143-161

Thinking About E-Commerce at Work

1. The case mentions "proof of concept." What is proof of concept, and why do investors usually want to see proof of concept before committing funds?
2. Examine the details. Was Lucy.com a pure online business, or was it a click-and-mortar business?
3. In February 2001, Lucy.com closed its Web business to become a one-store company in New York City. What do you think were the reasons for this failure?

WEB SOFTWARE

- Explain the role of Standard General Markup Language (SGML) and the difference between SGML and other markup languages
- Explain why HyperText Markup Language defines the Web
- Compare and contrast HyperText Markup Language and other Web programming languages
- Discuss the role of Extensible Markup Language and its contribution to electronic data interchange on the Internet
- Evaluate the different ways a Web server can establish an interactive link between Web browsers and databases
- Explain the contribution of three-dimensional renditioning on the Web

A "killer application" is a computer program that is so useful that people would purchase a computer just to use that program. In the 1980s, the most popular killer application was the spreadsheet. What is the killer application of our time? Undoubtedly, it is the Web browser. What enabled the Web browser? Initially it was HTML; later, XHTML, a combination of HTML and XML, became the standard programming language and the power behind the browser. A report by Nua.com, an Internet site dedicated to collecting Internet trends and statistics, estimated that as of March 2000 about 304 million people used browsers to log on to the Web. (Source: NUA, www.nua.ie/surveys/how_many_online/index.html, 2000)

The Internet is often confused with the World Wide Web. Actually, there is a difference between the two. The Internet is a physical, worldwide network of computers. It allows linked computers to send and receive any type of digital information. The Web is defined by the manner in which communicated documents are presented on the receiving computer. Therefore, the history of the Web started much later than the history of the Internet. In this section we discuss the standards and programming languages that have let us transform the Internet from a network that allowed us to transmit and receive only text into what we now know as the Web.

SGML: THE FRAMEWORK FOR PROGRAMMING WEB PAGES

How does your computer know how to interpret the streams of bits it receives over the Internet into sense-making text, pictures, and animations? The proper interpretation comes courtesy of a browser, a software application that is designed to correctly interpret and display such elements. Various programming languages help design documents that display text, image, and sound elements. Most of these languages conform to a general standard called **Standard Generalized Markup Language** (SGML). *Marking up* means adding special characters to indicate how certain parts of a document should be displayed. Programmers mark up elements as they design Web pages.

SGML is known informally as "the mother of all Web programming languages." In itself, however, it is not a programming language but a set of rules for organizing and tagging the elements of a document. *Tags*, such as "<", ">", "/", "{", and "}", determine how elements in a document—text, e-mail addresses, Web site addresses (URLs), pictures, sounds, and other elements—will be presented when someone opens the document with an application that can interpret it. SGML sets standards that are independent of any type of computer or of any operating system that sends or retrieves documents. This means that the marked-up document can be transferred from one machine to another, and from one operating system to another (such as from MacOS, Windows, or Linux), without losing information.

A *markup language*, then, is a set of conventions used for encoding texts and other elements. It details what markup is allowed, what markup is required, how markup is to be distinguished from text, and what the markup means. SGML mandates the essential rules for tagging document elements. The meaning of the markup is conveyed by the specific markup language used. Physically, markup tags are placed at the beginning, end, and within text.

SGML was developed and standardized by the International Standards Organization (ISO) in 1986, several years before the advent of the Web, when one could use the Internet only to retrieve text and download files by selecting from text-only menus. Again, SGML does not specify any formats but rather sets the rules. Two important markup languages have been developed in accordance with the general rules of SGML: HTML and XML. An additional markup language, WML, has emerged to accommodate wireless access to the Web.

HTML: THE HEART OF THE WORLD WIDE WEB

HyperText Markup Language (HTML) is practically SGML with a fixed set of tags. HTML defines a document's page layout, fonts and font sizes, text location, and graphic elements as well as hypertext links to other documents on the Web. Each link contains the URL of a Web page that resides on the same server or any other Internet server somewhere else in the world.

Tagged elements of an HTML page are surrounded by angle brackets (< and >). Certain tags determine the appearance of the elements when interpreted by a Web browser, such as font size and color, and certain other tags indicate that the element, text or graphic, is a link to another page or an e-mail address.

Figure 4.1 is an example of simple HTML tags. <body bgcolor="#FFFFFF"> instructs the Web browser to display white, encoded as FFFFFF, as the background color. Another color would have another set of six letters instead of FFFFFF. <p> instructs the browser to start a new paragraph. The <i> and </i> tags indicated the beginning and end of any text to be displayed italicized. The tag for centering the next line of text is self-evident. This text is also boldfaced by

F I G U R E

4.1 HTML TAGS (TOP) AND THE RESULTANT PRESENTATION (BOTTOM)

```
<html>
<head>
<title>Foundations of e-Commerce sample</title>
</head>

<body bgcolor="#FFFFFF">
<p><i>This text is italicized.</i></p>
<p align="center"><b>This text is centered and boldfaced.</b></p>
<p> <img border="0" src="file:///C:/narda.jpg" width="137" height="175"></p>
<p>This is my e-mail address: <a href="mailto:santa@northpole.com">santa@northpole.com</a>
</p>

</body>
</html>
```

This text is italicized.

This text is centered and boldfaced.

This is my e-mail address: santa@northpole.com

the tags <b> (for beginning of the text to be boldfaced) and </b> (for the end of text to be boldfaced). The image (img) source (src) is the file "narda.gif." Its measurements for presentation are also indicated (137 pixels in width, and 175 pixels in height). The text "santa@northpole.com" is tagged as an e-mail link by the tags <a href=mailto: . . . >. As you can see, both the text of the e-mail address and the link appear in the presented page. However, the link could have been associated with another piece of text or even an image. When clicked, the link would open a default e-mail application on the user's computer, and allow her to send a message to the tagged address.

HTML is a standard. It is important to set universal standards so that anyone, anywhere in the world, can send, retrieve, and interpret a document in the same way. A standard is a universally agreed-upon set of rules for doing or making something, in this case creating and interpreting Web pages. Like many other standards, each new standard has a version number. The Internet Engineering Task Force (IETF; see Chapter 1 for details about this organization) has standardized HTML 2.0 and newer versions. Subsequent versions include newer features such as eye-catching marquee graphics, blinking text, background, and other visual effects. Whenever a new version is standardized, all Web browsers must be updated to be able to appropriately interpret the new features.

Although HTML includes some types of statements that you would find in programming languages, it is to a large extent a *presentation language* rather than a programming language. In this sense, it is more similar to PowerPoint and other presentation programs than to Visual Basic and C++.

It is easy to look at an HTML page and see how a browser interprets it. Simply open the page with your browser. Now select Source from the View menu of Microsoft Internet Explorer, or Page Source from the View menu of Netscape. See Figure 4.2 for an example.

As soon as organizations and individuals started to show interest in building their own Web sites, software companies started treating HTML the same way they treated other languages: They developed programs called **visual HTML editors**. A visual HTML editor lets the programmer build all, or almost all, of the elements of a Web page by using graphical user interfaces (GUIs). The user may actually build very involved pages without knowing any HTML. The HTML code is

INTERESTING. . .

SO, WHO INVENTED THE HYPERLINK?

One bright day in June 2000, out of the blue, British Telecommunications (BT) announced that it held the U.S. patent for the hyperlink. BT said it had the Hidden Page patent, filed in the United States in 1976, and that the patent was granted in 1989. As you know, hyperlinks connect text, images, and other data on the Internet, allowing a user to click on a marked object on a Web page and open an associated item located elsewhere on the Web. The technology has been extensively used on the Web ever since Tim Berners-Lee developed HTML. Berners-Lee's work was based on earlier work by Ted Nelson, who coined the term *hyperlink* in his 1965 book *Literary Machines*.

Source: Rohde, L., "British Telecom claims to have patent for hyperlinks," *Infoworld*, June 26, 2000

4.2 A WEB PAGE (TOP) AND PARTS OF ITS UNDERLYING HTML (BOTTOM)

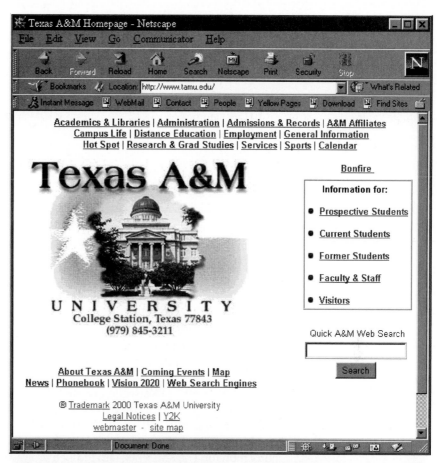

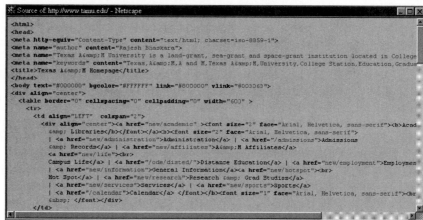

recorded for the programmer as he or she selects the tools available through menus and icons. Popular HTML editors include Microsoft's FrontPage, Macromedia's Dreamweaver, Adobe's GoLive, and Claris' HomePage.

XML: WHAT'S BEHIND THE SHOW

HTML is limited to the presentation of page elements; it does not tell what information the elements hold. The purpose of XML is to communicate this information to

4.3 HOW PLAIN ENGLISH, HTML, AND XML CONVEY INFORMATION
Source: Courtesy of Peter Tarasewich

Plain English	HTML	XML
Sport Utility Vehicle	\<TITLE>Automobile\</TITLE>	\<AUTOMOBILE TYPE="Sport UTILITY VEHICLE">
ABC Gremlin 300X SUV	\<BODY>	\<MANUFACTURER>ABC\</MANUFACTURER>
	\<UL>	\<LINE.Gremlin\</LINE>
	\<LI>ABC Gremlin 300X SUV	\<MODEL>300X SUV\</MODEL>
4 passenger	\<LI>4 passenger	\<FUEL UNIT="PASS">4\</PASSENGER>
145 maximum speed	\<LI>145 maximum speed	\<SPEED UNIT="MPH">145\</SPEED>
$19,280	\<LI>$19,280	\<PRICE CURRENCY="USD">19,280\</PRICE>
	\</UL>\</BODY>	

Web browsers. Like HTML, the **Extensible Markup Language** (XML) is a subset of SGML in the sense that it follows SGML rules. XML is a relatively new standard for structured documents on the Web. XML lets page developers define the tags used in terms of the *information* that tagged elements contain rather than their appearance. The importance of XML is indicated by the support it receives from companies such as IBM, Microsoft and Netscape, and the industry consortium CommerceNet.

Figure 4.3 provides a comparison of how information is conveyed in three manners: plain English, HTML, and XML. The \<UL> (Unnumbered List) and \<LI> (List Item) tags only tell a Web browser how to display the respective text items on the computer monitor. The XML code tells the Web browser what the information *is*: automobile type, manufacturer name, and so forth. Note that the XML code alone will not display anything on the computer screen. Only the combination of the HTML code and XML code will serve to display the list *and* tell the browser what the information is.

For example, the combined code *\<LI> 145 maximum speed \<speed unit="MPH">145\</speed>* would display the information on a monitor and also let the computer capture the information and do something with it, such as store it in a database or compare it with another fact. We see, then, that HTML is for viewing purposes only, while XML is for computer action. Note that the HTML and XML codes used in this example could appear one below the other, not necessarily combined horizontally. The effect would be the same.

Web pages can include both HTML and XML tags to make the content readable by both people and computers. Consider the following code:

```
<html>



<head>

<meta content="text/html; charset=iso-8859-1" http-equiv="Content-Type">

<title>Welcome to Gadget, Inc.</title>

<meta content="Microsoft FrontPage 4.0" name="GENERATOR">

</head>
```

```
<body bgColor="#aed7d7">

<div align="center"><center>


<TBODY>

    <tr>

    <td bgColor="#0000FF" width="100%"><p align="center"><font

    color="#c5e8fa" size="2">Gadget, Inc.<br>

    Tel. 1-123-555-3456<br>

    Fax: 1-123-555-6789<br>

    Wonderful Industrial Park<br>

    30 Swedesford Road<br>

    Malvern, PA 19355</font></p>

    <hr SIZE="1" width="85%">

    <p align="center"><font color="#c5e8fa" size="1">©Gadget, Inc.
2000</font></td>

    </tr>

</TBODY>

    </table>

    </center></div></td>

    </tr>

</TBODY>

    </table>

    </center></div>

    </body>

    </html>
```

If you view this simple homepage of Gadget, Inc., you will see the company's name, address, telephone, and fax number. However, because there are no XML tags in the code, you must view the information to infer which part of the text conveys what type of information. If you used a software application whose purpose was to capture the name, address, telephone number, and fax number of this company and place the information in the proper fields of a database, the software would not be able to do so.

Now consider the following HTML code, which also includes XML tags for information types:

```html
<html>

<head>

<meta content="text/html; charset=iso-8859-1" http-equiv="Content-Type">

<title>Welcome to Gadget, Inc.</title>

<meta content="Microsoft FrontPage 4.0" name="GENERATOR">

</head>

<body bgColor="#aed7d7">

<div align="center">/<center>

<TBODY>

    <tr>

    <td bgColor="#0000FF" width="100%"><p align="center"><font color=

    "#c5e8fa" size="2"><company_name>Gadget, Inc.</company_name><br>

    Tel. <telephone>1-123-555-3456/</telephone><br>

    Fax: <fax>1-123-555-6789</fax><br>

    <address1>Wonderful Industrial Park</address1><br>

    <address2>30 Swedesford Road</address2><br>

    <city>Malvern</city>, <state>PA</state> <zipcode>19355</zipcode></font></p>

    <hr SIZE="1" width="85%">

    <p align="center"><font color="#c5e8fa" size="1">©Gadget, Inc. 2000</font></td>

    </tr>

</TBODY>

    </table>

    </center></div></td>

    </tr>

</TBODY>

    </table>

    </center></div>

    </body>

    </html>
```

The appearance of this Web page when displayed by a Web browser is the same as before: It contains the same text, the table looks the same, the background color and the text color are the same, and the font type and size are the same. However, the company name now has the XML tags <company_name> and </company_name> before and after the company's name, respectively; special address1 and address2 tags indicate the two address lines; <telephone> and </telephone> indicate the beginning and end of the company's telephone number; and there is an XML tag for the fax number. In this format it is easy for a simple software application to pick up the name, address, telephone number, and fax number of every organization from its homepage and place the information in a database.

Similarly, the page could use codes for the industry in which the organization operates or for any other important information. For example, an invoice submitted in the form of an HTML document could include XML tags to convey all of the above information about the organization submitting the invoice as well as information about the items sold, amounts charged, grand total of the charge, and other pertinent details. As soon as the receiving organization gets the invoice, the details can be automatically channeled into the company's receiving, disbursement, and accounting information systems. This can save much labor and time. The use of XML also allows everyone, not only organizations that have used traditional and proprietary EDI systems, to use EDI. XML can be used for other handy purposes, too. For example, if your computer monitor shows a telephone number, you can instruct your computer to dial that number.

We have mentioned "standard" XML tags. Standards are exactly what the organizations involved in the development of XML are trying to set. It is important to set universal standards so that XML documents can be sent and interpreted the same way, much as everyone uses the same HTML tags to design Web pages. For example, the universal XML tag for telephone numbers is the pair <telephone> and </telephone> to indicate the start and end of telephone number data.

As HTML tags determine the appearance of a Web document and XML tags define the information contained in it, it is only practical that HTML and XML standards be consolidated. HTML 4.0 and XML 1.0 have been combined into a single standard called XHTML, which has quickly become the standard format for Web pages. With XHTML, developers can include different sets of data depending on the type of browser used to access the Web. This is benefiting businesses significantly.

XML holds the promise of making electronic communications between business partners quick and easy. IBM and Microsoft are the most aggressive participants in the efforts of setting XML standards.

The efforts have been focused on two initiatives. One deals with horizontal, or global, applications, such as the exchange of contracts between businesses in any market. This initiative has two goals:

1. To facilitate electronic transactions between companies that traditionally have not exchanged information electronically, and
2. To establish a set of universal tags that contains information about particular businesses, such as what they do and where they are located.

The second initiative focuses on the development of vertical applications to address the specific needs of information exchange of a large array of industries—from manufacturing to travel and lodging to health care to science.

Unfortunately, IBM and Microsoft do not coordinate all their efforts, either with each other or with other firms. It is expected that, in time, a single, universally accepted set of XML standards will emerge. While the issue of compatibility is being sorted out, several vendors, including DataChannel, Sequoia Software, and WebVision, are developing products that can support various XML types.

JAVA

Java is a high-level programming language whose great asset is that its code can run on several operating systems. Therefore, Java code is integrated into many HTML documents. The language was derived from the C++ programming language. Originally the language was called Oak by its developer, Sun Microsystems Corporation, and was designed for handheld devices and for set-top boxes that connect television sets to the Internet. In 1995, when it became clear that Oak was unsuccessful for that purpose Sun modified the language to take advantage of the fast-developing Web and changed the language's name. Supposedly, Java received its name from the large quantities of coffee that its developers drank. The coffee seems to have helped them develop a highly popular language that is simpler to use and less error-prone than C++.

Java **applets** are small Java programs that run on a client computer, namely, a computer that receives code from a server. Often, applets are embedded in HTML code. Translated Java code can run on all of the widely used operating systems, including Windows, MacOS, and Unix.

The source code of a Java program is translated into code called *bytecode*. The bytecode must be converted into machine-language code before it can run. When a Web browser encounters a Java applet in a Web page, it switches control to its built-in Java interpreter called a **Java virtual machine** (JVM). JVM translates the bytecode into machine-language code, which is then executed by the CPU. This is why Java programs are not dependent on any specific hardware; the JVM can execute the applets on any computer. JVM is available in the two most popular Web browsers, Netscape Navigator and Microsoft Internet Explorer.

When used by a server, Java programs are called **servlets**. Servlets are often compiled, rather than interpreted, by a special compiler called a *just-in-time* (JIT) Java compiler. In compilation of bytecode, the compiler simply takes the place of the JVM. (In Figure 4.4, the middle block would read: "JIT compiler translates the bytecode into the computer's machine code.") Compiling the code

INTERESTING . . .

RUMORS ABOUT ITS DEMISE HAVE BEEN GREATLY EXAGGERATED

Many people have thought that COBOL, the veteran programming language introduced in 1959, was dead. If all new business applications are adapted for the Web, all COBOL code must be replaced. Right? Wrong. A 2000 survey by International Data Corporation (IDC) revealed that 60 percent of U.S. corporations plan to continue using COBOL for the foreseeable future. Several companies have developed programs that convert COBOL code into Java code. Companies that wish to maintain their existing code and run it in a Java environment can use these programs to their advantage. The programs can save millions of dollars that would otherwise be spent on developing software from scratch.

Source: Vriody, D., "From pocket protectors to stock options?" *Infoworld*, June 26, 2000, p. 40

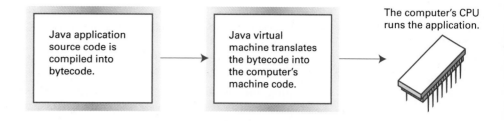

into machine code results in faster performance, but unlike applets, JIT compilers are not machine-independent. The servlet must be written with prior knowledge of the hardware on which it will run. The Java code is then said to have lost its hardware independence. Although Java is for general purpose, it is particularly suited to the Web thanks to the flexibility of JVM and its easy integration into HTML documents.

Like other programming languages, Java is available to developers free of royality for writing applications. However, JVM, the interpreter that translates and executes Java applications, is licensed to the companies that incorporate it into their browsers and Web servers. When using Java, programmers can write only one application, and that application can then run on many different types of computers with different operating systems. Professionals like to say that the application runs on "different platforms." This "write once, run anywhere" characteristic is what makes Java so popular with programmers. This is also why Java has become a leading programming language in just a few years since its introduction.

Unlike Java, which is a full-blown programming language, **JavaScript** is a programming language that uses syntax similar to Java's but was developed independently by Netscape. JavaScript's purpose is to enable Web page authors to design interactive sites. JavaScript can interact with HTML source code (code before it is translated to machine code), allowing the authors to enliven the pages with animations and other dynamic features. The syntax of the language is not owned by anyone and therefore does not require a license for use. Netscape supports JavaScript; however, Microsoft Internet Explorer supports only a subset of the language, which Microsoft calls JScript.

BROWSER-SERVER INTERMEDIARIES

One of the most important roles of Web sites in e-commerce is to serve as a conduit for interaction between the user of a Web browser and organizational information systems, such as databases, at the server end. These databases let remote users request, view, and manipulate data that come from sources beyond the immediate Web page. There are several tools with which to do this.

COMMON GATEWAY INTERFACE

Many Web sites offer data that clearly do not reside on the Web pages themselves. Such data may include lists of college classes available for registration, lists of available products, and current stock prices. The data are part of a database that resides either on the disks of the server or—more often—on the disks of another computer that is linked to the Web server. Some applications must take inquiries from remote client computers and produce the documents that show the desired information. Of the several types of software that facilitate such browser-server interaction, the oldest and most common one is a script called **Common Gateway Interface** (CGI).

A CGI script is a small program written in Perl, C, C++, or other programming languages that can function as an intermediary between HTML pages and other programs on the Web server. The scripts reside on the server. CGI scripts often allow remote users to fill out a form with data and send the data into a database, or to search a database with a query entered on a Web page. The CGI script sends the query to a database management system (DBMS) for searching the database files. When the required information is found, the script formats the results of the search as an HTML page and sends it back to the user.

HOW INTERMEDIARIES WORK

Figure 4.5 illustrates how a CGI script works when the user requests information from a database. One of the functions of the script is to parse the form that the user submitted. *Parsing* is the transformation of the request into a proper inquiry that the DBMS can process. Note that often the database itself is quite dynamic; the data in it may change every second or even every fraction of a second. This is evident in the Web sites operated by online stockbrokers. You can use your browser to check the latest price (*quote*, in professional lingo) of a certain stock. As the price changes, so does the value of the appropriate field in the database that you are accessing.

Many organizations still use CGI scripts to make Web sites interact with databases and other applications. However, more efficient and easier-to-use types of intermediary applications have been developed for faster processing. Microsoft

FIGURE

4.5 HOW A CGI SCRIPT WORKS

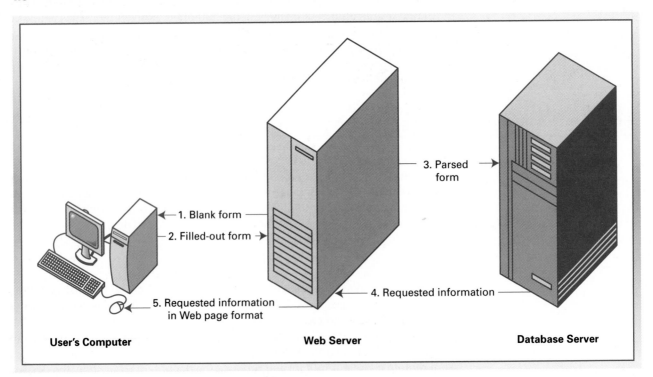

1. Blank form
2. Filled-out form
3. Parsed form
4. Requested information
5. Requested information in Web page format

User's Computer   **Web Server**   **Database Server**

developed **Active Server Pages** (ASPs) for Windows Web servers, and a Sun Microsystems and Netscape collaboration resulted in **JavaServer Pages** (JSPs) and Java servlets.

An ASP is a Web page that contains HTML and embedded programming code written in Visual Basic script or JScript, both programming languages that were developed by Microsoft. Either type of script works with Microsoft's **Internet Information Server** (IIS), which is software developed especially to manage Web servers. When the IIS server software encounters an ASP page that is requested by the browser, it executes the embedded program.

JSP uses Java scripts embedded in HTML pages; the HTML code is responsible for the formatting of requested information and returned information pages, while the Java script code processes the request and returns the requested information. All these methods result in the same effects that CGI scripts have, but they can be developed more quickly and they process interactive instructions faster.

WML: ENABLING THE WIRELESS BROWSER

In recent years we have witnessed the convergence of several types of electronic and communication devices. Many cellular telephones now offer some features that once were exclusive to computers; you can, for example, receive e-mail messages on and download information from the Internet to a cellular phone's small display. Handheld computers, also called personal digital assistants (PDAs), or palm devices offer such wireless connection to the Internet. Since these small displays cannot accommodate the same format and size of windows that larger computers can, they must use some software that converts Web pages into manageable size.

To this end, engineers developed a standard programming language called **Wireless Markup Language** (WML). Formerly known as Handheld Devices Markup Language (HDML), the language is part of the Wireless Application Protocol (WAP) that has been used by many manufacturers as a standard for wireless Internet communication. WML works alongside wireless communications standards to support handheld devices when they communicate with the Internet. Like HTML, the language is offered free of charge. Programmers use the languages to develop software known as *filters* that translate HTML pages into WML pages.

HOW SWEET ARE THESE COOKIES?

Interactivity on the Internet takes place not only between human and machine but also between machine and machine. Many Web surfers may not be aware that their computer stores information that is later used by a Web site's server. Such information may be very useful to the organization that operates a given site, and it may make browsing easier and more enjoyable for the user. However, it may also violate the surfer's privacy. The file containing such information is called a **cookie**. A cookie is a data file created by a server and stored on the hard disk of a Web user's computer. The cookie contains the URL of the server that stored it. When a browser encounters the URL again, it sends the cookie's content to the server. The server can then use the information when interacting with the user's browser as well as for further collection of information about the user's activity at the site.

Cookies can make the user's interaction with a Web site easy and useful. For example, if logging in requires a user identification code and the code was stored in the cookie, it would save that person from having to type in the same information all over again. Often, there is much more information that the user can avoid retyping. For instance, if you have registered with an online bookseller and entered a list of topics you like, you can see what new books are available on any of these topics. If you trade stocks online and would like to see how a certain portfolio (combination of securities) has performed and what its current value is, all you have to do is enter the symbols of the stocks once. From now on, every time you log on to the proper Web page, you will see the list of stocks and their values. Thus, cookies enable people to personalize the Web pages that they access. If you use a certain portal on a regular basis, you can personalize it to show the weather forecast for your region, the scores of games of the sports teams you designate, and the performance of your selected stocks.

Businesses love cookies because they allow them to customize service for individual consumers, to make the browsing experience at their sites more pleasant and informative, and to derive important statistics about the buying habits of consumers. We usually do not notice what pieces of information are stored in the cookies on our hard disk. We also do not know how, exactly, the information is used. Although many companies post privacy statements on their sites, telling people how information will be used, privacy advocates have found many violations of these policies.

FIGURE

4.6 PART OF A COOKIES FOLDER ON A USER'S HARD DISK

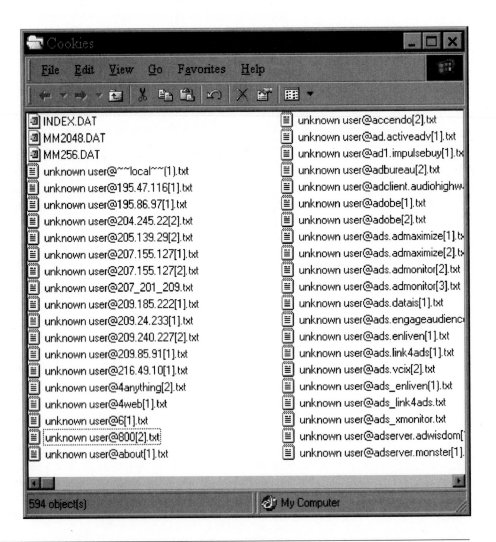

4.7 THE CONTENTS OF ONE COOKIE (THE NUMBERS MAY NOT MEAN MUCH TO YOU, BUT THEY ARE MEANINGFUL TO THE SERVER OF THE OPERATING ORGANIZATION)

4.8 USERS CAN DISABLE COOKIES WHEN BROWSING

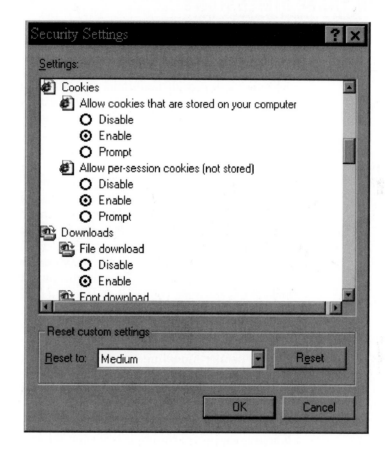

If you do not want to use cookies, your browser allows you to disable this feature; however, you will then have to live without the convenience that cookies afford users. Some Web sites offer downloadable software that enables you to detect whether a site sends cookies to your disk and what information it collects and leaves there. This way you can decide right then if you want to accept or reject cookies from that site. Cookies cause a major concern about privacy. We will discuss Internet-related privacy issues in more detail in Chapter 10.

Figure 4.6 is a screenshot of a cookies folder residing on a hard disk. Figure 4.7 shows the contents of one cookie. While the codes and numbers of a cookie may not mean much to the user, they are very meaningful to the server software operated by the organization that sends the cookie. Such numbers can indicate access codes, dates on which the server was accessed, and the IP number from which the server was accessed. Note, however, that a cookie does not have to hold more than one access code to enable the organization to create a file with your browsing and buying history; this information is usually held in a database that is connected to the server. If you delete the cookie, the site will not be able to identify you the next time you log on; you will have to reenter your access code, if one is required.

Figure 4.8 (page 69) shows how you can have your Web browser disable the acceptance of cookies. The specific example is for Microsoft Internet Explorer. To enable or disable cookies, you must go to the Tools menu of the browser, then select Internet Options, then click the Security tab. The window shown in Figure 4.8 will appear.

BROWSING IN THREE DIMENSIONS

Browsers can be combined with other applications to enhance a user's experience. These applications are called plug-ins. A **plug-in**, so called because it is conceptually plugged into the Web browser, is an application that collaborates with the browser to provide additional capabilities or effects. For example, a plug-in such as Macromedia's Shockwave enables a browser to present impressive object motion and sound. Other plug-ins enable users to zoom in and out on specific objects displayed at a site and let users "grab" objects and rotate them for closer examination, as if the users were holding the object in their hand and looking at it from several different angles.

It is possible to get a sense of a three-dimensional environment when accessing certain Web sites and using the appropriate software. When users work with a browser with 3-D capabilities, they can manipulate the content of a page. By using the arrow keys of a keyboard, they can "move" forward, backward, or to the side inside a building; "fly" over a city; or "drive" a vehicle on a road. The software that lets a user do these things is called a **3-D viewer,** or just *viewer* for short. Currently, there are several different viewers for this purpose. Web browsers usually do not include this software; you must download it and install it before the browser can interpret 3-D Web pages. After installation, the software becomes part of the browser. A 3-D viewer may create a sense of virtual reality.

There are several standards for 3-D viewers, the most prominent of which is **Virtual Reality Modeling Language** (VRML, pronounced VER-ml). The first viewer that followed the standard was WebSpace, which was developed by SGI Corporation. Other viewers include WebFX, WorldView, and Fountain for the Windows operating system, and Whirlwind and Voyager for MacOS. Companies that specialize in the development of 3-D Web pages often develop their own proprietary viewers. One example is Skyline Software Systems, Inc., which developed a viewer called TerraExplorer. Once users download and install TerraExplorer, their browsers let them "fly" over a city from any altitude, and at any angle, direction, and speed.

Figure 4.9 shows two screenshots taken while virtually flying over Washington, D.C. Note the tools at the bottom, which allow the user to change the experience of the tour. The user can also use a mouse to change directions. As the virtual tour proceeds, labels pop up with the various sites and buildings that come into view.

Real estate agencies use virtual reality viewers to let online shoppers view both the outside and inside of buildings offered for sale. Anyone can examine a house or an office building from anywhere in the world. Architectural, engineering, and manufacturing companies use 3-D viewers to collaborate over distance on projects involving the design of items from motor-vehicle parts to toys. 3-D modeling is important not only because it saves the huge expense of building a physical

4.9 ONLINE 3-D RENDITION OF
WASHINGTON, D.C.
Source: Skyline Software Systems,
Inc. 2000

model to test a concept or as a prototype for later mass production; it also saves money and time because engineers and designers can collaborate on projects regardless of their physical locations, and because their work results in an electronic blueprint that can be immediately translated into digital manufacturing blueprints and specifications.

The commercial potential of 3-D online viewers for individual consumers is great as well. Shoppers can walk through a virtual shopping mall, zoom in on products, and rotate the products to see them from every possible angle before making purchasing decisions. Figure 4.10 presents a demonstration site using such technology. The shopper selects an item from an array of pictures. The user can then grab the object and change the view by clicking and dragging with the mouse. Note that this is done on a single Web page; the page is not refreshed.

Used in . . .	Used for . . .
Manufacturing	Engineers build and examine 3-D models of newly designed parts and products; they collaborate from several remote locations.
Travel and Lodging	Shoppers conduct virtual travel in locations of planned tours, both in outdoor and indoor environments.
Architecture	Architects design 3-D models instead of drafting by hand; 3-D e-models replace blueprints and wood models of new buildings.
Real Estate	Realtors post 3-D models of land and buildings offered for sale; shoppers take virtual tours of the grounds and inside the buildings.
City Planning	Planners and utility engineers collaborate remotely on zoning and planned utility lines (water, electricity, and gas).
Retail	Shoppers view objects from all angles.

Figure 4.11 lists the major uses of 3-D applications on the Web. Currently, there are few standard 3-D viewers for the Web. Most of these viewers are proprietary, but visitors are invited to download them free of charge. When you visit a site whose owner would like you to view and manipulate its 3-D objects, you will be invited to download and install the viewer first.

SUMMARY

- One of the main reasons the Web is a superb means of communication is the use of special software that allows users to enjoy graphics, sound, and interactivity.
- The Web page composer uses special tags in documents that allow a user's Web browser, after retrieving the documents from a server, to display the different elements of a document in a way that is useful and visually pleasing.
- To do this, the composer uses the rules set by the Standard Generalized Markup Language (SGML). SGML is an overarching set or rules for markup languages used in Web pages. HyperText Markup Language (HTML) is a set of tags and of rules for using these tags to format text, pictures, and other elements in Web pages. Browsers are designed to properly interpret the tags and display the pages.
- While HTML can deal only with the format of page elements, Extensible Markup Language (XML) allows browsers to detect the *type* of data in each element. Once the browser detects the type of data, the computer can use it in several ways, such as automatically storing it in the proper fields of a database.
- To enhance Web pages and interaction between Web servers and Web browsers, a programming language called Java is used. Java code can run on many different operating systems.
- One of the most important roles of Web sites in e-commerce is to serve as a conduit for interaction between the user of a Web browser and organizational

information systems such as databases at the server end. To this end, servers link the organization's system with a user's browser. Special applications can facilitate the interaction. Some of the technologies that enable such interactions are Common Gateway Interface (CGI), Active Server Pages (ASPs), and JavaServer Pages (JSPs).

■ Interactivity between a Web user and a server also takes place by use of cookies, which are small files that the server stores on the hard disk of a user's computer. Cookies contain key information pertinent to the user, such as access codes, names, and account numbers. The information is captured from the user registration and logons. Cookies are used to identify users and their preferences as soon as they log on.

■ Cookies let users customize Web pages and the services they receive from the operators of Web sites, making the browsing experience more efficient and pleasant. However, cookies often also violate users' privacy because they let operators organize detailed dossiers about the users, such as their demographic features, tastes, and buying habits. Users can elect to disable cookies through their browsers.

■ A plug-in is an application that enhances a Web browser's features. Users can download plug-ins and install them on their computers.

■ One type of plug-in lets users view and manipulate three-dimensional objects on Web pages. A 3-D viewer produces 3-D models and lets a user virtually fly over an existing or a planned city, walk inside online structures, and examine items from various angles.

KEY TERMS

Standard Generalized Markup
   Language (SGML)
HyperText Markup Language (HTML)
visual HTML editor
Extensible Markup Language (XML)
Java
applets
Java virtual machine (JVM)
servlets
JavaScript

Common Gateway Interface (CGI)
Active Server Page (ASP)
JavaServer Page (JSP)
Internet Information Server (IIS)
Wireless Markup Language (WML)
cookie
plug-in
3-D viewer
Virtual Reality Modeling Language
   (VRML)

REVIEW QUESTIONS

1. A friend tells you that she uses SGML as her primary programming language to design Web pages. Does that make sense? Explain.
2. What does *marking up* mean in authoring Web pages?
3. What is the purpose of tags in HTML?
4. What is the difference between HTML and XML?
5. What is the benefit of using a Web page editor?
6. Why is Java so popular among developers of Web applications?
7. What is a Java virtual machine? How does it let programmers write code that can be run on many different operating systems?

8. What is the difference between Java and JavaScript?
9. What is a CGI? Why is it so important in Web-based business?
10. What is a cookie? Why are cookies usually small, and not big, files?
11. List four uses of 3-D applications on the Web. Can you think of additional uses?

DISCUSSION QUESTIONS

1. List 15 types of information that you would like tagged in XML. How can the tagging of these elements help in business-to-business or business-to-consumer operations?
2. How can individual users (rather than companies) use XML when retrieving Web pages?
3. Are cookies more of a convenience or more of a nuisance and privacy risk? Do you prefer to enable or to disable them when you surf the Web? Why?
4. Why do you think there are so many proprietary 3-D viewers on the Web? (Hint: What, usually, is the reason that organizations come up with proprietary applications?)

ASSIGNMENTS

1. There are several sites that offer ready-to-use JavaScript applets that you can integrate into an HTML file. First, use a Web editor to author a homepage for an imaginary firm you would like to establish. Ensure that the homepage shows all the necessary text elements (name, address, purpose, etc.) and a graphical logo. Then go to one of those sites, select a JavaScript applet, and integrate it into your page. E-mail the file containing the page to your professor.

2. Prepare a three-page research paper on the current status of XML. Describe the organizations involved in setting standards, which standards are and are not agreed upon by all parties, which elements have already been integrated into Web browsers, and so on. E-mail the paper to your professor, and be ready to make a presentation of your findings.

E-COMMERCE AT WORK

Competitive Intelligence on the Web

How can you discover which features of your Web site are appealing to customers? What makes their shopping and buying experience pleasant, and what turns them off? One of the best ways to learn how to best build Web software is to take a peek at your competitors' software. This is what Drugstore.com did, to its advantage.

Drugstore.com's CEO and cofounder Andy Cargile had to react fast. It was August 1999, and one of his competitors, PlanetRx.com, had just installed a convenient shopping tool for its online customers. You may be familiar with the digital shopping cart found on many retail Web sites—a shopping cart icon is linked to a list of items you have selected for purchasing. PlanetRx.com's feature, which Cargile describes as a "pervasive shopping bag," lets customers virtually drop items into an online shopping bag without having to return to a shopping-cart page with every selection. A shopping-bag list remained on the screen wherever a visitor went, making the shopping experience less time consuming.

Cargile had wanted to install a similar feature for some time, but he was busy with other things. When PlanetRx.com beat Drugstore.com to the punch, the shopping bag became the first item on Cargile's priority list. However, he wanted to be sure that the feature would indeed attract customers; furthermore, he wanted to know how well his competitor's feature was received, and what could be done to improve upon it. He knew that it could take several weeks and a lot of money to develop a prototype from scratch. Therefore, before Cargile spent any resources on the tool, he decided to find out how his competitors at PlanetRx.com were doing. Using that information, he could make decisions about how Drugstore.com should proceed.

To acquire the information, Cargile decided to use the very means that was the basis for his own company: the Internet. It has revolutionized the way information is collected, since so much material has been posted on the Web and much of the information is readily available and accessible to the public. Research can be done with much less effort than before. To survive, many companies must make decisions within days rather than weeks or months. To satisfy the need for information, a slew of companies sell "competitive intelligence" services, collecting information on rivals to help companies make decisions about their own businesses.

Cargile turned to Vividence, a San Mateo, California, firm that specializes in the collection of information about competitor Web sites and in researching what their customers think about the sites. The company maintains a pool of 125,000 "testers"—people who are willing to log on to sites and answer questions. Vividence considers its testers volunteers, but frequently it offers thank-you gifts for their time. The company employed 200 testers to examine PlanetRx.com's site. Each tester visited the site while using an analysis program provided by Vividence. The program included pop-up windows that gave instructions on what the testers should be doing while at the site.

A special browser let Vividence record each move the 200 testers made. As visitors traversed the site, the program asked questions as to why they made a certain choice and what they felt about PlanetRx's shopping bag. According to Artie Wu, Vividence's CEO and cofounder, Vividence shows its clients the world of their competitors through customers' eyes. This is reflected in the company's name, a contraction of "vivid evidence."

What did Cargile receive for his money? The knowledge that customers loved PlanetRx's shopping bag. However, they did wish that they could see not only what they had in the bag at any given time, but also how much the items cost. They also opined that some of the graphics and instructions about the shopping bag were confusing.

Armed with this information, Cargile quickly built what he claims was a better shopping bag at Drugstore.com's site. He feels his company discovered the benefits and flaws of the tool and avoided blindly following the competition.

Vividence usually charges $20,000 to $40,000 for analyzing a competitor's Web site. Because Drugstore.com contracted with Vividence for 22 investigations, the cost per investigation was significantly lower than these amounts.

Another feature that online drugstores use is the drug-interaction checker. This is software that determines the effect on the human body of taking two or more different drugs. Drugstore.com is now using Vividence to study the online drug-interaction checker of several major competitors. Drugstore.com will use the findings to develop its own checker.

Cargile notes that Vividence is only one of about 10 research companies that Drugstore.com uses to keep abreast of what its competitors do. There are several dozen other companies that sell similar services. These companies offer a variety of services, from recording what people are typing in chat rooms to retrieving the divorce records of a rival company's chief executive officer. Leonard Fuld, president of Fuld & Company, a Cambridge, Massachusetts, firm that teaches companies how to set up their own competitive intelligence units, estimates that this is a $100 billion industry.

Source: Dahir, M., "Getting the Dirt," *The Industry Standard*, June 26, 2000

Thinking About E-Commerce at Work

1. Is the use of the services of companies such as Vividence good for consumers? Explain.
2. Put yourself in the place of a chief executive officer of an online retailer whose site is being investigated by a competitor. Would you feel threatened, or would you welcome this act as an incentive for improvement?
3. Has the chief executive officer of Drugstore.com done anything unethical? Explain. Is Vividence doing anything that is unethical?

- Select and register domain names for Web sites
- Register a Web site with search engines
- Select a hosting company for a Web site
- Explain what is required to maintain one's own Web server
- Appreciate good Web site design principles and know how to avoid design pitfalls

H ow can you keep customers visiting your Web site? Apparently, fast-loading and easy-to-navigate Web pages are very important. cPulse, Gartner Group Company, which monitors visitor satisfaction through random polls at 250 sites, found that 79 percent of Web surfers polled said they considered ease of navigation to be the most important characteristic of a site, but that only 66 percent were "very satisfied" with the navigability of the site at which they were polled. Seventy-four percent said speed of page download was very important to them, but only 64 percent were highly satisfied with the speed of download of the site at which they were polled. (Source: *The Industry Standard*, April 24, 2000, p. 186)

DOMAIN NAME SELECTION AND REGISTRATION

The first thing that an Internet entrepreneur needs to do after deciding to establish a Web-based business is to select a **domain name**, or a name for one's Internet business. The registration itself is simple and inexpensive. The applicant can use the Web sites of any of the domain name registrars to find out if a desired domain name is available. A **domain name registrar** is a firm that is licensed to assign domain names to individuals or businesses and to register them in a global database. If the name is available, the applicant can pay for the registration online and have the name reserved.

Domain names must be associated with an Internet server, that is, an IP number. The domain name will not be associated with any Internet server until the name's owner designates one. Of the millions of domain names that have been registered, it is estimated that over half have not been associated with a Web site. Businesses often reserve a domain name with several top-level domains, such as .com, .org, .net, or country domains, such as .us, .uk, or .de. A **top-level domain (TLD)** usually indicates the general purpose of the business (e.g., .com for commercial and .org for nonprofit), but one may choose any top-level domain. Such action is to ensure that no one else registers the main name with any of these suffixes, especially if the business intends to use specific country domains for local operations in different countries. Often, domain names are registered simply so that others do not seize them first.

HOW TO REGISTER?

Figure 5.1 shows part of the homepage of Register.com, a domain name registrar. In this example, an applicant is checking the availability of the domain name

5.1 A DOMAIN NAME REGISTRAR'S WEB SITE

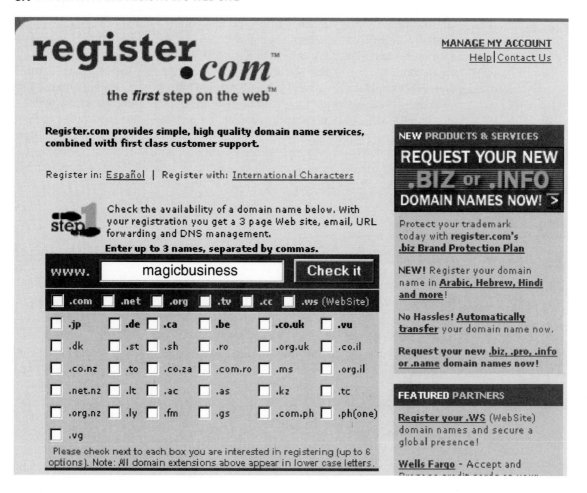

magicbusiness combined with a list of top-level domains. Clicking the "check it" button initiates a search that will yield a response telling the applicant if the name is available. If it is not, the applicant can see who owns it and how that individual or business can be contacted.

If a new business has not yet decided on which server to post its Web pages, it can ask the domain name registrar to "park" the domain name on the registrar's server. Some registrars, such as Register.com, do not charge a fee for parking, and some do. Registering and parking a domain name may cost from $15 to several tens of dollars per year, depending on the registrar one selects and on the number of domain names registered at the same time.

SELECTING DOMAIN NAMES

Branding experts recommend that a new Web business select a domain name that will draw attention to the site. (We discuss the importance of domain name branding in Chapter 9.) Whatever name you choose for your new Web site, it is important to keep several facts in mind.

People often misspell domain names. Therefore, you should register all the domain names that are spelled similarly to yours as well as those that may sound like yours, because some people may remember only the sound of a domain name. Thus, if your site's name is wunderbar.com, register vunderbar.com, wundebar.com, and other close names. Register the same name with .org and .net, and consider securing the same name with country-level domains, such as .de and .fr. Unfortunately, the registrars of some attractive country-level domains charge significantly more than $15 per year. For example, for some time, if you were adamant on registering a name with a .tv suffix (Tuvalu's country domain), you had to pay $1,000. Do not settle for an .org or .net as your ultimate domain name—especially if someone else has registered with a .com the same name that you chose—because when people do not enter the suffix, their browser will likely complete the URL to a .com address. Have all possible addresses point to your site.

Whatever domain name you select for your business, it should be either the literal name of the business or closely related to it. It should not be a slogan. For

INTERESTING . . .

A ROSE BY ANY OTHER NAME IS STILL A NUMBER

In 1984, there were only 1,000 computers connected to ARPANET, the father of today's Internet. However, people who used the fledgling network already realized they had a problem—they could not remember every 12-digit IP address that each computer had been assigned. Paul Mockapetris of the University of Southern California's Information Sciences Institute suggested a solution: To identify each machine, use a name instead of a number, and classify the names by the type of organization that owned them—.edu for educational institutions, .com for commercial enterprises, .org for nonprofit organizations, and so on. The system of domain names we use today was born.

Source: Tynan, D., "What to Name the Baby?" *The Industry Standard*, April 17, 2000

NEW DOMAIN NAME SUFFIXES FOR THE NET

ICANN selected seven new top-level domain names in late 2000: .info, .biz, .name, .pro, .coop, .museum, and .aero. These new TLDs will greatly increase the amount of Internet space available and boost the companies that offer domain name registrations. The new TLDs will simultaneously make finding Web site addresses more difficult. One of ICANN's intentions was to introduce more competition into the domain name market, which currently is dominated by Network Solutions. This is one of the reasons the .pro TLD was chosen; now Register.com, a competitor of Network Solutions, will have exclusive rights to the database of a TLD that competes with .com. ICANN also purposefully selected a limited number of new TLDs, which is why the proposed .info was selected but .web was denied. The .info proposal did not have the support of ICANN Chairwoman Esther Dyson. The selection of .info "doesn't foster competition in the sense that we've created a competitive market only to see cooperatives formed," says Dyson.

The selection of new TLDs will be the first test of ICANN's authority, according to Alan Davidson, the Center for Democracy and Technology's staff attorney, and others. ICANN had a slight balancing act to pull off in selecting an acceptable number of new TLDs, but some think it did a decent job. If ICANN had chosen any more TLDs, it would have caused complete pandemonium, says NetNation Communications CEO Joseph Kibur. The TLD suggestions that were not chosen will be reconsidered at a later date.

Source: Cha, Ariana Eunjung, "Seven New Domain Suffixes Approved," Washington Post (November 17, 2000) p. E1, *www.washingtonpost.com/wp-dyn/articles/A35598-2000Nov16.html*

example, if you operate NorthernAir Airlines, the domain name should be northernair.com, not something such as flynorth.com or flyingnorth.com. This is because if people do not know your business's domain name, their first guess most probably will be the business name with the .com suffix.

DIMINISHING IMPORTANCE

Currently a memorable domain name may be important, but this may change in a few years. Technology experts predict that more clever ways to reach a desired Web address will soon be developed. In fact, the way we reach an address now is already more sophisticated than it was just a few years ago. Previously, a single missed backslash in a URL would trigger an error message. Now, keywords and smarter browsers ensure that anything close will usually land users where they want to be. Also, browsers can "remember" a URL from just one or two characters, and bookmarks eliminate the risk of stumbling onto a site whose name is similar to the one we seek. The rise of portals will continue to make domain names and catchy URLs irrelevant, especially in the e-commerce world. (As explained in Chapter 3, portals are heavily trafficked sites that display links to many other sites. Millions of people turn first to a portal when they log on to the Web.)

INTERESTING...

THE SEARCH ENGINE LANDSCAPE

Establishing a Web site does not guarantee that people will visit it. In 2001, the number of online Web pages was estimated at more than two billion. More than 4,000 new Web sites are created every day, each adding several tens or hundreds of pages. With such a large number, how can you ensure that Web surfers looking for what you offer will find your site? You have to register with search engines. A **search engine** is software that helps Web users find sites, or particular pages at a site, based on certain keywords. A study by Zona Research, a market research consultancy, found that in 77 of 100 cases, people who look for information on the Web use search engines. This makes search engines the premier source of information on the Web. Positioning a site at the top of an engine's list can result in increased site traffic, additional revenue opportunities, and enhanced customer relations—all without investing a penny in advertising. The process works in several key ways.

There are several major search engine sites, most of which have turned into portals, such as Yahoo!, Excite, and AltaVista. The techniques they use for searching vary. Some, such as Ask Jeeves, use artificial intelligence applications that allow users to enter free-form questions rather than keywords. Figure 5.2 provides a list of the most popular search engines. Note, however, that "most popular" does not necessarily mean "most comprehensive." Figure 5.3 ranks search engines in terms of the number of Web pages they had indexed as of June 2000. The number of pages indexed by each of these search engines is growing constantly. For instance, by June 2001, Google had over 1.3 billion pages.

The search engines listed in Figure 5.2 are important because Netscape, Microsoft, and Internet Explorer have links to them. However, there are many smaller search engine sites. Search engines can be roughly classified into two types: *index engines* and *directory engines*. Index engines include AltaVista, Lycos, and Infoseek. They produce a list of all sites that have the keywords in their titles or metatags (explained below). Directory engines include Yahoo! and Excite. They take keywords and produce treelike directories that let the user "close in" from widely defined groups of sites to more and more specific ones, until the user finds the desired list of sites.

To date, most search engines have not been very effective; they produce a large number of Web site addresses in response to keywords. Their inability to pro-

Search Engines	. . . and Their Addresses
AltaVista	altavista.com
Ask Jeeves	www.askjeeves.com
AOL Search	search.aol.com
Direct Hit	www.directhit.com
Excite	www.excite.com
Fast Search	www.alltheweb.com
Google	www.google.com
Go (Infoseek)	infoseek.go.com
HotBot	www.hotbot.com
Lycos	www.lycos.com
Magellan	magellan.excite.com
Netguide	www.netguide.com
RealNames	www.realnames.com
Snap	www.snap.com
WebCrawler	www.webcrawler.com
Yahoo!	www.yahoo.com

duce a small set of URLs that closely relate to what the searcher is trying to find makes most searches frustrating. However, it is better to be on the index of a search engine that is mildly effective than be registered with none at all.

REGISTERING WITH SEARCH ENGINES

Most major search engines include a "submit URL" link on their homepage, usually tucked away at the bottom. For instance, Yahoo! has a "How to Suggest a Site" link on the bottom of its homepage. They require only that you submit a URL and your e-mail address.

These sites usually use only software to register your URL. Other sites use human "registrars." To register, you provide a description of your site and the category in which it fits. It may take several weeks or months until your site starts showing up in searches.

To ensure that the major search engines have your entry recorded correctly, without misspelled words, it is recommended that you do the submission manually. However, new businesses can also take advantage of the search-submission services of commercial companies that specialize in such activities. For a

Search Engine	Millions of Web Pages Indexed
Inktomi	500
Fast Search	350
AltaVista	350
Northern Light	340
Excite	340
Google	214
Go (Infoseek)	50
Lycos	50

fee, these companies will register your site with multiple search engines. For example, Register-It.com charges $40 for submitting sites to 400 search engines and indexes. If you want to save the fee, you can use selfpromotion.com, which will register your site with all the major search engines and about 100 smaller indexes.

If you do not want to submit your Web site manually, you can use software to automate the process. Once you install the software, you fill in the information and let the program register for you. Convenience and cost are the two advantages of using such software. The larger the number of search engines with which you intend to register, the more economical this method is. Submission Wizard is one such program. You can register as many sites and Web pages as you want, limited only by the amount of time you can use the service. In 2001, you could purchase a one-month key for $35 and a six-month key for $90. Submit Blaster, another registration program, is free. All you have to do is go to the site *www.rtlsoft.com/submitblaster*, fill out a form, and launch it to a list of search engines. You are guided through the simple, three-step process.

Similar to registering your domain name, when submitting keywords you should think of a set of words that best describes your business. This will determine the position of your URL when people search for the goods or services your site offers. You want your URL to appear at the top of the list and be noticed immediately. Therefore, if you sell women's tennis apparel, you should submit these exact words, not just "women's apparel" or "tennis apparel," because these word combinations will place your URL toward the bottom of any searcher's list. Basically, start by guessing which words users will enter as keywords. Then, broaden your thinking: some sites include misspelled words in their homepages, because they expect users to misspell words on occasion.

TITLES AND METATAGS

Most search engines list sites by their titles. Depending on how you have designed your homepage, your Web site's title may or may not be visible. Use important keywords in the site's title. Some search engines, such as Excite, order sites by popularity, defined as the number of links to a site from other sites. If there is any way you can convince other sites to create links to your site, do it. Some search engines record the description that the Web page developer enclosed in metatags. A **metatag** is an HTML tag that identifies the contents of a Web page. It does not appear on screen, so users will not actually see it when they view the site's pages. More than 50 metatags are available for use in HTML, but only two categories are commonly used by search engines for indexing and ranking: description metatags and keyword metatags. The following is an example of a keyword metatag in HTML code:

<meta name="keywords" content=
"My Wonderful Business, peripherals, store, MWB">

Anyone who uses a search engine to look for "My Wonderful Business," "peripherals," "store," or "MWB" will find your site listed.

Some search engines use description metatags. Here is an example of the HTML code for such tags:

<meta name="description" content=
"The best source for computer peripherals">

This type of search engine lists sites by their descriptions.

When you submit your site to a search engine, expect to be paid a visit. Some search engines use special software called a Web crawler. A **Web crawler**, also known as a *spider* or *bot*, is a program that visits Web sites and reads their pages. It picks up the most important elements of a site and creates keywords for the search engine index. Crawlers are usually programmed to visit the sites registered with the search engine. The entire site, as well as individual pages, can be indexed. Crawlers "crawl" the site one page at a time and follow links to other pages, until all pages have been read.

SEARCH ENGINE CHECKLIST

One trick to get noticed is to include in the HTML code of your homepage a long list of keywords. However, some search engines chop off any characters beyond the first 1,024. Also, if you provide a succinct description of your site, a search engine may place the site higher on the list of users. Remember the following points.

1. Include the most important keywords in the homepage's title. The title is the first item that search engines notice.
2. The higher the keywords appear on the page, the better. Search engines read pages the way we do: from top to bottom.
3. Tables and large pieces of JavaScript code placed before metatags push the text further down the page. This may result in a lower ranking of the site in search results.

There are sites that provide information and advice on how to attract the attention of search engines and on how to write metatags. One of them is *www.searchenginewatch.com*; another is *www.firstplacesoftware.com*. The latter provides free software that evaluates the effectiveness of titles and metatags for search engine positioning. It would be wise for any online business to utilize such resources. In addition, businesses should integrate the following elements into the routine maintenance of their sites.

1. *Stay current*. Search engines often change the manner in which they index sites. Stay abreast of such changes. Search for information in online newsletters.
2. *Watch your competitors*. Routinely use search engines to look for your own site, and see which 10 sites top the list. Examine the description and keyword metatags in their HTML source code to learn their secrets.
3. *Blow your horn*. Look for sites that may be willing to include a link to your own, or to cross-link with you. The increasing popularity of your site may place it higher on search engine indexes.
4. *Keep registering*. New search engines pop up every few months. There is no harm in registering with them—you do not know which engines people use.
5. *Update metatags*. Update metatags to reflect content updates in your Web pages. Check that your site's metatags reflect current industry terms, concepts, and buzzwords.
6. *Take advantage of software tools*. Be aware that several software applications assist with site registering, ranking, and metatags. Find the best ones, and use them.

To establish a Web business, one must have access to a server. Recall that a server is a computer that is connected to the Internet backbone. There are several options when establishing a Web site; you may use any of the following ways to connect your business to the Internet.

1. Your own server
2. An ISP site
3. A Web portal
4. A cybermall or storefront
5. A Web hosting service
6. A virtual Web server
7. A subdomain

In the following sections we discuss the advantages and disadvantages of each option for different types of businesses.

YOUR OWN SERVER

Installing and maintaining your own server is the most expensive option, but it gives you the greatest degree of control. Setting up a server requires expertise, which may or may not be available within your business. Specialists often must be hired to maintain the server. They may be employees of your company or employees of a consulting firm whose services you hire. Specialists purchase the appropriate server or servers, connect the server(s) to the Internet through a dedicated line (such as a T1 line), and install an operating system (usually Unix or Windows NT) and Web server software. Specialists are also the ones who "scale up" the server system when a business grows and handle issues such as load balancing to ensure quick response and to minimize the probability of a site crashing. A site crashes when too many people try to log on at once, and the software stops responding to anyone.

ISPs (Internet service providers) offer low-fee or free space for individual or business Web sites. However, because people may associate such online businesses with the "here today, gone tomorrow" phenomenon, using an ISP's Web-site service is probably more appropriate for individual Web pages than for business sites. A typical URL for a business of this sort would be *members.eoz. com/mybusiness,* if the hosting party is Eoz. (Do not look for this firm; this is a fictional example.)

Large portals are another option. Most large portals offer free hosting of personal Web pages. Some allow small businesses to maintain pages on the portal's servers. As with ISPs, this option is suitable only for small businesses. The space provided is usually limited, and businesses must comply with quite limiting templates.

CYBERMALLS OR STOREFRONTS

A **cybermall** is a shopping mall on the Web. A company hosts an entire business site consisting of a homepage and all the subpages that collectively make up the

Web site. That company develops the pages for the hosted businesses. This option of Web hosting, also called **storefront**, can be quite expensive. Service quality varies widely. Yahoo! and Lycos are two of the major portals that offer storefront service. Lycos, for instance, charges $99.99 per month for a storefront. One of the benefits of a storefront with a large portal is that millions of Web surfers visit the portals daily.

In many U.S. cities, local newspapers have added storefronts to their Web sites. On the homepage of the Web version of the newspaper, a list of participating local businesses appears, enhanced by text or images. The target audience of newspaper cybermalls are residents of the newspaper's city and suburbs. The main purpose of the client business is to attract customers to the physical site of the business. A client pays a onetime fee of several thousand dollars to have the newspaper staff build the pages of the site that relate to the business. The monthly fee for storefront service ranges from several dollars to several hundred dollars.

WEB HOSTING SERVICES FOR BUSINESSES

Several companies focus only on offering **Web hosting services** for businesses. Most of them specifically target small businesses. Of the 25 million small businesses in America, about one fifth operated on the Web in 2000; forty to sixty percent of the small businesses were expected to do so by 2002. The hosting companies offer space on their servers for free hosting of Web sites. All provide templates for pages, and some provide software tools for more flexible page development. Several of them offer services such as shopping carts, which allow customers the convenience of "dropping" an item into an electronic shopping cart, and credit card payment mechanisms. Most companies charge for the latter service. For example, a company named Bigstep provides "wizards" that walk you through the time-consuming process of setting up catalogs and reports. The service is free or quite low, but you are charged a fee if you accept credit-card payments through the hosted site. Free or low-cost Web site hosting firms include GeoCities, Tripod, Homestead, AllBusiness.com, bCentral, BizLand, SmartAge, Verio, and Go2Net, as well as Bigstep (see Figure 5.4). Due to the space and trading limits that these companies offer, free hosting is appropriate for individuals and small businesses only.

VIRTUAL WEB SERVER

To establish a **virtual Web server,** a business must have its own registered domain name. The effect of a virtual Web server is that potential clients may assume that the business maintains its own server, when in reality the domain name will point to the server of another company. To arrange for a virtual Web server, a business must ask the registration authority to associate the domain name with another company's server. This arrangement is popular and, usually, more cost effective for many companies than maintaining their own Web server or using a cybermall. The company owning the server provides all the relevant services, such as running the server management software, adding servers when the business grows, and keeping and updating security measures such as firewalls. The business is not stuck with a single company; it can move the Web pages to the server of another company and ask the domain name registration authority to update its databases with the details of the new server.

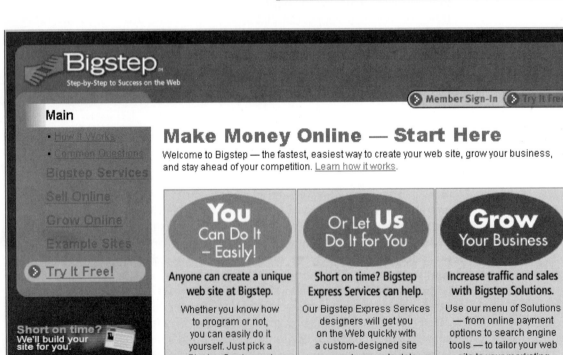

USING A SUBDOMAIN

A business can also use a **subdomain** instead of registering its own domain name and use the services of a hosting company for Web pages. For example, if your business's name is PoorSchnook, and if Eoz is the host company and owns the name *eozhosting*, it may host your site with the subdomain *poorschnook.eoz.net*. There are two disadvantages to this option: your business's domain name contains the name of another entity, and, unlike in the previous option, your business's online address (the URL) is associated with a single Web server. If you want to move the Web pages to another server, you will no longer be able to use this URL.

HOW TO SELECT A WEB HOST

If a business decides not to maintain its own server but to use the server of a hosting company, several factors must be considered. The first consideration should be the general type of help the business needs: does it need technology help, content services, or both? Some businesses need the technical help to set up a server and maintain it; others may need help with developing Web pages and marketing. Some, especially small businesses, probably need both. Figure 5.5 lists the major decision-making factors and provides a template for comparison. A simple method would be to compare each factor across the companies under consideration, weigh the big picture, and then make a decision. The comparison may use a point-scale method, assigning points to each factor for each company under evaluation.

Setup and monthly fees are self-explanatory. Monthly fees can range from several dollars to several hundred dollars. Some hosting companies offer large discounts to clients that sign annual contracts.

FIGURE

5.5 FACTORS TO CONSIDER IN WEB HOSTING SERVICE PROVIDERS

Factor	Hosting Company A (Points)	Hosting Company B (Points)
Quality of Technical Support		
Quality of Content Support		
Setup Fee		
Monthly Fee		
Amount of Disk Space		
Traffic Limits and Fees		
Availability of E-mail Accounts and Services		
Availability of FTP service		
CGI Scripts		
Scalability		
Support of Page Design Standards		
Total		

As a business grows and more information and services are provided, the number and complexity of Web pages also grow, and the business will need more disk space on the host's server. Thus, it is advisable to contract with a host that is responsive to requests for additional disk space. Large hosting companies often provide only a limited amount of disk space, and additional space may be costly. Smaller companies are usually more flexible and responsive to the individual needs of hosted businesses.

Some Web hosting companies charge extra fees if the site experiences activities above a predetermined size in terms of the amount of data that is downloaded from the site or the number of visits from Web surfers. These visits are called **hits**. Usually, the first 5,000 hits per month are free, and there is a charge per hit above this level. Web hosting companies price this way because the greater the number of hits, the more bandwidth they must allocate.

Most hosting companies provide e-mail services. The most popular type is a **Post Office Protocol** (POP) account. There is usually no extra charge for such accounts. Clients may want to inquire about additional services, such as mail forwarding (channeling e-mail messages to another e-mail address), autoresponding (automating e-mail reply), and access to mailing lists. Clients should clearly understand which e-mail services are free and which are not.

For many online businesses, it is important to have File Transfer Protocol (FTP) capabilities. FTP allows a site's owner to upload pages to the site and to post downloadable files, as explained in Chapter 1. Uploading enables site personnel to update Web pages whenever they need to, so that the personnel is not dependent on the services of other companies, including the hosting firm. The ability to post downloadable files lets a business serve its customers better.

The availability of CGI scripts (common gateway interface; see Chapter 4) is another measure that can be used to let visitors interact with the site. CGI allows site visitors to use a local "find" mechanism to find products by name, manufacturer, or style; fill out forms and submit them; or change the appearance of pages they often access. Most Web hosting companies provide CGI scripts and data access applications. A good hosting company should have a large library of such scripts and allow you to add your own CGI scripts.

Scalability, or the ability of a Web site to grow, is an important factor (scalability is discussed in greater detail later in the chapter). It is best to select a hosting company that has the hardware, software, and expertise needed to accommodate variable amounts of visits and that can help develop a site from a simple, static one to a heavily trafficked, interactive one.

The better hosting companies maintain software that supports a large variety of standards, so you can rest assured that all the features you develop in your pages will be supported by the companies' servers. For example, if you developed some ActiveX features in Web pages, which can run on a user's computer only if ActiveX is supported by the hosting company's server, you will want a server that can handle that. The same principle applies to features developed using the FrontPage design application. Some attractive features may not run correctly unless the proper software is installed on the server to support FrontPage.

MAINTAINING YOUR OWN SERVER

Establishing a Web site on your own server and maintaining it internally is usually more expensive than outsourcing it to an ISP. The cost involves not only purchasing hardware and software, but also employing skilled technical people. Because skilled personnel are scarce and in high demand, the human resource cost actually consumes the lion's share of a Web site budget. While experts often refer to the hardware and software required to establish a Web site and run it as "one-shot cost," the cost involved is not really one shot; as the site grows thanks to sharp advertising, good marketing, and improved service, more servers must be employed and more sophisticated software must be employed to run it. For these reasons, it is usually the larger and well-established companies that build and maintain their own Web sites. Usually, these large companies also have a high level of expertise in information technology in general and telecommunications in particular.

Personnel must include telecommunications specialists, Web designers, and transaction software specialists. The telecommunications professionals acquire the servers, link them to the Internet backbone, set up the **server management** software, and monitor communication speed and traffic load balance. When needed, they add servers, decide which servers will serve as mirrors or cache servers, and decide where the servers will be located (which can be anywhere in the world to ensure easy access to all potential parties that need it) and through which communication lines they will be connected.

Web design efforts are usually headed by a person whose title is **Webmaster**. The Webmaster's team must be well versed in Web design software, HTML, and programming languages such as Java and JavaScript; the team also must understand the purpose of maintaining the Web site and design text, graphics, animation, and links on the pages. At once, the designers must be good technicians and marketing experts.

If a Web site includes transaction software, qualified personnel must be available to support it. Even at companies that maintain their Web sites with in-house staffs, such software is usually purchased from a company that specializes in this type of application; therefore, it is usually the vendor's personnel who support this part of the Web site.

When an internal staff designs and maintains a Web site (regardless of who owns the servers on which the site is maintained), the site must be tested before it is linked to the Internet. Tests include downloading pages from a variety of computers with a variety of operating systems and equipped with different types and sizes of monitors. Content layout on Web pages may look quite different on different monitors. Web pages must also be tested with different browsers. Some features (such as marquees and other visual effects) may look fine through Microsoft's Internet Explorer but not through Netscape. Some features that work on the former may not run through the latter. The Web site should also be tested from computers in different locations in the country—and, if possible, in different parts of the world—to ensure proper download speed.

Companies have a choice of various communication speeds when they contract with an ISP to hook up their servers to the Internet. We discussed communication speeds in Chapter 2, but it may be helpful to consider again the problem of speed concerning the retrieval time of Web pages. The greater the speed, the higher the client's monthly fee to the ISP. If a Web site includes transactions and many graphics, the company cannot afford to opt for low bandwidth. Figure 5.6 illustrates how long it will take to download 10 MB from a Web site using different communications media, each of which in turn means a different speed. A 10 MB file contains about one minute of sound, one and a half minutes of a movie clip, or two and a half text-only books. Note that this speed is relevant only between the server and the Internet backbone. The actual speed at which a user downloads depends on the user's access line.

5.6 TRANSFER TIMES OF A
10 MB FILE BY DIFFERENT MEDIA

Medium	Transfer Time
14.4 Kbps modem	1.5 hours
28.8 Kbps modem	46 minutes
128 Kbps ISDN	10 minutes
1.54 Mbps T-1 link	52 seconds
4 Mbps cable modem	20 seconds
8 Mbps ADSL link	10 seconds
10 Mbps cable modem	8 seconds

Even with the fastest available communication links, Web sites often cannot deliver their content fast enough. This happens especially when many people try to visit a site or interact with it, and when the Internet as a whole is overcrowded with users. To overcome this problem, the operators of sites can employ a content delivery network. A **content delivery network** uses multiple servers that have copies of the site's Web pages. When too many people visit the site, some of the calls are directed to other servers, those maintained by the content delivery service. Because these sites create "mirrors" of the site, they are also called *mirroring services*; and because they cache a site's most frequently requested content so that that content can be transmitted faster, they are also called *caching services*.

There are many content delivery service firms, among which are Akamai, Adero, Digital Island, AT&T, XOSoft, and many others. Some of them use special software that monitors changes on the original site and mirrors the changes on their worldwide servers. All these firms employ security and load-balancing software. Fees are determined by the amount of data stored, the number of visitors, and other factors such as special services.

ISP SERVICES

Many businesses opt to hire the services of an ISP to host their Web sites. ISPs provide servers, connect the servers to the Internet, install security software such as firewalls (discussed in Chapter 10), and provide load balancing among servers. **Load balancing** ensures that requests are routed equally to the several servers used by the firm so that no single server is overloaded. This minimizes the chance of a crash.

A 2000 survey by Forrester Research showed that two thirds of the firms surveyed indicated a lack of internal resources as the main reason for contracting with an ISP to host their Web sites. Easier network connection was a reason cited by a third of the respondents. ISPs specialize in this activity.

The cost of maintaining a Web site with an ISP can range from $500 to $1 million per month, depending on the business needs. Consider the site of Bluefly, a New York clothing retailer. The firm uses Digex, Inc., as its Web hosting organization. Digex provides both the servers and the transaction software. It also monitors Bluefly's servers 24 hours a day to detect any mishaps that might stop traffic. It further ensures that enough servers are used to keep capacity at no more than 60 percent, so that a surge in traffic does not result in a crash. Interestingly, Digex does not provide Internet connectivity directly; it subcontracts connectivity to two other telecommunications companies. Digex charges its customers a monthly fee of $2,000 to $100,000 per server. Bluefly's vice president of technology estimated that it would cost his company several million dollars per year to set up the servers and maintain them in this fashion around the clock, every day.

Some Web-based firms prefer an arrangement called **colocation**. In colocation, the client company owns the servers, but the servers are maintained at the facilities provided by the ISP. Level 3 Communications, Inc., a telecommunications company that owns many miles of optical fibers, is one company that offers this arrangement. It rents out the physical facilities, such as secure racks that hold the client's servers. The client programs the servers and maintains (that is, updates and modifies) the software running on the servers. Level 3 connects the servers to the Net and ensures continuous connectivity.

Qwest, another telecommunications firm that offers colocation, was the choice of a children's site called Yourownworld.com. The site's chief technology officer (CTO) estimated that it would have cost his firm almost $2 million to set up the site's server facilities and another $500,000 per year in salaries for IT staff to maintain the servers. The colocation option allowed the site to be up and running almost immediately. Without it, it would have taken the company six months to set up the site, not to mention the fact that it could not obtain adequate funding for such set up.

If you decide to use Web site hosting by an ISP, you should make sure that the ISP provides several services (see Figure 5.7). First, the facilities must provide a high level of security. This includes access technology such as *biometric identification*, whereby special readers identify personnel by recognizing physical features such as a palmprint or retina map. Surveillance cameras should be on all the time. The servers must be housed in locked cages so they cannot be removed without authorization. This is especially important in colocation arrangements, because the servers are the client's property. The facilities must include smoke detectors and temperature and humidity control devices.

Load-balancing software should be employed. **Mirroring**, the duplication of server content on another server so that either one can be accessed and provide the same content and service to Web users, is important, too. Both practices are intended to ensure the availability of Web pages and business transactions and to reduce the probability of crashes due to traffic surges.

Caching (pronounced CASH-ing) is another key process. In Web **caching**, the most frequently used pages are retrieved from hard disks and maintained in the primary memory (RAM) of the servers. This way, users can retrieve these pages faster. Unlike with a mirror (a server that constantly maintains the same content as another server) caching lets the server retrieve for use only Web pages that are used frequently, thereby optimizing storage space. Until all Web users can access the Internet via high-speed communication lines, caching can alleviate slow downloading.

FIGURE
5.7 IMPORTANT SERVICES

To Maximize . . .	The ISP Must Provide . . .
Security	Biometric identification for access
	Surveillance camera
	Caged servers
Access Speed	Mirror servers
	Cache servers
Availability	Load balancing

Obviously, the speed of the communication line connecting the servers to the Internet is also important. The monthly fee increases as the speed increases. Thus, the decision on connection speed must be one that balances need and cost.

CONSIDERATIONS IN DEVELOPING A WEB SITE

Avoiding mistakes is a crucial consideration when developing a Web site. Businesses must also plan for company growth as they develop their sites and understand more about the basics of Web page design.

AVOIDING MISTAKES

This has probably happened to all of us. We log on to the Web site of a company that we want to contact. We search the home page, but there is no address or telephone number. We use the links provided, but there is no luck there either. Eventually, we find the address on some page that has nothing to do, logically or intuitively, with the link that took us there. This is just a small example of mistakes that organizations make when building their Web sites. Many of the mistakes have to do with design of the Web pages; others have to do with strategic decisions about building and maintaining the site. Jakob Nielsen, a Web design expert, offers the following list of top mistakes made by Web designers. Here are some of the mistakes he has observed in building organizational Web sites.

Not Knowing the Purpose   Companies should start their Web site projects only after they have found ways to add value for their stakeholders, especially customers. The Web site should be designed to give users benefits for spending time at the site. The site must be designed to attract them to do business with the organization. Many Web sites are built simply because some executive told someone to do it without telling that person the site's purpose. Executives in some organizations feel that their company must have a Web site because everyone else does. They believe that not having a Web site is like not having telephone or fax numbers. While this is probably true in this day and age, the purpose of building a site should still be clear, whether it is to merely establish a presence on the Web or other purposes as well.

Designing for Top Management   Mission statements and accomplishments are fine on the About Us page, but not on the homepage. Designers must remember that the target audience is customers, not corporate executives. Smart executives are likely to accept this notion. A site should not be built to the taste of top executives. Some companies build sites that tout mission statements and corporate feats. This should not be the purpose of a Web site, even if top executives may like it.

A Site That Mirrors the Organizational Structure   The site's structure should be determined by the tasks users will want to perform on your site, even if that means having a single page for information from two very different departments. It is often necessary to distribute information from a single department across two or more parts of the site, and many parts of the site will have to be managed in collaboration between multiple departments. It is tempting to let each department design its own part of a site, but this may result in a site that mirrors the organizational structure. Again, the focus of a site should be on the customer, not the organization. Therefore, the site must be designed to address customer needs and convenience, not to reflect organizational structure.

Outsourcing to Multiple Agencies   When all interface elements look and function the same, users feel more confident using the site because they can transfer their learning from one part of the site to another, rather than having to learn everything over again for each new page. Thus, it is recommended to have a single department be responsible for the design of an entire site. At the least, a group of representatives from various departments should be in control of the design templates. If the organization outsources pieces of the Web site to different design firms, the site may end up looking like a patchwork, so beware of this. Each firm has its own distinctive approach, which it will try to promote—not to mention that it will try to promote its own reputation through the client's site. Such a clash of approaches will not result in the consistency that is so vital to Web sites.

Forgetting to Budget for Maintenance   New features keep users coming back. Some organizations have a "launch and forget" approach. This is a grave mistake. As a rule of thumb, the annual maintenance budget for a Web site should be about the same as the initial cost of building the site, with 50 percent as an absolute minimum. Obviously, ongoing costs are even higher for news sites and other projects that depend on daily or real-time updates. However, even more static sites must be jazzed up on occasion to maintain the impression that the site is vital.

Treating the Web as a Secondary Medium   The Web is different from television, different from printed newspapers, and different from glossy brochures, so you cannot create a good Web site out of content optimized for any of these older media. The old analogy still holds: Movies are not made by filming a play and putting the camera in the best seat of the theater. The only way to get great Web content is to develop specific content *for* the Web. The designer must conceptualize the site with hyperlinks and other Web features in mind, ignoring creative work for other media.

Wasting Linking Opportunities   The Web is a linking medium: Hypertext links are what tie it together and allow users to discover new and useful sites. Most companies have recognized this phenomenon to the extent that they religiously include their URLs in all advertising and press releases. However, it is a mistake to mention the homepage URL in advertisements for particular products or services; rather, the specific address of the page providing information about these items should be mentioned. For instance, instead of mentioning the website *www.ourgreatcomopany.com,* mention *www.ourgreatcompany.com/kitchenware.* This way, you do not force an interested shoppers to meander through your site until they find the proper page.

Confusing Market Research and Usability Engineering   A Web site is an interactive product, and therefore its *usability* must be studied to see what happens during a user's interaction with the site. **Usability engineering** is the effort to design Web pages in a manner that makes navigation and absorption of information efficient and enjoyable. This has little to do with market research, which focuses on demand for products and services by various segments of the market and on which features are desired in the products and services that the organization wants to sell. Consequently, one cannot use market research methods to test the usability of a Web site. The organization must create a facility for the site's users to voice their frustrations and make suggestions for improvement. When a new idea is being implemented, the organization should study a small group of users to learn how they interact with the improved Web pages before the pages are put online. To do so, organizations can use usability engineers, who charge at least $15,000 in consulting fees for testing the usability of a Web site. They watch several users actually using the site to perform real tasks. This process is called **usability testing**. It is very important to test a site *before* it is activated on a server connected to the Internet.

Although the Web has been around for several years, it is still a new and rapidly developing medium. Learning from these common mistakes can be helpful but may not guarantee a successful Web site. Organizations must learn as they go along. The people who are in charge of the organizational Web site must listen carefully both to customers and their own staff.

BUILDING IN GROWTH

It is neither fun nor wise to establish a Web site without being optimistic. No one should build a Web site if the intention is for it to remain small. Don't just think big; think continuous growth. Therefore, when establishing a Web site, entrepreneurs must take measures that will allow them to support a growing business. As previously mentioned, the ability of a site to be modified to serve a growing number of needs is called scalability. This usually means adopting hardware that can be expanded relatively painlessly and inexpensively. More servers also mean additional communication lines and other hardware pieces as well as more or new software to support managing the hardware.

A television commercial for an Internet consulting firm shows the faces of several young people who built an Internet retail business and are now watching its first few minutes of operation. They are anxious until the first online customer places an order, smile when several hundred have ordered, and panic when hundreds of thousands of customers have flooded the site with orders. Why? Because servers are limited in the amount of traffic they can handle within a given period of time. When a business grows, the site operators must increase the site's capacity.

There are several ways to scale up a site. One is to speed up the site's connection to the Internet, another is to increase the server's storage capacity or add servers, another is to expand the capability of the database interacting with the server, and another is to reconfigure software that is already in place. The proper solution depends on the specific bottleneck. For example, a larger number of servers (or a *server farm*, in professional parlance) will not resolve the problem if the bottleneck is caused by limited bandwidth.

Greg Doherty, vice president of engineering at Onebox.com, noted in an article in *The Industry Standard* (Dahir, M., "Growing pains," March 20, 2000, pp. 216–218) that the most common scalability challenges are (1) database problems, (2) CPU (central processing unit) speed, and (3) bandwidth, in this order of difficulty. The latter challenge may be alleviated by the rapid spread and declining prices of fast links to the Internet, not only at the server end, but also at the client end. Cable modems and DSL services are quickly replacing dial-up modems.

What growth may cost depends largely on how much scaling up is needed. Companies spend between several thousand to several million dollars to install more, or faster, servers. By and large, scaling up hardware is less expensive than hiring scalability consultants and acquisition of better software. Some experts estimate that about one-third of the money spent on Web-site maintenance is earmarked for scalability.

Typically, a business's first need is to have more computers in order to serve a growing number of customers, often logging onto the site at the same time. Then, the software may have to be changed to add more services or to direct a growing number of callers to different Web pages and to different files in linked databases. Consider what happened at *WhatsHotNow.com,* a site that sells pop-culture items such as "cool" electronics, music CDs, and T-shirts. The site opened for business in July 1999. Within two weeks the number of simultaneous visitors jumped from 150 to 1000. The unexpected success made customers unhappy because many could not log on to the site, and when they did log on it took too long to complete orders. The site crashed several times. This caused lost sales and, worse, lost customers. The company solved the problem by separating the applications from the database: one server, the **database server**, holds the databases containing product catalogs and customer records, and the other server, the **application server**, lets visitors enter queries into catalog databases, select items for purchase, and process payments. This arrangement, illustrated in Figure 5.8, has been adopted by many online businesses. It accommodates scalability well. When traffic grows, or when more applications are added, several application servers can be linked, and several database servers can be linked to accommodate the growth.

PAGE DESIGN IMPERATIVES

Displaying information on the Web is very different from displaying information in print. On paper, you have much control over the material presented, and readers have control over how much time they want to spend on each part of the printed material. On the Web, how the pages are displayed depends on the type of monitor being used and on communication speed. There are several imperatives

F I G U R E

5.8 APPLICATION SERVER ARRANGEMENT

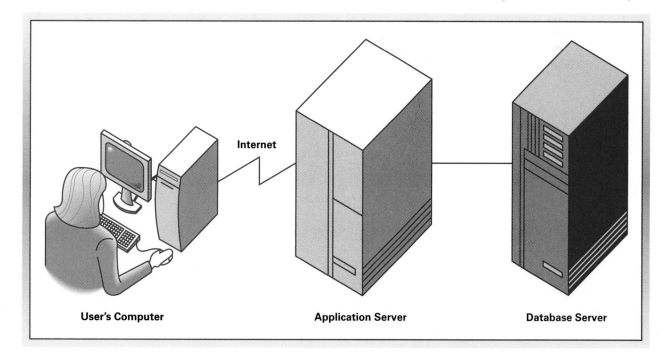

User's Computer   Application Server   Database Server

in Web design that should be kept in mind regardless of the type of online business you run. These principles are true for any type of site. In Chapter 9, we provide additional do's and don'ts specifically for the purpose of marketing, such as which colors to use for what purpose.

Different Views Remember that people use monitors of different sizes and qualities as well as more than one browser. Test your pages using monitors of different sizes and resolutions. A page developed for a 1280x1024 resolution and one million colors will not look as good on a monitor that supports only 800x600 resolution and 256 colors. Also, Internet Explorer may interpret shades somewhat differently than Netscape.

Quick Load Web site visitors do not like to sit and wait for pages to download. Therefore, it is important to construct pages that can download in a few seconds. Experts recommend a maximum of 10 seconds for a homepage to load and 30 seconds for other pages. If the pages take longer, you will probably lose that visitor, who will move on to another site.

To meet these recommendations, the homepage should be no bigger than 50KB (50 kilobytes), and other pages should be no bigger than 100KB. This is not much if you want to include pictures, and that is exactly the point: do not include too many pictures on your homepage. Too many graphics will slow down the load. Include the larger and more colorful graphics on other pages; if visitors are interested in what the homepage promises, they will be more patient with subsequent pages. As another rule, images should not be greater than 50KB, or they will load too slowly.

There are ways to reduce the size of image files without significantly degrading image quality. You can compress images so the files take a fraction of their original space. This way, the loading time will be significantly shorter while the quality of the image may seem the same, or almost the same, as the original. To use less space for pictures, convert all photographic images to the JPEG format, which uses less space than the GIF format. Provide thumbnail images to give access to enlarged images; users can click on the thumbnails to load their corresponding larger images.

Often, pages provide links to other sites. To speed up the loading of such pages, do not use the domain names of linked sites but rather their IP numbers. When you include a domain name, the name must first be looked up at a domain name system (DNS) server. The **resolver**, the software on the server that looks up the domain name to find the IP number, will take time to do so. By using the IP number, you save that time. Your site's visitors do not know how you indicated the link in the HTML code anyway, and if they do, they do not care.

Navigation Each page should be within three clicks away from the homepage, or visitors may lose their patience and leave your site. Follow the three clicks rule: click, click, click, and the users are at the page for which they were looking. Provide many links. It is a good idea to provide horizontal links to the major areas of the site on the bottom of each page. Most importantly, provide a Home link on every page. Visitors should be able to go back home and start a new search whenever they want.

Do not use content from other sites unless you receive permission. It is illegal to open other sites' pages in a frame within your site. You may, however, provide links from your pages to other sites. When developing your pages, design them so that a link to another site opens the page in the other site.

A Picture Is Worth . . . While the old adage "A picture is worth a thousand words" is generally true, it may not always be so on the Web. On the one hand, using icons saves words; on the other hand, many people may not understand the "hint" in the picture. You must communicate the function of each link directly and clearly. Therefore, use text in addition to or instead of icons. If you insist on icons, include the proper text underneath them. For instance, do not simply use an envelope icon; use the phrase "E-mail Us" as well. Do not use only an icon showing a little house; use the word "Homepage" for clarity. Note also that many people with slow connections to the Internet surf the Web with the graphics turned off in their browsers, so they can surf faster. If you provide only picture menus, they cannot navigate your site. (To automatically provide a text alternative to each image, you can use the HTML ALT tag in designed pages.)

People in non–English-speaking countries may not understand any or all of the English text on your Web pages. Using pictures will not solve the problem. If you want non–English speakers to read your text, provide the text both in English and in other languages. Icons and other graphics are not a good substitute for language.

Providing a Find Mechanism Experienced Web designers have learned that it is imperative to give as much control as possible to users. Do not force visitors to traverse the site in a pattern predefined by you. Let them decide how they want to proceed. The greatest feature you can give them is a mechanism to find information at your site, aptly called a **find mechanism** (or *local search engine*), especially if the site is large and involved. Go to any retail site and you will see a search feature somewhere at the top of the homepage. This is also true of noncommercial sites. All find mechanisms let users search by keyword.

If you include sound and long-playing animations, do not have these features start playing automatically as soon as a user loads the page. Provide links to these features and invite visitors to use them.

Frames Avoid frames when designing pages, if you can. **Frames** divide the browser's window into several independent panes. This reduces the useful window area and irritates visitors. The only useful type of framed pages is the one that has a narrow vertical frame on one side of the window for selecting from a long menu, alongside a major frame to display the content of each choice. This is logical and convenient. Avoid horizontal frames, because most people like to peruse lists top down, not sideways.

Flashing and Other Tricks You may have noticed that very few sites now contain marquees, flashing text, and similar features that are supposed to catch the visitor's attention. To many people, these features are annoying. If you insist on such features, have them do the trick once, not repeatedly. If you use animations, do not use more than one per page, because you may confuse the user.

Consistency and Proper Presentation Design all pages in a consistent manner, so the user quickly gets used to the structure. Keep the user's learning curve in mind; the user must be able to learn the ropes of your entire site within several clicks. For example, if you use a horizontal menu on the bottom, use horizontal menus on all the pages, even if the menus change to fit the content of a particular page. Similarly, use the same font and font size in these menus. If you use buttons, use text to ensure the users know where each button will take them when clicked. To the degree possible, design all pages with the same or similar general appearance.

Extend this rule to paragraph format, text size, fonts, and colors. To increase readability, use sans-serif fonts for titles, which are usually of large size. For paragraphs, captions, and long quotes, use serif fonts such as Times and Times New Roman, because serif fonts are easier to read. Ensure that there is adequate contrast between text and background. Remember that not all users have all the fonts that are available on your computer. If some users' computers are missing a font that you used in your pages, their browsers will select another font. Therefore, it is recommended that you only use fonts usually provided with operating systems. If you want to use a fancy font, make it an image. Then all browsers will present it the same way.

To control the presentation of text, use tables. This way, you ensure that text within a table cell remains in the cell.

Use a different color for all the pages of each section of the site. This will help users know in which section of the site they are. The color can be of the background or of the text. However, use color only to enhance the appearance of pages, not to dominate them. Users are interested mostly in content. Providing a color key on the homepage may be useful to visitors.

Flexible Sizing Remember that different users will be using computer monitors of different sizes. Therefore, it is best to use relative sizes for fonts and percentages for table sizes. You can specify "large" and "small" font sizes rather than specific sizes such as 10 points or 24 points. This will ensure that a large font is large in relative terms in any size of browser window regardless of the size of a particular computer monitor.

Similarly, size your tables using percentages. For example, if you designate 60 percent for a table's width, the width will take 60 percent of the browser's window in an 18-inch monitor as well as a 15-inch monitor. If you fix table sizes, they will stay the same size, so if a browser window is too small for a table, part of the table will not be displayed. Fixed table sizes are fine for tables small enough to be displayed in their entirety in practically every monitor in use.

For the Disabled As a courtesy to the visually and hearing impaired, design your pages so that they, too, can enjoy them. If the pages are designed for a government organization, you may have to do so under the law. For example, local, state, and federal sites must abide by the Americans with Disabilities Act (ADA). Blind visitors to your site can use text-to-sound software and hardware, but they will not be able to use this technology if you provide only pictures without text. It is another good reason to include text under all icons, and consider including text under other graphics as well.

Allow visitors to view larger sizes of any pictures by clicking the ones originally displayed in the page. This may help not only disabled people, but also many adults. About 90 percent of people over age 40 have imperfect vision. Remember: Your site should be inviting and inclusive, so all visitors feel welcome.

No "Work in Progress" Designing a Web site may take several weeks or longer, especially if the site involves sophisticated interactive and animated features. Wait for the design and construction to be complete—do not rush to put up a homepage announcing that you are "Coming Soon." No one cares how soon it is coming if you do not have a ready-to-go site. People who reach such a page are unlikely to return. Cute "Under Construction" animations will not save your site from this fate.

Unlike with a brick-and-mortar business, the location of Web-based business is immediately international, by default. Your site can be accessed by anyone from anywhere. However, while the presence of your Web site is universal, its legal status may not be. You should be especially cautious if you intend to attract consumers from countries whose laws are different from those of your own. Note that this has nothing to do with marketing techniques (which we discuss in Chapter 9), but with the practicality of using a Web site for doing business with businesses and consumers in various countries.

Consider the legal challenges facing companies that want to set up auction sites in France, Germany, and Italy—these European countries forbid auctions of new goods; only used ones can be auctioned. The countries established these laws to protect auctioneer guilds. Italy specifically prohibits electronic auctions under a law that was passed in 1998. In Germany, auctions are allowed only if licensed auctioneers conduct them. In the Netherlands, Internet auctions are practically infeasible because the law requires a notary public to witness an auction.

Similar laws forbid or limit other types of activities on the Web, such as online gambling and the sale of alcoholic beverages. If you intend to use your new Web site to conduct business with people from other countries, states, or provinces, it is advisable to discuss your plan with an attorney who specializes in the laws of these political units. We discuss additional legal issues in Chapter 11.

SUMMARY

- The first step in establishing a business on the Internet is to select a domain name. The applicant can use any of several domain name registrars and select a name that is not already reserved by someone else. Registrars' Web sites provide search mechanisms so you can check which names are available and who owns names that have already been assigned.

- Owning a domain name does not necessitate assigning it to a server; the owner can "park" the name with the registrar by associating it with the registrar's server until the owner has another server with which to associate it. To make it easy for Web users to find a site, the site's URL should contain the business name. The name should be registered with all top domain names, preferably also with some country domains.

- To help Web users find a site, a business should register it with search engine sites. The homepages of major search engines include a link for submitting new URLs. Applications for listing sites on search engines can be submitted manually or by using special software. Several companies provide application services for a fee. Some provide free online application forms. It is important to include the most important keywords between metatags in the homepage's HTML code. A metatag is an HTML tag that identifies the contents of a Web page.

- After deciding to go online, a business has several options: using its own server, using an ISP site, using a Web portal, using a cybermall, using a hosting site, using a virtual Web server, or using a subdomain. The first option is the most expensive. When selecting a Web-hosting company, the client should consider several factors: the quality of technical support, the quality of content support (if content is the host's responsibility), the setup fee, the amount of disk space, traffic limits and fees, the availability of e-mail accounts and services, the availability of FTP service, CGI scripts, scalability, and the support of page design standards.

- Maintaining a Web site on a business's own servers is not only expensive, but employees must be skilled at dealing with the technical side of hardware and telecommunications on the one hand, and of page design on the other hand. A business commonly employs a Webmaster to head a group to maintain its own server. Establishing and maintaining a communications link with high bandwidth to ensure speedy downloads by site visitors is important. Businesses that maintain their own Web sites bear the cost of hardware, software, and labor of skilled professionals.

- Many businesses opt to hire the services of ISPs. The cost of having an ISP maintain a Web site may be anywhere from several hundred dollars to about a million dollars per month, depending on variety and quality of services. Usually, the ISP provides space on its servers and a link to its servers so the Web site owner can update pages remotely. Some ISPs provide not only technical services, but also content services such as page development and updates. Some online businesses prefer the colocation arrangement, in which the client company owns the servers, but they are maintained by an ISP at its facilities.

- Before contracting with an ISP, a client needs to ensure that the facilities provide a high level of security; that load balancing software is employed; that mirroring, the duplication of server content on other servers, is available; and that the servers have adequate caching capability. The speed of the communication lines connecting the servers to the Internet backbone is also important.

- There are several mistakes that businesses often make when establishing Web sites: not knowing the purpose of establishing the site, and therefore developing an improper site; designing the site for top management rather than for customers; developing a site that mirrors the organizational structure rather than designing it for ease of use by customers; outsourcing the construction to multiple agencies, thereby losing coherence; forgetting to budget for maintenance of the site so that it can be constantly improved and updated; treating the Web as a secondary medium, whereby losing opportunities that only the Web, not other means of communication, provides; wasting linking opportunities by advertising the homepage rather than the specific page at which customers can find what the company is selling; and confusing market research with usability engineering.

- Since many Web sites expand in activity thanks to both growth in traffic and in the variety of services provided, an online business must take scalability into account. A scalable online operation allows for the addition of servers and the distribution of applications over several servers. The most common scalability challenges are database problems, CPU speed, and bandwidth.

- To overcome Internet congestion in general and site congestion in particular, site operators can purchase the services of content delivery networks. These networks mirror the original site on their servers throughout the Internet.

- Regardless of the purpose of a Web site, if it is to attract visitors, its designers must heed several rules. They must ensure that the pages look good on computer monitors that vary in size and resolution—using relative sizes for fonts and tables is often a good practice. They must design the pages so that they can be loaded within seconds. They must provide menus and buttons for easy navigation so that visitors can always use three or fewer mouse clicks to get to wherever they want to be at the site. They should provide text alongside pictures, both for browsers with disabled image loading and for blind users who visit the site (using text-to-sound software and hardware). They should provide a local search engine, especially if the site includes a large number of pages. They should use frames only for side menus and avoid irritating features such as flashing text. They should maintain consistency throughout the site and color code sections to help the orientation of visitors. In general, the designers should give as much control as possible to visitors and not force them to navigate in a rigid manner. Lastly, a site should never be posted before its design is complete.

■ When a site is put up on the Web, it immediately becomes international as it can be accessed from anywhere in the world. If the organization intends to do business outside the country where the site is operated, management must be aware of legal hurdles. Business practices that are legal in one country may be illegal in another. These facts must be taken into account when planning the site.

KEY TERMS

domain name	Webmaster
domain name registrar	content delivery network
top-level domain	load balancing
search engine	colocation
metatag	mirroring
web crawler	caching
web hosting service	usability engineering
cybermall (storefront)	usability testing
Virtual Web server	database server
subdomain	application server
hits	resolver
Post-Office Protocol (POP) account	find mechanism
scalability	frames
server management	

REVIEW QUESTIONS

1. How does one reserve a domain name? What does *parking* a domain name mean, and what is a good reason for doing so?
2. Enumerate the points one should keep in mind when registering a domain name.
3. What are metatags, and what is their purpose?
4. Often, an ISP provides not only access to the Internet, but also hosting services. Why?
5. Installing one's own Internet server is usually more expensive than hiring the services of an ISP. Why? What costs are involved?
6. What is a cybermall? Would a cybermall be a good option for a national retailer?
7. What is a subdomain? Give an example.
8. Explain the terms *mirror server* and *cache server*. Why are such servers important?
9. What is the difference between market research and usability engineering?

10. What is scalability? Why is scalability so important for Web sites?
11. Why do some online businesses opt to have an arrangement of two types of servers: application servers and database servers?

DISCUSSION QUESTIONS

1. You are to select a group of people to test the usability of a new Web site. The site sells sports clothing for the entire family. In terms of demographics, which people would you select for the usability test? Explain your choice.

2. Suppose you tested the usability of your new Web site and discovered that people respond well to icons without accompanying text. The test took place in several countries and included people who do not speak English. Someone suggests that since an easily-understood picture is great for international sites, you should not add text to the icons "to make the site truly international." Do you accept the suggestion? Why or why not?

3. You are a member of a team that is designing a new Web site for your company. The company intends to attract consumers from all over the world. Someone suggests using a lot of images and a wide variety of color, especially because the site is international and should be language-independent. You are concerned about load time. Fellow managers tell you that your concern is without merit because "eventually, everyone will have a high-speed link to the Internet." What is your response?

ASSIGNMENTS

1. You have a dog-walking business that you would like to expand to all major cities in the United States. You have no technical skills and cannot develop Web pages on your own. Yet, you would like to offer the services of your business through the Web. To open extensions in other cities, you would also like to use the Web to recruit dog walkers.

   Explore the Web for hosting services and make a list of at least 10 companies that offer them. Feel free to list the ones mentioned in this chapter. Use the table in Figure 5.5 to rank the hosting companies from most suitable to least suitable. In addition, provide a narrative to explain your ranking after you have examined the Web sites of at least one business hosted by each of these companies.

2. Use a Web page editor (such as FrontPage) to design the homepage of Kool Kollege Tee Shirts, an online retailer of T-Shirts. Use graphics, a side frame for a menu of different types of T-shirts, and a table (with invisible lines) for arranging text and pictures. Follow all of the advice given in the Page Design Imperatives section of this chapter. Test the page to ensure that it looks good using at least two different operating systems (e.g., Windows and MacOS) and the two major Web browsers, Netscape and Microsoft Internet Explorer. Test the site on several monitors of different sizes and resolutions. Submit a disk with the page, or e-mail it to your professor. Your professor will grade it based on the design imperatives listed in this chapter, and possibly on additional factors.

Triangulating Online Shopping

The new electronic economy has some interesting faces. One of them was discovered, and exploited, by a 31-year-old Mexican entrepreneur. Juan Carlos Garcia established DeCompras.com in 1999, a Spanish-language site that specialized in the sale of expensive consumer electronics. (The words *de compras* mean "going shopping" in Spanish.) He received funding from a former business associate and worked hard to grow the business. However, Garcia soon realized that he had a major problem. Internet access and use in Mexico is far from that in the United States, Europe, or even parts of Asia. In addition, few Mexicans use credit cards, which are essential for Internet-based purchasing.

A genius idea lit in his mind. There are 15 to 20 million Americans of Mexican descent living in the United States. They send an average of $500 per person per month to relatives in Mexico, a total of more than $10 billion per year. Since electronic appliances are more expensive in Mexico than in the United States, why not employ these facts in a business model? If he could only convince Mexican Americans to purchase electronics from his Web site and send them instead of cash to relatives, he could make millions.

Garcia began an intensive advertising campaign in the major concentrations of his target audience: Los Angeles, Chicago, and all over Texas and Arizona. The ads prompted Mexican Americans to send merchandise instead of cash. Several brick-and-mortar companies sell products in the United States and deliver them to Mexico, but DeCompras became the only one to do so online. In addition to this major change in strategy, Garcia also augmented the merchandise he offered to include many household items. This let him tap a significantly larger audience. Apparently, the great majority of Mexican Americans prefer purchasing refrigerators to handheld computers.

Unlike his brick-and-mortar competitors, Garcia stocks in Mexico rather than in the United States. This lowers his shipping costs and lets him serve his customers more promptly. Therefore, his service is cheaper and more attractive. Sales of the company are about $1 million per month, which is impressive relative to the Latin American online market of $350 million per year. In Mexico, online sales reached a mere $30 million in 1999. Once the Mexican business model is consolidated, Garcia plans to apply the model to other communities.

Source: Helft, D., "Say it with blenders," *The Industry Standard*, June 19, 2000, p. 157

Thinking About E-Commerce Today

1. What elements (text and graphics) would you include in a site that tries to generate revenue the way DeCompras does?
2. Which other communities in the United States would you tap in a manner similar to that of DeCompras? Which communities in other countries?
3. Could a venture such as DeCompras become a world brand name? Explain.

LEARNING OBJECTIVES
WHEN YOU FINISH
THIS CHAPTER YOU
WILL BE ABLE TO:

- Explain the concept of Electronic Data Interchange (EDI)
- List the benefits of EDI
- Explain the notion of virtual private networks
- Articulate the benefits of EDI conducted via extranets
- Illustrate a typical scenario of EDI-based transactions

One of the earliest needs for the standard communication of commercial documentation arose in 1948 during the Berlin Airlift. The city was blockaded by the Soviets. The task of coordinating airfreights of food and other consumables was daunting because the shipments arrived with differing shipping lists, also known as manifests. Because several Western-bloc nations took part in the effort, which also involved many organizations, the manifests were in different languages and formats. So a standard manifest was devised. Later, when the electronic transmission of commercial documents started during the 1960s (initially in the rail and road transport industries), standardization of the documents was essential. The concept of electronic data interchange was born.

WHAT IS EDI?

Electronic data interchange (EDI) is the exchange of electronic documents in standardized form between organizations, directly from a computer application in one organization to an application in another organization. Such organizations are referred to as **trading partners**. EDI speeds up the interchange of information and the execution of transactions between trading partners. Typical documents exchanged between computers include purchase orders, shipping lists, invoices, and remittance advices. Instead of using regular mail, telephone, and fax, the parties use computer-to-computer communications to exchange formatted documents. The documents must be formatted according to an agreed-upon standard so that information can be properly encoded at the sending end and properly decoded at the receiving end.

This communication can take place in a **value-added network (VAN)**, which is composed of lines leased from a telecommunications company that also manages the network. (Note that the provider of such service is often called a VAN, not a VAN provider.) VAN services ascertain that business partners with different hardware or operating systems can communicate seamlessly.

An EDI message contains a string of data elements, each of which represents a fact—such as a company name or address, part number, or price—separated by delimiters. (A delimiter is any character or space that denotes the end of a piece of information.) The entire string is called a *data segment*. One or more data segments framed by a header and trailer form a **transaction set**, which is the EDI unit of transmission. An EDI transmission is equivalent to a message. A transaction set usually consists of information that would otherwise be contained in a business document or form, such as a purchase order or an invoice.

In an EDI arrangement, Company A sends formatted documents via the network to Company B. Special software is used by the trading partner at the receiving end to translate the electronic documents into human-readable documents or to channel the data directly into Company B's system, which also uses special software. Company B can respond using the same type of software. A typical series of EDI transactions is depicted in Figure 6.1. EDI's many benefits are summarized in Figure 6.2.

Perhaps the strongest benefit is that EDI reduces business cycles tremendously. Sellers can quickly send price lists and price proposals from their databases directly to potential clients. Data are recorded much more accurately because they do not need to be re-keyed into information systems; business data

FIGURE

6.1 TYPICAL EDI TRANSACTIONS

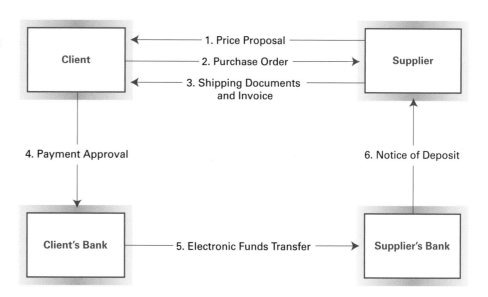

Cost Savings and Accuracy	Onetime data entry
	Reduced amount of data-entry errors and improved error detection because data are not re-keyed
	Automatic reconciliation (of shipments, debts, etc.)
	Reduced manual labor; greater productivity
	Elimination of lost documents
	Reduced stock held; closer to just-in-time operation
Time Savings	Elimination of postage and shipping charges
	Rapid exchange of documents (minutes vs. days)
	Shorter production cycle
	More timely response to clients
	Data are already in electronic form and can flow automatically into internal systems (such as accounting and disbursement); no need to re-key data
Uniform Communication with . . .	Customers
	Suppliers
	Banks
	Government agencies

are already in electronic form and can be routed to the proper information system, such as the accounting or disbursement system of the target company. EDI significantly reduces manual work and paperwork, ultimately resulting in less need for physical storage such as file cabinets. When trading partners establish enough trust, they can move from paying upon the receipt of invoice to paying on the basis of delivery of goods matched against a purchase order. This may result in further cost savings for both partners.

When payment is made, it too can take the form of electronic signals instead of a check mailed in a paper envelope. **Electronic funds transfer (EFT)** occurs between banks. Upon instruction from an account holder, a bank electronically debits the account by the amount specified and authorizes the payee's bank to credit the payee's account with that amount. EFT is the oldest form of EDI. Whenever we wire money, we actually order the bank to use its EFT system.

VAN SERVICES

EDI VAN communications services provide trading partners with an asynchronous mail-box service. (Recall that normal e-mail systems that we use are asynchronous—the receiver does not have to receive the message immediately after it was sent.) A trading partner dials into a VAN access point in a way similar to dialing up to connect to an Internet server from a PC. The trading partner then uses a file transfer protocol to send the electronic document to the VAN. The VAN then routes the document to the receiving trading partner's VAN mailbox. (The trading partners may use two different VANs.) The receiving trading partner dials into the VAN and downloads the document from its VAN mailbox. Trading partners check their electronic mailboxes several times daily.

EDI IN ACTION

EDI is not a new concept. It traces its roots back to the 1970s. It was the only way to conduct e-commerce before the Internet became available to commercial organizations. Detroit's big-three automakers and the large retailers such as Wal-Mart, Sears, Dayton Hudson, and Kmart have had EDI systems set up with their suppliers for a long time. For example, Kmart developed a proprietary EDI application that it has used to conduct business with 500 suppliers. Large companies submit the lion's share of their purchase orders through EDI networks. For example, 80 percent of the orders that Home Depot, the home improvement chain, issues are transmitted through EDI. According to the research company the Gartner Group, from as early as 1987, 1,000 companies used some practical form of the concept, and in 1996 an estimated 100,000 companies used EDI. By another estimate, of the 6.2 million U.S. businesses operating in 2000, only 80,000 used EDI.

The majority of America's largest buyers have made great efforts in setting up EDI relationships with their largest suppliers, enabling them to purchase most of their inventory electronically. A few, Dell Computer and Wal-Mart included, have required all their suppliers to implement EDI. However, most buyers followed the 80/20 rule: Connect the top 20 percent (in terms of supplies' worth) suppliers into your EDI or VAN EDI network so that 80 percent of inventory is purchased electronically; this works because the other 80 percent of suppliers provide only 20 percent of the inventory's worth. This business practice has left the majority of suppliers out of EDI arrangements.

GREAT EXPECTATIONS

Despite proven benefits, EDI has not become ubiquitous, and its success has been only moderate. According to the Boston Consulting Group, a business strategy and management consultancy firm, only seven percent of the $9 trillion business-to-business commerce conducted in the United States in 1998 was done through EDI or other electronic means. The rest of that business was conducted with some combination of telephone calls, faxes, and paper mail, involving much manual labor.

Why doesn't every company use EDI? First, EDI systems are costly to install and operate, especially in the early period after implementation. Training costs are particularly high. This is why no company has ever connected with more than the top 20 percent of its trading partners. Even the more optimistic estimate of 100,000 businesses using EDI constitutes less than 2 percent of all U.S. businesses. Furthermore, the cost burden of installing EDI systems is usually asymmetric: the purchasing party usually ends up paying less than the suppliers. This has been a disincentive for many small companies to join EDI arrangements.

The exploding adoption of the Internet may encourage more companies to embrace EDI—even small businesses can afford it with the new medium. Experts now expect a great majority of manufacturing businesses to use Internet-based EDI in just a few years. EDI on the Internet is implemented using the concept of *extranet*, explained in the following section.

INTRANETS AND EXTRANETS

As we mentioned in Chapter 2, the communication protocols of the Internet are TCP/IP (Transmission Control Protocol/Internet Protocol). Soon after commercial

WANT TO SELL TO THE U.S. GOVERNMENT? GO EDI.

In October 1993, then-President Clinton ordered his administration's agencies and departments to begin using EDI. In October 1994, the Federal Acquisition Streamlining Act was passed, requiring the entire federal government to use EDI. Anyone who wants to sell goods or services valued at under $100,000 to the federal government must be EDI capable.

businesses were exposed to the Internet, they realized that they could use the same protocols on their local area networks (LANs). Furthermore, they could conveniently link their LANs to the Internet and create internal organizational networks for their employees. This arrangement is especially useful when an organization consists of several sites miles or thousands of miles apart. The arrangement is called **intranet** (*intra* for "within" as opposed to *inter* for "between").

To ensure that an organization can limit access to a Web site only to employees and other authorized parties, security and access control measures must be installed. In addition to access codes, such as passwords, cautious organizations have installed robust software applications called **firewalls**. The term *firewall* comes from the automotive industry, where a firewall is a sheet of metal placed between a vehicle's motor and cabin to prevent fire from reaching the passengers in case of accidental combustion. Similarly, firewalls in an Internet context are hardware and software that prevent unauthorized parties from accessing any resources that an organization has connected to the Internet but deems private. Such security measures create an environment in which employees perceive both the LAN and the Internet to be part of a private and secure network, just as a network used only by employees of the company would be. The network seems private and therefore is called a **virtual private network** (VPN), as explained in Chapter 2.

We might say that a VPN is a private network configured within a public network. While the public part of the network can be used by anyone with access to the Internet, proper measures by the VPN's owner ensure that only authorized people can use the Internet to access the VPN's information resources.

VPNs are used not only for intraorganizational communication, but also to establish efficient communication with business parties. Companies open some of their resources to both suppliers and corporate clients. A network like this is called an **extranet** (*extra* for "outside"). In practical terms, an extranet is a Web site for existing customers or clients rather than the general public. When a site is built for clients, it can provide them with sole access to paid research, current inventories, and internal databases. When established for suppliers, the site becomes an excellent means to conduct EDI. Similar to an intranet, an extranet uses the Internet as its transmission system but requires passwords to gain access.

Traditional EDI formats are X12, a U.S. standard; EDIFACT (EDI For Administration, Commerce, and Transport), an international set of standards backed by the United Nations; and TRADACOMS (TRAding DAta COMmunications Standards), a European standard used mainly in the retail industry in the United Kingdom. The Internet is making EDI very popular, but not by using the traditional EDI data formats. Rather, XML connects businesses together over the Web. We discussed XML in Chapter 4.

There are two types of Internet Protocol EDI: EDI without use of Web technology, and Web-based EDI. Both take place on the same network, but the former does not make use of the Web. Instead of using a VAN, the partners use the Internet. The transactions are transported via FTP (File Transfer Protocol) and e-mail. The downside of this approach is that the parties cannot enjoy the services provided by the VAN firm. Web EDI lets the partners use Web interface and pages for the same purposes that traditional EDI has been used, but with more convenience. Employees can simply fill out forms embedded in Web pages. In our discussion, we will refer to Web-based EDI, as this is the direction in which most companies are heading. Because all Internet EDI is carried out via extranets, we will refer to it as extranet EDI.

The benefits of extranet EDI are:

1. *Global network availability.* The Internet is available to any party that can establish a link to the network. The network itself already exists, and an organization that wishes to establish EDI relations with partners does not have to lease communication lines. Businesses can use very inexpensive dial-up modems or expensive T1 lines and DSL services, whose availability is growing fast.

2. *Free software.* To use traditional EDI, companies need to purchase proprietary software, which is quite expensive. To use EDI on the Web one needs only to use a browser. Browsers can be obtained free of charge. XML formats are integrated into browsers as soon as they are agreed upon, much the way HTML standards have been incorporated into the most popular browsers. In fact, HTML and XML have already been merged by W3C (the leading Internet standard setter discussed in Chapter 1) into a single language called XHTML.

3. *Existing universal equipment.* Subscribing to the EDI services of a VAN provider usually requires special equipment for connection to the privately held network. In using the Internet, there is no need for such equipment. All that a business needs is a PC and a link to the network, which can be established via a low-cost modem. Practically all newly purchased PCs come with a built-in modem. Many PCs are sold with built-in DSL modems.

4. *Low training costs.* It is easy to learn how to use a Web browser, and millions of people already know how to use one. Organizations can avoid the burden of training employees to use complex EDI software. The same application, the Web browser, is used to interpret non-XML as well as XML elements on Web pages.

5. *Single set of standards.* Over the years, many companies have committed themselves to an EDI standard, such as X12, EDIFACT, and TRADACOMS. As business develops and they wish to practice EDI with a company that uses another standard, they must employ special software to translate communicated documents. On the Web, XML provides a single, universal standard for business information. This eliminates the needs for translation software and the cost involved in employing it.

6. *Fast communication.* In general, VANs have lower bandwidth than that of the Internet, because much of the Internet is made of broadband channels.

However, extranet EDI has some shortcomings compared with VAN EDI:

1. *Inferior security.* Even if the utmost security measures are implemented to protect communication from being intercepted by unauthorized parties, organizations must keep in mind that such risks always exist because the

Benefits of Extranet EDI
Global network availability
Free software
Existing universal equipment
Low training cost
Single set of standards
Fast communication

Shortcomings of Extranet EDI
Inferior security
No speed control
Only partially developed XML standards

Internet is a public network; the communication lines are shared by millions of users and are not under the control of the EDI partners. EDI over the Internet is not and cannot be as secure as VAN EDI, where the lines are leased for the sole use of subscribers.

2. *No speed control.* As mentioned previously, communication is faster over the Internet than over VANs. However, when communication lines are leased, communication speed is practically guaranteed for the EDI partners. The amount of data transmitted depends only on them. The amount of traffic on the Internet, however, depends on millions of users. No individual can control it. Thus, at times a company may want to rush a document to a business partner but if traffic is heavy just then, the document may take a long time to reach its destination.

3. *Only partially developed XML standards.* It took many years to establish EDI standards for different industries (e.g., trucking, health care, manufacturing, etc.), but the standards are now well established. XML has been developed for EDI for just a few years. There are some standards already, but not as many as supported by EDIFACT. It will take some time until XML standards satisfy a large variety of business needs.

The benefits and shortcomings of extranet EDI are summarized in Figure 6.3.

STANDARDIZATION OF EDI ON THE INTERNET

VANs can provide several services that are not yet available in Internet-based trading. VANs have administrative responsibility for maintaining the trading partner accounts and for ensuring that the accounts are valid. VANs also provide several levels of service that allow a trading partner to track the progress of a document being communicated through the VAN. Trading partners can subscribe to *mailbox delivery notification* or *mailbox pick-up notification.*

Mailbox delivery notification is sent by the VAN to the sending trading partner when the EDI document is delivered to the receiving trading partner. Mailbox pick-up notification is sent by the VAN to the sending trading partner when the receiving trading partner downloads the document. The services provided by the VAN ensure three important conditions:

1. **Transaction integrity**, which means that the entire transaction is communicated without interference. The integrity of transactions may be violated when parts of electronic documents do not reach their destination or reach it too late.
2. **Privacy**, which means that only the parties exchanging information are aware of such exchange, or, at least, that only they can read the information exchanged. Private networks such as VANs provide higher levels of privacy than public networks such as the Internet.
3. **Nonrepudiation**, which is the inability of a business partner to deny sending or receiving a document. A business partner may claim that it did not receive an electronic document, although it did. That is, the partner may repudiate the receipt of the document. A VAN's mailbox delivery notification and pick-up notification establish solid nonrepudiation. If a trading partner sent or received a document, it cannot deny this fact.

The Internet is not overseen by anyone. Therefore, neither a third party such as a VPN provider nor software controls ensure that these elements are supported on VANs. The Internet Engineering Task Force (IETF), whose role we discussed in Chapter 1, has a task group that seeks to provide standard solutions to challenges faced by EDI over the Internet. The group is called EDIINT (EDI Internet). The group's initial effort was to produce standards for packaging X12 and EDIFACT documents with security measures that provide a secure environment for the exchange of documents following traditional EDI standards. The group has continued its effort to address the issues of transaction integrity, privacy, and nonrepudiation.

When business partners use traditional EDI, many security measures and other business procedures are the responsibility of the VAN provider. When VANs are used, all communication passes through the VAN's servers, which are equipped with proper software for these measures. For example, the software verifies the information that appears in the header of EDI documents, such as sender ID, receiver ID, a control reference (for future tracking), and communications agreement ID. On the Internet, the parties must be able to communicate in a peer-to-peer manner, without the use of EDI exchanges. Therefore, all these procedures and assurances must be devised for the Internet. The EDIINT group's focus is to recommend solutions for each of these concerns, using existing standards whenever possible. The group recognizes that many of the standards will be fully integrated into XML.

Eventually, XML standards will enable any two trading partners to exchange commercial information directly. This is the great promise of Web-based EDI. In other words, partners will not need any intermediary for exchanging electronic documents, because all the elements now provided by VANs will be incorporated into browsers. For the time being, most Web-based EDI is executed through Web sites that take the place of VANs, providing transaction integrity, security, nonrepudiation methods, and other necessary EDI procedures and assurances.

As Figure 6.4 shows, buyers can link their manufacturing requirement planning (MRP) systems to special XML servers whose purpose is to process XML documents. According to manufacturing master plans and other information, MRP systems produce purchase orders that can be automatically sent to a vendor via the firm's server and the Internet. The vendor's XML server interprets the order and sends the information from the interpreted order into the appropriate modules of its enterprise resource planning (ERP) system. This system helps plan the availability of resources such as human resources and raw materials required to manufacture the items ordered.

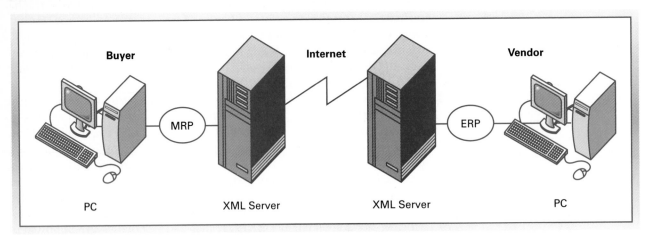

BUSINESS USE OF EXTRANET EDI TODAY

The answer to the question "Who uses extranet EDI?" is "Who doesn't?" Members of practically every industry have either started using extranet EDI or are in the process of establishing such relationships. Here are just a few examples.

TARGET

Target Corporation, one of America's largest department store chains, uses Web-based EDI with its suppliers. The main purpose of deciding to use EDI was to improve the company's inventory management, and the major reason for adopting Web-based EDI was to offer vendors the ability to easily exchange documents using a Web browser without having to purchase software. The software Target has installed lets its vendors exchange complex documents, such as the Advance Ship Notice and bar-code labels, over the Internet. The vendors can print out necessary documents on their own printers.

PIPS AND ARROW ELECTRONICS

In the computer component and electronics industries, dozens of companies have adopted a standard for applications called *Partner Interface Processes (PIPs)*. PIPs are XML exchanges that let manufacturers, distributors, resellers, carriers, and cus-

INTERESTING . . .

VERY DIRECT MARKETING

A 1999 survey of more than 500 members of the Direct Marketing Association (DMA) revealed that 95 percent of the responding organizations use the Internet for sales and marketing. Fifty-one percent of the companies use EDI.

Source: DMA, 1999

tomers along the supply chain carry out business processes in a standard manner, rather than each employing custom-developed procedures. PIPs determine how trade partners interact with one another as they execute day-to-day business activities in areas such as partner-product review, product information exchange, order management, inventory management, marketing information management, and service and support. As this list indicates, the partnership between businesses goes beyond the electronic transfer of documents; businesses can actually peek into each other's inventory and production schedules.

Arrow Electronics, Inc., the world's largest distributor of electronic components and computer products, is one of the companies that have adopted PIP. In February 2000, Arrow implemented a PIP with Intel to speed up orders for a high-valued chipset the company buys from Intel. In the past, Arrow had to accumulate change orders throughout the day in its inventory-management system, and then submit them overnight through an EDI transmission. The next day, Intel checked its sales order-entry system to see if the chipsets were available, then responded that night with an EDI message to Arrow. This cycle took 36 to 48 hours. By using a PIP, the purchase-order change occurs immediately.

TRANSPORT CLUB AND SWIFT

The bulk of extranet EDI now takes place through hub sites. One such hub was established by two large European organizations. Transport Club (TT Club) is a giant mutual insurance company for shipping companies. The Society for Worldwide Interbank Financial Telecommunications (SWIFT) is a cooperative owned by several banks. It handles secure messaging and international EFTs for more than 7,600 banks worldwide. The two international commerce giants have launched *Bolero.net*, a new business-to-business hub on the Internet that establishes an online center for importers, exporters, shipping organizations, and financial institutions. Through this hub businesses can automate the paperwork associated with international transactions.

SWIFT managers say that on average the cooperative transfers more than $5 trillion dollars daily. The TT Club management says the company provides liability and equipment insurance to ship operators, stevedores, terminal and depot operators, port authorities, freight forwarders, and other transport businesses in more than 80 countries. The company also insures more than two thirds of the world's container fleet and more than 1,700 ports and shipping terminals.

The Web site was tested in the fall of 1999, as trials were conducted with 120 multinational corporations involved in international commerce, including Mitsui, Maersk Lines, Citibank, HSBC, Cargill Coffee, Federated Department Stores, Marubeni, and Statoil, the state-owned oil company of Norway.

An arrangement such as this may save companies millions of dollars. It can totally eliminate the use of paper and the expensive handling of paper documents. United Nations statistics show that seven percent of the cost of international trade, which amounts to about $420 billion per year, is caused by inefficiencies in trade administration. Using EDI over the Internet can reduce much of this amount.

Executives at the Japanese Sanwa Bank, a member of the Bolero.net group, estimate that the bank can cut its administrative costs by 30 percent simply by sending documents electronically through the Internet rather than by mail or fax. Statoil tested Bolero.net between its Statfjord terminal in the Norwegian North Sea and oil traders in the country's Flotta crude market. The instant transmission of key documents saved the company more than $200,000. Thanks to the speedy transmission of documents, shipments arrived faster at their destinations. This saved the company an additional sum of $80,000, which would otherwise have been paid in interest for the longer period between drilling and receiving payments from customers.

Bolero.net's executives cite inefficiencies that result from the fact that business partners often use a multitude of proprietary EDI software. Apparently, the applications do not always "talk to each other" properly, which may cause technical problems and loss of time. A single hub such as Bolero.net—and the fact that all partners use the same software and Web browsers—eliminates such mishaps.

SUMMARY

- Electronic data interchange (EDI) is the exchange of paperless documents that takes places between two organizations. The organizations are referred to as trading partners. Typical documents include purchase orders, shipping lists, invoices, and remittance advices. For many years, owners and providers of value-added networks (VANs) have provided EDI services.

- EDI reduces business cycles, reduces the need to send and store paper documents, minimizes the need to re-key data into information systems, and saves much of the cost of manual labor. For these reasons, the number of companies that have adopted EDI has grown fast since 1987, when only some 1,000 companies used it. Yet, the great majority of businesses still do not use EDI. The main reason is the high cost of implementation. This may change as extranets continue to be an economically feasible solution for small and midsize companies.

- Extranet EDI offers several benefits: the availability of a global network, the Internet; free software in the form of browsers that already incorporate XML, the software that supports Web-based EDI; existing universal equipment in the form of personal computers, with no need for special hardware; low training cost; a single standard, the Web standard, rather than at least three incompatible standards that require special software for conversion; and communication lines that generally support greater speeds than VANs. However, extranet EDI also has some shortcomings: security, lack of control over communication speed, and the fact that current XML standards are incomplete.

- VAN firms lease to their clients the use of networks and maintain the appropriate hardware and software to guarantee several important elements of EDI: transaction integrity, a high degree of privacy, and a way to ensure nonrepudiation. Privacy cannot be as strong on a public network such as the Internet as on a private network. Nonrepudiation is a major challenge over the Internet, because there is no trusted third party to ensure it, unless the parties use a commercial hub, or exchange, such as Bolero.com. Yet it is expected that a growing number of companies will start using EDI via the Internet because the benefits outweigh the costs.

KEY TERMS

EDI	firewall
trading partners	extranet
VAN	transaction integrity
transaction set	privacy
EFT	nonrepudiation
intranet	

REVIEW QUESTIONS

1. What is EDI?
2. What are VANs, and what are their functions in EDI?
3. EDI reduces the need to reenter data into information systems. How?
4. Why is Web-based EDI less expensive than VAN EDI?
5. In relative terms, large companies have adopted EDI in greater numbers than small companies. Why?
6. What are the three important elements provided by VANs for EDI? What are the challenges of Web-based EDI in regard to these elements?

DISCUSSION QUESTIONS

1. EDI is supposed to promote uniform communication with business partners. Does EDI do that? Explain.
2. It is said that XML standards will eventually enable any two trading partners to exchange commercial information directly. Do you have any reservations about whether this will actually occur? Explain.
3. Do you think Web-based EDI will encourage fraud? Explain.

ASSIGNMENTS

1. Use the Web as your resource for researching the state of XML. Prepare a two-page report explaining the challenges that XML standardization is facing. Open your report with a listing of the organizations involved in XML standardization and why each is involved in the talks.

2. Obtain the source code of a Web page that contains XML tags. Highlight the first five XML tags. Type up a page that lists the tags and explains the data information that is communicated by each tag.

E-COMMERCE TODAY

Will the Tortoise Beat the Hare?

Like so many other small companies, U.S. Lambswool has never been on the leading edge of technology. The five-employee company, operating out of Freeport, New York, makes mops and supplies them to the largest hardware retailers in America, including Ace Hardware, Do It Best Corporation, and TruServ.

Until 1998, the company conducted business with those large retailers through an awkward maze of electronic, fax, and paper communications. For example, a Chicago-based commissioned-sales representative could receive purchase orders from the hardware chains in EDI form over a VAN run by Sterling Commerce. The salesman's primary role: translate the EDI data into human-readable form and then fax it to U.S. Lambswool.

EDI was supposed to be the common language of electronic business, but the reality for many small companies has been different from that vision. Most large buyers—the GMs, Costcos, and Intels of the world—have long been able to place, track, and settle orders with their largest suppliers using software built around EDI. But small suppliers such as U.S. Lambswool could not afford the thousands or tens of thousands of dollars that need be spend on set-up, licensing, and ongoing service fees traditionally charged by dominant EDI/VAN vendors.

The difficulties small companies have in adopting EDI make the use of XML over the Internet so attractive. However, the complexity—or perceived complexity—of XML causes many small businesses to hesitate. This is where companies like that of Andrew Duncan come into the picture.

Duncan is the president and chief executive officer of the EC Company. Based in Palo Alto, California, the company provides a service capable of translating any digital transaction data format—EDI, XML, or any other of myriad transactional data standards—into any other format. By acting as a link between the information systems of any two companies, the EC Company is something like the Rosetta stone of business-to-business transactions.

Duncan's company sells its service to more than 1,000 suppliers and 100 Fortune-500 buyers, all conducting business on EC Exchange.net. So far, the 65-employee firm has handled an average of no more than 32,000 transactions per month. It is questionable whether the firm will be able to grow its market share significantly, because leading EDI companies such as IBM Global Services, Sterling Commerce, GE Global Exchange Services, Atlanta's Harbinger, eB2B Commerce, and SPS Commerce have plans to accommodate small and midsize companies in their ventures. The latter two companies intend to offer translation services that directly compete with those of the EC Company's; they are targeting the small and midsize businesses that hope to link electronically to their big buyers.

One observer equated such ISP services to households: Households wanted a simple solution to their Internet hook-up challenge. They wanted to be connected without hassle. Their needs have been satisfied by the likes of AOL. Now, small businesses are looking for the AOL of EDI.

Duncan founded the EC Company in 1996, after spending four years running an IT consulting group. One regular lament Duncan heard was the large-business managers' frustration with being unable to include small suppliers in their emerging transaction networks. He realized there was a great opportunity to create value by building a network that would help all suppliers in the same network. The EC Company is based on the premise that a third-party manager of these electronic trading relationships could create scalability (discussed in Chapter 5) that had previously been missing in traditional EDI/VAN packages.

What is the firm's business model? The EC Company gives the big buyers free accounts, and then uses those relationships to persuade smaller suppliers to join the network. These smaller companies would be assessed a per-transaction fee for less than what they were likely paying to manage paper-based transactions. Buyers and sellers can upload transactional data to the network in any format they choose, as long as each company consistently uses only that format. The EC Company translates the data according to the needs of the recipient, then forwards it to its destination. One reporter called the scheme "EDI for dummies."

In the beginning, the company did not do well. For several months its only large buyer was Ace Hardware, the large hardware store chain. The EC Company was running out of money. However, with Ace Hardware signed on, Duncan began going through the list of Ace suppliers, armed with a letter from the hardware chain admonishing those suppliers to sign up for the service or risk losing Ace as a client. The strategy worked. While the move sounded like a threat, Duncan used his wit, rather than his muscles, to convince Ace suppliers that his company could help them. Some of these small firms had wanted to join the EDI bandwagon for a long time anyway; they welcomed Duncan's proposals. One of these firms was Power Poxy Adhesives, a 50-employee company in Waukesha, Wisconsin. Another was U.S. Lambswool. Lambswool is now using the service with all of its buyers, not only with Ace.

The EC Company's list of large customers includes Walgreen's, General Mills, and Sears. In addition, the firm entered strategic alliances with American Express, Ariba, CMGI@Ventures, webMethods, and VerticalNet. Ariba and webMethods sell Internet-based trading software. The companies see the EC Company's service as complementing their own. For example, webMethod's customers have 160 clients worldwide. Some of the customers want to extend their clientele by going beyond Web browser integration. The EC Company helps them trade electronically. American Express invested money in the firm, but its presence also brings an association with a globally recognized financial-service brand, along with thousands of corporate clients that can be tapped by the EC Company.

The company is facing fierce competition. In 1997, GE Information Services (now GE Global Exchange Services) launched TradeWeb, an online service where companies large and small could do business using EDI in a per-transaction fee arrangement. IBM Global Services and Harbinger, both leading EDI/VAN service providers, have built pay-per-transaction services to run alongside their traditional EDI VANs. Two other companies, SPS Commerce of St. Paul, Minnesota, and eB2B Commerce of New York, offer Web-based electronic transaction services.

Duncan is well aware of the competition, and he is braced to deal with it. He claims that his company is now well funded and gets more business than it can handle.

Source: Nickell, J.A., "The paper chaser," *Business 2.0,* June 13, 2000 Copyright © 2000. Reprinted by permission.

Thinking About E-Commerce Today

1. Can the service that the EC Company offers be equated to that of professional interpreters? Explain.
2. Do you agree that the service the firm offers is "EDI for dummies"? Why? Is sophistication the only allure, or does the service offer other benefits.
3. Strategically, does the EC Company have an advantage over its competitors who have been in the VAN-based EDI industry a long time? Explain.

BUSINESS-TO-BUSINESS:
A VARIETY OF MODELS

LEARNING OBJECTIVES

WHEN YOU FINISH
THIS CHAPTER YOU
WILL BE ABLE TO:

- Explain the contributions of online markets to individual firms and to the economy
- Describe e-commerce business models and give examples of how revenue can be generated on the Internet
- Explain how application service providers facilitate e-commerce for small and midsize businesses
- Explain the principles of auction and matchmaking online business
- Discuss business alliances and cite real-world examples across several industries
- Evaluate the benefits of government-related Web sites to citizens and governments

Brian Stengl is a restaurateur whose story was brought up in the May 21, 2000, issue of the *Philadelphia Inquirer*. The only way he could find Ecuadoran shrimp for his seafood restaurant chain in Tampa, Florida, was to make an endless number of phone calls, send faxes, and wait for shipments. Sometimes the shipments came, and sometimes they did not. He decided to join Gofish.com. Gofish.com is an online marketplace where sellers and buyers meet electronically. It functions as an open marketplace where a seller can see what every other seller charges. Even while shrimp are still on the boat, fishermen can log on by satellite and post an offer of so many pounds of shrimp. At a moment's notice, fishermen can post a product for sale, make it temporarily inactive, or take it off the market entirely. Actual transaction prices are available to subscribers, so they better know how to negotiate the best prices. A special feature lets sellers and buyers receive messages about the status of their offers even if they have left the Web site. As part of the general information posted at the site, Gofish provides the exchange rates of countries that are the most involved in fishing, such as Japan and Norway.

THREE CONTRIBUTIONS OF ONLINE MARKETS

According to a study by the Boston Consulting Group, business-to-business e-commerce will explode in the next several years. If the market maintains its expected growth rate of 33 percent per year, the Internet will account for one fourth of all business-to-business (B2B) purchases by 2003, a total value of $2.8 trillion.

In his article arguing why online B2B will grow more than analysts predict ("The Sky Is . . . Rising," *Forbes ASAP,* February 21, 2000 Vol. 165, no. 4, p. 149), Kevin Jones lists three ways businesses save money and create new revenue: inventory squeezers, value creators, and product creators.

Inventory squeezers save buyers money by enabling them to quickly find information on price, availability, and guaranteed arrival dates of items the buyer needs to make products. For example, e-Steel.com lets steel makers reduce the extra inventory they keep to ensure that delivery delays do not prevent them from meeting customer demand. The site links 1,441 companies from 65 countries.

Value creators are companies that would never have existed without the Internet and whose value for customers could be created only with such a large network. For example, Alibris.com, a Web hub for used books, helps buyers and sellers find each other by availing the inventories of used-book dealers to online book vendors such as Amazon.com and Barnesandnoble.com. Alibris helps sell books that might otherwise never be sold. Value creators provide intermediary service.

Product creators are Internet markets that provide services that eventually enable the creation of physical products that would otherwise not have been developed. For example, the Patent and License Exchange (*www.pl-x.com*) helps universities, businesses, and research groups exchange intellectual property so that an idea that one organization might never turn into a product can be manufactured and marketed by another.

Another way to look at B2B online markets is by the target buyer. In this simple framework there are two types of market Web sites: horizontal and vertical. In a **horizontal market**, many companies within an industry market to companies from different industries. The term *horizontal* is used because all these companies operate in the same market, as if it were one plane. For example, a business exchange can attract companies from a variety of industries to purchase their office supplies online. Sellers of office supplies offer their products at that site to all business customers (see Figure 7.1, page 122).

In a **vertical market**, trade takes place among companies that operate in the same industry. The term *vertical* refers to the various phases in the supply chain. For example, a logging company can offer its logs to a lumber company that offers its products to a furniture factory that offers its products to a furniture store chain. All participants buy and sell products at various phases of their production and assembly (see Figure 7.2, page 122). Online vertical markets often consist of only two levels of the supply chain, such as automakers and parts manufacturers. This makes most online markets seem like horizontal markets but with all buyers in the same industry. Thus, it is likely that Figure 7.2 would include only lumber companies and furniture makers, rather than all four types of organizations as shown.

7.1 HORIZONTAL MARKET

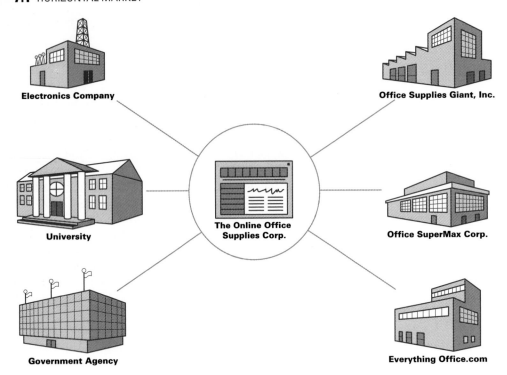

Electronics Company

Office Supplies Giant, Inc.

University

The Online Office Supplies Corp.

Office SuperMax Corp.

Government Agency

Everything Office.com

7.2 VERTICAL MARKET

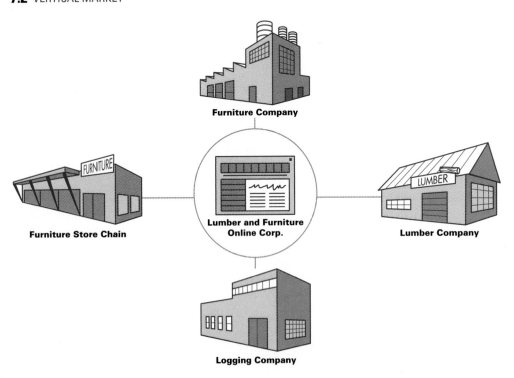

Furniture Company

Furniture Store Chain

Lumber and Furniture Online Corp.

Lumber Company

Logging Company

In our discussion, we will focus less on the horizontal or vertical nature of trading and more on the various techniques and activities that generally take place in online markets. In each type of electronic market, firms must find a way to sustain themselves financially. They must define what value they are creating for others and who would be likely to pay for the service they provide. In other words, they must create a **business model** for themselves.

BUSINESS-TO-BUSINESS MARKETPLACES

Electronic marketplaces are the Internet's greatest contribution to the economy. An **electronic marketplace** is an environment where businesses (and individuals, for that matter) can trade through communications technology. Unlike a physical marketplace, trading is done in cyberspace, with no need for the parties to convene. Without need for a physical location or travel, thousands of organizations can sell and buy within seconds, with full disclosure of transactions. The availability of information to all market participants, a condition that has always been a key principle of competitive markets, has finally been accomplished through the Internet. This brings us significantly closer to what economists call a **perfect market**: No single entity, seller or buyer, can affect prices. Prices are truly determined by the combined forces of all participants.

Near-perfect markets have been established in industries that until recently were quite limited in their use of information technology for transactions, such as the construction industry. For example, BuildNet, Inc., created a vertical market system for the residential construction industry. People who would like to build a new house, for example, can obtain materials and labor after competition by multiple bidders. The competition significantly brings down the total cost to the buyer. BuildNet sells software and services that help link the information systems of general contractors, subcontractors, suppliers, and manufacturers. The company's services also go beyond trading; they include project management as well, which involves all the players in the project.

BuildNet intends to link the enterprise applications (often called *ERP systems*) of manufacturers, suppliers, subcontractors, and builders to its Web-based central system for project management. When a house is to be built, the BuildNet system generates a schedule for every activity in the project, from delivery of supplies to the final touches. If there is a delay in one assignment, the software automatically adjusts the schedules of all the remaining dependent tasks. Studies show that four to eight percent of the cost of a product in the construction industry results from redundancies in information processing. BuildNet's system was developed to reduce these costs.

The use of BuildNet services may save up to 35 percent of total construction costs, some of which can be passed to the consumer. The rest goes to builders. Since profit margins in this industry range from one to three percent, such cost savings are extremely important.

Not all B2B electronic marketplaces follow the same pattern. Some serve as auction sites, some serve only as matchmaking sites, and some, such as BuildNet, link buyers, sellers, and service providers. Some electronic marketplaces offer a specific service to all businesses, such as application service providers, and some are instruments for creating alliances of several competing organizations that collaborate on specific activities, such as the acquisition of goods and services. We will elaborate on all these business models soon.

While the Internet fosters near-perfect markets, in some circumstances the Internet can be used by one party to exert more, not less, bargaining power. This happens when a handful of powerful organizations band together to establish a single Web site through which they purchase from many suppliers or sell to many buyers. In a later section, we will give several examples of such sites.

WHAT IS A BUSINESS MODEL?

Understanding what technology enables us to do is key to our understanding of the infrastructure of e-commerce. It is equally important to understand how different business models work, both on and off the Web. In fact, in recent years the Web has brought greater ingenuity to business more by spurring the creation of innovative business models than by introducing a new technology. A business model is the principal manner in which a business operates. In for-profit organizations, a business model is the way the organization generates revenue.

For example, one of the most pervasive business models on the Web is to provide free information that attracts traffic, then generate income by selling advertisements. This model for generating advertising income is the same one used by noncable television networks to generate theirs. Another business model is to directly sell content. On the Web, *content* means information: news, entertainment, sports statistics, and the like. To generate income, such a site sells subscriptions. Subscribers, who are often referred to as members, pay monthly fees for the content and gain access via passwords. (Log on to the sites of some of the major consulting firms, such as the Gartner Group and Jupiter Research, and you'll find that while some of the research findings can be accessed free of charge, most require passwords.) Practically all fee-paying clients are businesses. In another e-commerce business model, auction sites generate income from the fees that they charge sellers whenever a transaction is executed via the site.

The Web has created opportunities for business models that could not exist in other environments. For example, no sane executive would sell merchandise below cost to attract large numbers of customers, but on the Web, Buy.com and its competitors do sell below cost. What's the business model? Buy.com expects to generate its profits by enticing companies to advertise at its site, which is frequented by millions of customers. The crux of it is this: Entice heavy traffic by selling merchandise below cost and generate profits through advertisements. In reality, such companies are not so much in the retail business as they are in the advertising business. All hope that in time, when they have created a loyal clientele, they will be able to make profits on the merchandise that they sell, too. The approach is risky.

No business model, whatever the technology behind it, can be successful if it does not, in the end, generate income. Thus, the owners of a new venture on the Web must clearly plan how their site can bring in money. If they sell content, the content must be attractive enough for people to pay for it. (By and large, people do not like to pay for content.) If they intend to attract advertisements, companies must constantly provide interesting or useful information to maintain a high volume of traffic. If they provide an auction site, they must plan how they will execute transactions and charge fees. Taking an approach of "If we build it, they will come" is not good enough, because they may not come. It must be clear who, eventually, pays the site owners: consumers, businesses doing business through the site, advertisers, or another group.

Regardless of business model, B2B commerce has generated the greater portion of online commerce: In dollar terms, about 80 percent of what we call

Industry	Estimated Online Sales in 1999 (billions)	Projected Online Sales in 2003 (billions)	Increase (%)
Pharmaceutical and medical	$1.4	$44.1	3,050
Motor vehicles	9.3	212.9	2,189
Paper and office products	2.9	65.2	2,148
Shipping and warehouse	2.9	61.6	2,024
Consumer goods	2.9	51.9	1,690
Construction	1.6	28.6	1,688
Food and agriculture	3.0	53.6	1,687
Petrochemicals	10.3	178.3	1,631
Heavy industries	1.3	15.8	1,115
Industrial equipment	1.3	15.8	1,115
Utilities	15.4	169.5	1,001
Computing and electronics	50.4	395.3	684
Aerospace	6.6	38.2	479

Source: Forrester Research, 2000

e-commerce is trade between two businesses and about 20 percent is between businesses and consumers. The projected volume of B2B commerce for the next decade varies among observers, but all agree that it will increase manyfold. The Gartner Group, based in Hartford, Connecticut, estimates that B2B volume will reach $7.3 trillion by 2004. Forrester Research, another research firm, estimated the dollar volumes of B2B sales in 1999 and made forecasts for 2003. The firm's estimates are shown in Figure 7.3. A short list of B2B Web sites is given in Figure 7.4 (page 126). In addition to these sites, which specialize in products of particular industries, there are exchanges that bring together buyers and sellers from a wide range of industries. They include Ventro in Europe and Vertical.net in the United States.

Some investment groups specialize in establishing and supporting B2B initiatives. Internet Capital Group, Inc. owns many such firms, wholly or partially. The company's CEO did not set the goals of its group in terms of profit but rather in terms of how much business his organization processes. The company wants a significant portion of the U.S. gross domestic product (GDP) to pass through its sites, he said in 1999. This may not sound modest, but it reflects the shifting of much of global economic activity to the Web.

AUCTION AND MATCHMAKING BUSINESSES

Numerous Web sites serve as virtual meeting places for auctions. Corporate sellers can reach many more buyers than they could in physical space, and corporate buyers have access to many more sellers than they do through trade journals. These **auction sites** create highly competitive environments in which buyers can obtain the lowest prices for given products and quantities. Some of the earliest auction sites were in the chemical and metal industries. MetalSite started as an Internet exchange for scrap steel, with only three steel mills as sellers. Thanks to its success, management augmented the exchange to include nonsteel and nonscrap metals. Membership had grown to several thousand within two years. The site ran out of cash and stopped operating in June 2001.

Site Name	Activity
Altra	Natural gas
CarStation	Auto-body shops
ChemConnect	Chemical industry
Collabria	Commercial printing
Digital Think	Corporate training
E-Steel	Steel industry
Extensity	Back-office automation
Fair Market	Custom corporate purchasing
Iprint	Commercial printing
Medibuy	Medical supplies
National Transportation Exchange	Transportation
Neoforma	Medical supplies
Noosh	Commercial printing
Portera	Knowledge workers
TradeOut	Surplus inventory
Universal Access	Broadband networks
Web Methods	Business integration software
WorldRes	Travel industry

In the chemicals industry, sites run by ChemMatch in Houston, Texas; ChemConnect in San Francisco, California; and e-Chemicals in Ann Arbor, Michigan, match buyers with sellers in a real-time auction environment. They help buyers streamline their procurement process. Salespeople and procurement officers in the industry had been accustomed to complex deal making and tight, long-term contracts. Web-based auction sites replaced complex negotiations with open bidding and shortened the length of contracts. Since buyers have many more choices in this auction process, they do not have to obligate themselves to long-term contracts.

Several sites specialize in selling what outside of the Web environment has been extremely difficult to sell: surplus goods. For instance, ZoneTrader.com specializes in selling surplus capital equipment, such as computers. Ford Motor Company selected this site as a preferred auctioneer of its surplus assets. When Ford wants to sell surplus items, it auctions them off through ZoneTrader.com.

I N T E R E S T I N G . . .

WEBRICULTURE

The 1.9 million farmers in the United States feed not only their own country but also other nations throughout the world in need of grains and other agricultural products. Foreign purchases of seeds, fertilizers, and other products in the U.S. market total $285 billion per year. Farmers have adopted the Internet faster than other industries, using the Web to check weather conditions, read about their industry, and check commodity prices. Many farmers buy commodities and even livestock vaccinations online. In fact, one site, Farmbid.com, receives seven million visits daily.

While some B2B sites exist for pure auction deals, others do not provide auction services per se but rather are **matchmaking sites.** They match parties who wish to buy with parties who wish to sell, letting them decide on final quantities and prices.

Some sites are limited to a single industry; others are not. One is VerticalNet.com, which is home to hundreds of auction and matchmaking sites serving a wide variety of industries. Categories include communications, utilities, financial services, food, hospitality, health care, human resources, and many others. Some categories include several exchanges. VerticalNet is one of the largest commercial matchmakers in the world's online B2B sector.

Several sites cater especially to small businesses. Figure 7.5 is a short list of matchmaking sites that operate in this environment. The sites mainly serve small businesses of 100 to 500 employees. There are about 30 million such small businesses in the United States (on and off the Web), and they account for approximately half of the country's gross domestic product.

REVENUE MODELS AT B2B SITES

How do auction and matchmaking sites make money? Usually, the business model is simple: A cut of an agreed-upon percentage is charged for each transaction. The B2B site's software automatically calculates the dollar amount and charges it to the seller, the buyer, or both. Some sites also charge a monthly membership fee. The fee is almost always charged to sellers, and in some cases to buyers as well.

The major challenge of a B2B site is to quickly reach a critical mass of sellers and buyers. Although no one has ever specified what that critical mass is, each B2B firm can calculate a break-even point for itself. Once potential sellers feel that "everyone is using that site," they are likely to join. The same principle applies to buyers. Early joiners usually pay no membership fees, or very low ones, because the site's value to sellers and buyers grows as more companies become members or regular participants.

The fact that auction and matchmaking sites need a large number of participants to succeed has caused many experts to argue that in a few years there will be only a few such sites; small sites simply will not survive, either going out of business or merging with the big sites.

FIGURE
7.5 ONLINE MATCHMAKERS FOR SMALL BUSINESSES

All-Purpose	Helping Buyers	Helping Sellers
AllBusiness.com	Webango.com	SmartAge.com
At YourBusiness.com	Works.com	
Bcentral.com		
Business.com		
BuyerZone.com		
Onvia.com		
ZoneTrader.com		

Until just several years ago, an organization that needed to use software had to purchase it and install it on employees' computers. Today, one solution to this problem is gaining popularity fast: Using the service of an application service provider (ASP). Instead of purchasing or renting software applications, the client firm pays a monthly fee that authorizes its employees to access the applications remotely via telecommunications lines. The applications are stored on the ASP's hardware at its site and can be accessed with a Web browser. The client's employees use the applications and create documents that they can save either at the ASP's site or on their own hardware, depending on the contract terms. The ASP usually charges the client for each user for each month of availability. For example, eAlity, Inc. (www.eality.com) charges $7 per application per user per month, and Corio, Inc. charges from $5 to $795 per user per month, depending on the application.

CLIENT BENEFITS

Purchasing services from an ASP is similar to leasing a car rather than buying it: You can use the car as if it were yours, but you do not have to have much cash up front, and you are not burdened with maintaining the car. If you want, you can stop using the car and paying for its usage after the lease is up. ASPs offer businesses, especially small and midsize businesses, several benefits:

1. The client does not have to commit a large sum of cash to purchase applications for its employees. The client has the flexibility to drop certain applications and "lease" new ones with relatively short periods of commitment (usually several months).
2. The client does not have to pay for upgrades; as soon as an upgrade of an application is available, the ASP installs it for use by clients.
3. The client does not have to maintain a costly technical team to install, upgrade, and maintain applications. This is the responsibility of the ASP. There is also less need for help-desk professionals, because help-desk services are the ASP's responsibility.
4. The client can save on hardware costs, because all applications, and possibly documents, are saved on the ASP's hard disks.
5. The client has a fixed cost for the use of software applications over a period of one to several years. This helps in the budgeting and cash allocation process.
6. The client can save deployment time. Since the software is already installed, there is no need to spend time and money on installation. This helps the client to respond to its own customers in a timely manner.

It is no wonder, then, that the ASP market is growing so fast. From nonexistence in 1998, this market grew to $889 million in 1999. The Gartner Group predicts the market for ASP services will grow to more than $22.7 billion by 2003.

ASP clients usually fall into one of four categories:

1. Small companies that do not have the cash to pay upfront but must use office, telecommunications, and operations applications.

2. Companies that are growing fast and rely on software for the deployment of their operations.
3. Midsize companies that need expensive software, such as enterprise applications for their operations, but cannot afford the immediate payment of large sums (examples are enterprise resource planning [ERP] applications from companies such as SAP and PeopleSoft).
4. Organizational units at geographic sites where it is difficult to obtain desired software or personnel to install and maintain the software. These sites are located far away from a regional headquarters, typically in a less developed country. The office at that site can use applications from a more developed country.

To gauge the potential financial benefits of using an ASP, one can look at the cost of purchasing and installing an ERP package. Depending on how many modules of the package an organization purchases, the cost is usually several million dollars. The labor cost of installing the software usually exceeds one million dollars. When using an ASP, however, the organization pays only several thousand dollars for an ERP application use. Management saves not only the cost of installation, it avoids the hassle of searching for certified software professionals to perform the installation, which may take a relatively long time.

Note that while some software vendors offer their own software through an ASP service, many ASPs are not in the software development business. Furthermore, some vendors have ASP divisions that offer competitors' applications in their application portfolio. ASPs sign contracts with the owners of the intellectual rights of the applications to allow them to offer the service to third parties (that is, the end clients).

Some observers are sure that two things will eventually happen: (1) all software vendors will use the Internet as one of several channels to generate revenue, and thus all will become ASPs; and (2) virtually all businesses will, at least to some extent, become consumers of ASP services.

There are some needs that ASPs currently do *not* satisfy. For example, their services do not support mobile employees, such as traveling salespeople and insurance claim agents. To access the applications, employees must be able to connect to the ASP's site from a specific location.

CAVEAT EMPTOR

The rush to employ the services of ASPs is reminiscent of the rush to outsource services in the early 1990s. Many companies soon discovered that outsourcing was not the optimal way to fulfill their needs. The same awakening has started to occur in many companies that hired the services of ASPs. *Caveat emptor,* or "let the buyer beware," applies here as it does in so many instances.

Michael Solter is the solution manager for continuity services for e-business in IBM's Business Continuity and Recovery Services Unit. He suggests that customers ask potential ASPs the following questions to prevent problems after the service contract is signed.

1. *Who will be responsible for keeping track of, and maintaining an inventory of, the technical environment in which my applications are supported?* The customer wants to be assured that qualified personnel are working to ensure that applications are always available and updated with new versions and add-ons.

2. *How will my database be backed up on an ongoing basis?* Transactional and archival databases must be backed up. If a database fails, there must be a way to update it from a backup copy.
3. *What is your company's ability to scale up capacity, network access, and processing capability should my site get a surge in visitors?* Scalability is extremely important, especially for new businesses that cannot accurately estimate their future growth. The ASP must be able to provide more network access without communication delays and more hardware for storage of databases and documents.
4. *How quickly can you scale to accommodate surges in business volume, and how do you charge for this?* Customers want to be able to estimate cost for scaling up ASP services to better plan their finances.
5. *Assuming that critical data are being backed up, where are the backups stored and on what medium? How safe and accessible are these backups?* Protection against natural disasters is important. The measures taken to reduce the effect of such events should be disclosed to the customer.

BUSINESS-TO-BUSINESS ALLIANCES

The leaders of numerous industries have realized the potential of the Internet and collaborated to establish marketplaces. A Web-based marketplace can take any of the forms we discussed in this chapter. However, when industry leaders band together to establish a site, they have one of two goals: (1) to save money and time on purchasing, or (2) to save money and time on sales. Each site is the result of a **business alliance** among several companies for a specific purpose: selling or buying. Here are some examples of such alliances.

B2B IN THE GROCERY INDUSTRY

In the summer of 2000, the Grocery Manufacturers of America (GMA) announced plans to create an online marketplace for its members. GMA members employ 2.5 million people in all 50 states of America and generate U.S. sales of $460 billion

INTERESTING . . .

THE BIG LOSER IN ONLINE B2B

As more and more business-to-business activity has moved to the Internet, state and local governments in the United States have become concerned about lost tax revenue. As long as new laws for collecting online sales tax are not enacted, governments do lose revenue. The majority of states in America charge sales tax. According to professors William Fox and Donald Bruce of the Center for Business and Economic Research at the University of Tennessee, because of online B2B sales, these states lost $106.6 billion and $244.9 billion in 1999 and 2000, respectively, and were expected to lose $486.6 billion, $821.8 billion, and $1,297.8 billion in 2002, 2003, and 2004, respectively.

annually. Executives for the new ventures in e-commerce come from some of the largest grocery manufacturers, including Kraft Foods; Procter & Gamble; General Mills, Inc.; Nestle USA; Bestfoods; and Unilever.

The GMA says that initially the marketplace will bring in multiple buyers and sellers to support catalog purchasing, bidding and price quotes, and online sourcing and auctions of raw materials, packaging supplies, and other goods and services essential for their operations. The joint Web site may also provide services such as capacity planning, demand forecasting, production planning, financial services, payment facilities, and logistics planning.

One major purpose of the initiative is to negotiate reduced prices on joint bids, in which several companies that are in need of the same item consolidate their demand. Suppliers see the large quantity posted in the bid and are willing to sell this quantity for a unit price lower than they would for the same total quantity bid separately in smaller batches. This way, competitors collaborate to reduce their purchasing costs.

RETAIL ALLIANCES

Retailers can save costs by concentrating their purchasing at a single online procurement center. Eleven leading global retailers, including Kmart, Target, and Safeway, announced the formation of the WorldWide Retail Exchange, a collaborative venture. They were soon joined by Albertson's, CVS, and the Gap in the United States; Tesco, Marks & Spencer, and Kingfisher in the United Kingdom; Auchan and Casino in France; and Royal Ahold in the Netherlands. Together these companies operate 30,000 stores around the world, and their combined sales in 1999 was more than $300 billion. The exchange launched by this alliance links some 100,000 suppliers, partners, and distributors, all of whom provide products and services to the retailers.

THE AUTOMAKERS' ALLIANCE

In February 2000, the three largest U.S. automakers joined forces to establish a central online procurement center to pressure suppliers into more competitive prices. The new venture is called Covisint and is described by the automakers as a purchasing hub. General Motors, Ford Motor, and DaimlerChrysler together purchase more than $250 billion worth of auto parts and services annually.

The purpose of the site is to cut costs, improve communication, and streamline purchasing decisions. The companies convinced the French automaker Renault and the Japanese automaker Nissan Motor Company to join Covisint. Volkswagen AG, Europe's largest automaker, declined membership. By the end of 2000, 40 suppliers had subscribed to Covisint. By the end of 2002, 7,000 were expected to trade through it with the automakers.

While the automakers expect to save billions in purchasing costs, suppliers fear that the cost savings will mean lower profits for them. They also find it difficult to leave behind a culture in which price negotiations are made face-to-face and with a high level of confidentiality to assure them that competitors do not receive information provided to the buyers.

This way of doing business is in sharp contrast to the concept of Covisint. The idea behind the alliance is the sharing of information—all bidders are aware of what each of them proposes, so that the practical effect is an open auction in which the lowest bidder wins. Having purchasing decisions so vigorously connected to price does worry some observers, who argue that practices encouraged by this site may drive down quality. These fears drove two giant auto-parts makers, Dana Corporation and Delphi Automotive Systems Corporation, to consider a supplier-managed online parts exchange. In such an exchange, the suppliers are at the center of business activity, and the automakers order parts through the suppliers' online site. However, the idea was later abandoned.

ALLIANCES IN THE COMPUTER INDUSTRY

Even fierce competitors in the computer industry have decided to collaborate in online purchasing. Compaq, Hewlett-Packard, Gateway, and many other firms established an alliance in May 2000 to set up a central Web exchange for computer components. Like the three automakers, they intend to have computer-parts makers compete with bids on lots of processors, disk drives, and other parts used in the assembly of PCs.

AIRLINE ALLIANCES

Two alliances of airline companies were consolidated in 2000: Star and Orbitz. Star (at *www.star-alliance.com*) is an international airline network whose main purpose is to concentrate purchases in the global airline industry.

Similar to the automakers' Web site, Star is an online exchange that lets all participating airlines purchase supplies through the Internet. The site is operated independently of any airline and offers participants a selection of goods and services typically used by airlines, from aircraft parts and ground equipment to general office supplies. In addition to lower prices, the exchange lowers the airlines' administrative costs.

American Airlines, Delta Airlines, Northwest Airlines, and Continental Airlines first collaborated to establish Orbitz. Within months, the alliance grew to include 30 of the world's largest airlines. The purpose of their site is to offer online discount airfares and ticketing. The site enables the airlines to control the entire travel process, which includes providing information, booking tickets, assigning seats, and recording frequent flier miles. In addition, the site also includes reservations for hotel rooms, car rentals, cruises, and vacation packages.

By developing their own Web site, airline companies can avoid paying the five- to ten-dollar commission fees that they usually pay to online travel brokers. Other fees that can be eliminated are those paid to online database companies that link travel agencies, airlines, and other travel companies. This end-to-end control is the reason travel agents claim that Orbitz undercuts their commissions, and even their livelihoods.

While the commissons may seem quite small, they add up. Consider the huge size of the online booking industry. According to Forrester Research, about $12.8 billion in business and leisure trips were booked online in 1999. The firm predicts that by 2004, the value of travel booked online will reach $64 billion.

HEALTH-CARE ALLIANCES

In March 2000, health-care giants Johnson & Johnson, GE Medical Systems, Baxter International, Abbott Laboratories, and Medtronic announced plans to create a privately held online exchange to streamline purchasing for manufacturers of health-care equipment and drugs. The exchange is supposed to streamline the purchasing, sale, and distribution of medical equipment and devices, health-care products, and related services worldwide. It will also provide access to extensive clinical information. When the site is complete, it will be accessible to all health-care manufacturers, suppliers, distributors, providers, group purchasing organizations, and other trading partners.

Unlike other online exchange sites, the firm that will run the health-care alliance site does not intend to charge service fees. Experts have opined that this alliance exchange may dramatically reduce the capital investment in information technology that health-care equipment and pharmaceutical suppliers must make for procurement and for obtaining vital information.

B2B IN THE HOSPITALITY INDUSTRY

Large hotel chains have used the Internet predominantly for room reservation, but they have been quite slow in using it for business with their business partners. However, in summer 2000 the Hilton hotel chain became a leader in B2B. Interestingly, Hilton has organized a B2B Web site that allows the firm to buy online from multiple sellers.

The hospitality procurement network handles almost all of the company's purchases of goods and services (totaling $1.5 billion annually) from thousands of suppliers. Two subsidiaries, Doubletree and Embassy Suites Hotels, also use the site to order goods and services. By inviting suppliers to bid, Hilton and its subsidiaries buy large quantities at once and therefore enjoy lower prices than before. The hotels have access to more than 21,000 suppliers.

EXCESS PRODUCTS AND EQUIPMENT

Manufacturers often cannot find buyers for their excess products. One estimate places the annual value of excess products worldwide at $350 billion. In the United States alone, companies overproduce and subsequently must unload $60 billion worth of products. Before the Internet was commercialized, manufacturers in North America could not find buyers outside North America. Similarly, Asian manufacturers were not able to sell excess quantities outside their own region. Manufacturers still sell most of their surplus goods the old-fashioned way: by phone, fax, mail, and e-mail. However, several industries are fast moving toward online exchanges. Several entrepreneurs have seen a matchmaking opportunity between manufacturers and buyers from different world regions.

One site that brings together manufacturers and buyers specifically for trading excess consumer products is Rebound International. Clients pay the company a four- to eight-percent fee on each deal, depending on the transaction size. Paying these fees costs less than assigning excess stocks to liquidators. The average Rebound transaction is $50,000.

A site with a similar purpose is ZoneTrader.com. However, ZoneTrader does not match sellers and buyers of excess quantities; instead, it serves large companies that want to sell surplus capital equipment, such as furniture and computer equipment. One such company is Ford Motor, which designated ZoneTrader as its outlet for the disposal of a wide variety of items the company does not need.

Several other companies have entered this lucrative market: TradeOut.com, Redtagbiz.com, RetailExchange.com, Liquidation.com, iSolve.com, and CloseOutNow.com all vie for billions of dollars of excess merchandise. AMR Research, a market research firm in Boston, Massachusetts, estimated that in 2000 the volume of online excess-product trade was $600 million. The firm's estimate for 2004 was $22.4 billion.

An estimate by the Gartner Group puts the number of Web-based marketplaces, or exchanges, at 600 for the year 2000 and a predicted 4,000 by 2004. However, it is unlikely that a single industry will have many exchanges. The whole premise of an exchange, especially if it serves the same industry, is to be a central place for an entire industry to do business. This is one reason why only a single or a few exchanges are expected to survive in each industry. To survive, an exchange must reach a critical mass—that is, a certain minimal number of subscribers whose fees can cover the site's operating costs. This is another reason why observers expect only a handful of exchanges to last in each industry: Only those that reach a critical mass relatively soon after inception will survive.

GOVERNMENT E-BUSINESS

In 1999, Pennsylvania became the first political unit anywhere in the world to include its URL address on automobile license plates. This might be only the most visual manifestation of a growing movement. An increasing number of national, state, and local governments continue to move some of their business to the Internet. While this is not exactly business-to-business activity—few people would consider government a business—it reflects a similar use of the Internet for communications and transactions.

Government can enjoy great degrees of efficiency by moving activities to the Internet. There are roughly three types of electronic activities in government:

1. Government-to-citizen transactions
2. Government-to-government transactions
3. Government-to-business transactions

In government-to-citizen transactions, government agencies, for example, let citizens file online applications for licenses and for renewing them. Citizens can find zoning information online and pay fees and fines via the Web. By allowing residents to apply for driver's licenses and renew vehicle registrations online, the state of Alaska not only made the lives of its citizens easier but also saved millions of dollars. In Georgia, two thirds of the state's physicians renew their licenses online, saving state employees many labor hours.

Several private companies serve as intermediaries between governments and citizens on the Web. GovWorks.com accepts electronic payment for parking tickets, utility bills, and real estate taxes for some 36,000 towns and cities. In this arrangement, a local government does not have to be linked to the Internet; GovWorks interacts directly with citizens via the Net and sends the local government a (paper) check if it is not wired. EZgov.com provides similar services. Figure 7.6 shows the homepage of this firm and some of the services it provides. The baby pictured on the site one day will "wonder why people once stood in line for government services," the site claims. You may wonder already.

Government-to-government transactions include intragovernment exchanges of information—that is, interaction between two agencies of the same government—and transactions between two governments, such as sharing employment information and cross-checking tax files.

Government-to-business transactions include mainly purchasing arrangements for goods and services by governments from private businesses. These sites

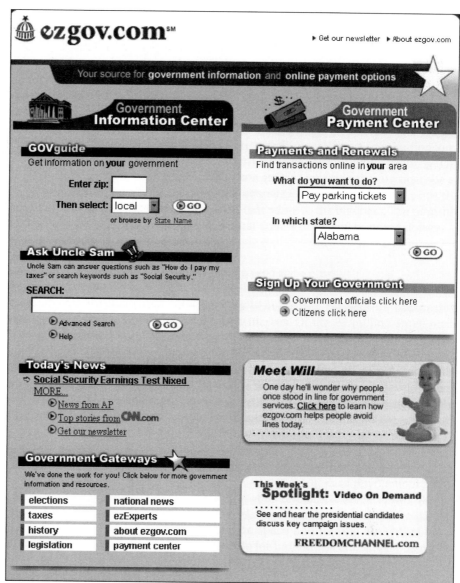

©1999 EZGov, Inc. All rights reserved.

I N T E R E S T I N G . . .

A LITTLE COUNTRY BIG ON E-GOV

Estonia, a small Baltic country with a population of 1.4 million people, has taken a great leap forward in e-government. Cabinet ministers read proposed laws, make comments and suggestions, and vote entirely online. Parliament sessions are broadcast online. Full-text transcripts are posted soon after meetings conclude. Ordinary citizens can access a wide range of information via the Internet. Estonia's government is almost totally paperless.

Source: Perera, R., "The little country that could," *The Industry Standard,* December 4, 2000

function similarly to corporate procurement sites, such as the one the big automakers established. Business firms whose expertise is the setup and operation of central procurement Web sites benefit the most. Some states have started establishing their own sites dedicated to the procurement of goods and services. Pennsylvania's government is using Web auctions to find the lowest prices for a variety of goods and services, from office furniture to telephone installation to coal.

The U.S government is the largest purchaser in the world, so it makes sense that at the federal level the business of helping the government purchase online is quite lucrative. It is estimated that the U.S. government spends at least $1 trillion per year on purchases. Several private firms have set up Web sites to help the government. One such firm, Digital Commerce of Reston, Virginia, maintains FedCenter, a site that matches government purchasing officers with the vendors of a great variety of goods and services: alcohol for military post exchanges, laboratory supplies for Department of Veteran Affairs hospitals, and many others. The site lets the purchasing officers compare prices while complying with federal acquisition regulations. The site's list of subscribed vendors is growing fast. In January 1999 it had 80 vendors; by March 2000 the number had reached 500. As with all sites that serve as electronic marketplaces, their operators generate revenue by charging a percentage of the value of each purchase made through the site.

In the first wave of federal sites, several U.S. government agencies established "local" sites. One agency, the General Services Agency (GSA), was charged with linking all the sites and services. In 2000, it established and began maintaining the portal site FirstGov. The agency merged 20,000 government sites and about 27 million Web pages. FirstGov is a single site that serves as an entry for all federal and some state government sites. It can be accessed by using either the URL *www.firstgov.com* or *www.firstgov.gov*. Figure 7.7 shows the homepage of the site.

FIGURE

7.7 FIRSTGOV, THE U.S. FEDERAL GOVERNMENT PORTAL

WELCOME to FirstGov

Featured Subjects

- Millennium
- Holiday Mailing Tips
- U.S. Government for Kids
- Internet Fraud
- Greetings to U.S. Military Abroad
- 2001 Consumer Action Handbook
- Online Transactions
- Federal Asset Sales
- Federal Business Opps.

- **Past Features**

U.S. Government

- Executive Branch
- Legislative Branch
- Judicial Branch

State & Local

Home | Privacy & Security | Help | FAQ | Site Map | First-Time User

Keyword Search

Search for: [   ] [Search]

Search Tips | Advanced Search

Interesting Topics

Agriculture and Food
Farms, Food, Nutrition

Arts and Culture
Museums, History, Grants

Business and Economy
Business Advisor, Statistics, Trade

Common Interests
Kids, Disabilities, Seniors, Veterans

Consumer Services and Safety
Recalls, Complaints, Safe Workplaces

Home and Community
Your Home, Mail, Emergencies

Learning and Jobs
Students, Jobs, Training

Library and Reference
Laws, Regs, Stats and Pubs

Money and Taxes
Your Money, Taxes, U.S. Budget

Public Service Opportunities
Government Jobs, Volunteering

Recreation and Travel
Parks, Passports, Air Traffic Advisory

Anyone needing help from any government agency can save time by logging on to "Your First Click to the U.S. Government."

In 2000, the Pennsylvania state government entered an agreement with Microsoft to augment the services the state provides through its Web site. Users were expected to swarm to the site because it would allow them to renew their driver's licenses, obtain hunting and boating permits, and more. Students at public schools would be able to download the latest homework assignments posted by their teachers.

In addition to these initiatives, the federal government took a big step in October 2000 when it started operating Pay.gov, a site managed by a government agency called Financial Management Service (FMS). FMS is the world's largest collection and disbursement system. It collects more than $2 trillion and disburses more than $1.2 trillion annually in Social Security, veterans' benefits, tax refunds, and other payments.

Federal agencies can link their own Web sites to www.pay.gov and collect monies from organizations and individuals who owe the government. Users can pay taxes, fees, licenses, and leases by credit card, electronic transfer, or a number of other electronic means. Initially, the site was designed to accept payments only by credit and debit cards, but it also plans to make use of digital cash, electronic checks, and machines similar to automatic teller machines. In the future, the site will save the U.S. government millions of dollars now spent on labor in the huge collection effort.

The government of Singapore (see Figure 7.8) operates one of the most advanced and helpful government portal sites. It is predominantly organized to help citizens. The site is set up so that users can click on the picture of a building and find information on specific matters such as education, military service, and employment. When a user clicks the building, she enters it virtually and can direct herself to the department whose services she needs. A citizen can select forms to fill out and launch, may interact with government officials, and can retrieve fur-

F I G U R E

7.8 THE SINGAPORE GOVERNMENT INTEGRATED SERVICES SITE

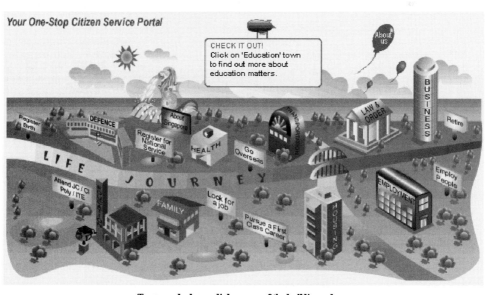

To proceed, please click on one of the buildings above.

E-GRIPES

In 2000, Senator Ron Wyden urged the U.S. government to create an Internet portal capable of recording and sorting citizen complaints about the government so that those comments could be automatically routed to the appropriate officials. The senator observed, "At present, a citizen with a significant complaint about a product, a service, or a government function may not know which agency or office to contact, and might therefore fail to lodge the complaint. . . . The Internet offers consumers a much better way to make sure their complaints get to the right officials." He suggested that an electronic complaint box be added to the U.S. government's portal FirstGov.com.

Source: McGuire, D., "Sen. Wyden calls for government complaint portal," *Newsbytes,* November 21, 2000

ther information. The site is organized by life experiences, not by government departments. The Singaporan government allocated $870 million dollars for the site, which the GSA called "the most developed example of integrated service delivery in the world." The site saves the government an estimated $23 million per year, predominantly in labor and paper. In 2000, 40 percent of Singaporan taxpayers filed their tax forms and paid their taxes via the site. Another soon-to-come site that accommodates businesses is expected to save the government $46 million per year.

SUMMARY

- Business-to-business (B2B) is commercial activity between businesses. Online B2B is growing fast in both vertical and horizontal markets. In a horizontal market, companies in one industry sell to companies in other industries. In a vertical market, trade takes place among companies operating in the same industry in a sequential supply chain.
- However we look at electronic commerce among companies, the greatest contribution of the Internet to the economy is the ability to create electronic marketplaces. These electronic marketplaces potentially can bring together an unlimited numbers of sellers and buyers, a situation that would never be feasible in a traditional manner.
- However a business operates on the Internet, it must generate revenue to survive. The scheme through which a business generates revenue is called a business model, and business models are as vital in e-commerce as they are anywhere else. Revenue can come from consumers, another business that pays for doing business through the site, advertisers who pay for posting banners at the site, or another party. So far, several business models have taken hold in e-commerce. In most of them, the site that serves as a marketplace receives a fee for each transaction executed through the site. In many cases, sellers and buyers also pay a periodic membership fee for the privilege of using the site.

- An auction site holds electronic auctions on goods and services. Sellers simply list their products and services, and buyers bid on them. A matchmaking site provides a virtual place for sellers to find buyers for their goods and services.

- In recent years, application service providers (ASPs) have provided a service that has been in demand. ASP companies sell organizations the permission to use application software online. The software is maintained on the ASP's hardware. The software is not necessarily one developed by the ASP. Client organizations find many benefits with this type of service: they do not have to pay large sums of money upfront, but pay for each period of use; they do not have to upgrade software, because it is upgraded by the ASP; they can save money on hardware because they need less of it for storing software; and they can save money and time because they do not have to recruit and pay professionals to install and maintain the software.

- Online commerce enables same-industry organizations to take advantage of their aggregate purchasing or selling power. Automakers, airlines, hotels, grocery chains, and other organizations have established shared sites where their suppliers can bid on purchase orders. To outbid competitors, suppliers reduce prices, and buyers enjoy reduced costs. Some suppliers band together to sell to bidding buyers. Commerce on the Internet also helps organizations find buyers outside their immediate global region. This is especially helpful to manufacturers that are left with large quantities of excess merchandise.

- Local, state, and federal governments have recently joined the e-commerce bandwagon after a relatively slow start. While many online services are rendered to individuals, governments also use online technologies to interact with other governments and especially to execute transactions with businesses. Using Web sites to solicit bids on government purchases is a process similar to solicitation by industry alliances. Governments can save costs and provide more timely services through their Web sites.

KEY TERMS

horizontal market	perfect market
vertical market	auction sites
business model	matchmaking sites
electronic marketplace	business alliance

REVIEW QUESTIONS

1. Online businesses can be categorized into three groups: inventory squeezers, value creators, and product creators. Explain each category.
2. What is a vertical market? Give an example not mentioned in the chapter.
3. What is a horizontal market? Give an example not mentioned in the chapter.
4. What is a hub on the Internet? Why should a hub attract businesses?
5. What is a perfect market? Why do economists say that the Internet can facilitate a near-perfect market?
6. Examine Figure 7.3. B2B activity in the motor vehicles sector is expected to grow more than in any other except the pharmaceutical and medical sectors. What developments in the motor vehicle sector have taken place to support this projection?

7. What is the business model of an ASP? What could be a company's reasons not to use the services of an ASP?
8. B2B alliances are usually formed for one of two purposes, or both. What are these purposes, and how can B2B alliances realize these purposes through the Internet?
9. What are the purposes of government Web sites?

DISCUSSION QUESTIONS

1. Examine Figure 7.3. Companies in the computing and electronics sector already conduct more business today through B2B sites than any other and are expected to continue to be the leader in 2003. What are the reasons for this?
2. In 2000, there were several hundred B2B Web sites. Some analysts argue that in just a few years there will be significantly fewer B2B sites. Why?
3. The governments of the United States and other countries have probed several B2B alliances for possibly violating fair trade practices. How can such alliances encourage or facilitate unfair trade practices?

ASSIGNMENTS

1. Brainstorm with another student from your class to generate a new B2B business model. Write a report explaining how the business model would generate income for you and your partner.

2. Browse the sites of at least three state governments. Prepare a list of the features offered: services to organizations and citizens, bidding for state purchases, and so on. Explain how each feature works and how it can save taxpayers money. Make a list of features that could be added: What activities have state governments not yet offered via the Internet that they could? What costs would they possibly save?

E-COMMERCE TODAY

Levi Strauss: A Blue Experience

Many companies have traditionally sold their products only to other businesses. The Web's growing role as a sales outlet has tempted some of them to *disintermediate*—that is, to cut out the so-called middleman and sell directly to the consumer. Such was the attempt of the world's most famous maker of blue jeans.

In 1873, a Bulgarian immigrant named Levi Strauss saw an opportunity to benefit from the California gold rush and began making rugged pants for gold miners. Strauss's invention, the blue jean, has been cited as the greatest contribution of the United States to international fashion.

By 1990, the Levi Strauss Company sold almost half of all jeans purchased in the world and was well regarded as a clothing brand by fashion-minded young consumers. However, since 1990 the company has seen its market share slip to 16.9 percent of total jeans sold in 1998. After a peak of $7.1 billion in sales in 1996, sales dropped to $6.9 billion in 1997 and then to $6 billion in 1998. Some analysts blamed missed opportunities in not meeting fashion fads head on—baggy pants, hip huggers, and so on. Studies indicated that the typical young consumer wanted more stylish jeans, such as those made by Tommy Hilfiger or Ralph Lauren. A marketing survey reported that in the population of U.S. teenage males, Levi's image as a "cool" brand had dramatically decreased from 21 percent in 1994 to 7 percent in 1998. Another bit of bad news was that discount stores such as Wal-Mart and Sears were also capturing some of the market share previously held by Levi.

An article in *Fortune* magazine blamed Levi Strauss's loss of market position on the management priorities of its CEO Robert Haas. The article stated that the extensive use of re-engineering in the 1990s had allowed the company to take its focus off its product. In this re-engineering project, Haas was focused on making Levi Strauss the model of a socially responsible company. But while doing so, "nobody was minding the store," and decision makers apparently did not notice that the company's traditional market of baby boomers was aging and that an entirely new generation of consumers had appeared. The resulting shift in consumer tastes led to closing 11 plants and a layoff of 7,400 employees in 1997.

Connecting with young people became a top priority for the 146-year-old company, as its "must have" jeans had lost much of their appeal. According to the company, it was a need to gain direct consumer feedback that led to its decision to try selling online. The information gained from online sales would be used to determine product and marketing efforts.

The first talk of a Web site began in 1994, an action that would later label Levi as a pioneer in e-commerce. The first site was community oriented and contained information related to esoteric, "hip" subjects. However, a consumer looking to buy jeans would be out of luck; one could not purchase anything online. Over the next three years, the site was modified but always remained designed to entertain, not to sell. Levi's executives stated that they just wanted to put something on the Web and learn more about Internet opportunities as they went along.

During these early Internet years, Levi reported receiving thousands of requests from customers asking for online buying capabilities. Heeding these requests, in spring 1997 Levi organized a task force to investigate online sales. The task force was named SOTI (Selling On The Internet). By January 1998, the task force convinced top management to proceed with online selling, selecting Canada as the first test site. Within 60 days, a virtual Levi store was available to Canadian users.

At this time, Levi's sales in retail stores provided nearly all of the company's $7 billion in annual sales. Therefore, to minimize complaints from its retailers, Levi told its Canadian retailers that the Web site was only an experiment that would help all parties sell more jeans. In addition, Levi represented the trial site as an excellent opportunity to gain information on customers, again benefiting both the manufacturer and the retailers.

One month after the Canadian site opened, Levi began work on a site to serve U.S. customers, dedicating 50 staff members to the project. The work on the site was kept confidential, and the sales force knew nothing about the project until approximately one month before the online date. In November 1998, the U.S. online retail store went live. According to the company, online sales from the first two weeks exceeded the sales volume of one of its flagship stores in San Francisco.

From the start of its online retail project, Levi forbade its retailers from selling Levi products online so that the company's Web site was the exclusive online retailer. This strategy drew criticism and was called overly stringent by many analysts. A vice president of Estee Lauder went so far as to label Levi Strauss as "stupid dot-com" and recommended that Levi "needs to remember who brought you to the dance." In response, Jay Thomas, the digital-brand manager for the project, declared that Levi Strauss had no apologies for the retail partners who helped build the brand; further, he stated, "it wasn't about them. It was about the customer."

Levi Strauss opened two online sites offering more than 120 items with 3,000 possible variations (i.e., combinations of clothing), allowing its customers to buy directly from the company. The sites employed innovative tools: a "fit calculator" that suggested the best sizes, a "changing room" that allowed the buyer to mix and match tops and bottoms, and a "style finder" that used filtering technology to recommend apparel based on a person's taste for music, fashion, and lifestyle. Levi's use of interactive filtering for personalization was the first time this technology was used in the online fashion industry. In addition to product offerings, the Web site also included many entertainment activities and promotional gimmicks, such as contests, chat rooms, and games.

According to senior marketing manager Kevin McSpadden, the immediate goal of the site was to boost awareness of Levi's wide product line and to open a new distribution channel beyond its 1,600 U.S. retail partners. Thomas affirmed that the online selling of Levi's brand was part of the company's new priority to establish a direct relationship with consumers.

Yet the new sales channel did not improve the company's finances by much. More plants were closed, and the company decided to hire low-paid foreign workers to cut and sew its blue jeans and other apparel. An additional 5,900 workers, nearly 30 percent of Levi's 19,900 employees, lost their jobs.

To improve its presence in the physical world, Levi opened a new 24,000-square-foot flagship store in its hometown of San Francisco. The store offered consumers the chance to get a 3-D body scan, customize their own jeans with help from a Levi's designer, and sit in a tub of hot water for special "shrink to fit" jeans. Analysts saw this store as a further attempt by Levi to change from its orientation as a manufacturer to a manufacturing and marketing company.

In late 1998 and early 1999, major changes also took place in management. Chairman Haas relinquished the chief executive officer post to Philip Marineau, formerly with PepsiCo, in a move to expedite the changes facing the company. There were also major changes in other key executive positions, including the chief international marketing officer.

Traffic to the Web site greatly decreased. According to the Web rating firm MediaMetrix, by the spring of 1999, Levi.com was attracting fewer than 10,000 unique monthly visitors in the age range of 18 to 24 years. By comparison, more than 200,000 young adults visited Yahoo! monthly. The low traffic was not related to a lack of promotion. Over the few months after the November launching, Levi had spent an estimated $5 million to $7 million to promote the Web site; the actual cost of development was not made public.

Less than one year after announcing the opening of the online retail Web site, Levi Strauss announced that it was closing the site after the 1999 holiday season. Instead of offering all of its products for sale directly to consumers, Levi Strauss selected a few e-retail partners (including Macy's and J. C. Penney's) for online sales. Management decided to maintain the site only as a merchandising vehicle and for linking customers to the retailers' Web sites.

A company spokesman stated that running a first-class e-commerce site was unaffordable. "We learned that it's costly to run a world-class e-commerce business," said Jeff Beckman, spokesman for Levi Strauss. "When we looked at what are the priorities for the next year, we decided this was a great time to allow our retailers to offer our products . . . [and] that selling online was more difficult and less profitable than the company had expected." The company maintains a Web site but does not use it for sales.

Sources: "Heritage and pricing outweigh status," *Time Women's Wear Daily,* November, 1999; Kane, M., "Levi's to end direct sales online," *ZD Net,* October 29, 1999; Kroll, L., "Digital denim," *Forbes,* December 28, 1998; Sutter, S., "Levi's slow fade," *Marketing,* November 22, 1999; Weaver, J., "E-Denim: a good fit for Levi's?" *ZD Net,* November 12, 1998.

Thinking About E-Commerce Today

1. Levi's tried to use Web technologies to expand its mode of operations from B2B commerce to B2C commerce—and failed. Was this part of a pattern? Would this be a futile attempt for any B2B company, or do you find this a generally viable approach that will see only occasional failures?
2. Was Levi's failure a matter of bad luck, or did management do something wrong? What would you do to make this move successful?
3. Do you know of any manufacturers that have established a successful B2C commerce Web site? Name the companies and try to state their ingredients for success.

BUSINESS-TO-CONSUMER E-COMMERCE

8

LEARNING OBJECTIVES

WHEN YOU FINISH THIS CHAPTER YOU WILL BE ABLE TO:

- Summarize the principles of the main types of online business-to-consumer (B2C) activities
- List the major players in the B2C arena
- Explain the challenges of B2C firms
- Articulate the difficulties of e-retailing in general and delivery in particular
- Explain the concept of channel conflict
- Contrast failure and success factors in online B2C ventures
- List the major future developments that are anticipated in online B2C commerce

In January 2000, Autobytel.com, an online intermediary, announced its strategy for selling cars online. The firm would enter into agreements with car dealerships to set fixed prices for the same models. A customer would shop for a car online and order a car from a dealer who is party to the arrangement. Does this sound like a revolutionary idea? Why should car dealers need Autobytel.com or similar intermediaries? Consider this business model: You examine car models at the carmaker's Web site. You then go to a nearby dealership to test-drive the car. That car is the only unit of this model at the dealership, because the dealer does not need to maintain more than one unit of each model. If you like the car, you close the deal. The carmaker will deliver the car to your front door. Thus, the Web may turn dealerships into mere test-driving and car-service centers. If you do not need to test-drive the car, you do not need the dealership at all. You certainly do not need it to apply for financing: Both the purchase and the financing can be executed directly with the automaker via the Web. This is just one example of how the Web may cut out an inter-mediary—and fewer intermediaries means lower costs, and hence, lower prices.

BUSINESS-TO-CONSUMER HOOPLA

While venture capitalists and the corporate world may have most of their attention directed to business-to-business ventures and models, millions of people are exposed to online business mainly through business-to-consumer (B2C) activities. The reason is simple: There are more consumers in the world than there are businesses. Since the mid-1990s, when very few people purchased anything through the Internet or even had the hardware and telecommunications means to do so, B2C has developed into a multibillion dollar activity. A study by the consulting firm the Boston Group pegged the 1999 B2C volume at $33.1 billion and estimated it almost doubled to $61 billion in 2000 (The Boston Group, "The State of Online Retailing 3.0," April 17, 2000). Equally important is the finding that 85 percent of Internet users are also Internet shoppers ("The Interactive Consumer: Charting the Online Shopping Revolution," a survey commissioned by *Parade Magazine*).

Consumers prefer to shop and buy on the Internet for three major reasons: convenience, saving time, and comparative shopping. Shoppers can shop from anywhere in the world, at any time. They can shop in the middle of the night, sitting at home in their pajamas, and with a single click of the mouse execute a purchase order. Shoppers can visit numerous vendors' sites within a short period of time. While it could take several hours to drive to shopping malls and browse the brick-and-mortar stores, they can accomplish much more shopping from the comfort of home in a few minutes.

One of the Web's greatest advantages over traditional shopping is comparative shopping. Numerous sites let shoppers compare items and prices in preset categories. If customers know what item they want it is easy to find the site that sells it for the lowest price. If they are looking for a price range of an item, they can easily find the brand that provides the best overall quality of that item. In consumer surveys, respondents have cited additional reasons for shopping online, including the ability to buy from nonlocal merchants and shopping without sales pressure.

The lion's share of B2C activities fall into two categories: electronic retailing and reservations. We will address these and other B2C areas, such as auctions, content, grocery shopping, and bill presentment and payment.

THE BUSINESS OF E-RETAILING

In the last few years we have witnessed significant growth in retailing over the Internet. According to the research and consulting firm Forrester Research, retail sales on the Internet will reach nearly $185 billion by 2004. Many companies were established especially for retailing online, and some brick-and-mortar retailers augmented their operations by bringing them onto the Web (turning themselves into click-and-mortar businesses), while others moved completely from physical structures to the Internet. In this section we discuss the characteristics, issues, and challenges of **e-retailing**, or operating retail businesses through the Internet.

In historical perspective, we can discern three waves in retailing, as Figure 8.1 shows. The relationship between the consumer and the retailer in the groceries sector can be highlighted as an example; the relationship is similar in other retail sectors. For centuries, shoppers bought groceries at relatively small stores, usually owned by a single proprietor. The service was personal: The corner grocer and customer were on a first-name basis. The grocer was service oriented and responsive. He knew the customers' needs—and did everything to satisfy them: their preferred cuts of meat, the types of tomatoes they liked, how many loaves of bread they needed each week. When a fresh supply of a preferred product came in, he notified the proper customers, or, better yet, set aside an amount for them knowing that they would buy it. He offered diverse services, such as check cashing and credit, or even free delivery.

The next wave was supermarkets. Customers served themselves in stores several times the size of the corner grocery. Customers enjoyed the beautiful aisles of colorful produce, lower prices, and great sales. Choice and lower prices replaced intimacy and service. The lower prices and choice were partly available because now shoppers, not the grocer, did the picking, packing, and delivery. Procter & Gamble, the giant consumer products company, estimates that in that manner shoppers save supermarkets 13 percent of the total cost of sales.

We are now at the beginning of the third wave: shopping and buying through the Internet. We have no intimate relationships with the retailer; we do not even know where the retailer is. We miss the colors and smell of what we are shopping for, and we do not experience the immediacy of shopping physically—what we buy is not immediately in our hand or bag. However, we do enjoy a huge variety of items to choose from, and the retailer picks, packs, and delivers. Some experts say that in these waves we have moved from full service to self-service and back to full service. Understanding the limits of intimacy and immediacy is important for online retailers; to succeed, they must compensate consumers with other advantages, such as very low prices, excellent service and product return policies, and superfast delivery.

Online grocers and other retailers will probably enjoy their greatest leap in efficiency when a new technology is implemented: the cheaply embedded radio-frequency electronic chip. This tiny, very flat chip will replace the universal product code (UPC). Instead of passing items over a UPC reader or reading

FIGURE

8.1 RETAIL WAVES IN THE GROCERY MARKET

them with an electronic wand, items will be identified remotely on the shelves and placed in a cart. When leaving the warehouse's gate, a special reader will capture all the information at once: a list of items and their prices. The invoice (which in most cases will actually be a receipt by this point, thanks to prepayment upon ordering) will be transmitted to the customer via the Internet. This will save much of the manual labor involved in picking and shipping. The technology already exists. One challenge, as with many new technologies, is to bring down the price. A chip will have to cost less than a penny to make its use economically viable.

ELEMENTS OF E-RETAILING

The purpose of e-retailing (or *e-tailing*, as some people like to call it) is to sell goods to consumers via the Internet. Generally, this entails a site that (1) promotes the items offered for sale; (2) provides a mechanism to search for items by attributes such as brand, size, color, and price; and (3) has the means to accept a purchase and the payment for it.

Promotion of items is executed through the Internet itself but also through more traditional means of advertising and public relations: print media, radio, and television. On the Internet, advertising is typically carried out through clickable banners.

Companies that specialize in the development of online transaction software offer comparison software. The software enables users to search for items with common features and compare prices, delivery times, and other variables. Web retailers do not have to develop their own software, although they may ask the software vendor to tweak the software to fit their special needs. Ariba, Commerce One, IBM, and numerous other companies sell and support such software.

These companies also offer software to support two other key transaction elements: order acceptance and payment. Orders are channeled into a database from which workers at various stations receive them electronically and fulfill the order: picking from shelves, packaging, and preparing for shipment. Large e-retailers maintain warehouses in many geographically remote sites. Workers at these warehouses receive electronic information about the orders they should fulfill.

Payment software is usually purchased and installed as an off-the-shelf package. The least expensive packages, typically used by small e-retailers, cost as little as $80 and can be purchased in stores. The companies mentioned above offer more complex systems. The most common method of payment on the Web is by credit card. To process credit card payment, retailers must enter into arrangements with credit card issuers. However, there are other ways to accept payments online. We discuss these methods in Chapter 12.

DIMINISHING IMPORTANCE OF BRAND NAMES

How important are brand names in e-retailing? Apparently, their importance is diminishing for online shoppers. Brand names used to connote high quality and guarantee of support. People decided to purchase a certain brand-name item because they assumed there was no better, similar item. This attitude saves comparison time and hassle. But the Internet changed our shopping habits.

Nicholas Carr, in his article "Bonfire of the Brands" (*The Industry Standard*, March 13, 2000, p. 298), announced the death of the brand name. His explanation: A brand name is a shortcut we take when we do not have convenient access to information about a product. In the age of plentiful, convenient information on the Internet, there is no need to go out and buy a Sony when we are looking for a new DVD appliance; we can compare the quality and prices of many DVDs on the Internet. When we "Web shop," we are more rational and less sensual. Thus, brand names are important to us when we shop physically, but not when we shop on the Web.

What does this mean for e-retailers? It means that they can attract and retain consumers by providing all of the goods available on the Web rather than relying on selling only brand-name items. E-retailers should maintain items from a wide variety of manufacturers and provide the consumer with the tools to compare qualities and prices at their sites. On the Web, the brand name should be of the e-retailer, not of the manufacturer. If you ask regular online shoppers about the electronic devices they have purchased, you may notice that the site where they made a purchase is more important than the brand name of the item they purchased. Experienced online shoppers are more likely to go back to Amazon.com or Buy.com rather than look for the items of a specific manufacturer.

REPEAT BUSINESS CHALLENGE

Retailers approach Web surfers as missionaries approach "lost souls." Masses of Web surfers pass by retailers' electronic stands, and the e-retailers must do two things: Attract the surfers to spend some time at the site, and then convert the visitors into buyers. When these two goals have been accomplished, the final challenge is to turn the buyers into repeat buyers.

According to Forrester Research, in 1999 more than 70 percent of Internet retailers had a conversion rate of less than 2 percent, which is to say that of every 100 visits to a retail Web site, only two resulted in purchases. The **conversion rate** is the rate at which visitors are converted into buyers. Industry experts suggest that market leaders such as Amazon.com have conversion rates no higher than 15 to 20 percent. Conversion is one of the most difficult challenges with which online retailers must deal.

INTERESTING . . .

IF THE SHOE FITS . . .

Raindrop Geometric, Inc., a software company in Durham, North Carolina, makes applications that scan objects and create precise 3-D digital models. Here is how the software could be used for the online ordering of personal goods. You go to a Kinko's store, or to any authorized chain, and make a 3-D scan of your foot. Then you visit the Nike Web site to order a shoe, e-mailing the file containing your foot scan. A few days later, Nike ships you shoes made exactly for your feet.

Source: Chris O'Brien, "E-Commerce effects: Something for the imagination," *The Philadelphia Inquirer,* May 21, 2000

Peter Fader, marketing professor at the University of Pennsylvania's Wharton School of Business, cites the issues on which managers of e-retailing enterprises must concentrate.

1. The professor observed that most firms do a poor job of analyzing data to arrive at useful information. Most managers do not perform separate analyses; rather, they look only at "the bottom line," which is visitors and revenues. That is insufficient information to figure out consumer behavior.
2. Managers must break up overall sales figures into their component parts. These parts should be the amount of traffic that comes to a Web site; the conversion rate; the frequency with which buyers return for repeat purchases; and whether buyers spend more money when they come back.
3. The ultimate goal of B2C firms that focus on e-retailing should be to convince visitors to come back and purchase more. Without proper information, managers cannot know how to accomplish this purpose.

When managers analyze data, they also need to acknowledge that there are great differences among shoppers. It may not be enough to state that the conversion rate is 10 percent. A 10 percent conversion rate may indicate that all visitors buy something one out of every 10 times they visit, but the truth may be that 10 percent of the people buy on every visit while 90 percent of them never buy at all. Both truths produce the same statistic: 10 percent of visits end up in purchases. However, the company must use completely different resources and methods for enhancing the firm's sales performance for each truth. It takes one measure to convince buyers to buy more, and another to convince mere browsers to purchase something.

Some observers argue that roughly 20 percent of buyers bring in 80 percent of the total revenues of many online businesses. The other 80 percent of buyers bring in significantly less revenue. To convince these buyers to buy more, the firms must devise incentives that are comparable to frequent-flyer miles or reward points.

DELIVERY CHALLENGE

A funny television commercial aired in 1999 showed people receiving consumer items by fax that they had ordered; the fax machine spat out diver fins, a compact disk player, and other items. If only this could be real. Unfortunately, though it may take only a few seconds to purchase an item, it may take another few weeks to actually receive it at your door. Indeed, the greatest challenge for online B2C businesses is *prompt delivery*. Some companies have accepted the challenge and are trying to do something about it. Kozmo.com, for example, was an online company that promised to deliver a variety of items within one hour (see Figure 8.2, page 150). Apparently, the challenge is difficult; in April 2001, after three years of existence, Kozmo went out of business. Another company that promises delivery in under an hour is LastMinute.com.

CHANNEL CONFLICT

Internet pundits keep telling us that successful online businesses are those that entered the new frontier first. Supposedly, they gained experience and brand-name recognition early, and that gave them a significant leading position. However, reality shows that the rule is not universal. Take Reebok, for instance, which is one of the world's largest producers of sports apparel, especially sports

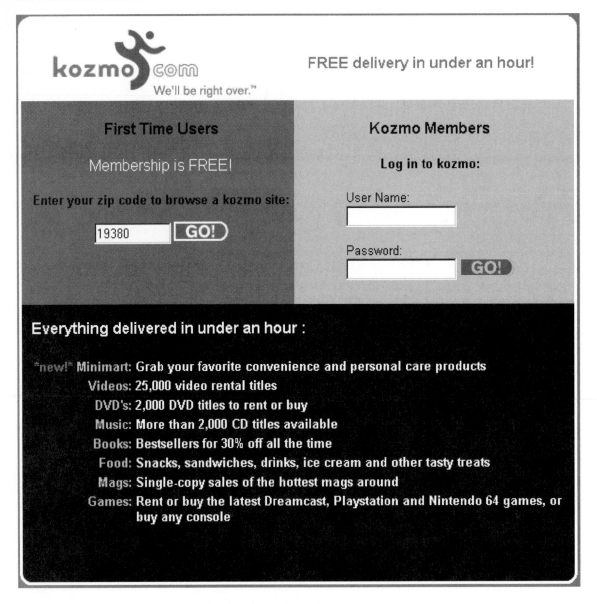

shoes. In 1994, it was the first in its industry to launch a Web site, assuming that its Internet presence added to its credibility as a pioneering, "cool" brand. Yet, from 1997 to 1998 the company's sales dropped 14.6 percent. In 1999, the company hired an executive whose task was to develop a global e-commerce plan for the company's brands, including Reddbok, Weebok, and Rockport, as well as its licensed apparel lines. Apparently, the approach did not work well. It was discovered that Reebok's e-commerce ventures were taking away sales from its traditional bricks-and-mortar distributors. The strategy for the Web site was changed: Instead of using it for selling, the company is now using it only to promote its products.

Reebok's bad experience was not unique. The phenomenon is called **channel conflict**. Manufacturers realized that establishing a direct manufacturer-to-consumer distribution channel may be successful when measured on its own merit, but the overall result is negative: The manufacturer becomes a competitor to its traditional distribution allies. While manufacturers' outlets are not new, traditional outlets (which are typically located at the manufacturer's factories) require that you travel to the single (or one of few) physical location where the goods are actually manufactured and purchase them there. On the Internet, these "outlets" are as ubiquitous as those of the retailers.

Some e-retailers have warned manufacturers that they may switch to other vendors if the manufacturers continue to sell directly to consumers online. For example, consider Home Depot's move. When the hardware retailer planned to unveil its own megasite, it sent letters to its vendors that said, in part, "We too have the right to be selective in regard to vendors we select and trust. You can understand that a company may be hesitant to do business with its competitors." It was a polite, yet emphatic warning to any vendor that valued its relationship with Home Depot that the company would not tolerate its own suppliers functioning as direct competition online.

Apparently, a similar struggle may have caused the quick demise of Levis.com as a sales outlet. (See "E-Commerce Today" in Chapter 7. The site still exists, but not for direct sales.) The Web site of the famous maker of dungarees invited online shoppers to order tailor-made clothes. While management did not publicize the reasons for folding the practice, it is possible that Levi's was encountering some negative feedback from retailers that carried its brand and resented the new competition.

There may be ways to circumvent channel conflicts. One approach is to sell online items that are not distributed through retailers. For example, Black and Decker, a leading hardware manufacturer, sells a product line that is available only on the Internet. Direct competition does not exist, but the manufacturer needs to consider if it would be beneficial to not use traditional retailers for a new product line, which often is a key investment. A company could also sell online-only catalog items that the manufacturer has decided not to sell through retailers. If management believes that brand names may make a difference (which is waning on the Web, as we discussed above), it can avoid channel conflicts by selling online the same items sold through retailers but under another brand name.

CHALLENGING WAREHOUSE-TO-RETAIL TRANSITION

Recall the Levis.com case. Direct competition with its retail allies might have been a reason for the Levi Strauss Company's shutting down of its online retail operation, but this might have been only one reason. The site moved the company away from one that produces for warehouses to one that tailors clothes for individual consumers. There is a great difference in logistics between the two business models, and the transition might have been too drastic to sustain.

Any e-commerce transaction that involves the purchase of a physical product requires getting that item to the customer's home or office. Labor and transportation costs thus shift from the customer to the retailer. The store suddenly comes to the customer, instead of the customer going to the store.

This issue was articulately addressed in an article titled "The Longest Mile" (*Business 2.0*, December 1, 1999) by Mohanbir Sawhney, a professor of electronic commerce and technology at the Kellogg Graduate School of Management at

Northwestern University. The "last mile" is a term for the last phase of an online purchase: delivery, also called fulfillment. According to Sawhney, there are five essential strategies for solving the "last mile" problem: *portal, buildover, caching, speed,* and *niche* (see Figure 8.3).

PORTAL STRATEGY

With the **portal strategy**, a firm offers many different, but related services to consumers. By aggregating service requests, the firm achieves economies of scale. Economy of scale occurs when a business manufactures a large quantity of the same product or provides a large quantity of a service. By handling a large quantity, the business saves resources because only a small additional effort goes into adding a large quantity of the product or service. For instance, a superstore saves money by selling food in large quantities, because employees spend time on a single buyer who purchases a lot instead of spending multiples of the same time on several buyers who would yield the same combined revenue.

Boston-based Streamline.com and Westwood, Massachusetts, based ShopLink.com promote themselves as "one-stop shopping" home delivery and errand services. They aim to ease the lives of busy suburban families by providing Internet-based order centers for a wide range of products and services and delivery of these items directly to customers' homes. Items include groceries, prepared meals, pet food and supplies, postage stamps, dry-cleaned clothes, video and video game rentals, and processed film.

Unlike Webvan.com and other large online grocery stores, these companies attempt to deliver a "wholesome" service. In order not to waste customer time in attending deliveries, these companies install drop-off boxes outside the house or in the garage, access to which is given only to authorized delivery personnel. The larger parts of these boxes are refrigerators in which the workers put perishable groceries. In addition to the high cost of delivery, these companies bear the high cost of the delivery boxes. It should be noted, though, that these companies collect subscription fees to offset such costs.

BUILDOVER STRATEGY

The **buildover strategy** is so called because the firm builds its own infrastructure rather than relying on other firms' infrastructure. It is highly ambitious and requires large sums of investment capital. Instead of fulfilling customers' orders from other supermarkets and stores, the company establishes its own large warehouses called *fulfillment centers*. Pickers fill boxes with ordered items, and large trucks haul the boxes to the subscribers' homes. Webvan, once the world's largest online grocer, adopted this approach. The company spent $1 billion on building 26 fulfillment centers in the United States. Because the infrastructure is so expen-

F I G U R E

8.3 APPROACHES TO SOLVING THE "LAST MILE" PROBLEM

Approach	How It Works
Portal	Aggregate demand across categories; achieve economies of scale.
Buildover	Maintain your own warehouse.
Caching	Aggregate orders for delivery at a single location.
Speed	Charge more for fast delivery of convenience store items.
Niche	Charge more for specialty items that are difficult to find elsewhere.

sive, the company had to attain a large number of subscribers in each market (i.e., a region in which it has a fulfillment center). Moreover, it had to attain a large sales-per-subscriber-per-year ratio to break even and maintain profitability. Webvan could not attain that ratio and closed its doors in July 2001.

CACHING STRATEGY

The **caching strategy** is so called because filled orders are aggregated, or *cached*, in one delivery location. Apparently, HomeRuns.com used to deliver this way but later delivered to homes. Groceries and prepared meals were delivered to collection centers located in places such as corporate parking lots, gas stations, and office buildings at the end of the working day. HomeRuns.com stopped operations in July 2001. Collection centers are more convenient than home deliveries both to the online firm and the customers, because there is no need for attended delivery.

SPEED STRATEGY

The **speed strategy** relies on quick delivery of products. A Los Angeles-based firm called PDQuick, for instance, functioned like a combination of a 30-minute pizza delivery store and a convenience store. It promises to deliver groceries, ready meals, sandwiches, and beverages within 30 minutes. For the convenience, customers pay more than they would if they purchased the items in a traditional way. The challenges of this business model are that orders are typically small and traffic congestion may foil the 30-minute delivery promise.

NICHE STRATEGY

The **niche strategy** focuses on a niche market in which the firm specializes. It does not require new infrastructure. Typically, firms adopting the strategy sell a relatively narrow selection of products that can be efficiently delivered or that require a specialized fulfillment infrastructure that is already in place. For instance, Drugstore.com focuses on prescription drugs that are cost effective to ship. These are items with a high ratio of profitability to physical volume and weight. EthnicGrocer.com specializes in nonperishable and ethnic products that are hard to find at local groceries. All the products provide high margins of profit.

It is not easy for online retailers and grocers to combine several delivery approaches. Indeed, a company such as Webvan probably could add the installation of drop-off boxes but could not afford the added costs. These companies have already spent millions of dollars on fulfillment centers and vehicle fleets, so the installation of such boxes would add costs that they do not want to bear. Niche companies would lose their delivery efficiency and profitability if they augmented their product selections into perishables. Similarly, "speedy" online convenience stores would not be able to charge higher rates if they offered all grocery items. Webvan, on the other hand, could not practically promise a 30-minute delivery nor charge the higher rates that PDQuick does.

Seemingly, the only two avenues for guaranteeing dominance in online markets that involve physical delivery are by

1. gaining a large customer base over a short period of time, or
2. devising more efficient methods for delivery.

The latter can probably be accomplished through innovative online software applications that can expedite the order-picking-packing-shipping chain.

SUCCESSFUL B2C BUSINESS MODELS

Certain business models are well suited to B2C e-commerce, although some may not be perfect. The following sections detail several models for services and goods delivered over the Internet from businesses to consumers. Despite challenges, all of these have achieved at least a degree of success in recent years.

RESERVATION SYSTEMS

Reservations for any type of service seem to be an ideal activity for the Internet. After all, the reservation process is in-demand, information-intensive, and does not require the physical delivery of goods. An online reservation for any service can be more convenient and less time consuming than making one the traditional way—that is, by physically going to an office of the seller or even by telephoning. If a reservations site is built properly, it is easy to find the service desired and easy to reserve it. This is true of reservations in any industry. Successful online reservation systems have been set up in the travel, entertainment, and sports industries.

However, more than convenience is gained in such systems. They encourage fierce competition among companies for consumers' money. The systems have become highly efficient markets. This is manifest mainly in the travel industry, a market in which consumers spend $300 billion every year.

The Travel Industry Association of America (TIA) reported in 2000 that the number of travelers booking airline flights and hotels over the Internet has increased 146 percent from 1998 to 16.5 million travelers in 1999. The association found a strong correlation between frequent traveling and booking reservations via the Internet. Of the 16.5 million who purchased travel over the Internet in 1999, 8.2 million were frequent travelers, making five or more trips during that year. The Gartner Group predicted that travel e-commerce would increase from $5 billion in 1999 to an annual $30 billion in 2001, a sixfold expansion within two years.

In addition to saving human labor, what can online reservation systems do for the travel industry? They may reduce the number of unsold flight seats. Every week, about 3.5 million airline seats are unfilled. Priceline.com, with its reverse auction site, sells about 100,000 flight tickets per week. As explained in the following section on reverse auctions, Priceline invites travelers to quote prices for flights, and then airlines can decide if they are willing to offer a seat for that price. The traveler is obliged to pay for the ticket if an airline is willing to sell it for no more than the traveler offered to pay. Microsoft's Expedia.com offers a similar service. Another company, Orbitz, sells tickets at discounted prices, but the prices are fixed and the consumer is not obligated to purchase an offered ticket. The company is financially backed by such prominent airline companies as United Airlines, American Airlines, Northwest Airlines, Continental Airlines, USAir, and America West.

These developments in the travel industry may eventually demonstrate how e-business is good for the consumer but not so good for participating sellers. Once customers learn that they can buy the same ticket for less money, they may postpone the purchase until a few days or even a few hours before the flight takes place to obtain the discounted price. They also may visit Orbitz to get a price for a flight, and then head to Priceline.com and place a slightly lower offer for the same ticket.

Online reservation systems in the entertainment and sports markets function similarly to those in the travel industry. Some of these systems are actually integrated into travel reservation systems so that customers can be offered tickets to shows and sports events when they reserve their flight tickets, lodging, and rental cars. TicketMaster and several other ticket reservations agencies have quickly expanded their operations to the Web as soon as the technology was available for online operations.

CONSUMER AUCTIONS

In Chapter 7 we discussed online auctions among businesses. General auction sites provide similar services to the general public. Online auction sites practically turn the entire world of people who have access to the Internet into one huge virtual auction room. Rather than 30 or so people huddled in a single room where an agent of a professional auctioning firm conducts an auction, the Web site becomes a "room" that can accommodate millions of sellers and millions of bidders. While traditional auctions limit the time of bidding to a few minutes, online auctions allow days—and can extend the bidding indefinitely. Similarly to traditional auctions, the auction house—in this case, the owner of the online auction site—generates revenue by taking a percentage of the sale price from the seller. Forrester Research forecasts that the consumer online auction market will grow from $1.4 billion in 1998 to $19 billion by 2003.

Because auction site firms act only as intermediaries and transactions take place between one consumer and another, some people like to call this type of activity consumer-to-consumer (C2C) e-commerce. The best-known C2C auction site is eBay.com, which managed to capture a large audience before competitors such as uBid.com started their own sites. EBay was profitable within less than two years of its operations, probably because its business model relied on transaction revenues from the start. In recent years auction sites have been burdened with hoax propositions (such as putting up body organs for sale), fraud, and auctions of items that are illegal in some countries. Nonetheless, as Figure 8.4 (page 156) indicates, Jupiter Media Metrix expects revenues in the auction market to grow at an annual compounded rate of more than 40 percent.

REVERSE AUCTIONS

Auctions were not new to the Web. In auctions, the few—the businesses or individuals who offer items for sales—try to sell to the many. Thus, the auction model was practical before the Web and has only been enhanced by it: many

FIGURE

8.4 GROWTH OF C2C ONLINE
AUCTIONS

Year	Net Revenues (billions)
1999	$3.0
2000	6.4
2001	8.8
2002	11.6
2003	13.3
2004	15.1

Source: Jupiter Media Metrix, March 2000

more parties offer items for sale to many more potential buyers. Reverse auctions, on the other hand, could not be practical without the Web. In a **reverse auction**, the masses of potential buyers name their prices for items, either goods or services, and the few have an opportunity to sell for the named price or below it.

Priceline.com was the first company to offer online reverse auctions. The company was granted a U.S. patent for this business method. The company now offers reverse auctions for airline tickets, hotel rooms, home mortgage loans, rental cars, and new cars. Companies that offer these products and services sign up with Priceline, and the company's list of reverse bidders is open for competition and offers. The company generates revenue by skimming a fee from the companies for every sales transaction.

Most intriguing and complex of Priceline's categories was groceries and gasoline. Groceries were handled through Webhouse, a private subsidiary of Priceline's CEO, Jay Walker. The name of this organization reminded consumers of warehouse clubs, where for a monthly fee members could shop in a huge, warehouse-like store for groceries at reduced prices. Priceline stopped grocery and gas sales in October 2000. It claimed that further investment in infrastructure to make such operations profitable would be prohibitively high, and that it could not secure the high sums from investors. Yet the business model is likely to be repeated by this company or other companies, and it is worth a discussion.

Webhouse charged a nominal membership fee ($3 in 2000). Their business model relied on four parties: the consumer, the retailer, the sponsor, and the producer. Figure 8.5 illustrates the model. The consumer logs on to Webhouse to bid for products. Within a minute, the site responds with a list of approved prices, and the consumer's credit card account is charged for that grocery list. The consumer prints out the list. The consumer picks up the items at a participating supermarket. The supermarket sells the items to the customer at the reduced, agreed-upon price, but it eventually collects a retail price because the producer subsidizes the product. Sponsors advertise at the site and can offer "Webhouse dollars" to consumers who buy the sponsor's products. For example, a magazine publisher may offer so many dollars of discount for purchasing groceries through Webhouse if the customer subscribes to the magazine. The most critical party in this complex scheme is the producer, who must subsidize the items. In early 2000, when gasoline prices reached a historical peak, Priceline offered reverse auctioning of gasoline the same way it offered groceries.

While the first experiment with this business model failed, it may not be doomed. Some experts say that when the number of registered members increases to millions, producers will flock to such arrangements for the huge number of buyers, and that the large sales volumes will compensate for the deep

8.5 GROCERY REVERSE-AUCTION
MODEL

discounts. To succeed, however, the investment must be large enough to sustain the business for several years until a massive clientele is built up.

STOCK TRADING

No one traded stocks and other securities on the Web in 1994, but, by the first quarter of 2000, 38 percent of all stocks traded by U.S. discount brokerage houses were traded online. Discount brokerage company Charles Schwab is an example of a firm that was not a leader in adopting a new technology but did become the leading exploiter of the technology. In October 1995, when the chief executive officer of Schwab decided to start offering stock trades online, there were two other companies that offered the service: E-Trade and Lombard Securities. E-Trade was an online-only broker, while Lombard extended a traditional business onto the Net. Schwab noticed that "low-end" customers were steadily flocking to these services. (*Low-end customers* in this industry are individual investors—as opposed to institutional investors—who trade stocks for relatively small amounts of money and who shun the expensive services of analysts and investment advisers. The latter are often called *full-service* brokerage houses.)

In the 1980s, Schwab was a pioneering discount broker, a firm that offered stock trading services for commissions significantly lower than those charged by full-service stockbrokers. Many individuals embraced the service because they were willing to give up the expensive analysis and advice provided by full-service brokers such as Merrill Lynch. Schwab became the leading discount broker, cutting into Merrill Lynch's business. In the mid-1990s, the company's CEO decided not to allow E-Trade and company to do to Schwab what Schwab had done to Merrill Lynch. Within 90 days and after spending a mere $1 million, Schwab's own Web team, headed by a recently recruited executive who specialized in Web business, established an online stock trading site. Soon, the online trading service accounted for about half of all revenue.

Merrill Lynch, on the other hand, declared that it would never launch an online trading service and regarded it as a fad. But, the growing number of online traders started to put pressure on the management of America's largest broker. In June 1999, the company's CEO announced it was going to offer online trading. The company's challenge was not technological but organizational: What to do with the several thousand brokers whose services may no longer be needed?

Online stock trading prompted some entrepreneurs to offer after-hours trading, namely, trading outside the regular opening to closing times of stock exchanges, such as 9:30 A.M. to 4 P.M. at the New York Stock Exchange. After-hours trading was not a new invention. Financial institutions had practiced it for many years; the "newness" of it was that it was now available to individuals. To some people this was and is disturbing, because it worsens a negative social phenomenon: the day trader.

Day-trading is practiced by investors (usually nonprofessional investors) who try to make a living by reaping gains on stocks that they buy and sell several times on the same day. Practically speaking, the activity has all the elements of gambling. While gambling is against the law in many countries, day-trading is not: and there is no practical way to stop it even if governments passed laws against it.

GAMBLING

If you have ever visited a casino, you have seen electronic gambling machines. In fact, *all* gambling machines now in casinos are electronic. If you see a handle on their sides, remember that it is there only because some people prefer pulling a handle to pressing a button. Now, you do not have to travel to Las Vegas to use these machines; you have one at home, and it is your personal computer.

Gambling sites usually require that you allow a precharge to your credit card for a minimum amount (some require as little as $10). Your winnings are credited to your personal account, which the firm establishes and which you can check online at any time.

It did not take long for gambling entrepreneurs to realize that instead of offering gambling only in casinos, they can offer it to anyone who can browse the Web. Some countries, such as the United States, forbid online gambling (except in Nevada), and the United States and some other countries have taken several additional legislation initiatives specifically to close possible legal loopholes. However, such legal restrictions have not stopped entrepreneurs from setting up offshore online gambling sites. (*Offshore* is a relative term; a site is offshore if it is not stationed physically in your country's territory.) Apparently, online gambling is flourishing both in the United States and other countries, regardless of legality. We discuss the legal aspects of it in Chapter 11. At this point we should recognize one simple fact: While it is relatively easy to block the movement of physical goods and the rendering of services requiring physical presence, it is practically impossible to block online gaming. (You will not find the word *gambling* used in any U.S. casino, only *gaming*.)

CONTENT

The word *content* in e-commerce means information, such as news, research results, statistics, and other useful information. Almost all of the information that you can find on the Web is free of charge. Thus, it should not be surprising that Jupiter Research discovered in 1999 that 78 percent of Web users had never paid for content. The greatest content category for which users did pay (6 percent of all

Web users) was Adult Text/Image, or, to use a noneuphemistic word, pornography. The next two categories were Financial Information and Shopping Aids.

The public at large has shunned sites that charge for information. However, some firms have managed to convince some audiences to pay for periodic subscriptions to their information services, or at least to some specialized information. The majority of content providers fall into one of three classes:

1. A publication, such as a newspaper or professional magazine, that is available both in print and on the Web
2. An online newsletter, and
3. A per-download-basis content provider

In the first class you will find *Consumer Reports* and the *Wall Street Journal*. These are the two content sites with the largest number of paying subscribers. *Consumer Reports*, a shopping guide, has 560,000 online subscribers, and the *Wall Street Journal Interactive*, a financial news site, has 591,000 subscribers. The *Journal* was one of the first newspapers that successfully created a profitable content Web site. Taking a great risk, management decided to implement an interactive Web-based version of the daily. Within months, tens of thousands of corporations and individuals had subscribed, a number large enough to achieve profitability. Subscriptions to the *Journal* and similar newspapers are typically less than $100 per year. The *Journal*'s Web page is shown in Figure 8.6; note the login field.

FIGURE

8.6 THE *WALL STREET JOURNAL* OFFERS FEE-BASED CONTENT ON THE WEB

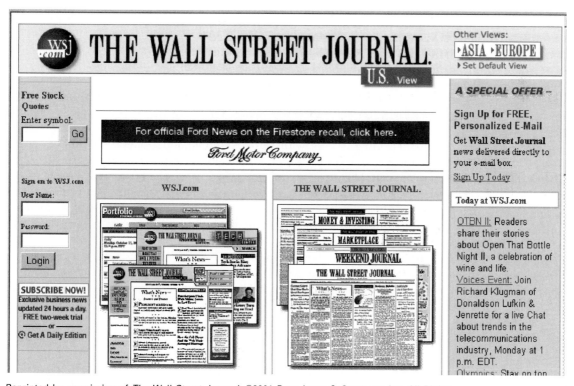

Numerous newsletters providing research results and expert advice in narrowly defined areas are posted on the Web or e-mailed to subscribers. When posted on the Web, reading requires login information. Like their print counterparts, these newsletters require subscription fees that range from tens to hundreds of dollars, depending on the field of expertise.

Per-download services let anyone download a desired article for which readers must pay before they are allowed to view or print out the article. Per-download sites include scientific journals as well as trade magazines.

Selling content on the Internet remains a serious challenge. Few firms have seen profits from content sale alone. Since so much information can be obtained online free of charge, the public at large mostly refuses to pay for information. Newspapers such as the *Wall Street Journal* are the exception rather than the rule. Although statistics are not available (at least not free of charge), it seems that almost all content revenue comes from businesses that pay for their executives' subscriptions and from universities that purchase the right to use the sites' content for their faculties and students.

Jupiter Research analysts predict that although content sales on the Web will grow significantly, they will still amount to only about $1.4 billion in revenues by 2003. The most successful categories for paid content will be general news and research, adult content, broadband-oriented video programming, and financial news and information. Broadband video will grow as more and more people have access to fast communication lines such as DSLs and cable modems.

SOFTWARE SALES

We discussed application software providers in Chapter 7. ASPs contract with other businesses and therefore are considered to be in the B2B arena. The model of renting the use of service through the Internet has not crossed the B2B line into the B2C arena. Households cannot enter into agreements for personal software use with ASPs. However, an increasing number of software applications can be purchased through the Web. Surprisingly, in 2000 no more than 2 percent of all software was sold on the Web.

This is surprising because software is a perfect product for electronic delivery. Interestingly, free software is downloaded daily by millions of people. Such software includes drivers for peripheral equipment (a driver is software that enables the use of printers, scanners, disk drives, and other peripheral equipment), utility applications, and more. However, when it comes to purchasing software, it seems that many of us still expect to buy it in a box. The explanation many people give is that they prefer a box because it also contains a manual; this preference is unfounded in reality, since the manual, too, can be downloaded. Also, an increasing number of these manuals are integrated into the software as electronic help and technical facilities anyway.

Experts such as Lawrence Ellison, chief executive officer of Oracle Corporation, opine that moving from physical sales of boxes of software to purchasing it online is only a matter of time—our cultural habits will change. Indeed, online sales of personal software is increasing, albeit slowly.

PERISHABLES ONLINE

Among online retailers, grocery service organizations are of special interest. The industry became quite crowded by 2000 despite the fact that none of the organizations was profitable. All compete for the $200 billion to $1.5 trillion (the figure varies considerably among sources) that Americans spent on food annually. The online grocery industry has included, at one time or another, Webvan, HomeRuns, Streamline, and several other, relatively small firms. As mentioned in previous sections, all online operations that must deliver physical goods face challenges. Online groceries face a particularly difficult problem: efficient picking and delivery of perishable physical goods.

It is interesting to follow what has happened in the online groceries sector. Peapod, the veteran online grocer, used supermarkets. Its employees shopped, picked, packed, and delivered for subscribers. Peapod lost an estimated $56 per order over its 10 years of operations—it never broke even, much less made a profit—and went out of business in 2000. It was purchased by the online grocery giant Webvan, which itself went out of business in 2001. Streamline, a smaller company, added other errands to its grocery service. It used supermarkets for products, but it installed refrigerated boxes outside subscribers' homes so customers did not have to be present at delivery. The company enjoyed an operating profit and was growing slowly. (The firm stopped operations in November 2000.) Webvan took a different approach to make operations more efficient: It owned warehouses in which it stored products before shipping them to customers. The company had not made a profit. To succeed in this business, the firms must increase the number of orders per warehouse per day.

Online grocery firms face great challenges because the products they sell are perishable. A highly efficient logistical infrastructure is a major key to success. These companies must also overcome a cultural hurdle; many people like to touch and smell such food as apples before buying them.

BILL PRESENTMENT AND PAYMENT

For years, utility, telephone, and other companies have spent millions of dollars annually on billing. The cost includes labor, paper, and postage. In the age of global networks, the need for paper billing falls fast. Every person with an e-mail account could save these companies money by agreeing to receive monthly bills by e-mail, through the Web, or both. **Online bill presentment** does not involve selling anything, yet it is an activity that significantly increases efficiency in B2C commerce. Interestingly, although we tend to associate electronic billing with B2C commerce, more than half of the 20 billion bills issued annually in the United States are sent to other businesses. Online presentment and payment of bills saves resources both for the payer and the receiver.

According to the Electronic Payment Association and Bill Payment and Presentment Resource Center, traditional paper-based payments cost the paying party $0.50 to $1.50, whereas an online payment costs only $0.24 to $0.80 (when there are about 25 monthly payments). The cost of traditional payment includes stamps, envelopes, checks, and the labor and time involved in opening envelopes and printing checks, all of which can be eliminated in electronic payment. Both companies that present and accept payments online and companies that accept and pay this way have reached savings of up to 50 percent of their bill presentment and payment costs compared with the cost of the traditional method.

Typically, a service subscriber agrees to receive bills by e-mail or to be notified by e-mail and click on a link to the provider's Web site for a detailed bill. The agreement may include an **online bill payment** clause that allows the company to charge the subscriber's credit card, or the subscriber can simply pay by check. Figure 8.7 (page 162) shows the top and bottom of a typical Web-based bill. By clicking on market information, such as telephone numbers and time durations, the subscriber can receive further details.

AT&T ONLINE CUSTOMER SERVICE
It's all within your reach

end session

Good Afternoon Effy Oz!

Your AT&T Statement

August 24, 2000

Customer # 231-555-1234

HOME ○
BILL REVIEW ●
MY PREFERENCES ○
AT&T SERVICES ○
WHAT'S NEW ○
ASSISTANCE ○

EFFY OZ
3621 CONIFER DR
WEST CHESTER PA 19380-2107

<u>Customer Service
Questions?
Moving?
Who did I call?</u>

Summary of charges

Previous balance......................................156.09
Payment received - Thank you.........................-156.09
AT&T Long Distance Services..........................134.78

Total amount due   **$134.78**

Automatic payment date   **September 3, 2000**

Direct dialed calls

HOME ○
BILL REVIEW ●
MY PREFERENCES ○
AT&T SERVICES ○
WHAT'S NEW ○
ASSISTANCE ○

	Date	Number called	Where	Time	Rate	Type	Min	Amount
60	Jul 19	718 263-		2:24pm	night	direct	4	.20
61	Jul 24	212 678-		4:36pm	night	direct	3	.15
62	Jul 25	248 557-		9:44pm	night	direct	1	.05
63	Jul 25	248 557-		9:56pm	night	direct	9	.45
64	Jul 26	410 289-		7:15pm	night	direct	1	.05
65	Jul 26	410 289-		7:16pm	night	direct	5	.25
66	Jul 27	410 289-		5:17pm	night	direct	2	.10
67	Jul 27	410 289-		5:44pm	night	direct	12	.60
68	Jul 27	410 289-		9:22pm	night	direct	5	.25
69	Jul 28	856 727-		12:59pm	night	direct	37	1.85
70	Jul 28	410 289-		4:42pm	night	direct	2	.10
71	Jul 28	410 289-		4:44pm	night	direct	14	.70
72	Jul 28	410 289-		7:29pm	night	direct	1	.05
73	Jul 29	410 289-		8:28pm	night	direct	6	.30
74	Jul 29	718 263-		8:43pm	night	direct	23	1.15
75	Jul 31	828 253-		5:31pm	night	direct	1	.05
76	Jul 31	952 929-		5:32pm	night	direct	1	.05
77	Jul 31	954 735-		5:34pm	night	direct	8	.40
78	Aug 3	206 241-		12:27am	night	direct	1	.05
79	Aug 4	814 865-		8:29am	night	direct	3	.30

FIGURE

8.8 EXPECTED GROWTH OF ONLINE BILL PRESENTMENT AND PAYMENT

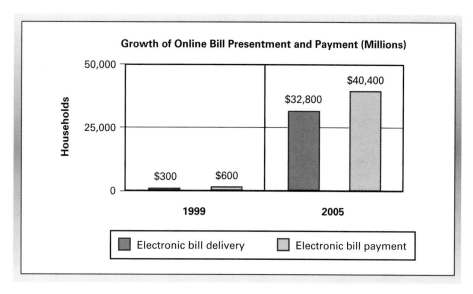

Chart "Growth of Online Bill Presentment" © Ovum. Reprinted by permission.

The details of a bill are channeled directly from customer files that are part of the electronic information systems of the company. This ensures a high level of accuracy. It also gives customers the convenience of easily retrieving their bills whenever they wish. A bill cannot be lost; clients only have to remember their access code to retrieve the bill from the company's Web site.

As Figure 8.8 shows, in the United States, online bill presentment and payment between businesses are expected to grow quickly, as the number of Internet users grows and they recognize the convenience. The figure shows the amount of dollars paid this way in 1999 and the expected growth. In the B2C arena, Jupiter Media Metrix predicts that by 2005 more than 40 million U.S. households will receive and pay at least some of their bills online. This is a huge growth from the mere 100,000 households that paid online in 2000. U.S. companies spend $18 billion annually on sending bills to consumers.

To implement electronic bill presentment and payment (EBPP, in professional jargon), companies usually outsource these tasks to organizations whose expertise is in this area. International Data Corporation predicts that revenue of the EBPP industry will reach $1 billion in 2004.

When deciding to pay electronically presented bills, subscribers agree to have a specific credit card charged several days after the bill is presented. Transmitting their credit card account number only once through secured communication lines does not pose a serious security threat.

DO WELL BY DOING GOOD

E-commerce has enriched many people, but it also offers a way to support non-profit community causes and charities. Companies that use e-commerce in this way serve as shopping portals for people who wish to support their communities or nonprofit organizations with specific causes. The nonprofits and charities benefit by receiving a percentage of each purchase that the retailers are willing to donate. The rule followed by all parties involved is "do well by doing good," and it supports a win-win situation. The portal companies are usually for-profit organizations. They make a profit, but they share it with nonprofit organizations.

Schoolpop, Inc. is an organization that helps U.S. elementary schools raise funds. Anyone can register at the company's Web site and designate a school to which their contribution will be made. Consumers do not make direct contributions. They have access to more than 200 retailers through links on the site. They pay regular prices for what they purchase. Up to 20 percent of the price of each item purchased is rebated to the designated schools. The school receives about 75 percent of the rebate, and Schoolpop receives the other 25 percent. Schoolpop manages the fundraising and transfers the appropriate sums to the designated schools. The company has signed up more than 16,000 schools nationwide.

Similarly, Shopforcharge, Inc. promises to donate five percent of every purchase made through its site to organizations such as Amnesty International, Sweatshop Watch, and Greenpeace. If you go to the Greatergood site, you can choose to donate part of your purchase to a special-cause organization, an elementary school, or a college.

ONLINE CUSTOMER SERVICE

Consulting firms stress the need for a human touch in online shopping. Apparently, many people who shop online back off before they click the "Add to Shopping Cart" button because they are not sure about some features of the product they were about to purchase. According to a study by Yankelovich Partners, 63 percent of Web surfers will not buy anything online until they feel they have had adequate human interaction. Forrester Research estimates that after they found the product for which they were looking, 66 percent of people who would otherwise buy online decide not to do so because of service-related reasons. Even people who are used to buying online need human help, especially when they purchase an expensive item, such as a car or jewelry, or items that are technically complex.

The solution to this concern may be in *streaming voice* over the Internet. To help consumers, some online retailers have implemented the same technology that has been used for telephoning. For example, the online jeweler Miadora.com allows shoppers to speak with a customer service representative by clicking on a button that initiates the call. A staff member noted that customers like to maintain anonymity when they purchase luxury items, which is perhaps why they are shopping on the Internet. However, the more important factors are that customers want to hear the warm voice of a human helper before they buy an expensive item. The Internet voice option satisfies this expectation and does not require an additional communication line to the one already used by the online shopper. American Express, the giant financial services provider, uses the same technology for customer service. Applicants for a credit card may improve their chances of receiving one if they answer certain follow-up questions after filling out online forms, and cardholders can voice their concerns as they view their account information online. Statement disputes may be resolved as both the company representative and cardholder view the statement and discuss it.

Viewing information online while talking to a customer representative has been a problem for customers who use a single telephone line. When they are asked to call the company, they must log off. Using Internet voice technology, they can use the same single line for both viewing information and discussing it with the representative. To the company, using representatives to serve online customers does not add cost; the same representative serves both customers who call via the phone and those who call via the Web.

According to a survey released in August 2000 by the Gartner Group, even the most popular e-retailers fail to provide high-quality online customer service. Of the top 50 consumer e-retail sites, Gartner did not rate a single one "good" or "excellent" for online customer service. Twenty-three percent were rated "average." Seventy-three percent were rated "fair," and four percent were rated "poor." The sad conclusion of the firm's researcher was this: "For customer service on retail Web sites, pick up the phone." Of the surveyed sites, half were pure play (selling only online) and the other half were online arms of brick-and-mortar retailers.

Apparently, the majority of e-retailers do not take advantage of enabling technology to improve their **customer relationship management** (**CRM**). CRM includes all the activities that help customers make purchasing decisions, receive prompt answers to their questions, and get satisfactory help both with the service and the products they purchased. Gartner found in its survey that only 10 percent let customers track inquiries from start to resolution; only 6 percent offered a feature that enabled customers to ask a representative to telephone them; only 24 percent implemented instant messaging; and only 28 percent had a policy of acknowledging that they had received a customer e-mail inquiry. Ninety percent of the surveyed sites did have a frequently asked questions (FAQ) page. However, this static feature is a minimal necessity for CRM and does not come close to satisfying all customers' needs. Gartner experts opined that by improving online CRM, e-retailers could increase their revenues by up to 15 percent.

The importance of good CRM is also evident in a study conducted in December 1999 by Forrester Research. The researchers found that 90 percent of satisfied customers are likely to visit a Web site again, and 87 percent will tell others about the site. Many software companies offer CRM software. Among them are Microsoft and virtually all of the firms that also offer enterprise resource planning (ERP) applications, such as Oracle, SAP, and PeopleSoft. According to Dataquest, a unit of the Gartner Group, the worldwide market for Internet-enabled CRM software was estimated at $19.9 billion in 2000, an increase of 28 percent over 1999.

FAILURES: NOT ALL THAT GLITTERS IS GOLD

Despite the overall success of commercial activity on the Internet, there have been hundreds of casualties. As Figure 8.9 (page 166) indicates, failure occurs for various reasons: lack of a solid business model, bad financial planning, or simply an inability to compete with larger, better-funded, or better-known firms. Often, the reason for failure is simply the lack of a solid business model: management cannot envision how the site can generate profit or how it can compete with other firms in the same market. When that happens, potential investors refuse to infuse more money into the site, and when financial resources run dry, the site ceases to exist. Sometimes, the business model is solid—that is, the firm intends to sell a product or service for which there is a sizable demand—but management underestimates the amount of funds necessary to sustain the firm until it has established a strong brand name and adequate logistical assets. Some firms bank on future advertisements but cannot generate the traffic necessary to generate advertising revenues. Here, we bring to light just a few examples of failure.

BOO? POOF . . .

Boo.com, based in the United Kingdom with offices around the world, including U.S. headquarters in New York, made the headlines as a young, splashy company specializing in retailing expensive clothes. It described itself as "the first truly

Reason for Failure	What Happens
Poor business model	There is no demand for the products or services the firm tries to sell online.
Insufficient logistical means	The firm runs out of funds before it has fully established an adequate logistics infrastructure.
Competition	The firm cannot compete against stronger players in the same market.
Overreliance on advertising	Traffic at the site is too small to generate advertising revenue.
Critical mass	The firm fails to reach, within a reasonable period of time, a consumer base large enough to break even and profit.

international e-commerce site." Boo.com was established in 1999, went online in November of that year, and for several months was considered a huge success. The site was a pioneer in online retailing technology. It featured cutting-edge design, including three-dimensional photographs and software that let customers zoom in on various parts of a product and dress virtual mannequins in various outfits. In May 2000, however, Boo.com was on the verge of bankruptcy. Apparently, the company had struggled from the start: In the beginning it had technical problems that postponed its debut, and then it simply could not become profitable. The young founders quickly spent the entire $120 million they had raised as venture capital. An additional cash infusion of $30 million by one of the initial investors could not save the company. In October 2000, Fashionmall.com purchased Boo.com and relaunched it.

Why did Boo.com fail? Apparently, management spent much money on its technology and on advertising in print and broadcast media. Some analysts also say that Boo.com spread its initial resources too thin by targeting 18 international markets at once. The site was available in seven languages and offered customers in many markets free shipping and free returns. Boo.com also staffed its customer call centers with multilingual representatives. There was no reasonable proportion between the resources the company spent on these efforts and the amount of sales it could generate.

FOOFOO FIZZLES

Foofoo debuted in the summer of 1999, offering content from prestigious magazines and access to products from specialty e-retailers such as SharperImage.com. Like other portals, the company generated revenue from collecting a percentage of the purchases made from its affiliated e-retailers. The site was well organized, but the firm's business model had a major flaw. Once users had experienced the novelty of visiting Foofoo, there was nothing to attract them back, since the site did not offer much original content and since they could bypass the links and access directly much of what was offered. Foofoo went out of business a short time after it opened. This is a classic case of an ill-conceived business model. The founders should have foreseen the customers' behavior.

In some cases, the failure of an online business stems not from its business model, but from the manner in which it funds its operations. The delivery challenge did not deter CookExpress.com. In January 1999, the company launched a service geared to busy professionals and time-pressed families who did not have the patience to cook but did have an appetite for healthful food. The San Francisco firm offered same-day delivery in the San Francisco Bay area and overnight delivery in other parts of the United States. It quickly had more than 5,000 customers and was an immediate success. Yet, one year after the start of operations, CookExpress's kitchen closed. The reason: lack of funds (or, as investors prefer to call it, a cash flow problem).

CookExpress's president admitted that the founders did not take into account an important fact associated with this type of operation: They should have raised much more money initially because they had to augment their market significantly before they could start enjoying a positive cash flow. Establishing the logistics of this type of operation requires a very large capital investment, significantly greater than the $3.5 million raised. CookExpress ran out of money after only a few months and stopped operations before it had a chance to obtain further funding from an IPO.

TOY SMART

Toysmart.com was established in Waltham, Massachusetts, with funding from the Walt Disney Company. Toysmart sold safe and educational toys—"good toys," defined as "toys that help children learn, grow, and develop by being high quality, educational, open-ended, and with a high play value." In addition, the site offered curriculum guides, teacher resources, classroom decorations, and art supplies.

Within one year, the company grew from 20 to 200 employees and increased its product list from 20,000 to 70,000. Holiday season sales in 1999 were 10 times greater than the year before.

Yet the company failed. It found itself competing with giants such as the online arm of Toys R Us, Amazon.com, and eToys in a market that leaves narrow profit margins. It pulled the plug in May 2000. Apparently, the founders of Toysmart underestimated the hurdles of brand-name recognition, which the sites of Amazon, eToys, and Toys R Us already had. They also did not learn from the experience of these very companies, which may have had a large market share but had not seen profits by the time Toysmart entered the market.

INGREDIENTS FOR SUCCESS

One must keep in mind that the Internet has existed as a vehicle for commerce for a relatively short time, less than a decade. Almost daily we hear of new business models, models that lost their clout, and businesses that are reshaping themselves. Internet entrepreneurs are taking great risks when establishing a new online business in general and a B2C business in particular, because the Internet environment is changing fast: The number of online consumers is still growing, consumers are becoming increasingly sophisticated, retention of consumers on the Internet is significantly more difficult than in "traditional" commerce, and Web technologies are getting more and more sophisticated. Therefore, it would be presumptuous of anyone to prescribe guaranteed ingredients for success. We can only learn from what has happened so far and identify which business models have succeeded, and which have not. Figure 8.10 summarizes the major lessons learned.

MEET A CONSUMER NEED

Most consumers do not purchase an item only because it is "cool." They purchase it because they need it. If they have not needed it so far, you must convince them that the item can make their lives easier or more enjoyable, or show them that the item can save them time or do something more conveniently. The principle of perceived need is equally important on and off the Internet. It is doubtful that people will buy a book on the Internet that they would not buy in a bookstore. However, if you offer them a convenient way to purchase that same book, they will buy it online. What you offer them, really, is not another book but another *way* of acquiring that book. In other words, you offer them a *service* that was not available to them before. You have met the consumer need to save time and hassle.

If you examine the online business revolution carefully, you will see that almost always it is the manner in which products are sold, not the products themselves, that attracts people to Web-based purchasing. As for services, you must offer a wide selection, easy means to browse the selections, easy means to compare items in terms of quality and price, an easy way to pick an item, and an easy and safe way to pay for it. When physical items are involved, a no-questions-asked return guarantee will make the purchase more attractive.

The Internet uniquely satisfies certain needs that cannot be satisfied through any other channels: the convenience of accessing information and purchasing from home, privacy, and 24/7 service. Regardless of one social view about adult materials, no one can deny the commercial success of adult-oriented Web sites. All estimates indicate that these sites sell more content than any other type of online business. What do they offer that is so attractive? One can access their materials at one's privacy and receive the information in quantities larger than from any printed source.

Entrepreneurs need to think along these lines: What information or services do people prefer to receive with a high degree of privacy? What pictorial or other

FIGURE

8.10 SUCCESS FACTORS FOR ONLINE B2C FIRMS

Success Factor	Reason for Success
Meeting a need	Consumers buy only what they need; offer them a product or service they need at a reasonable price, and they will buy it.
Total service	Offer a host of related services as one package. Aggregate online products and services offered in a traditionally fragmented industry.
Interaction and personalization	Enable customers to conduct live human-to-human interaction with the firm. Create consumer profiles and "own" your relationships with them.
Use of technology	Use the latest technology to update your site; visitors will expect technology as accommodating as that of your competitors.

information could we offer which people could not receive in large quantities from other sources 24/7? When you come up with an idea that answers these questions, you may have a successful business idea for a Web site.

PROVIDE A TOTAL SERVICE

Think of supermarket shelves: What do you see next to the 20 kinds of spaghetti? Twenty kinds of spaghetti sauce as well as other items that are normally used with spaghetti. This diversity should be reflected in the mind-set of successful online retailers and service providers when they plan their mix of offerings. Consider the difference between two companies that we have mentioned in this chapter, Webvan and Streamline. Webvan was an online grocer. It delivered groceries to people who ordered them online, but consumers could purchase only groceries, and they had to be at home to accept deliveries. Streamline saw itself in the errands market. Its philosophy was: "You are busy; you have to shop for groceries, pick up your clothes from the dry cleaner, and buy stamps at the post office. We will bring the groceries to you and place them in the box we installed in your garage or next to your entrance door; we will pick up your clothes and purchase the stamps for you; and you do not have to be home for our delivery." Streamline was gaining subscribers at a rate faster than any grocery-only online firm.

INTERACT AND PERSONALIZE

Some Web sites do not interact with consumers. Studies have shown that sites that implemented software to interact with consumers have increased their revenues by up to 15 percent. Interaction can be achieved through the use of phone lines whose numbers are displayed at the site, or via synchronous e-mail such as Instant Messenger. Experts recommend that online retailers allow live interaction with the site's personnel to be successful. Many customers become alienated and may not visit the site again if they wish to make an inquiry or file a complaint and cannot do so through human-to-human live interaction.

Who does not like to feel unique? Everyone does, including online consumers. They want to know that their wishes are known and that the firm is interested in them personally. To succeed, online firms should track and "own" their relationships with their customers. As consumers keep visiting a site, additional information can be collected about their preferences through cookies and click streams. Many retailers keep track of the types of products that people purchase; when they revisit a site, it offers them special deals for the same or similar product. Over time, special software prepares and fine-tunes a shopping profile for every visitor. The offers and presentation of Web pages become increasingly personalized. Banners draw visitors' attention to items in which they have shown interest in the past. For example, online booksellers provide pop-up messages about books on topics in which the visitor has shown interest. The message that firms must project to each consumer is: "We know and respect your wishes; we are here to serve *you*."

The motto is true not only for retailers. It is at least as important for online services of all kinds. For example, online stockbrokers e-mail customers reports detailing the day's performance of their stock portfolios (see Figure 8.11, page 170), and they provide a monthly analysis of their portfolios complete with color diagrams. The customers can import the tables and diagrams into widely used applications such as MS-Excel for further processing. Customers can ask to change some of the presentation features of these e-mail reports.

UPDATE WITH THE LATEST TECHNOLOGY

Staying abreast of technological developments is a must for any online business. Technology is the underlying element that makes the shopping and purchasing experience more efficient and enjoyable. It enables features such as the ubiquitous virtual shopping cart, one-click purchasing, on-site searches, product comparisons, wish lists, and customer reviews. Being on the cutting edge of technology may be costly, and it may not be necessary for long-term success. Eventually, all Web technologies move from expensive proprietary software to off-the-shelf applications. However, it is important that a site does not stay behind technologically for too long and thereby make competitors' sites more attractive.

F I G U R E

8.11 A PERSONALIZED DAILY REPORT FOR AN ONLINE INVESTOR

Good evening, EFFY. "My Ameritrade Portfolio" was up $15.67 as of 5:35 pm EST today:

Market and Portfolio Update				
Index	6-month graph	Close	Change	% Change
Dow Jones Ind.		10847.4	+81.9	+0.76%
NASDAQ		3803.7	-25.1	-0.66%
S&P 500		1448.7	-0.3	-0.02%
Russell 2000		518.8	+4.5	+0.87%
My Ameritrade Portfolio		$28,809.38	+$15.67	+0.1%

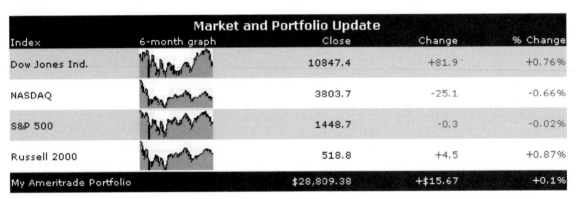

Stock Performance (% Change)

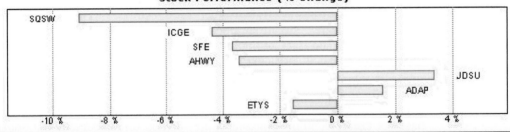

Today's Portfolio Activity								
Symbol	Close	Change	% Change	High	Low	Volume	Shares	$ Change
SQSW	8.750	-0.875	-9.1%	9.563	8.625	265K	480	-$420
ICGE	23.125	-1.063	-4.4%	23.250	21.625	5,427K	27	-$29
SFE	23.063	-0.875	-3.7%	23.875	22.750	956K	100	-$88
AHWY	0.875	-0.031	-3.5%	0.969	0.844	40K	380	-$12
JDSU	107.000	+3.500	+3.4%	107.438	97.875	25,058K	130	+$455
ADAP	24.000	+0.375	+1.6%	25.000	21.875	1,539K	300	+$113
ETYS	5.906	-0.094	-1.6%	5.969	5.719	772K	40	-$4

Professor Gerry Lohse of the Wharton School of Business found that in 1997 the average online purchaser spent $420 a year and that in 1998 the figure more than doubled to $911. In 1999, however, the increase was less than 30 percent, rising to $1,136. These statistics reflect three phases in public response to the new economy: *exploration, enthusiasm,* and *educated procession.* Some observers might say that the initial exploration enthusiasm is over, and that people have quickly embraced the Internet as a normal way to do business. People are no longer enthused with the phenomenon itself; they know how to use the Web to do more selective and comparative shopping.

As the Internet becomes an integral part of the mainstream world economy, B2C commerce is expected to change. Here are some developments that we may see in the next decade.

MERGERS OF B2C FIRMS

As mentioned several times in the previous chapter and in this chapter, online businesses must quickly reach a fairly large consumer base to sustain themselves, let alone make a profit. As venture capitalists become impatient and refuse to wait years for profit, the pressure on these businesses grows. Other, financially stronger firms have acquired many B2C firms. There is a trend of mergers and acquisitions that eventually will create an environment with significantly fewer firms on the Internet. Some experts believe that by 2005 we will see only 10 percent of the number of current B2C firms, especially in the retail sector.

CLICK-AND-MORTAR GRAVITATION

A growing number of brick-and-mortar businesses augment their operations on the Web. In fact, the Web arms of traditional retail chains have been more profitable than their pure play counterparts. Apparently, logistics infrastructure and experience is very important in running a retail operation on- and offline. From the other side, pure play companies increasingly have become similar to traditional chains. The ideal virtual retailer was supposed to have no warehouses and few employees. However, look at what happened to Amazon.com and similar businesses: They operate huge warehouse and packaging operations, or, as they like to call them, "fulfillment centers." These fulfillment centers are labor intensive, not technology intensive. Thus, we should expect to see e-retailers that perhaps have no physical stores but do have an electronic storefront and multiple labor-intensive fulfillment centers. This is the shape that both traditional retail chains and pure play firms are taking and probably will continue to pursue.

SOUNDER BUSINESS MODELS

It is doubtful that any new e-commerce business will set sail on the Web that does not have a sound business plan and can bring in profit within months of launching. When Jeff Bezos, the founder of Amazon.com, declared that the company did not plan to realize profit before 2003, investors accepted this approach. The approach was: Let us first establish the most recognizable brand name on the Web and capture a huge market share. Companies such as Amazon.com and Buy.com forwent short-term profits for branding and market share, especially by selling at cost or below cost. What will happen when the brand name is built and the market share is satisfactory? Then, executives said, we will increase prices; customers will continue to buy at our site because of our brand name.

Indeed, these companies do build formidable brand names, but customers are not stupid. They use search engines and comparison technology to find the sites that sell at the lowest prices. A site's brand name is important only because it puts the company at the top of the list of Web sites when consumers "go shopping." However, firms with top brand names are not the only ones visited when consumers shop online.

Therefore, new B2C firms will either offer unique products and services or offer experiences that competitors' technology cannot offer. They will have to improve that technology continuously, so that other firms do not catch up with them. Technologies such as virtual shopping carts, one-click shopping, and site search engines have been easy to emulate. They are not the type of technology that would give any firm an advantage.

Building a successful site on the sole basis of obtaining high traffic to sell advertising banners will not happen often. There are already too many content sites and other sites that attract a lot of traffic. Entering this crowded market is economically infeasible.

M-COMMERCE

Several technological developments may make e-commerce, especially B2C commerce, more popular than it is today. The most important one is mobile commerce, or **m-commerce**: online commerce executed from wireless devices such as cellular phones and PDAs (personal digital assistants, also known as handheld computers).

The consulting firm Strategy Analytics projects that by 2004 130 million consumers will execute 14 billion m-commerce purchases worth $200 billion per year. Cliff Raskind, a senior analyst for the firm, predicts that expansion of m-commerce will come in three waves. In the first, similar to early uses of the Web itself, people will make simple transactions that take advantage of the novelty, such as paying with a mobile phone at gas stations. In the second wave, m-commerce will use more advanced technology, including satellite-driven global positioning system (GPS) devices. Combining the technologies will enable customers to purchase perishable items on the go and let merchants announce interesting promotions. For example, merchants will alert passersby to special sales. People who are within a certain radius of a store will be able to participate in "blue light" sales as if they were actually in the store; they will simply walk over to the closest store of the chain and buy the special-sale item. If they are driving, the handheld device will direct them to the store. The third wave may involve universal shopping carts, enabling users with handsets to purchase any product from anywhere in the world. In this phase, handheld e-commerce may reach a larger scope than personal computer-based e-commerce. We further explore the future of m-commerce in Chapter 13.

SUMMARY

- About one fifth of e-commerce takes place between businesses and consumers (the other four fifths take place between businesses). B2C is of greater interest to the public, because most online buyers are not organizations but people—millions of them.

- We have witnessed waves in retail. From intimate relationships, small variety, immediate service, and personal delivery at the corner store, we have moved to no intimacy, huge variety, and no service immediacy at online sites.
- An online retailer (e-retailer) needs to promote items that are on sale; provide a mechanism to search for items by attributes such as brand, size, color, and price; and have the means to accept a purchase and the payment for it.
- Online, the importance of product brand names has diminished; shoppers use comparison software to find items of the best quality at the lowest prices regardless of brand name. The benefit of brand names has shifted from product makers to sites, as consumers buy from sites that they recognize and that they trust to reliably deliver what they need.
- E-retailers face two major challenges: the repeat business challenge, and the delivery challenge.
- The ability of manufacturers to interact directly with consumers tempted some to open B2C sites. This has created tension with retailers who had for many years sold the product, creating channel conflict. To save their relationships with the retailers, several manufacturers have backed off and stopped selling directly to consumers.
- Typically, e-retailers have adopted one of five strategies to deliver the items they offer. In the portal strategy, a firm offers many different, but related services to consumers. Aggregation helps accomplish economies of scale. In the buildover strategy, a company builds and relies on its own infrastructure (such as warehouses and a truck fleet) for delivery. In the caching strategy, a firm delivers goods to predetermined sites at which customers pick up items. This practice significantly reduces delivery cost. In the speed strategy, a firm charges high prices for fast delivery. The higher rates help cover costs. Companies that specialize in a narrow array of items whose availability is limited have adopted the niche strategy. Customers agree to pay higher prices for such hard-to-find items.
- Reservation systems have been one of the most successful applications on the Web, serving the travel, lodging, car rental, entertainment, and sports industries.
- Auctions are a "natural" feature of the Web. They virtually turn the entire world into one big auction site for any item offered for sale. Reverse auctions have been conjured up especially for the Web, because they are practical only in this medium. In a reverse auction, the customer offers a maximum price for a good or service, and the sellers are the bidders. Reverse auctions such as the one operated by Priceline.com may involve several parties: the consumer, the auction site, the producer, and the seller.
- Stock trading is moving fast from the traditional relationship between broker and investor to trading on the Web. Software lets investors receive real-time quotes and execute buy and sell orders within seconds.
- Much casino gambling has moved to electronic machines over the past decade. Using the technology over public networks such as the Internet seems to be a natural extension. Despite laws against gambling, millions of Web users have tried online gaming.
- Few firms have succeeded in sustaining their business on sales of content alone. The most successful ones are financial news and consumer information providers, and to some extent pornographic sites. Most people refuse to pay for online content of any type.
- Although it makes good business sense to sell software through the Internet, only a small fraction of software sales have been executed online.

- Online grocers face special challenges because they deal with perishable products. Because of the great investment in warehousing and delivery infrastructure, they must acquire a large customer base within a relatively short period of time to break even or perhaps become profitable.
- A growing number of companies, especially utility providers, have adopted electronic bill presentment and payment. A growing number of customers agree to receive and pay bills this way. Businesses that bill other businesses have also implemented the practice. The concept saves millions of dollars.
- More and more businesses use information technology to serve customers over the Internet. Among the technologies is streaming voice. Most consumers are not willing to purchase online unless they have had adequate human interaction via the site. Surveys show that B2C sites generally fail to adopt technology to support customer relationship management (CRM).
- Many online B2C firms have failed. The main reasons are poor business models, not creating sufficient logistical means before funding is exhausted, strong competition, overreliance on advertising, and inability to achieve a critical mass of customers.
- To succeed in B2C commerce on the Web, firms must meet customers' needs, provide total service, interact with customers and personalize their relationships with the firm, and use the latest technology.
- In the future, B2C firms will continue to merge into larger, stronger firms. Traditional brick-and-mortar retailers will continue to establish online extensions to their businesses, and pure play e-retailers will continue to augment their brick-and-mortar components such as warehouses and fulfillment centers. As venture capitalists expect profits sooner than they did in the second half of the 1990s, new business models will need to be sounder than before, depending less on brand-name recognition and market share and more on cost recovery and profit. Mobile commerce (m-commerce), which relies on handheld devices with wireless links to the Internet, will become prevalent and may eventually exceed e-commerce in personal computers.

KEY TERMS

e-retailing	niche strategy
conversion rate	reverse auction
channel conflict	day trading
portal strategy	online bill presentment
buildover strategy	online bill payment
caching strategy	customer relationship management
speed strategy	m-commerce

REVIEW QUESTIONS

1. Why does B2C receive more attention in the media than B2B?
2. For consumers, what are the advantages of shopping and buying online?
3. What features offered by online retail sites diminish the importance of brand names?

4. What are the factors that turn Web surfers into buyers, and why? What are the top three factors that can turn you into a buyer at a site?
5. In Web retailing parlance what does *conversion rate* mean? Why is conversion such a huge challenge?
6. What does *channel conflict* mean? If you were a manufacturer of a popular line of products, would you try to retail the products online? Why or why not?
7. Why do online grocers face particularly difficult challenges?
8. Priceline.com used its reverse auction technique to sell nongrocery perishable items. What are these perishable items, and why are they so appropriate for reverse auctions?
9. What are the necessary factors for B2C enterprises to succeed? Can you think of other factors that are not mentioned in this chapter?
10. What is CRM? Why is it so important for businesses in general and for online businesses in particular?
11. Why are so many B2C Web sites expected to die or be merged into larger sites?

DISCUSSION QUESTIONS

1. Do you expect to see faster growth in B2C than in B2B commerce on the Web? Explain.
2. What items (goods and services) will you never purchase online? Why?
3. What opportunities for fraud in B2C commerce could the Web seem to invite?
4. Do you agree with the assertion that brand names are diminishing in importance because of the Web? Explain.
5. How do the portal, buildover, caching, speed, and niche strategies work?
6. Would reverse auctions be feasible without the Internet? Explain.
7. What costs do online bill presentment and payment save? List and explain each type of cost.
8. Compare the initial business model of Amazon.com with that of eBay.com. Why was eBay profitable almost from the start of operations while Amazon still did not show a profit even five years after its establishment?
9. Why do experts expect the wave of mergers and acquisitions to continue among Internet B2C companies?
10. It is predicted that many consumers will use wireless handheld devices to shop online. Will you be one of these shoppers? What will you prefer to purchase the "old-fashioned way" from a personal computer but not from a handheld device? Do you foresee any undesirable social phenomena as a result of m-commerce (mobile commerce)? Explain.

ASSIGNMENTS

1. The chapter mentions several examples of Web firms that, while making a profit, help schools, charity organizations, and other worthy social causes. Brainstorm with another member of your class and come up with an idea for a site (or a series of sites) that can help such causes. Your idea may be for-profit or nonprofit, but you must be able to convince your professor and classmates that the idea is viable.

2. Customer relations management has been cited as being neglected by many online B2C sites. Prepare a software-based presentation (using PowerPoint, for example) listing the techniques you would use at an online retail Web site. Explain all the techniques both from technological and business points of view.

E-COMMERCE TODAY

Will You See Webvan in Your Neighborhood?

What could have more B2C flavor than letting consumers do their grocery shopping online? The concept is not new; it was first implemented in 1989, years before the Web existed. Several entrepreneurs have since brought the idea to the Web. All found it challenging, including the biggest of them all: Webvan.com.

Webvan was the brainchild of bookstore chain entrepreneur Louis Borders. It was founded in 1998 and started operations in San Francisco in 1999. It invited online shoppers to order groceries, videotapes, books, and housewares at its Web site. Webvan could schedule a next-day delivery that would occur within a 30-minute time slot. The orders were processed at an automated distribution center, packed into boxes, and shipped out in refrigerated trucks for delivery at customers' doors.

George Shaheen, who was lured from the giant consulting firm Andersen Consulting to lead the company, admitted he had underestimated the challenge. He did not realize how hard it would be to convince shoppers to change their habits and trust Webvan employees to pick, pack, and deliver tomatoes for them. According to some surveys, about 40 percent of people would like someone else to do grocery shopping for them. Yet, the "Build it, and they will come" rule has not worked well for online grocery service firms.

The profit on groceries is low, only 1 to 2 percent of sales. For online grocers, there are additional challenges. Groceries can rot in transit. Packaging, handling, and storage requirements vary from product category to product category. Online grocers must deal with meat that spoils, eggs that break, and picky customers with a tight schedule. Thus, if supermarkets have little room in which to maneuver, online grocers have even less of it.

The firm raised $1 billion in its initial public offering of shares in 1999. Yet the financial reports did not show a rosy picture. Revenue rose from $16 million in the first quarter of 2000 to $28.3 million in the second quarter, mainly thanks to Webvan's expansion into Sacramento and Atlanta. The important figure at which its CEO, Shaheen, was looking was average order size. This figure rose in San Francisco. Analysts estimated that the company had to reach a gross margin of 32 percent to be profitable.

Gross margin is the difference between what the consumer pays for the items bought and what the company pays to buy the items. Obviously, the company also had to pay for its own operations, which reduced the gross margin to a much smaller percentage, which is profit. Unlike most online retailers, online grocery service firms must run huge warehouses, and they must do so very efficiently. Webvan had several such warehouses from which the groceries were distributed. One must also bear in mind that almost all of the items were perishable, which complicated the logistics. Webvan had to have at least 3,500 orders per day to have a positive cash flow at each warehouse.

The company was experimenting with several marketing strategies. For instance, it did not advertise both on television and radio in the same city at the same time. It used practices that financial institutions and airlines have long used: data mining for profiling and finding consumer shopping habits, and e-mailing special offers to frequent shoppers much as the airlines do with frequent fliers.

Peter Relan, senior vice president of technology and business process at Webvan, did not find the challenges easy, either. It was his task to build the infrastructure that serves as the foundation for the company's operations. He connected the Web site with the order processing and order fulfillment systems, and he synchronized the entire system to ensure that couriers deliver the appropriate items to the appropriate place within the allotted time.

If the task is so daunting, why are entrepreneurs so attracted to it? The answer is in the figures. The potential for profit, if you know how to make it, is huge. The current size of the U.S. grocery industry, which is dominated by supermarkets, is $1.5 trillion per year. (The figure depends on the source you consult. One source estimated the current market at "only" $450 billion.) A typical shopper visits a grocery store 2.2 times per week and spends a tenth of his or her weekly earnings there, which is $60 to $100 for the average household. The *online* grocery market was projected to grow from $350 million in 2000 to $3.5 billion by 2002.

The key to success in this business, Relan said, was to merge immediacy with convenience. When we shop at a supermarket we have immediacy: The items we choose are immediately in our hands. However, it would be more convenient if someone else spent the time and did the buying for us. The challenge is to change shopping habits that have been the norm for more than a century. The Web cannot, as yet, deliver the sensory experiences that grocery shoppers enjoy—the rich colors and feel of fresh produce or the smell of fresh baked bread. He saw his mission as conquering the "last mile of e-commerce." Practically, this means changing the grocery shopping habits of millions of people.

Although subscribers were happy with its service, Webvan went out of business in July 2001.

Sources: Mullaney, T., "George Shaheen: Driving Webvan through the dot-com lean times," *BusinessWeek Online,* July 19, 2000; Sanborn, S., "Webvan senior VP takes on retail challenge," *Infoworld,* July 17, 2000, p. 42; Tapscott, D. and Ticoll, D., "Retail evolution," *The Industry Standard,* July 24, 2000, pp. 220–221.

Thinking About E-Commerce Today

1. What challenges did Webvan face that other retailers, such as Amazon.com, do not?
2. Why was the number of orders per warehouse such a critical indicator of the financial viability of Webvan's business?
3. Assume you are an executive for a firm such as Webvan. Which medium would you prefer to use to advertise the firm's service? Why?
4. Think CRM. What would you do to maintain your customers and make them recommend the service to friends?
5. Would you subscribe to the services of an online grocer? Why or why not?
6. Do you think Webvan's business model is viable? Explain.

- Explain the marketing value of domain-name recognition
- Recognize important design elements in Web pages geared to various demographic groups
- Compare various affiliate models in Web marketing
- Articulate the pros and cons of e-mail marketing
- Propose statistics and ratios for measuring success in Web marketing

According to a report published by the Internet Advertising Bureau, online advertising spending reached $1.953 billion during the first quarter of 2000. There was an increase of 182 percent in advertising spending between the first and last quarters of 2000. At the same time, studies have shown that online consumers start their searches for a product with a search engine and follow with comparison mechanisms to evaluate prices. The effect of advertisements at portals and other high-traffic Web sites is not significant. Are Web businesses spending their marketing money on the proper channel? Do they measure the right factors to gauge marketing success?

CYBERMARKETING

Marketing is the effort of promoting goods and services and trying to sell them. Marketers try to draw attention to their products and services, to convince people to purchase them, and to turn first-time purchasers into repeat purchasers. In general, marketing on the Internet is similar to marketing through other mass communication media such as newspapers, radio, and television. However, research results show that convincing people to purchase goods and services on a Web site may be more challenging than convincing them to purchase from brick-and-mortar vendors.

Consider these findings of the consulting firm ActiveMedia, LLC: Buyers who know exactly what they want to buy before logging on make *70 percent* of product purchases; and buyers who had decided which vendor they were going to visit before they logged on make *two thirds* of purchases. Both phenomena make Web marketing highly challenging, because they reduce or significantly alter the in-store "just looking" effect that often ends up in a purchase. Online shopping involves fewer impulse purchases than in-store shopping. In addition, when shopping online, the competition is just a click away.

The Web lets marketers use both the printed word and information conveyed in images and sound on the same page. Therefore, on the positive side, marketers can use the Web as a combination of newspaper, radio, and television. On the other hand, there are significantly fewer radio stations, television stations, and newspapers than there are Web sites. Finding the information you need—if you don't know specifically where you are going—is much more difficult on the Web than it is in other media. The intrinsic nature of the Web, then, provides both opportunities and challenges in trying to reach consumers.

In this chapter we discuss the major issues of marketing on the Internet. Note that online business use of off-line marketing methods will not be discussed here; we are concerned only with marketing that takes place online. Marketing on the Internet utilizes two applications: the World Wide Web and e-mail. Since the former is more complex and offers more opportunities, we devote the lion's share of the discussion to how marketers make use of Web technologies for business. We start by examining the issues of domain name selection and Web site design. We then discuss the important perceptual differences in marketing between Web sites and physical stores, and we address typical mistakes made in Web site design and how they may affect marketing. We devote a full section to the important issue of organizing a site's menus. Finally, since the Web is an international medium, we discuss how cultural differences affect marketing and how to address them on the Web.

The Web provides excellent opportunities for referring business from one site to another. The section on affiliate marketing explains current models of this popular Web marketing approach. We devote a brief discussion on two of the oldest advertising methods on the Web: *cross-linking* and *cross-luring*.

Many Web businesses are still in learning stages. We discuss the major mistakes that annoy customers and suggest ways to avoid these mistakes.

One of the greatest assets of the Web from a marketing standpoint is the ability to electronically profile consumers. We discuss methods of consumer profiling, touching upon the controversy that such methods create regarding privacy. (A full discussion of this ethical issue is included in Chapter 10.) We then discuss the importance of market research and statistics for online target marketing. Businesses often accompany target marketing with one of the least expensive marketing methods, e-mail. Finally, whatever method an online business uses, managers must know how to measure the success of their marketing effort. We discuss measurement techniques and how they are used, both correctly and incorrectly.

DOMAIN-NAME RECOGNITION

Every business, online and offline, wants a name that is easily recognized. A recognizable name is critical for an online business because Web users often search the Web for names they recognize before they resort to general searches. Ideally, managers of a Web-based business would like potential customers to easily remember their site's name so that they can type it in the Web address window of their browsers (e.g., www.iremember.net). Most people remember only a small number of such names, which makes the competition for memorable names fierce. What makes a Web domain name recognizable? There is no decisive answer to the question.

When trying to come up with a domain name, you must abide by the rules: Domain names with a .com, .net, or .org top-level domain cannot exceed 67 characters, and domain names with country codes (such as .de and .il) cannot exceed 26 characters. Domain names can use only letters, numbers, and dashes and cannot include spaces. Otherwise, you can choose whatever domain name you like as long as it is not already registered. However, the overall selection of domain names is fast becoming small. A typical English dictionary holds 200,000 words, but there were already more than 11.5 million domain names registered in 2000. A growing number of domain names are not English words, and many are combinations of several words.

Some of the lucky few who were quick to register generic domain names such as www.business.com and www.drugs.com later managed to sell the names for millions of dollars. Yet such names do not make them more recognizable than others. For example, there is nothing in Amazon.com that even hints of what this company sells. (The name comes from the Amazon jungle, implying "huge" or "vast.") *Yahoo* does not imply that the owners of Yahoo.com operate a popular Web portal that was organized around a search engine. What makes these domain names so recognizable is not the name itself but the fact that they were among the very first online businesses in their respective categories. Since they made a tremendous impact and captured a large market share at an early phase of the Web era, their names are associated by millions with the type of business they run, regardless of how strange the name may sound to some ears.

Selecting a domain name is not easy. Daniel Tynen, a journalist for *The Industry Standard,* compares the process to selecting a name for a new baby. The parents want the name to reflect good traits, to sound nice, to reflect some of their wishes or memories, or to honor a tradition or family member. While this is not an easy task, selecting a domain name is much more difficult. On top of selecting the right name, the new business must also select a name that is unique. Imagine if you were not allowed to name your new baby Michael or Jennifer because the name was already taken.

For a long while (in Web terms), businesses adopted domain names that started with an "e," "i," or "my," such as in eBusiness.com, iWon.com, and MyJob.com. Thousands of such domain names exist. Consultants who specialize in the selection of domain names opine that such names are not more recognizable than others. Often, businesses select an exxx.com, an ixxx.com, or a Myxxx.com name simply because the xxx.com name has already been registered by someone else. The next phase included a spate of exotic names with meanings in non–English languages: *Xuma* (Chinese), *Flooz* (Pharsi), *Esus* (Greek), and the like, all with a .com at the end of their domain names. While the names may have something to do with the purpose of the site (*Xuma* is an ancient Chinese battle cry; *Flooz* was a Persian marketplace currency thousands of years ago), it is doubtful that people know or pay attention to the meaning. It is the exotic look or sound of the word that is intended to attract customers. Out of curiosity, some people type in the address and browse the site.

How do e-businesses decide on a domain name? They work through a process that is similar to how businesses adopt company names. Either the founders

CADAVERS IN THE AMAZON

The name that Jeff Bezos first selected for his new Web-based bookstore was kadabra, as in abracadabra. His attorney convinced him that the name reminded English speakers of the word *cadaver*. So instead, Bezos named the business Amazon.com, which is now the Web's most recognizable domain name.

decide on the name by themselves and pay nothing but brain effort, or they go to an expensive consulting firm. Several such firms now specialize (so they claim) in selecting domain names. Landor Associates, The Nuancing Group, and NameLab are such firms. Landor and Nuancing sell branding advice. A *branding consultation* may cost a client up to $100,000. The goal of such a consultation is to select a name that is consistent with brand identity and site structure. Typically, the firms also include in their service domestic and international trademark searches, market research, and linguistic screening to ascertain that a name does not sound or imply something ridiculous or offensive in any language. Ideally, the name that is ultimately suggested also is significantly different from other names, although there is no way to guarantee that someone will not register a similar name later.

Marketing experts argue that, in the final analysis, a brand name on or off the Web is as good as the product or service the business delivers. This is evident from Figure 9.1, which presents the findings of a survey of 3,121 online consumers. Most consumers do not go to any specific site first, regardless of its "recognition." They simply use search engines and type in the name of the product in which they are interested. Thus, if managers of a new Web business select a name they

F I G U R E

9.1 HOW CONSUMERS REACH PRODUCT INFORMATION
Source: Jupiter Media Metrix/NFO Consumer Survey, March 2000

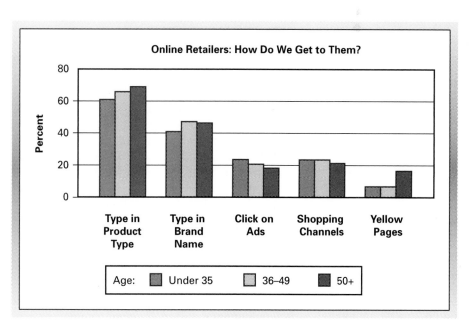

THE GOOD SAMARITAN

Since 1997, Rob Moritz has registered hundreds of domain names containing names of famous people. The devout Christian decided to do so when he was shocked to learn that jerryfalwell.com and woodyallen.com were pornographic sites. Moritz has registered more than 500 domain names, but he does not collect these names to make a personal profit. He has given more than 430 of them to people whose names he registered. In return he asks the recipients to make a donation to his Christian foundation. One recipient was Ralph Nader, the well-known consumer advocate who ran for U.S. president in 2000 and wanted to use ralph-nader.com, which was registered to Moritz.

Source: "Saving domain souls," *The Industry Standard*, October 2, 2000, p. 41

believe will be good advertisement, they may want to note what Mickey Belch, a marketing professor, says: Nothing will kill a poor product faster than good advertisement. While an attractive domain name may help, it is the quality of what you deliver that will make the difference between failure and success.

APPEALING WEB SITE DESIGN

For a business to market products through a Web site, the site must be appealing. Wise use of organization and color plays an important role in design. This section gives some examples of the importance of these elements.

PAGE ORGANIZATION

One of the primary concerns in Web page design is determining where on the page users should go first. Designers need to know the psychology of users. For example, a study by Stanford University and the Poynter Institute found that people read news online differently from how they read news from print media. While newspaper readers direct their eyes first toward visual elements on a page, such as photographs, online consumers of news first view headlines and news briefs. Pictures are not the entry points for people who read news on the Web: 50 percent of the study participants looked at text first. Although 64 percent eventually viewed photos, only 29 percent were attracted to the photos as the first element on the pages. It was also found that the participants viewed 45 percent of the banner ads. The study was conducted with participants who wore special lightweight headsets that recorded their eye movement and the amount of time the eyes paused on each page element.

The results of studies like this are building the case for informed Web design; this information should be taken into consideration when choosing which elements to include in Web pages and where to position them. For example, if the site provides news and sports statistics and generates its revenue from advertising, it should avoid pictures on its homepage, except for small logos or graphics.

Interestingly, online retailers must have noticed that people read before they view pictures, because many announce special sales the same way online news sites list headlines. The news is presented with a headline and the first few lines of the news, while the link to more information is marked "read more." In the case of retailers a "headline" first appears announcing the name of the item (or type of item) offered on a special sale (usually at a significant discount), and a link to more information follows. The page with full information also includes a large picture of the item. Some sites include a feature that allows users to visually rotate an item in 3-D. We discussed this technology in Chapter 4.

COLOR

Color is another important element of Web page design. On a page, color must be appealing either to the general public or to the demographic group that the site tries to attract. For example, the favorite color of 13-to-18-year-olds in the United States is slimy green. Why? They grew up with this color watching the television shows on the Nickelodeon cable channel—a green slimy substance is a staple in almost every broadcast of this channel. If you design a Web site for this group, you may attract more of these people by using this color. However, what single color is the most appealing to the general public? Many studies have found out that blue is the most popular color. Indeed, much blue appears in backgrounds and pictures on many commercial sites. Professional advice about Web page colors can be found online at sites such as www.pantone.com.

A simple rule to follow in using color is this: Use bright colors to attract visitors to a site, and use cooler colors to make visitors comfortable at the site. Yellow and red are considered bright colors. Our eyes are strained when we view these colors; we tend to look at anything that is yellow or red first, before we examine other colors, before our eyes get too tired. (This is the reason that most road signs are yellow or red.) Blue and green are easier on our eyes, and therefore we prefer these colors when we need to look at something for a long period of time.

Knowledgeable Web page designers have used these color principles. Many buttons and banners that intend to attract you to a Web site are yellow or red. One such button is Adobe's "Get Acrobat" button, which you might have seen at sites that offer downloadable PDF (Portable Document Format) documents (see Figure 9.2). Notice also the yellow text and other areas of the homepages of online retailers. Often, the items to which the retailers want you to go first are yellow. Other sections of a site appear in cooler colors so that visitors can read and browse in a comfortable visual context, one without eyestrain.

While aesthetics are a matter of taste, the basic principles of Web site design are similar to those that underlie all professional graphic design. Good Web design is supported by what research has discovered about people's choices when it comes to organization, color, font types, and other elements that attract users to a site and may make them stay there. We have discussed some of the important elements in Chapter 5.

FIGURE

9.2 YELLOW AND RED DRAW ATTENTION MORE THAN OTHER COLORS

PIZZAZZ

In the physical world, we may or may not be attracted to stores by bright lighting, splashy signage, or moving toys that draw our attention and make us want to at least "check it out," if not stay there longer. Similarly, Web sites can attempt to attract and even retain visitors by adding *pizzazz:* small interactive programs such as crossword puzzles, trivia, and eye-popping animations, or more serious attractions such as prize-bearing competitions. However, similar to the brick-and-mortar world, it is largely advisable not to confuse customers with too much of this material.

To gain repeated visits, experts advise that sites offer "a little something" for free. For example, the words *Free Downloads* can attract many people. We like to receive something for nothing. If a site sells software, such offers are natural, but even if a site has nothing to do with software, there is always some application that it can give away, such as an attractive screen saver or a computer game.

Because visitors can get tired of sites that look the same for a long time, many Web businesses change their site's appearance every few months or even every few weeks. Sometimes the change is the result of improved features, but often the change only sends a signal: "We are alive, and there is something new here." When changing the appearance of a site, the designer should be careful not to change the fundamental organization of its menus so as to not confuse frequent visitors.

THINK WEB, NOT STORE

We often refer to a Web site as an "online store," a fine figure of speech, a misleading one if implemented literally. Companies established specifically for operation on the Web usually design their sites with all the features that the Web offers in mind. These companies, called pure play companies by experts (for their "pure" Web operations, as mentioned in Chapter 8), are usually not biased by their previous history—they do not have any. On the other hand, companies that extend their operations to the Web often make the mistake of importing ideas from brick-and-mortar operations. Retailers in particular regularly commit this "sin." Some retailers that have done remarkably well with information technology in general have not been able to capitalize on the Web's full potential. We discuss why below.

TRADITION, TRADITION

Wal-Mart, the world's largest retailer, is an example of a firm that had some difficulty making a marketing transition from brick-and-mortar operations to the Web. Philip Evans and Thomas Wurster of the Boston Consulting Group cite the site's "store map" (Figure 9.3) as an image that tells about the online strategy of brick-and-mortar retailers that almost literally carry their floor plans and philosophies to the Web. Note that the company has changed the original design of its site.

If you go to any pure play online retailer, such as Amazon.com, Buy.com, and many others, you will not see any store map because they have no need for one. Figure 9.4 (page 186) provides an example. The homepages of all these sites include category tabs across the top and down on the left side, and a facility for a keyword search below the category tabs. Keyword searches are probably the most useful tool for anyone who shops at an online retailer, because customers know either the exact name or the type of product for which they are looking. If they want information about a category of items, they can enter the category into the search tool and receive more information on a larger range of related items. Categories are organized on one

9.3 THE "STORE MAP" OF WAL-MART'S ORIGINAL WEB SITE

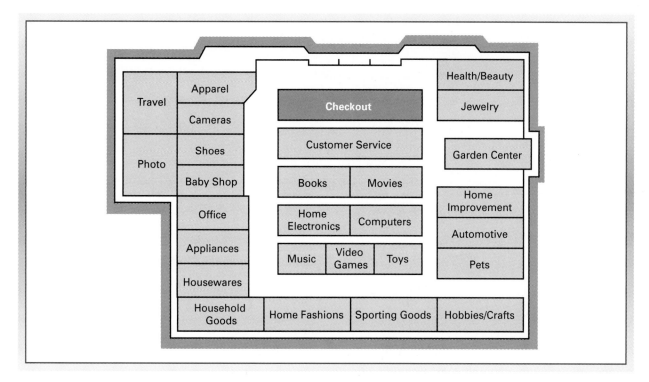

side. The homepage features only a few, small pictures; limited screen space is reserved for short textual links, which are more useful to a potentially time-pressed shopper than large, slow-downloading pictures augmented with bright colors. This type of design is a more efficient use of the Web site. The layout of tabs on the top and categories on the side has practically become the standard followed by many pure play as well as brick-and-mortar sites.

Brick-and-mortar retailers often limit their selections to those offered before they went online. However, once a retailer goes online, the possibilities change; there is no reason to limit the number of items offered because there are no physical stores in which space is limited.

CHOICE AND CONTROL

With the amount of choices online stores offer, it makes sense that they provide more than a single way to navigate and traverse the site rather than a rigid hierarchy of links. Experts also recommend that online stores offer more information than atmosphere—and hence more text than pictures and colors, as explained previously. Menus should take several forms: vertical, horizontal, and layered. Each page should offer quite a few links to other pages.

Experts also observe that pure play sites attract shoppers more than other sites, thanks to higher *interactivity*. Pure play sites often include chat rooms, consumer reviews, product ratings, and other features of "commercial democracy" in which consumers can voice their opinions. Few of the large brick-and-mortar retailers allow consumers to post their opinions on products.

FIGURE

9.4 ONLINE RETAIL STANDARDS
(OUTPOST.COM AND
AMAZON.COM): TABS, SEARCH
TOOLS, AND CATEGORIES

Interactive features put some control in the hands of consumers. You may go to the site of Buy.com and read some negative reviews of products the site sells. Managers of Buy.com and Amazon.com are not afraid of posting low ratings of a product; they probably embrace this as a learning process that leads to good decisions about which products to discontinue. Consultants Evans and Wurster applaud the help pure play retailers extend customers in making choices and expressing themselves. They refer to this seller-buyer relationship as *symmetry of information* whereby dialog, community, and transparency take the place of the old one-to-many asymmetries of traditional media.

THE IMPORTANCE OF MENUS

When designing menus, the use of color and interesting bullet shapes are important, but the order of the items is significantly more important. Menus should take advantage of the way we tend to examine new information in print or on screen. Most people examine a new book this way: They quickly look at the first few pages, then they look at the last few pages, and then they look inside the book or read it from start to end. Readers look at lists in a similar manner, and menus are indeed lists.

Consider the FedEx site. The homepage simply lists languages in which you can interact with the company. Once you select a language, the Web page shown in the top part of Figure 9.5 (page 188) appears. Menus in languages that are read left-to-right are often located on the left side because readers' eyes turn to that side of the page first. About 80 percent of the people logging on to the site are customers who want to track their shipment. Yet, the tracking option is not located on the left side. The company wants you to open an account (Open an Account) and order supplies (Order Supplies Online). Items that are less important to the company's business are located neither at the top nor at the bottom of lists. The least important items are not located on the left side at all (News). If you are already a customer and want to track your shipment, the assumption is that you already know where the tracking option is. The tracking window is not located on the left, but is outstanding sufficiently for existing customers' convenience. These rules of menu item location are even more important if the list is long.

The bottom part of Figure 9.5 shows the menu that appears on the homepage of First National Bank of Chester County. The great majority of visitors to the site use only one item: Online Banking Log-in. One might expect this item to appear more prominently, either in a larger font or in a different color. Yet it is just another item among others, and it appears on the right side of the page. Again, it is visitors who are not familiar with the bank's services who are "courted" by the homepage. The bank already has as customers those who click the most-used item, and they know where to find it.

Note that the FedEx menu is clearly divided into several distinct lists: Services listed at the top are those that are most important in engaging new customers and helping existing ones; next come the informational services; and lower come the services in the "other" category, such as employment opportunities. The bank's menu is divided into groups in a similar manner.

CULTURAL DIFFERENCES

In China, a local Web site was ignored by consumers because of its inappropriate use of gold and red colors. Historically, colors have had significant connotations in

© First National Bank of Chester County. Reprinted by permission.

China. Traditionally, red and gold could be used for painting houses and to dye clothes only by the nobility. Peasants and other members of the so-called lower classes used green and blue. Red and gold colors now connote prosperity, which, apparently, had little to do with what the site was trying to communicate.

This is just one of many examples of what may happen when cultural differences are not considered in building and operating Web sites. A **culture** is the aggregate of perceptions, gestures, and daily priorities of a demographic group. Often, the demographic group is a nation. Nations differ in how they use colors for different occasions, the hand and face gestures they use, the forms of payment they prefer, the foods they eat, and the manners they employ, along with many other behaviors too numerous to mention. In dealing with people from another culture we must learn about the culture both to communicate meaningfully and to avoid embarrassment. In the case of commercial activities, misunderstanding may cause loss of great business potential.

E-commerce organizations, especially in the B2C arena, face a challenge. On the one hand, they want to be global companies, with shared visions and mode of operation; on the other hand, they must be attuned to the culture of each world region that they target. This is why executives in some of these companies use the term **glocalization**, a combination of globalization and localization. The challenge in glocalization is to organize a Web site as a global portal for business that also reflects sensitivity to local cultures. Some companies that have not been able to meet this challenge with a single Web site have decided to operate several, parallel Web sites.

WATCH YOUR LANGUAGE

Some firms specialize in helping companies globalize their sites. One of them is Uniscape, Inc., of Redwood Shores, California. The company makes sure that Web pages are translated correctly and use appropriate currencies and characters. Client companies submit their under-development Web pages, and Uniscape sends them to a network of translators in many countries who translate the material into 42 languages. The company warns clients about unintentional cultural blunders. An image, gesture, or reference that may be innocent in one culture may be offensive in another.

Preference of language and "kinship" are also important when an international site tries to sell online in local markets. For example, 75 percent of consumers in China and Korea prefer to frequent sites that communicate in their native language. The same proportion of consumers also prefer to purchase from sites of local merchants in spite of the smaller selection of goods and services. Preference of local businesses to a national or global business is a reflection of kinship. Sensitivity to national identity is high in some regions of the world. For this reason America Online does not spell out its name outside the United States; it is simply AOL.

THE LITTLE THINGS THAT MATTER

Attention to simple but often ignored details may save embarrassment and ensure effective communication with users in various countries. For example, many U.S. sites do not allow online submittal of forms from users who do not fill in fields for U.S. postal zip codes and telephone area codes. These companies lose many international consumers. Another example of this problem happens with names. People in some countries have only one name rather than two. Most U.S. and European sites do not accept forms unless the user provides a first name and a last name.

Many U.S. companies assume that all citizens of the world prefer to pay the way their citizens do. This is a grave mistake. Relative to population size, Americans hold more credit cards than any other nation. They are more willing to use their credit cards when making online purchases than people of any other country. Japanese people, for instance, prefer to pay cash. How can you sell online to people who prefer to pay cash or by check? Sony found a way to sell online to Japanese consumers. They can shop and order online. The company ships the product to a store close to the buyer's residence, where the buyer pays for and picks up the item. How many U.S. companies would think of this simple solution?

Strategize	Develop a strategy before you develop a site, or multiple sites, for an international audience.
Translate properly	Use local interpreters to translate content for local audiences. Trust only the human touch. Do not use software or other automated methods, unless humans review the translated material. Professional translators are attentive to contemporary nuances and connotations.
Know the audience	Understand cultural preferences, convention differences, and legal issues. Tailor the local site to how the local people prefer to do business.
Be egalitarian	Plan a process for keeping all your sites (or national sections of a site) in sync with each other so you do not offend any audience. Do not let any audience feel second class because the content addressing this audience is not as good as that for others or because it is not updated.
Avoid cultural imperialism	If a local language or culture has a word or picture for communicating an idea, use it; do not use those of your own country.

LOCALIZE

Companies that wish to cater to local users must localize their sites. Figure 9.6 lists the five important points to follow when localizing sites.

LetsBuyIt.com is a good example of how each national audience can feel "at home" just one click past the homepage. Figure 9.7 shows sub-homepages for three of the site's 16 sections that cater to multiple nations and people who speak different languages and dialects. The three examples cater to people in the United Kingdom and other English-speaking countries (top), Finland (middle), and Italy (bottom). Notice how similar in format and content they are. The company makes every effort to keep all 16 sections "in sync." No audience is made to feel inferior to other audiences, and the English section, which probably serves many more customers due to the internationality of the language, does not include any element that the other sections do not.

AFFILIATE MARKETING

Because it is so easy to link various Web sites, firms can use a marketing tool that is unique to the Web: affiliate programs, which are among the most effective marketing methods on the Internet. In an **affiliate program**, a Web site includes on its pages advertising banners and icons that link to another merchant's Web site. When consumers "click through" to the other merchant and purchase something, the hosting firm, also called *affiliate*, receives a commission for the purchase (see Figure 9.8, page 192). The commission is based on a predetermined scheme, such as a percentage of the purchase's total sum of money. Usually, merchants offer a different percentage for each category of items. Typical commissions range from 2 percent to 20 percent; usually, the higher the profit margin of a category, the higher the commission rate. The commission is often called **referral fee**.

FIGURE

9.8 HOW AFFILIATE
PROGRAMS WORK

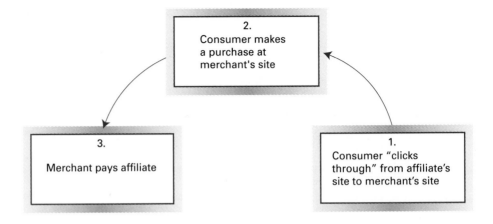

In addition to referral fees on sales, merchants occasionally offer referral fees for new customers. The commission scheme determines how many dollars are paid to the affiliate for each new customer who clicked through to the merchant's site and made a first purchase there. Usually, the affiliate receives a certain sum for the first one thousand new referrals, a larger sum for so many thousands more new customers, and so on. Obviously, an affiliate can collect a commission for each new customer referral only once. Merchants credit their affiliates' accounts and pay them on a periodic basis—when the commission reaches a certain amount, or every month when the commission due reaches a certain minimum (such as every month when the commission is at least $25). The specific affiliate program scheme depends on the type of site as well as the nature of the merchandise.

Several firms provide affiliate program services. Among them are LinkShare Corporation (at *www.linkshare.com*) and Commission Junction (at *www.cj.com*). They provide online forms for firms to register as affiliates and help for new affiliates in entering into agreements with merchants. Merchants provide their own icons to be posted at the affiliate's site and the software associated with the icons.

There are several models of affiliate programs. The following schemes are the most prevalent.

PAY-PER-SALE MODEL

In the *pay-per-sale* model, the merchant pays the affiliate a percentage of the actual sale value when a consumer makes a purchase immediately after he or she has clicked through to the merchant's site. Some merchants pay the commission if the customer makes a purchase within a longer period of time. For example, Internet News Bureau pays a 10 percent commission on purchases that a customer makes within 90 days after the initial visit to its site from the affiliate's site. This pay-per-sale model offers the largest commissions.

According to some surveys, about 15 percent of the revenues of online merchants in 2000 came from consumers who clicked through from affiliate sites. Among the sites that offer such affiliate programs are Amazon.com and Buy.com, but there are many others. It is difficult to find any online retailer that does not offer an affiliate program. Organizations that sell high-priced items, such as research services, offer commissions of several thousand dollars per referred customer. For example, Forrester Research offers affiliate sites $10,000 for each customer who purchased the firm's basic research package. Figure 9.9 displays Amazon.com's page inviting operators of other sites to join the firm's referrals program.

PAY-PER-CLICK MODEL

Many sites do not sell anything; they provide content free of charge and make money only by advertising. Because businesses prefer to advertise at high-traffic sites, these firms want to show that many people click through to their site. They pay affiliates for the sheer number of click-throughs in this *pay-per-click* model. For example, AOL runs the Digital City program, in which it provides data to local audiences through multiple sites. It is striving to drive traffic to these sites so that the exposure value for potential advertisers at the sites increases. If you are willing to post a link to the sites, you will receive three cents for each visitor click-through from your site.

F I G U R E

9.9 AN INVITATION TO SERVE AS A REFERRAL SITE

PAY-PER-LEAD MODEL

Some firms pay affiliates for referring qualified leads in a *pay-per-lead* model. What qualifies a lead depends on the merchant's definition. Usually, a lead qualifies for a commission if the consumer who clicked through filled out and submitted a registration form or an agreement to receive periodic information, such as a newsletter or e-mailed promotional messages.

HYBRID PROGRAMS

A *hybrid program* is one in which the merchant pays affiliates for more than one element of the referral. For example, Amazon.com sometimes pays for referrals of new customers in addition to paying commissions on sales. That is, when a new customer makes a purchase after clicking an affiliate's link, the affiliate receives a commission on the sale as well as a commission for the referral. The first commission is based on the amount that *all* referred customers spend; the second commission is based on the number of *new* customers who are referred.

MULTITIERED PROGRAMS

What happens when an affiliate recruits other affiliates? This situation is a *multitiered* arrangement, which is similar to a multilevel marketing plan: Affiliates at all levels of the arrangement receive a portion of the commission paid by the merchant. The recruited affiliate is referred to as a *subaffiliate*. Typically, when two levels are involved the subaffiliate receives four fifths of the commission and the affiliate receives one fifth.

CROSS-LINKING AND CROSS-LURING

The Web provides opportunities to advertise in ways that are not possible in any other media. Two such methods are simple and effective: cross-linking and, for lack of a better term, cross-luring. In **cross-linking**, two firms agree to place each other's clickable icon or banner. Often, no money changes hands in such deals. Obviously, you will not see cross-linking between competitors. Usually, it happens between two businesses that sell related products or services. Often, the items offered are complementary.

The wise move is to cross-link among Web sites that have something in common: a demographic (e.g., age or gender), related interests (e.g., nature conservation and hiking gear), or vertical goods or services (e.g., real estate, home financing, and the moving industry). This is a win-win relationship. However, there is a risk in cross-linking: You may be so successful in sending your visitor to a linked Web site that the visitor does not come back to your own site.

While cross-linking is collaborative, **cross-luring** is competitive; one site is trying to gain business at the expense of another. You might have noticed the practice when you last looked on the back of a supermarket sales slip. You purchased a bar of soap of a certain brand, but on the back of the slip you find a coupon printed for soap of a competing brand. The competitor pays the supermarket chain to print its coupon whenever an item of a competing brand is rung up at the cash register.

A similar "trick" can be executed when people use a search engine on the Web. A Web business can contract with a search engine operator to produce the following effect: An online consumer types in the name of a company. A list of Web sites appears. The first on the list is not the desired company's URL but that of the competitor. If the consumer looked for the original site not because he or she is interested in the site itself but in its products or similar products, it is likely the consumer will click the first site that appears on the list. This is all that the competitor wants: to lure shoppers to its site. Whether this practice is ethical depends on one's own set of values, but the practice is perfectly legal.

The same effect can be produced with the use of online shopping tracking bars such as "dash." You can download the software and configure it to work whenever you use a Web browser. A narrow window opens on the bottom of your browser window that is linked to a special server that constantly collects information about your purchases. Your incentive to employ the software is the discounts you receive from the retailer through the dash company. However, the company promotes only the companies with which it has contracts. So, for example, when dash is up and you link to *www.staples.com*, a message appears in the dash window: "Dash saves you 4 percent when you shop at OfficeMax.com instead."

HOW NOT TO ANNOY THE CUSTOMER

In its February 7, 2000, issue, *Business Week* published a list of 10 things that irked holiday online shoppers. The list—shown in Figure 9.10—is ordered from the least irritating to the most irritating. The ranking was based on a survey conducted by the management consulting firm Andersen Consulting. It does not take a genius to see that some of these problems could be rather easily fixed.

Bear in mind that some complaints are limited to a customer's interaction with a Web site and how it was designed to serve customers, while other complaints relate more to the full scope of a business's decision making. The interesting point may be that customers do not often *care* what aspect of a business produced an annoyance or failure—he or she just wants the job done well. This is another version of the classic maxim "The customer is always right" that traditional marketing embodies. Let us analyze the complaints and see what the site operators could do about each complaint.

Number 10: If a site does not carry a wide variety of items, or does not have agreements with suppliers who can ship a wide variety of items, it simply cannot offer many items. This is a business decision that is dependent on an e-commerce model but has little to do with the site's design.

Number 9: Price-setting is a business decision that has nothing to do with the fact that a business sells through a Web site.

FIGURE

9.10 TYPICAL CONSUMER COMPLAINTS

10	Site didn't offer enough gift ideas
9	Prices weren't competitive
8	Site didn't provide enough information
7	Site was hard to navigate
6	Selections were limited
5	Didn't get a confirmation or status report
4	Connection trouble
3	Paid too much for delivery
2	Item wasn't delivered on time
1	Product was out of stock

Source: Andersen Consulting, in *Business Week,* February 7, 2000

Number 8: Not providing enough information is a real sin on the Web. It would take relatively little time to provide product descriptions, specifications, and other information, such as customer reviews of products. Product information can be recorded directly from manufacturers' files, and customer reviews and other feedback can be collected from input entered by customers who had made purchases. There is ready-to-use software that can capture such information and post it at a site.

Number 7: Navigation must be well planned and tested before Web pages are posted. One of the best ways to ensure easy navigation is to ask representatives of different demographic groups to navigate the site and provide feedback before the pages are posted.

Number 6: A limited selection is closely related to Number 10, not enough gift ideas at holiday time. Scope of product selection is a business decision independent of the fact that a business uses a Web site.

Number 5: Confirmation of order receipt can be generated automatically, immediately after the order is recorded in the order database. Only credit card information may involve human intervention. Customers of all businesses expect order and credit card confirmation.

Number 4: Connection trouble is something that is largely out of a business's control. The business can ensure that its own servers are fast and that there are enough servers with the capacity to serve a large number of consumers at peak times; however, connection problems may also be related to difficulties at the consumer end and to network congestion.

Number 3: Prices of products and of shipping are pure business decisions. However, some online retailers believe that they can lure customers by offering a product at a low cost while charging a relatively high shipping rate. The practice rarely works.

Number 2: Delivery, much like prices, has little to do with the fact that a business operates on the Web. Web businesses, however, have learned that they must be careful about making delivery promises in high-volume times and must work closely with their suppliers and delivery service providers.

Number 1: Apparently, many sites have not been ready for peak times such as a holiday season. How much stock to maintain is a business decision. However, Web businesses should be courteous and inform shoppers about items that are out of stock. If an item is out of stock, reliable information must be posted that tells the shopper when the item is expected to be available. Then, the shopper can decide whether to purchase the item and receive it late, or to look for it elsewhere.

Professor Gerry Lohse of the Wharton School of Business found three major factors that cause consumers who had made purchases on the Web to stop the practice. In ascending order of concern, they are:

1. Too much spam (unwanted e-mail) following online purchases.
2. A low level of trust when it comes to online retailers.
3. A high level of concern about third-party monitoring. Although not all consumers know about cookies, they know that information is captured about every move they make on the Web, and that bothers them.

E-retailers can solve all three problems. First, they can give consumers more control. Consumers can decide whether or not to receive e-mail if e-retailers provide the *opt-in* rather than *opt-out* approach.

The low level of trust will take longer to solve. This problem can be solved by providing excellent service: prompt shipping of goods and services ordered online, prompt response to customer inquiries, a generous return policy, and a general approach of continuously listening to customer complaints and suggestions and of learning from mistakes.

The third concern can be resolved much like the first one, by adopting an opt-in policy. Consumers must be assured that no information will be collected about them as long as they are at the site, unless they so choose. Consumers may choose to allow full or partial collection of information about their shopping behavior if they receive something in return.

One reason for consumer frustration stems from poor technology or a lack of clarity of how to use a Web site. In 1999, the Boston Consulting Group conducted a survey of 12,000 consumers in the United States and Canada. The typical online purchaser completed 10 transactions and spent $460 online over the preceding 12 months. The researchers found that 28 percent of attempted online purchases failed. First-time online purchasers approach the act with great concern. Twenty-eight percent of those who experienced a failed attempt stopped shopping online. Twenty-three percent stopped purchasing only at the site that disappointed them. Apparently, frustration with a site may result in further damage; 6 percent of disappointed shoppers stopped shopping at the brick-and-mortar stores of the firm.

Consumers who had a satisfying initial experience were likely to spend more time and money online. On average, satisfied customers made 12 online transactions and spent $500 during the 12-month period; disappointed customers made only four purchases totaling $140.

CONSUMER PROFILING

An advertisement by a firm that specializes in online consumer profiling consists of two pictures: One shows the incomplete mosaic of a young woman, presented in the style of ancient Rome; the other shows a complete mosaic of the same woman. Knowing more about consumers has always been a major desire of all commercial enterprises. Wanting to know more about online consumers is no different. Finding out can be accomplished by capturing a person's "electronic footsteps" on the Web.

Consumer profiling is the process of building dossiers about consumers with the goal of targeting the consumers who are most likely to purchase what a firm offers and tailoring marketing to the tastes and shopping habits of individual

INTERESTING . . .

ANYTHING ELSE, SIR?

Web technology has created interesting marketing opportunities—from the marketer's perspective, at least. ATMs, those famous machines in the wall from which we squeeze cash, can become a major marketing channel. Having a profile of every customer visiting an ATM, a bank can display personalized advertisements and offers for services likely to be of interest to the customer. High-speed Internet connections will enable the customer to actually order the advertised services and pay for them through the ATM.

Source: Acey, M., "Common Web code could save banks money," *TechWeb,* January 24, 2000

shoppers. In the process, companies build massive databases containing personal data that indicate demographic membership, shopping habits, payment habits, and other types of behavior. E-commerce provides great opportunities for consumer profiling because entire shopping, buying, and payment activities can be electronically recorded and are immediately available for analysis.

While some large companies conduct their own data collection, many firms prefer to use the services of companies that specialize in consumer profiling. Many of the banner ads displayed on Web pages are not selected and delivered by the proprietors of the Web site but by companies that manage and provide advertising for numerous unrelated Web sites. The major player in the industry of Web-based data collection and profiling is DoubleClick, Inc. Other companies include Net Perceptions, Inc.; Alexa (a subsidiary of Amazon.com); CoreMetrics, Inc.; Engage, Inc.; Personify, Inc.; and Predictive Networks. These companies do not merely supply banner ads; they also gather data about the consumers who view their ads.

Like other such companies, DoubleClick asserts that the company "collects non-personally identifiable information about you, such as the server your computer is logged onto, your browser type (for example, Netscape or Internet Explorer), and whether you responded to the ad delivered." Although the information gathered by network advertisers is often anonymous (i.e., the profiles are linked to the identification number of the advertising network's cookie on the consumer's computer rather than the name of a specific person), in some cases, the profiles derived from tracking consumers' activities on the Web are linked or merged with personally identifiable information. Some experts estimate that DoubleClick has collected data on more than 100 million consumers.

Data collection and profiling firms collect at least the following data: your IP number, from which the firm infers your geographic location, company, and type and size of the organization whose server you use; your top-level domain, such as .com, .net, and .edu, from which it can infer, for instance, whether you are a member of a commercial business or an academic institution; your browser version, operating system, and Internet service provider (e.g., AOL or MindSpring); and data reflecting how you use the pages you visit within the site of the firm's client (e.g., which pages you viewed, for how long you viewed each page, and which buttons on the page you clicked). Privacy advocates claim that DoubleClick and its competitors also use personally identifiable information.

Some companies give consumers a degree of control over their profile. One such company is eCustomers.com. The firm maintains clusters of consumer profiles that are updated with data collected from visits to any site that subscribes to eCustomer.com. When a Web user first visits any of these sites, a consumer profile is established and records any demographic and lifestyle data provided by the customer or collected through mouse click streams. The data are not personally identifiable. Site behavior during each visit is added to the profile. All businesses using eCustomers.com have access to the updated profiles. Customers are allowed to log on to eCustomers.com and edit their profiles.

Unlike those who practice covert data collection, some companies invite consumers to willingly provide their profiles and agree to be monitored. We have already mentioned dash, which tracks your shopping and purchases whenever the dash window is open while you use a Web browser. Similarly, AllAdvantage pays registered users 50 cents per hour to run highly targeted ads at the bottom of their screens. AllAdvantage's revenue comes from the companies whose ads the company places. AllAdvantage also runs a program called MyPoints, which awards points that participants can use to pay for purchases. The firm has persuaded about 6 million customers to accept targeted ads in return for points that they can use to bid on prizes auctioned by affiliated online businesses. WinWin.com, a company with a similar scheme, collects personal data from registered users, who are paid for their registration forms and for clicking ad banners. Dash, AllAdvantage, and WinWin collect information on users' viewing and clicking habits, interests, and responses to ads and use the aggregated data to sell more ads.

TARGETED ADVERTISING

In the early years of the Web, there were no tools to gauge which consumers purchased what and what was driving them to purchase certain items at certain sites. Almost all firms used the unsophisticated "spray and pray" method: Place as many advertisement banners as you can and hope that consumers will flock to your Web site. Now, many companies provide survey findings that can help target the audiences most likely to visit a business's site and make purchases.

Consumer profiling is one way to obtain information for targeted advertising. Another way is the use of statistics, available free or from research companies. While consumer profiling often involves the use of personally identifiable data, the use of statistics does not and therefore does not evoke complaints about violation of privacy.

Using statistics is a major key to succeeding in target marketing in general and on the Web in particular. Statistics are compiled from directed questions a marketer asks a sample of people. The primary questions that a target marketer should find answers for are: Who is most likely to purchase my products? What is the most effective way to attract this audience? Which sites attract these audiences so that I can place links there and bring customers to my site?

READING THE NUMBERS

Marketing experts do not have to spend money on every bit of information they need for their analyses. Much useful information is available to the public from multiple sources, online and offline. All researchers need to do to access this information is to scour the media for survey reports from consulting and research firms such as the Gartner Group, Jupiter Research, the Boston Group, Forrester Research, and many others. An example of such survey results is given in Figure 9.11. The survey was published in February 2000 by Forrester Research. It reveals that men and women differ in their activities on the Web. E-commerce marketing managers would find such information useful.

The results of another key survey could help all online retailers fine-tune their marketing efforts. These findings were reported in May 2000 by many online news

FIGURE

9.11 MEN'S AND WOMEN'S USE OF THE WEB

Online Activity	Men (%)	Women (%)
Purchase online	50	40
Read daily newspaper	35	30
Read product or entertainment reviews	25	18
Visit adult entertainment sites	22	6
Play online games	19	23
Visit family sites	13	18

Source: Business Week, February 7, 2000, p. 114 (Data: Forrester Research)

outlets that focus on e-commerce. The survey found that in 1999 only 13 percent of people who had been online for less than six months had purchased online. Twenty-four percent of people who started surfing the Internet in 2000 had bought something in the past three months. A very useful finding for marketers turned out to be the fact that the average online shopper is not a young, technically savvy male, as previously supposed. The majority of online shopping is done by baby boomers aged 35 to 54, with an average age of 42. Fifty-five percent of shoppers were male, and, according to the survey, gender differences were shifting at a rapid rate. Another survey later in 2000 revealed that as of June 2000 a greater number of women surfed the Web than men, and the amount of dollars spent by women on the Web was growing faster than the amount spent by men.

For several years, online retailers held onto an incorrect picture of who shops online: young men from affluent households. The survey found a different picture: There is no difference between spending patterns offline and online. The people who are spending most of the money online are the same people who are spending most of the money offline: middle-class people in their thirties and forties. Or, as one analyst said, "Middle America is driving e-commerce, not some digital elite." One must keep in mind that the great majority of marketing surveys like these consider only U.S. residents. A smaller number of surveys include Europeans, and a very small number of them also include online shoppers from other world regions. However, judging from the U.S. patterns that other countries have followed when it comes to the Internet, there is little reason to believe that there are vastly different socioeconomic patterns on the Web in non–U.S. populations.

AND MORE DEMOGRAPHICS

A March 2000 Jupiter Research survey revealed that when it comes to finding products and retailers, online shoppers are self-directed and tend to find online stores by going to search engines and typing in product types and brand names. Looking at navigation trends by segment, however, the survey revealed interesting differences among age groups. Younger shoppers were more likely than older shoppers to click on online advertisements to reach retailers. Twenty-six percent of those under 35, compared to only 16 percent of those over 50, click on online advertising. Meanwhile, older shoppers were more likely than younger shoppers to find products by using the Internet Yellow Pages. Thirteen percent of those over the age of 50, compared to only 7 percent of those under 35, use the Internet Yellow Pages. Older shoppers appear to be more focused when searching for retailers and products, whereas younger shoppers appear to be more impulsive and therefore more likely to be swayed by online advertising.

For example, consider these findings by the ratings firm Nielsen/NetRatings for June 2000: In the United States, children in the age group 2 to 11 clicked on Web ads more than any other age group, 0.87 percent. This is considered a high rate. The ad click rate for the entire Web surfing population was 0.45 percent. Youths 12 to 17 years of age clicked at a rate of 0.19, and young adults in the 18 to 20 age group clicked only 0.11 percent of the ads, the lowest of any age group. (Nielsen/NetRatings used a sample of 65,000 people in the United States.) This and similar studies report on specific online ad campaigns that generated the highest click rates in the different age groups. Advertisers can study the elements of such campaigns and emulate or improve upon them for their own products and services.

The economics of target marketing for e-commerce advertisers as well as traditional advertisers are simple. They should ask "How much does it cost me to acquire a customer?" They must also consider the average sums that members of different demographic groups spend online; from there they can focus their advertising dollars in ways that yield the greatest number of purchases.

Advertisers should further realize that the Internet influences purchasing both online and offline. According to a study conducted by Harris Interactive in July 2000 with a sample of 3,878 participants, 69 percent of Web users in the 13 to 24 age group research the availability, quality, and prices of products online before buying them in traditional brick-and-mortar outlets. Such information is especially important for brick-and-mortar businesses that also operate on the Web. Among the items 13- to 24-year-olds are most likely to purchase are clothes, music, books, and video games.

CAREFUL WITH THOSE DEMOGRAPHICS

Note that there is a great difference between catering to demographic groups and devoting entire sites to a demographic group. Experience shows that members of a demographic group such as women or teenagers may be attracted to a "demographic" site for content and advice, but Web users are not likely to shop at a certain site only because it caters to their gender, age group, or ethnic background. For example, iVillage.com was established especially for women. So was Oxygen.com. Both sites still provide content, but they stopped direct online sales that were targeted only to women. Experts have observed that demographically centered sites can still do well if a Web site's look and content cater to a demographic group, but only if the site directs its "demographic" visitors to a section or another site that caters to the general public.

For instance, MsMoney.com caters to women. The writers of its articles are women, the advisers are women, and all the pictures at the site show women. However, when you click the "Find a Car" icon, you are taken to the site of CarsDirect.com, which serves the general public. The same principle applies to other marketing efforts at the site. Visitors click through to other sites. MsMoney.com generates income from advertising and affiliate referrals.

WHERE TO ADVERTISE?

The Pew Internet and American Life Project published research findings in May 2000. The researchers interviewed 3,500 Americans by phone. The findings can help online merchants place ads efficiently on different Internet media and Web sites. Efficiency in this context means receiving the attention of the largest target audience possible for a given advertising expenditure. Apparently, people under 30, both male and female, like to use instant messaging services such as those provided by AOL Instant Messenger, ICQ, and Quick Dot. Similarly, young people flock to sites from which they can download music files. It is not hard to conclude that such services and sites may be just the right places for advertisers to reach young people.

If businesses are looking especially for the attention of men, they probably should advertise at sites that publish sports information. Three times as many men as women check sports scores online. If women are the target audience, businesses should advertise at health-oriented sites; twice as many women as men look for health information online.

Where should businesses advertise for the general public? Sites, or pages of sites, that report weather conditions may be a good choice. Pew researchers found that on a typical day online, many more people check the weather (16 percent) than buy a product (4 percent), participate in an auction (3 percent), make travel reservations (1 percent), or gamble (1 percent). Another efficient ad placement would be at government sites, if possible. Forty-eight percent of the surveyed people have looked for information at a government site.

E-MAIL MARKETING

So far we have devoted our discussion to how Web sites are used for marketing. The simpler cousin of Web marketing is marketing by e-mail: Advertising a business's goods and services by sending e-mail messages to prospective customers. E-mail marketing is one of the least expensive methods of marketing. If the organization already has lists of e-mail addresses, the cost comes down to the time it takes to type, organize, and send the messages. If the firm must purchase a list, the cost is usually 10 to 30 cents per address. Since the business already pays for Internet service, there is no additional cost.

However, before managers decide to use this method, they must understand that many recipients consider unsolicited e-mail rude and delete it readily. Most of us are familiar with the term for unsolicited e-mail—**spam**. Several states in the United States and some other countries have passed laws forbidding such communication, for reasons similar to those leading to forbidding unsolicited commercial fax communication. Recipients pay for spam with their own time in sifting through unwanted messages and by the use of disk space and server time. It is highly recommended that if you are in a position to make a decision for your organization, do not engage it in spamming because of the public resentment and possible violation of local laws. Remember that spam is spam, even if recipients are offered an opt-out option. With an opt-out option they can make the message the last one they will receive from you, but they must go through several operations such as accessing a certain Web site and clicking an opt-out icon or replying with a message bearing a certain subject or content (usually: "Unsubscribe").

A legitimate alternative to opt-out e-mail is opt-in e-mail. **Opt-in e-mail** is sent only to people who have expressed their consent to receiving commercial messages before the first message was sent to them. You can create opt-in lists by offering site visitors the option to receive messages about special offers and useful information. You may convince more people to consent if in addition to the advertisement you offer them noncommercial content. It is courteous to add a line on the bottom of each message reminding the recipient that he or she opted to receive the messages. Obviously, you should always add information on how to unsubscribe and ensure that the process of unsubscribing is convenient and takes only one easy step.

Another way to contact opt-in subscribers is to purchase e-mail lists. Organizations can purchase e-mail address lists from several firms that specialize in collecting, organizing, and maintaining such lists. Among these firms are PostMasterDirect.com, E-Target.com, and Bulletmail. PostMasterDirect.com offers more than 9,000 e-mail lists containing the e-mail addresses of more than three million people. These organizations obtain e-mail addresses from information provided by visitors to partner sites. Usually, the sites that provide the opt-in addresses enjoy high traffic. For example, PostMasterDirect.com has partnered with CNET, ICQ, Internet.com, and CBS Sportsline. It charges 10 to 30 cents per address, and the minimum charge is $1,000.

While e-mail marketing is inexpensive and may reach millions of people, the response rate of this method is low. In other words, it leads very few people to buy the companies' products and services. However, if the ad is well targeted, the rate is usually higher than that of regular direct mail promotions. Traditional direct mail promotions yield a 1 percent to 2 percent rate, while e-ad campaigns have yielded response rates of 10 percent to 35 percent. One must be careful about the term *response rate*. In e-mail advertising campaigns it often means simply the number of recipients who clicked through to a featured Web site or who forwarded the message to friends.

E-mail advertising has one feature that other forms of advertisements lack: It can be easily forwarded to friends. In addition, advertisers can also track who views ad e-mail, for how long, and to whom it was forwarded. This low-cost feature has prompted *offline* businesses to use e-mail. According to *Forbes* magazine (Meredith, R., "You've Got Ad-Mail," *Forbes* online, October 2, 2000), a television-like commercial digitized and packaged as an e-mail attachment costs as little as $5,000 to $40,000, and distributing it costs but pennies, as opposed to the several million dollars that would be spent on television broadcasting.

Consider some e-mail ad campaigns and their relative cost versus their effectiveness. In March 2000, the U.S. television network CBS e-mailed a video commercial to 230,000 fans of the band 'N Sync to promote a new album. Thirty-four percent of the recipients forwarded it to friends or clicked through to the band's Web site. Later, in May 2000, when CBS wanted to draw attention to its new TV show *Survivor*, the network obtained e-mail addresses of 29,000 viewers and e-mailed them a small version of a television commercial. The huge success of the show might be partially attributed to this strategy. In the same month, MindArrow, a firm that specializes in online advertising, conducted one of the largest e-mail ad campaigns. The firm sent 1.3 million fans of the singer Britney Spears an e-ad featuring the singer's latest single. Nine percent of the recipients passed the ad on to their friends or visited Spears' Web site.

The rate of actual purchases resulting from e-mail promotions, however, is significantly lower than the current 10 percent to 35 percent response rate. For example, Toyota e-mailed an ad to 112,000 people to promote the company's Celica, Spyder, and Prius cars. Toyota expected to sell only 60 cars through the campaign, a low sales expectation. Yet the e-ad cost the company only $18,000, a very low sum relative to the potential sales revenue.

INTERESTING . . .

YOU'VE GOT SPAM

Messaging Online, a New York research firm, estimated that at the end of 1999 there were 570 million e-mail addresses in the world. Most of these addresses were accessed by people in the United States. The firm estimated that, on average, a user had one e-mail address at work and another four for personal mail. The research firm Jupiter Communications estimated that Americans sent 132 billion messages in 1999, and that the number would reach 432 billion by 2003. The pace of growth of spam (unsolicited marketing e-mail) is greater than the growth of e-mail addresses; it is expected that by 2005 one fourth to one third of all personal messages will be spam.

Source: Lake, D., "Message in a packet," *The Industry Standard*, July 24, 2000, pp. 202–204

As in traditional marketing, it is not a trivial task to measure the success of marketing for online goods and services. If a new, small online company spends $3 million for 30 seconds of advertising during the Super Bowl and the company's sales jump 3,000 percent the next day, then the ad undoubtedly contributed to that result; the television commercial was even more effective if sales volume is sustained over the following months. However, measurements of surrogate variables such as site visits and onsite click streams are not always a good measure of marketing success or failure. (A surrogate variable is related to the variable we would like to measure but cannot; thus, we measure visits and click streams because we assume there is a relationship between these variables and revenue.)

Consider the findings of two researchers from the University of Pennsylvania's Wharton School of Business. In their paper "Capturing Evolving Visit Behavior in Clickstream Data," Peter Fader and Wendy Moe point out that commonly used measures of Web business success—such as number of hits, page views, and average time spent at a site—provide only general information about customers. These statistics lump together everyone from brand-new Internet surfers to serious repeat buyers. The researchers argue that to market effectively, sites must analyze the behavior of individual consumers. They suggest a model of consumer behavior that, they posit, yields a wealth of knowledge. This knowledge can help e-retailers market more successfully.

For their study Fader and Moe analyzed click-stream data collected by the research firm Media Metrix. At that time, the firm maintained a sample of some 10,000 participating households who had installed special software on their personal computers so their Internet behavior could be recorded, page by page, over time. The researchers gleaned variations in online "store visit" behavior as well as recorded changes over time in consumers' behavior as they gained experience with two particular sites, both of which were leading e-commerce enterprises.

Over multiple visits, the behavior of Web users changes, the researchers learned. In early visits to a site, the novelty element plays an important role. Over time, visitors return to the site only if they believe they can receive information there that they cannot get elsewhere. By examining data recorded about the two sites, the researchers concluded that although overall traffic increased, visits by individuals decreased. Fader and Moe concluded that if such a pattern were to continue, future prospects for the sites would appear less promising, especially when the arrival of new users inevitably begins to subside.

The study corroborated what had been believed for some time: That the more frequently people visit an online store, the more purchases they make. Thus, the real measure of marketing success on the Web is the degree to which the marketer can entice people to make repeat visits. People who decrease their visits to a site spend decreasing amounts of money there. In other words, marketing success on the Web should not be measured in terms of *traffic* but in terms of *conversion*.

Eventually, the measure of marketing success is the ratio of profit to marketing cost. However, for firms that are in their early stages and therefore cannot be expected to have profit, the "interim" proper ratio is revenue to marketing spending. This is not different from the ratio for offline firms. However, there are other ratios that may be used to gauge trends that lead to the success or failure of a marketing effort. Some are marketing spending per new visitor and marketing spending per repeat customer. Obviously, the term *repeat customer* may mean different things to different firms. The definition depends on the number of purchase visits that qualify the customer as a repeat customer, or visitor-turned-buyer. A firm can use its own definition only for a limited-period comparison of its own progress, not for comparison with other firms. There is one ratio that has not been used: repeat customers lost as a proportion of first-time visitors. Measured for a defined period of time, this ratio may serve as one good indicator of the overall success of acquiring and retaining visitors. It can be used within and among firms. The lower the ratio, the more successful the firm's marketing.

SUMMARY

- Domain-name recognition is still considered a marketing asset by many online businesses. Therefore, businesses make efforts to select memorable domain names that are brought to public attention through search engines.
- To attract visitors and convince them to spend a long time at a site, businesses must design their Web site's pages carefully. Among the important elements are the balance between text and pictures, color, and pizzazz.
- Designers of retail Web sites must remember the great differences between a physical store and an online one. Web users are comfortable with a familiar homepage design that features horizontal tabs and vertical menus. They do not expect a visual simulation of brick-and-mortar stores. They do expect a search mechanism, easy-to-use menus, and clickable icons.
- Give visitors as much control as possible over how they use a Web site.
- Menus are not only for selection; they should also serve to attract new visitors. Menu items catering to new visitors should be conspicuous to make it easy to explore the site's goods and services. A site's menu should be organized with due consideration given to different audiences: While veteran users are familiar with the menu and tend to find what they need quickly, new users are not and therefore should be "courted."
- Every Web site is international, because people from all over the world have access to it. Sensitivity to cultural differences is especially important for businesses that target audiences in different regions of the world. A Web site must accommodate people by using their native languages and respecting their countries' laws, ethics, cultural practices, and aesthetic preferences for color and art.
- The challenge of maintaining a global site that at the same time caters to a local audience defines the concept of glocalization. Businesses should develop a strategy that meets this challenge before building their sites. They must know the individual audiences, be egalitarian across audiences of various cultures, and avoid cultural imperialism.
- One unique way to market and sell on the Web is the use of affiliates. Affiliate organizations earn a portion of a merchant's revenue when visitors to the affiliates' site end up purchasing something at, or at least visiting, the merchant's site.
- Different types of incentives in affiliate marketing include pay-per-sale, pay-per-click, and pay-per-lead models. There are also hybrid models that combine two or more of these systems. A site that already is an affiliate can recruit other affiliates, and the joining affiliate will receive the larger share of the incentive.
- Businesses in different but related markets can collaborate by cross-linking, in which each business posts a link to the other's site. In contrast, cross-luring is a process in which a business contracts with a search engine to bring up its site's URL first whenever a search for a competitor's site is being conducted.

- Consumers have complained about annoying problems with retail sites. Most of these problems can be resolved by providing more information, more choice, an easier way to navigate the site, and ensuring product availability and prompt delivery.
- Specialized software makes it relatively easy to track consumer movement at a Web site. This enables businesses to create an electronic dossier that provides a detailed profile of the consumer and his or her shopping and buying habits.
- Much research is conducted on online consumer preferences. The results of many studies are available online free of charge. Businesses can better target their markets after learning the relevant statistics and trends.
- Demographic segmentation on the Web may be effective for content and advice, but it is ineffective for selling. Online retailers must cater to the general public to be successful.
- Marketing through e-mail is inexpensive, but many potential customers consider receiving spam a nuisance. However, the use of e-mail marketing is often effective in spreading news about a new product. E-mail ads receive a high response rate and are easily forwarded to others. Advertisers can include clickable text and graphics to link e-mail recipient to their sites.

KEY TERMS

culture	cross-luring
glocalization	consumer profiling
affiliate program	spam
referral fee	opt-in e-mail
cross-linking	

REVIEW QUESTIONS

1. What aspects of the organization *of* pages and *within* pages are most important for ensuring a long visit by Web users?
2. U.S. Web sites are often accused of cultural imperialism. What is cultural imperialism? Give some examples of cultural imperialism that you have seen on the Web.
3. What does egalitarianism mean regarding Web sites? Why is being egalitarian in localized Web sites so important?
4. Explain the differences among the various affiliate marketing programs. Can you think of an original scheme that was not mentioned in this chapter?
5. Is a multitiered affiliate program a Ponzi scheme? Explain. (If you do not know what a Ponzi scheme is, use Atomica or another online source to look it up.)
6. What makes consumer profiling technically easier on the Web than in traditional marketing?
7. How are statistics about the shopping and buying habits of different demographic groups important for e-retailers? If you ran an online retail site, which statistics would you act upon, and which would not matter to you?
8. What are the elements that make e-mail advertising cost-effective?

DISCUSSION QUESTIONS

1. Advertising on the Web is different from advertising in print, radio, and television. What are the differences between Web advertising and advertising in each of these media? What additional techniques can Web advertisers use that they have not yet used?
2. What pizzazz that you have recently seen at a site would attract you to revisit it? Why? Have you seen anything that puts you off?
3. Do you find anything unethical in cross-luring? Explain your position.
4. Figure 9.10 lists typical consumer complaints about online retail businesses. What are your complaints (in general, not against a particular site)? What could sites do to satisfy you?

ASSIGNMENTS

1. Make a visit to the Web sites of Brodia (*www.brodia.com*) and InstaBuy (*www.instabuy.com*). Write a two-page report explaining (1) how these organizations generate revenue, and (2) why they are called digital wallets, smart shopping companions, or credit cards 2.0.

2. Surf the Web and find a site that you think truly caters to a variety of audiences and follows the advice given in Figure 9.6. Prepare a software-based presentation (using PowerPoint or another presentation application) highlighting the elements that you like about this site and giving examples from the site's pages. If you can read and understand any non–English language used at the site, evaluate the accuracy of the translation across the site's local sections.

E-COMMERCE TODAY

Quest for Knowledge

College students are a huge market for products and services. What needs do they have that haven't yet been satisfied online? In the early days of the Internet, an Israeli student created quite a stir when he invited students to post research papers on any and every subject at his Web site. The purpose: Let any student who needs a finished term paper download it and use it. Plagiarism? Ethics? That's up to the individual students to decide, the young innovator said. (To his credit, one could say, the young man did not charge anything for the service.) Needless to say, many disagreed with his position.

Several years later, Questia Media, Inc. is taking the general idea many steps forward: It is a serious business that has massive funding from a venture capital firm. In its own words, the firm "is building the first online service to provide unlimited access to the full text of hundreds of thousands of books, journals and periodicals, as well as tools to easily use this information. For millions of college students, the Questia service will enable them to research and compose their papers at any time, from every connected corner of the world."

The firm's business model is simple. Executives expect millions of college students to pay $25 per month for the privilege to access its site, where they can search a huge database. It cross-references the full texts of 50,000 liberal arts textbooks, journals, and classic works of literature. The database also enables students to access the works online and incorporate passages into their term papers, saving many hours of research and typing. Questia also developed software to help students by generating footnotes and reference lists automatically as they use the source material.

Questia is trying to create a legitimate new industry. Founder and CEO Troy Williams says the company is targeting the entire population of 12.3 million U.S. undergraduate students. At $25 per month for nine months per year (the length of an academic year), the potential market is $2.7 billion. Williams hoped to capture this entire market within 5 to 10 years after the company started to offer the service in January 2001.

Questia is not the only player in the online library industry. However, it has an asset that no competitor has: its unique software, in which it invested over two years and $100 million. The software uses XML (extended markup language, discussed in Chapter 4) to build a cross-referencing system that lets students pinpoint searches and customize footnote formats. While there are other referencing applications (such as EndNotes), the combination of searches, cross-referencing, and automatic reference listing is unique to this software.

The company's team consists of 250 full-time employees and 4,000 part-time workers. It was funded with $130 million. Both the size of the investment and the number of employees are larger than the typical investment and workforce of new Internet firms. The company has agreements with 95 publishers, including major publishers of college textbooks. One of the investors in the company is Pearson Publishing (parent of Prentice Hall), which gave Questia the electronic rights of at least 100 books. An additional partner is the higher-education software company WebCT, which will offer the 6.8 million students it serves access to Questia service. The combination of unique, expensive software and these contracts gives Questia a strategic advantage over potential competitors.

Will Questia be able to convince millions of college students to pay $25 per month for its service?

Source: Cohan, P. S., "The Paper Chase," *The Industry Standard*, October 2, 2000, pp. 186–188

Thinking About E-Commerce Today

1. How would you market Questia's service to college students? Prepare a list of ideas.
2. Would you market the service differently to undergraduate and graduate students? Explain.
3. Would you target parties other than students for the service? Who and how?
4. For the first two years of operations, how would you measure the success of the marketing effort?

■ List the major threats to networked information systems

■ Suggest a security measure for each threat to networked information systems

■ Explain encryption and how it supports electronic signatures and digital certificates

■ Contrast the legitimate data-gathering needs of businesses and government with individual privacy concerns

■ Discuss how the increased use of the Internet increases threats to privacy

■ Explain the relationship between consumer profiling and privacy issues

According to an estimate by the consulting firm Price-waterhouseCoopers, the business world lost $1.6 trillion to hacker attacks in 2000. The firm based this estimate on a survey of about 5,000 information technology professionals in 30 countries. Viruses launched on the Internet carry out the most financially damaging attacks. The infamous Love Bug of 2000 alone caused an estimated $2.6 billion in damages. The FBI has listed virus attacks and employee violations of company Internet policies among the chief network-related crimes. While the FBI is beefing up its cadre of professional "cybercrime busters," some critics claim that the agency itself may violate one of America's most important civil rights: privacy. The accusation arises from the FBI's use of hardware and software to intercept e-mail in a stated attempt to prevent crime and terrorism.

What is the primary factor that turns online shoppers who merely browse into customers who buy? If you guessed price or quality of products, guess again. As a Jupiter Research survey of 1,147 people revealed, security is the primary factor that influences purchasing decisions of 68 percent of the respondents. Price came in second (see Figure 10.1).

From a corporate perspective, **online security** is the ability to protect information resources from unauthorized access, modification, and destruction. Information resources in this context are hardware, software, and telecommunications. From a consumer viewpoint, security is the perceived guarantee that no unauthorized parties will have access to communication between the consumer and the online business while the communication takes place and after communicated information has been captured by the business.

Business runs on trust. Online security in its broadest sense is vital not only because it is required to protect the information assets of organizations and individuals but also because of the long-term effects to both businesses and individuals that security breaches can have on e-commerce. When businesses hear about an unauthorized break into the Web site or databases of a business partner, they reevaluate doing business with that organization, both online and traditionally. When consumers read in the newspaper that a database operated by their bank has been accessed, let alone altered or destroyed, by an online intruder, they are highly likely to stop banking online with this bank or any other. Perhaps more significantly, they may transfer their account to another bank. For these reasons, companies today are spending increasing amounts of money and effort to ensure that unauthorized parties do not access their information resources.

F I G U R E

10.1 SECURITY IS THE PRIMARY FACTOR IN TURNING BROWSERS INTO BUYERS

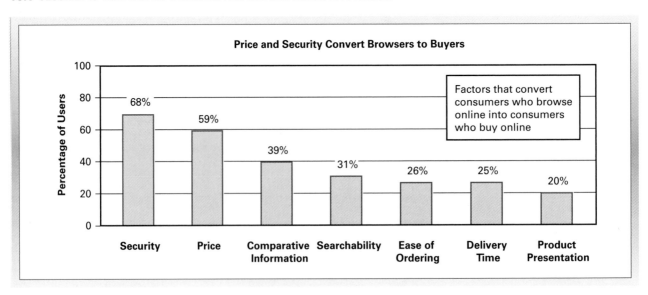

Source: Jupiter Research, June 2000

Still, the Internet is a public network. Doing business online continues to be a double-edged sword. Companies open their information systems to other businesses and to the public to increase sales and to make shopping, purchasing, and service more convenient for their clients. However, the more businesses allow access to their services and systems through the Internet, the more they are vulnerable to security breaches. This is akin to opening the door to your house so that more people can visit, while at the same time trying to ensure that no one peeks where he or she is not supposed to peek. Therefore, executives must realize that there is no absolute guarantee against security breaches. They can only employ measures to minimize them, which in turn minimizes damage to information and service.

Along with concerns about security, consumers are concerned about *privacy*. Most people resent losing control of the collection and use of their personal information, especially if personal data are collected and maintained without their knowledge. The potential for violation of privacy in e-commerce has been an issue of significant controversy ever since business on the Web began.

In this chapter we first discuss the major categories of online security breaches, along with the remedies organizations can take to prevent them. We then discuss important privacy issues related to e-commerce.

THE THREATS

The range of threats to e-commerce is broad, from "benign" unauthorized access and computer viruses to destructive attacks and denial of service. The following is a discussion of the major types of security breaches and attacks that may affect businesses operating on the Web.

HACKING

What do we mean by *hacker*? In this book we use the term **hacker** for a person who, without permission, accesses an information system resource. (Some authors prefer the term *cracker*.) Benign unauthorized access may only be a prelude to more serious activity, such as the destruction or alteration of computer files. Destructive hacking often results in **Web page defacement**, that is, the malicious alteration of text, graphic, and audio content of pages. This activity is considered criminal in virtually every country.

Hacking for the purpose of theft or fraud was a threat decades before the Internet was used by millions of people and businesses. Banks, credit card companies, and telephone companies have been subject to information theft for a long time. The Internet only exacerbates the problem because it links so many people to so many different organizational resources.

Unfortunately, hacking is almost a daily event. For some people it has become a second career. The first person to be tried and convicted under the U.S. Computer Fraud and Abuse Act of 1986 was a teenager named Kevin Mitnick. In 1990, the young man hacked into the information systems of Motorola, Sun Microsystems, NEC, and Novell, stealing software, product plans, and valuable data whose estimated value was $80 million. Mitnick did not reap any financial gains from the theft, and he paid for his crimes with several years in prison. Nonetheless, the companies sustained significant financial damages. In September 2000, a hacker stole the credit and debit card information of about 15,700 Western Union customers who used the company's Web site to transfer money. Hacking occurs all the time, even while you read this chapter.

Although hacking alone may not cause damage if the hacker settles for simply entering the system, hacking rarely stops at that point. It is almost always the first step toward criminal activity, such as data alteration and destruction or theft of information. Also, even if a hacker has not stolen, altered, or destroyed anything, the labor required to figure out what happened and prevent it from happening again costs money, and, therefore, there *is* financial damage, while the intangible negative effects of the security breach are damaging in their own right.

WEB SITE DEFACEMENT

Somewhere, almost daily, an organization's Webmaster comes to the office in the morning, heads to the site he or she manages, and is shocked to find out that the homepage—and possibly other pages—has been defaced. In the best-case scenario, Web defacement is the cyber equivalent of street graffiti; someone adds offensive text or pictures to the page. In the worst-case scenario, pages are totally replaced with offensive content. This causes several types of damage: First-time visitors are not likely to stay around long enough or revisit so they can learn about the true nature of the site, and they may associate the offensive material with the firm; frequent visitors may never come back; and shoppers who have had a good experience with the site may leave it forever because they no longer trust its security measures.

To deface a Web site, an intruder needs to know the site's access code or codes, which allow the Webmaster and others authorized to work on the site's server and update its pages. The intruder may obtain the codes either from someone who knows them or by using special software that "tries and errs" until it succeeds in accessing the pages.

Examples of such incidents are numerous. In one case, the Web site of Germany's Free Democratic Party (FDP) was defaced. The home page was "rearranged." The attacker destroyed files that contained the FDP's political credo, set up icons that led nowhere, and scrambled the site's hyperlinks so that they brought users to the homepage of another German political party, the Christian Democratic Party, instead of to the FDP's original links. Many of its files were destroyed. It was an embarrassment to the organization.

VIRUSES

A **computer virus** is a malicious program that spreads among computers through the exchange of files on disks or through computer networks. In 1998 the Internet was used to spread a virus for the first time. A destructive program, which slowed

UNWELCOME EDITING

In October 2000, a hacker changed three stories on the *Orange County Register*'s Web site. The hacker changed one story to read that Microsoft Chairman Bill Gates was arrested for breaking into NASA computers. Gates's name was substituted for the name of a real hacker arrested on charges of breaking into NASA Web sites. In the case of the altered news report, the hacking was noticed and fixed within 45 minutes.

down affected computers and filled their disks with useless data, spread to 6,000 computers. Since then, unscrupulous people have launched thousands of viruses onto the Internet. In recent years, the more infamous ones have been the Melissa virus in 1998 and the Love Bug virus in 2000. Both spread through opened e-mail messages, and both caused millions of dollars in damage. An assessment of financial damage is based on lost telecommunication time in infected networks, loss of valuable information in destroyed files, and the labor required to purge the virus from each computer and recover lost information. Some experts estimate the total damage caused by the Love Bug virus was $10 billion.

Computer viruses that actively spread through networks are sometimes called **worms**, because these files "crawl" through the network. Worms reach victim computers on their own; they do not have to be actively downloaded by anyone. Many other viruses are actually downloaded by their victims. Unfortunately, some are hidden as part of benign, useful applications. The user who downloads the file is not aware that in addition to the useful code, the file contains destructive code, which erupts either immediately or some time after the download. Such a virus is called a **Trojan horse**, after the wooden horse left by the ancient Greeks at the entrance gate to the city of Troy, as told in Homer's *Odyssey*. When the huge wooden horse, thought by the Trojans to be a gift, was hauled into the city, Odysseus and ten of his soldiers climbed down from inside the horse and opened the gate for their invading comrades.

DENIAL OF SERVICE

One day in February 2000, the stock brokerage firm National Discount Brokers Group experienced an unpleasant event. Its online servers were flooded with transaction requests. About 200,000 customers were unable to place stock orders through the firm's Web site, forcing them to relay orders on the telephone. Apparently, someone assaulted the site to produce a *denial of service* (DoS). **Denial of service** occurs when, due to hectic malicious activity, an organization cannot serve its clients. Usually this is accomplished by flooding the network with multiple login requests from one or just a few client computers, or through orchestrated login requests from many hackers at the same time. Since servers are designed to take only a certain maximum number of calls, legitimate users of the site soon find that their repeated login requests are not satisfied.

The information request in the National Discount Brokers Group case came from two URLs. To solve the problem, the company decided to disconnect the two addresses from its servers. Shortly afterward, it was able to restore its services.

This was not the first DoS of a major online business. In the second week of February 2000, Web surfers found that they could not visit some of the Web's most popular sites, such as Yahoo!, CNN, E*Trade, ZD Net, and Buy.com. Apparently, cyberhooligans attacked these businesses by finding a way to clog their servers. Buy.com, the popular online shopping site, was hit with a DoS on the day of its initial public offering of shares, which could have (and some people say did) hurt the amount of funds the firm raised from the public.

While DoS can be perpetrated by a single person who programs an application to repeatedly access a site, *distributed denial of service* is either the work of several people or one person's unauthorized use of multiple computers for the same purpose. In **distributed denial of service** (DDoS), the attackers "hijack" hundreds of computer systems (known as *zombies*) that are then instructed to access a site or network simultaneously. In such an attack, a network literally can be paralyzed when it is flooded with a high volume of visits. Many innocent Internet users do not realize that their computers might be used as vehicles for such attacks.

The Computer Emergency Response Team (CERT) has warned that computer vandals are scouring the Internet for computers vulnerable to the installation of automated "toolkits" that allow the intruder to control the affected computer for use in an attack against another computer or network. (CERT was established as the Internet's official emergency body after the first Internet virus crippled networked computers in 1988.) For example, CERT reported that more than 560 hosts at 220 Internet sites around the world unwittingly had participated in one particular DDoS attack.

When the flood of visits comes from a single source or only from a few sources, the technical staff at the attacked site can simply deny access to that URL, thereby ridding itself of the attack. However, DDoS is impossible to stop. One reason is that the zombies may change over the duration of the attack. Another reason is the risk of shutting out legitimate visitors. On top of this, it is impractical to burden personnel with the task of tracking down hundreds, and possibly thousands, of zombies.

Criminals who have launched DDoS attacks have never been caught. Tracking down the original computer that started the flood is practically impossible.

I N T E R E S T I N G . . .

RISKS AND THEIR COSTS

The Internet security firm ICSA conducted a survey on corporate security breaches and security budgets in 2000. Of the 1,897 technology and security professionals who participated, 37 percent said their company experienced denial of service attacks by outsiders, and 41 percent reported that company employees had destroyed or distributed confidential corporate information. Consulting firms had the largest annual budgets for security measures, about $2 million. Organizations having the next highest security budgets were banks and other financial institutions ($950,000), high-tech service providers ($900,000), and high-tech hardware and software manufacturers ($775,000). Educational institutions were spending the lowest amounts; their average annual budget was reported to be $100,000.

Source: Enos, L., "Report: Cybercrime outpacing security spending," *E-Commerce Times*, October 6, 2000

Imagine a person standing before your store and diverting people to a competing store. Now imagine that the person is invisible. This is what some people have done for some time on the Internet. **Spoofing** on the Internet may mean satirizing a Web site. But in recent years spoofing has also meant deception for the purpose of gaining access, or deception of users to make them think they are logged on to a certain Web site when actually they are logged on to another. This is the type of spoofing with which we are concerned in this chapter. Spoofing is a mechanism that lets hackers hijack traffic from a legitimate site and redirect it to a bogus site.

Most spoofing attacks are designed to embarrass Web site operators, but security experts worry that spoofing techniques may take a more sinister angle: A serious spoofing attack may result in massive fraud. When spoofing, the perpetrator takes advantage of certain vulnerabilities in domain name system (DNS) software. When a user types a domain name into her browser, the local DNS server sends a query through the Internet's distributed hierarchical DNS to look up the matching IP address for that domain name. Spoofers manipulate the DNS software so that the path to the IP address is redirected; the Internet user then believes that she is connected to the requested server when in fact she is connected to another server. This is akin to someone switching your name with someone else's in a telephone directory so you can receive all calls directed to that person's phone.

The most famous Web site spoofing incident happened in 1997, when a computer consultant working for the state of Washington redirected traffic from Network Solutions' InterNIC Web site to his own AlterNIC site for several days. It was an inside job. Network Solutions had the sole license to register domain names for several years. The company had received the license from InterNIC (Internet Network Information Center), a U.S. government agency. The offender pleaded guilty to computer fraud and received two years' probation.

A similar incident—this time for political purposes—took place on June 21, 2000. A group of computer hackers calling itself S-11 redirected traffic from www.nike.com to servers at a Scotland-based Web hosting company. The hijacking lasted 6 to 24 hours, depending on the schedules of different ISPs reloading the Nike Web site. During the range of the incident, Web users who tried to access Nike's site were instead sent to one that criticized the company and the World Economic Forum, a procapitalism group of which Nike is a member. Nike's sales through its Web site did not suffer significantly, but the spoof shook many online businesses. Many of those companies are still looking in earnest for a practical response to this kind of security breach.

THE REMEDIES

Some security breaches cannot be effectively eliminated. One type is DDoS, as discussed earlier. There is not much that an online business can do to prevent such an attack, but its staff can be aware of the possibility, know how to detect it, and have clear instructions on what to do when it happens. Other types of security breaches do have remedies. Any business that has resources connected to a public network should be primarily concerned with control of access (or authentication of users) and confidentiality.

To minimize hacking, online systems must be able to authenticate the identities of those who attempt to log on, allowing only legitimate users—employees, customers, suppliers, or others with permission—to access the system. **Authentication** is the ability of the system to verify that users are who they "say" they are. To this end, organizations must establish some kind of access code. A password, which the user is expected to keep secret, is the most prevalent type of access code. Often, approved users have another string of characters that is assigned to them, such as an employee ID or an account number. To log on, users are typically asked to enter both strings: the user ID (also called **username**) or account number *and* the password. The former is not meant to be secret; the latter is. The combination of the two strings serves as a key and gives the user access to the entire system or to a limited number of resources.

Security analysts often categorize access codes into "what you know" and "what you are." *What you know* are the codes, such as passwords and user IDs and account numbers; you are expected to remember what you know. The disadvantage of passwords and other codes, of course, is that people forget them. *What you are* is biometrics. **Biometrics** are unique physical features that people have and their use for authentication. Examples of biometric identification include use of fingerprints, voice signatures, and retina maps. Special devices at the user end can read a user's biometric and compare it with thousands of prerecorded biometrics available in a database. If the biometric is found in the database, it means the user is legitimate, and he or she can access the system.

Once the authentication has been made satisfactorily, it is often necessary to keep confidential the exchange of information between the remote user and the system. **Confidentiality** means that no one except the user and the system, or the user and his or her counterpart to the exchange, is able to know the content of an exchange.

When using a public network such as the Internet for information exchange, maintaining confidentiality requires some sophisticated technology. Usually, confidentiality is accomplished by using encryption methods. Encryption is used for authentication as well, when the user does not have a predetermined access code such as a password. We discuss encryption later in this chapter.

TRANSPARENCY

Whenever security measures are implemented, there is a trade-off between security and convenience. Consider what happens at an airport. As passengers, we collectively experience a higher probability of secure flights if each of us is stopped for questioning and if our luggage is scanned for suspicious items. However, the procedure is inconvenient. A similar trade-off occurs whenever we visit a secured site. We cannot immediately use the resource we seek. We must go through security.

To minimize inconvenience, security planners should subject users to as little delays and hassles as possible. You can notice security measures in two ways, either visually or in terms of performance speed. Complete **transparency** is accomplished when security measures are in place but are not noticeable to the users. Transparency is highly important for customers and business partners, and also for employees. Customers do not want to be inconvenienced; they do not want to pass through several layers of questioning to be authenticated by the sys-

OPEN FOR HACKERS

A 2000 study by the General Accounting Office (GAO) revealed disturbing security holes in government Web sites. The GAO, serving as a watchdog for the United States Congress, studied computer security in 24 agencies. Among its findings were the following: Personal information about individuals can easily be obtained from government computers; defense secrets are at risk of exposure; IRS data can be modified or destroyed; Social Security information is unprotected; and EPA (Environmental Protection Agency) computers are highly vulnerable to tampering. Access control was the major weakness cited. The GAO also found that though the same alerts had been published previously in its 1998 report on the subject, nothing had yet been done to fix the problems. As are all GAO reports, this one was posted at GAO's Web site, *www.gao.gov*. Apparently, no one at the GAO thought it was a bad idea to expose the findings for the reading pleasure of every hacker and terrorist in the world.

Source: GAO, "Critical federal operations and assets remain at risk," a report released on September 11, 2000

tem. When communication occurs between a user and the system or a user and another user, the parties should not notice any delays due to the fact that the information undergoes security checks and encryption. Businesses are constantly looking for the fastest security software they can implement while not compromising security.

INSURING SHIPS, LEGS, AND E-COMMERCE

Lloyd's of London, one of the world's largest insurance firms and well known for taking on atypical insurance risks, has partnered with San Jose, California–based Counterpane Security, Inc. to offer insurance against business losses due to mischief by hackers. An e-commerce policy can cover loss of business income as well as liabilities for damages related to public relations, intellectual property, difference in conditions, interruption of service, and electronic publishing. In general, companies with revenues of $1 billion or less can expect to pay premiums of about $25,000 to $125,000 per year for at least $25 million in coverage. Coverage limits can be as high as $200 million. Lloyd's notes that denial of service (DoS) attacks and other e-commerce risks are not covered by typical business insurance policies, while e-commerce insurance policies will usually cover the cost of computer consultants and lost income during the time an e-commerce site is down. Lost income can include lost sales for e-retailers and lost click-throughs for content provider sites.

Source: Enos, L., "Lloyd's of London to offer hacker insurance," *E-Commerce Times,* July 10, 2000

In the future, when biometric devices become part and parcel of every computer or other devices from which users log on to the Internet, the highest degree of transparency will be achieved, because authentication will be executed automatically.

FIREWALLS

To minimize the risk of fire in case of an accident, automakers install a metal plate between the engine and the vehicle's cabin. The plate, called a firewall, may save the lives of passengers. The term has been borrowed by the Internet world. A **firewall** in Web parlance is hardware and software whose purpose is to block access to certain resources. As Figure 10.2 illustrates, a firewall controls communication between a trusted network and the "untrusted" Internet. Firewalls often are programmed to work in both communication pathways, controlling communication coming into and moving out of a server linked to the Internet.

Employees typically are barred from accessing certain types of Web sites, such as adult sites or others that cannot possibly help them do their jobs. A firewall can accomplish this. In a system with a firewall, people who use the server to access company resources are barred from accessing certain databases, Web pages, and other files. Robust firewalls may stop hackers from altering and destroying data and from defacing Web pages.

To increase security, some companies take the **DMZ** (DeMilitarized Zone) approach. The DMZ is the link between two servers, one of which is a proxy server. A proxy server "represents" another server for all information requests. The proxy server is often the one operated by an Internet Service Provider (ISP). The DMZ

FIGURE

10.2 A FIREWALL

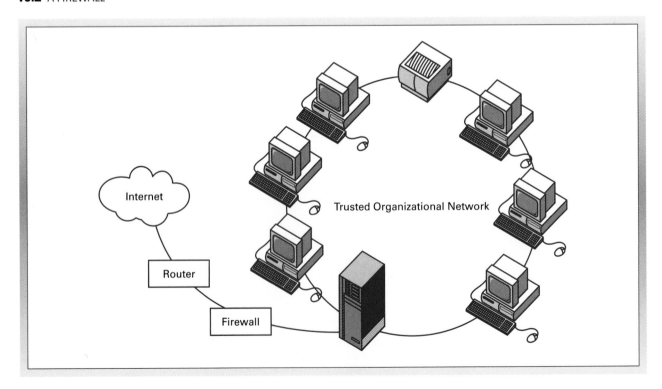

provides a barrier between the Internet and a company's organizational network, which is often, practically speaking, an intranet. Both the organizational network server and proxy server employ firewalls. In Figure 10.2, the firewalls would be installed on the gray server of the organizational network and the router. The router is often called a *boundary router*. The double firewall architecture adds an extra measure of security for the intranet.

As with other security measures, firewalls must be as transparent as possible to minimize inconvenience for system users. Customers may get frustrated if they have to wait too long for a response from a Web site. They may turn away and decide to shop and buy at a competitor's site. Business partners may complain about inconvenience. Companies are usually less sensitive to employee inconvenience.

ANTISPOOFING MEASURES

To overcome vulnerabilities to spoofing, individual sites can do nothing; rather, the telecommunications companies that operate their parts of the Internet must adopt spoof-proof software and use it throughout the Internet. The method to tackle this challenge is the same as the one for other online communication: encryption. In 2000, a new security mechanism called DNSSEC (DNS Security) was offered for that purpose. DNSSEC lets Web sites verify their domain names and corresponding IP addresses using *digital signatures* and *public-key encryption,* methods we discuss later in this chapter.

For DNSSEC to work most effectively, the user's local DNS server and the Web site's DNS server must support the DNSSEC system, along with the Internet's root and top-level domain servers. When all of these pieces are in place, the Web site's DNS server uses public-key encryption to send out a digital signature to the local DNS server to verify the authenticity of the Web site. Once authenticity of the site is confirmed, the user can access it.

BACKUP

Backing up is as important for an individual processing a text document as it is for a large online firm processing orders. Software applications and data files may be corrupted or destroyed for many reasons, some of which are malicious, such as viruses, and many of which are not. Businesses must back up all applications and data on their computer systems. To minimize the time between discovery of a mishap and a response to employees, clients, and business partners, backed-up files must be immediately available.

However, it is not enough just to *have* backup files. Ideally, the files should be updated in real time, so that the backup fully reflects the original. Backup files also must be stored off-site, so that natural disasters, hackers, or viruses cannot physically reach the files at the original site. To this end, businesses use the services of companies that specialize in duplicating files and storing them at their own sites. Some companies have cross backup agreements: Each company agrees to save at its site the files of the other company. The businesses "trade" their duplicate files on a regular basis—every day or every week, for example—through a communication network.

Some companies, such as Comdisco and Sungard, provide entire hardware and software facilities for businesses whose information systems may experience a massive attack or failure. The client business can continue operations from the off-site facilities.

For millennia, people have used many methods to prevent unauthorized parties from being able to read secret messages. Such methods, collectively called ciphering or encryption, have also been used to ensure the authentication of the sender. As use of public computer networks has increased, the need for encryption methods has increased as well. In this section we discuss encryption and its most widely used applications.

ENCRYPTION

To send private messages over public networks such as the Internet, one must encrypt them first. **Encryption** is the conversion of data into a secret code. **Decryption** is the conversion of the secret code back into readable data. Special mathematical algorithms (which are series of mathematical manipulations) are used to make the sequence of deciphering difficult. The assumption is that whoever intercepts the message will know the encryption algorithm. Thus, the effort of cryptologists has not been on the secrecy of algorithms, but the difficulty the interceptor faces when trying to figure out the particular key used with the algorithm. It is the necessity to find the proper key to unlock the message that makes the decryption process so long that decryption is practically infeasible. In other words, the difficulty is not in how complex the lock is, but in finding the key that unlocks it. The only practical difference between physical locks and encryption algorithms is that the latter allow the use of a different key for each new locking.

A key used in encryption is a binary number. Usually, this number is made up of 40 to 128 bits. The larger the key, the longer it takes to figure it out, and, therefore, to decipher the data. The data included in an electronic document is ciphered using the key. The result is text in gibberish, a picture that does not look like a picture, or a sound that is far from its original form. The key must also be used to decipher the message back into its original form. When two parties wish to communicate, both can share a secret key known only to them. Initially, they decide on the secret key either in a meeting, or by mail or courier. Then they can use the key on their data sent through public communications networks. A single, agreed-upon, secret key is called a **symmetric key**, because both parties in the communication use the same key. However, when people communicate with many other people over public networks such as the Internet, using secret keys becomes impractical. The solution is **asymmetric keys**, whereby the sender uses one key to encrypt the message, and the receiver uses a different, but related, key to decrypt it.

The common asymmetric key method is the *public-key–private-key* method, which is known more commonly as the **public key** method. A person may apply for a private key and a public key. The private key is secret and known only to that person. The public key is not secret; it is freely distributed. The keys are mathematically related. However, it is computationally infeasible to deduce the private key from its related public key. This is where the strength of the method lies. The sender uses the receiver's public key to encrypt the message. The receiver uses the receiver's private key to decrypt it. Only the public key can encrypt a message, and only the related private key can decrypt it.

ELECTRONIC SIGNATURES

In June 2000, the United States Congress removed one of the last hurdles in electronic commerce: It approved a bill that legitimizes electronic signatures in commercial transactions. The Electronic Signatures in Global and National Commerce Act, in effect since October 2000, establishes that electronic contracts with electronic signatures have the same legal force as paper contracts. The law defines the term **electronic signature** as "an electronic sound, symbol, or process, attached to or logically associated with a contract or other record and executed or adopted by a person with the intent to sign the record." By the time the federal law was signed, 40 states had their own laws validating electronic signatures for commercial deals. Ireland was the second country to legislate electronic signatures as a valid instrument in e-commerce. With such laws, consumers can sign documents electronically with the same legal validity of paper signatures.

Electronic signatures can take several forms. In one form, instead of signing on paper, the user signs with a stylus on a special pad. The signature is recorded as a graphic. Along with it, some systems also record how quickly the signature is written and how much force the signer uses against the pad so that subsequent signatures can be compared with these characteristics for authentication. You may have already used this system when you signed an authorization to charge your credit card at OfficeMax or when you received a package delivered by UPS.

Another electronic signature method records a biometric of the signer. (Again, a biometric is a physical characteristic of a person, such as a fingerprint, retina pattern, or voice.) A person's biometric is recorded once and then compared with subsequent signatures for authentication. For example, Sony, the electronics giant, offers a product that digitally records a user's fingerprints. The users can then access their electronic signature only after placing a finger or thumb on a scanner for comparison.

DIGITAL SIGNATURES

Every electronic signature is digitized or it could not be stored and processed by a computer. However, it is expected that in the great majority of electronic signatures, no physical characteristics will be involved. Rather, people will use signatures that do not require any signing. These signatures are called digital signatures. A **digital signature**, to differentiate it from an electronic signature, is an encrypted digest of the text that is sent with a message, usually a text message, but possibly one that contains other types of information, such as pictures.

Two phases are involved in the creation of a digital signature. First, the encryption software uses a mathematical formula called a **hashing algorithm** to create a **message digest** from the file you wish to transmit. A message digest is akin to a unique fingerprint. Then, the software uses your private (secret) key to encrypt the message digest. The result is a digital signature for that specific file. A digital signature authenticates the identity of the sender of a message. The digital signature also guarantees that someone other than the original sender has not altered the sent document; it is as if the message were carried in an electronically sealed envelope.

DIGITAL CERTIFICATES

To authenticate a digital signature, both buyers and sellers must use digital certificates (also known as *digital IDs*). **Digital certificates** are computer files that serve as the equivalent of identification cards. Financial institutions, such as banks and credit card issuers, issue them. Many financial institutions have special divisions or subsidiaries whose entire business is to create and sell digital certificates. These entities are called **certificate authorities**. (Hence the "CA" in the names of many of these firms.) One prominent CA that is not a financial institution is VeriSign, Inc. Certificate authorities also issue public and private keys.

A digital certificate contains its holder's name, a serial number, expiration dates, and a copy of the certificate holder's public key (used to encrypt messages and digital signatures). It also contains the digital signature of the certificate authority so that a recipient can verify that the certificate is real. To view the digital certificate of a secure online business, click on the lock icon at the bottom right corner of your browser. Figure 10.3 shows the certificate window that you would open (left). Click the Details tab to view the version, serial number, signature encryption method, issuer name, and other details of the certificate (right).

Digital certificates are the equivalent of tamper-proof photo identification cards. They are based on public key encryption techniques that verify the identities of the buyer and seller in electronic transactions and prevent documents from being altered after the transaction is completed. Consumers have their own digital certificates stored on their home computers' hard disks. In a transaction, a consumer uses one digital key attached to the certificate that he or she sends to the seller. The seller sends the certificate and his own digital key to a certificate authority, which then can determine the authenticity of the digital signature. Completed transaction documents are stored on a secure hard disk maintained by a trusted third party.

HOW DOES IT WORK?

As stated earlier, the public key method is standard practice for authentication and maintenance of confidentiality on the Internet. We explained the concepts of digital signatures and certificates. How does the public key method work? Take a look at Figure 10.4 and follow this example. Assume that you wish to send the draft of a contract to your business partner in another town. You want to assure her that

F I G U R E

10.3 A DIGITAL CERTIFICATE

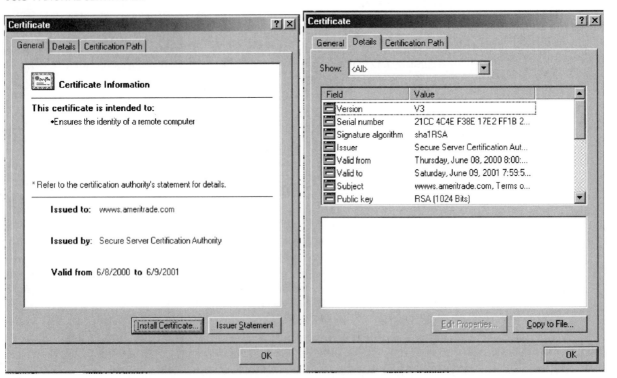

10.4 CREATING AND VERIFYING A DIGITAL SIGNATURE

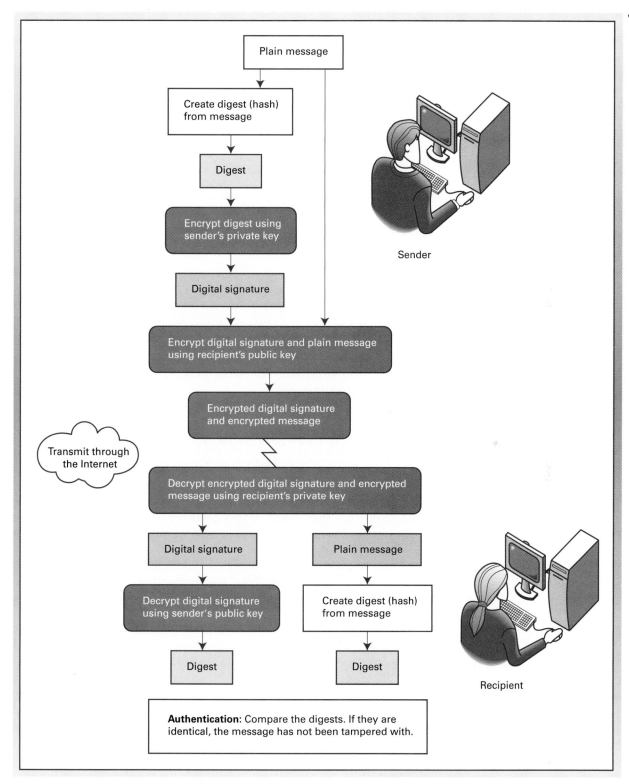

Source: Digital Signature Trust Company, *Infoworld,* June 19, 2000, p. 8

the document you intend to send will indeed be the one she receives, that it has not been altered in route. She wants the assurance that the document that she receives is really from you.

1. You attach the contract to an e-mail message. The entire communication is practically one message.
2. Using special software, you obtain a message "hash," which is a mathematical summary of the message. The hash is also called a message digest.
3. You then use a private key that you previously obtained from a public-private key authority to encrypt the hash.
4. Your computer uses your private key to turn the message digest into a digital signature. Since the message digest is different for every message, your digital signature is different each time you send a message.
5. Your computer encrypts both the digital signature and the plain-text contract using the recipient's public key.

Your business partner receives an encrypted message, which has two parts: the encrypted digital signature and the encrypted message.

1. To ensure that the message has not been changed, your business partner's computer uses her private key (which is mathematically related to your public key) to recreate the digital signature and plain text of the contract.
2. Her computer uses your public key to decrypt the digital signature into a digest. It also uses a hash algorithm to create a digest from the plain-text contract.
3. If the two message digests are identical, the received message is, apparently, the one you sent, unchanged.

SECURE SOCKETS LAYER, SHTTP, AND PGP

Public key encryption is used in **Secure Sockets Layer** (**SSL**). SSL is the most widely used security standard on the Internet. The software was developed by Netscape and has been merged with other authentication methods by the IETF (Internet Engineering Task Force) into a protocol known as Transport Layer Security (TLS). The software is integrated into all the popular Web browsers.

Consumers use SSL daily in their transactions with online businesses. When a consumer's browser contacts a merchant's server, both sides determine which encryption standard both support. They also exchange a *session ID,* which is a unique code that identifies the session. This is important, because the secret key about to be generated will be valid only for this session.

Next, the server "presents" the merchant's digital certificate. The browser authenticates that the server is one operated by the merchant. The server and browser have just completed a phase called *the handshake.* The browser now uses the certificate's public key to generate a secret (private) key. Only this consumer's browser and this merchant's server share this key, and the key is valid only for this session. Using this unique key, the browser and server can exchange sensitive information such as the consumer's credit card number or bank balances. A third party that intercepts the communication receives only encrypted data. When the consumer logs off, the key is useless. When the consumer logs on to the secure site, the entire process occurs again, and a new secret key is produced.

You can tell if you are logged on to a secure server. A secure session is indicated by an icon, usually a little key or lock, at the right or left bottom corner of your browser. Note the lock icon in the right bottom corner of Figure 10.5.

There are several public key methods on the Internet that work similarly to SSL. For example, SHTTP (Secure HyperText Transport Protocol) is such a method and standard. The difference between SSL and SHTTP is that SHTTP works only with HTTP, while SSL can work independently of HTTP. When your browser recognizes a secure server that supports SHTTP, it changes the "http://" prompt in the URL field to "https://". See the Address field in Figure 10.5.

Recall our statement that both buyers and sellers must use digital certificates. This is true if neither is using a predetermined secret code. Usually, individual consumers do not use digital certificates. Therefore, they must use a secret code provided by their online stockbroker, bank, or any other entity with which they wish to exchange authenticated, confidential information. This is why you first must enter a secret code when you wish to view your portfolio or purchase stock online. Your browser authenticates the identity of the broker's server using the

FIGURE

10.5 A WEB BROWSER IN A SECURE SESSION

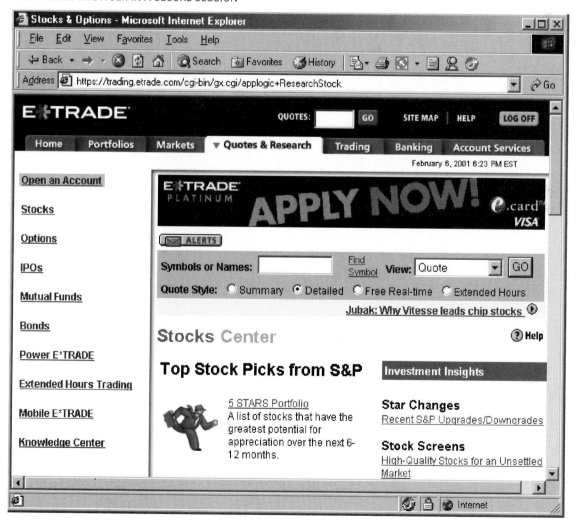

broker's digital certificate; the broker's server authenticates your browser's identity by your secret code. The secure session starts as soon as your secret code (along with your user ID or account number) has been verified by the server.

The public key method has been mainly applied to merchant-consumer communication on the Internet, whereby only the merchant authenticates the consumer. If two private people wish to encrypt their messages, they can download a program called PGP (Pretty Good Privacy) and apply for their public and private keys. The program is free for individuals and bears a relatively low cost for corporations. It was developed in 1991 by Phillip Zimmerman and is now managed by Network Associates, Inc. (formerly PGP, Inc.).

To use PGP, you download or purchase it (at *www.pgp.com*) and install it on your computer system. It contains a user interface that works with your e-mail program. You register the public key that your PGP program gives you with a PGP public-key server so that people with whom you exchange messages will be able to find your public key. Network Associates maintains a public key server that has several hundred thousand registered public keys. All public key–private key software use the same principles. What differentiates them from one another is the different hashing algorithm each uses.

BUSINESS CONTINUITY PLANS

It is fair to say that almost all businesses are dependent to one degree or another on the continuous availability of information systems. However, while some organizations can continue limited operations without information systems, online businesses rely on them. To online businesses, computer networks are like the arteries and veins in the human body: without them, there is no life. In professional parlance, the time during which systems are not functional is called *downtime*. Figure 10.6 illustrates how costly downtime can be, based on a survey and estimations performed by the research firm Dataquest.

Evidently, if a business cannot use its information systems for several hours, let alone several days, it may reach the brink of insolvency. For all Web-based companies, and for the e-commerce arms of other companies, downtime can be deadly. Companies must have a clear **business continuity plan** in place. The plan usually lists the people who are in charge of specific activities when servers or other parts of their networks are down, or when another serious interruption occurs, such as a denial of service or a computer virus attack. A list of the specific tasks to be taken and their sequence is another part of a business continuity plan.

Employees move to other positions, and information systems are modified along with the services that companies offer business partners and clients

F I G U R E
10.6 COST PER HOUR OF
SYSTEM DOWNTIME

Industry	Business Operation	Cost per Hour of Downtime
Financial	Brokerage	$6,450,000
Financial	Credit card authorization	2,600,000
Financial	ATM fees	14,500
Retail	Home catalog sales	90,000
Transportation	Airline reservations	89,500
Media	Ticket sales	69,000

Source: Dataquest, 2000

through these systems. There are many reasons business continuity plans must be reexamined periodically. Many companies reexamine their plans every three months and modify the plans if necessary. It is common every several months for all employees at a company to participate in dry drills that emulate a real mishap, to make them ready for the possibility of a real one.

Business continuity plans are sometimes called *business recovery plans,* and there is no question that they are vitally important. However, a key goal for management must be to avoid negative effects on the business in the first place. A good example of proper precaution measures can be seen in how Charles Schwab, the world's largest online stockbroker, handles its information system needs. In 1998, although the company had not experienced any server overload, Schwab's chief information officer decided to double the number of servers that route and process customer inquiries and transactions. The firm has never experienced any downtime, and clients have never complained about slow response. On the other hand, the world's largest auction site, eBay, has had to apologize to clients several times for long hours of un-responsiveness due to unforeseen load or DoS attacks.

Business continuity plans encompass hardware, software, people, and tasks. Chief information officers and chief technology officers can brush up on how to cope with adverse situations by reading trade journals that specialize in the subject; these publications provide model plans and analyses of real disaster cases. One such journal is *Disaster Recovery Journal.*

PRIVACY

Privacy has never been under so much attack as it has been since the dawn of the information age in the late 1950s. Computers make the collection, maintenance, and manipulation of personal data more possible, faster, less expensive, and more effective than manual methods. The growth of the Internet and its use for educational and commercial purposes makes such activities all the more faster, less expensive, and effective. A serious concern for individual privacy is growing right alongside the growth of e-commerce.

In this context, **privacy** is the ability of individuals to control information about themselves—what and how much is collected, how it may be used, and so on. In practically every country in the world, the law does *not* give people ownership of information about themselves. However, some laws limit the lawful collection and dissemination of personal information. Privacy is not specifically guaranteed by the

INTERESTING . . .

THE FBI ON FRAUD

By now we are all aware of the extent to which the Internet provides a fertile ground for fraud. What are the numbers? In 1999, Americans filed almost 18,000 complaints with the Federal Trade Commission about various types of Internet consumer fraud. The Securities and Exchange Commission receives 200 to 300 complaints per year about possible securities fraud schemes on the Internet. The FBI keeps track of the complaints and investigates many of them.

Source: Federal Bureau of Investigation, 2000

U.S. Constitution, nor by the constitutions of many other democratic states. However, the right to privacy is *implied* in the U.S. Constitution, and several laws in the United States and in other countries provide a measure of privacy to their citizens. We have come to expect that evidence of our existence will be known, but we do not expect or desire information about ourselves to be misused.

As Figure 10.7 conveys, individuals are subject to violation of their privacy by two types of organizations: government and business. All societies must deal with the natural tensions between individuals on the one hand and organizations on the other. Governments need individuals' information for planning of infrastructure and education and other services, as well as to facilitate law enforcement. Businesses collect consumer information to better target their marketing and service efforts. As employers, they monitor employees to ensure productivity and enforce corporate policies. All of these needs are legitimate. On the other hand, individuals often feel that too many organizations know too much about their pri-

F I G U R E

10.7 THREATS TO INDIVIDUAL PRIVACY

Business: Marketer

Government

Business: Employer

Individual:
Citizen
Consumer
Employee

vate lives. Some people commonly mention Big Brother in the same breath as threats to privacy. (We have come to know Big Brother, the fictional totalitarian government described by George Orwell in his 1949 classic book, *1984,* as the ultimate symbol of antiprivacy.) Therefore, many people try as hard as they can to minimize the amount of information collected about them, or, at the least, they demand that their consent to use their personal information be obtained.

INFORMATION OF THE PEOPLE, ABOUT THE PEOPLE, FOR THE PEOPLE?

Despite some fears, governments have used the Internet very little to collect information about citizens. U.S. citizens enjoy a high degree of privacy vis-à-vis their government. Agencies must disclose to individuals the purpose of any information collected about them, who will maintain it, and for how long. Citizens do not have to furnish information unless it relates to taxes or criminal investigations. A major concern of citizens in democratic countries is government monitoring of their communications. Several governments, including those of the United States, United Kingdom, and France, have either tried or succeeded in obtaining permission to monitor private communication. Because technology allows it, we are subject to monitoring of our cellular telephone conversations and Internet communications. Cellular communication uses radio waves that can be picked up by anyone with the proper equipment, an increasing amount of Internet communications, too, is carried out through radio waves, and governments have wiretapped physical communication paths as well.

Law enforcement agencies argue that they cannot effectively prevent crime and bring criminals to justice without monitoring the private communications of suspects. Because much of our communication now is digital, we can effectively foil tapping by using encryption. However, if honest citizens can do it, so can terrorists, criminals, and the intelligence agencies of hostile nations and of our own. For this reason, some governments do not allow the use of strong encryption schemes by private organizations and individuals. The U.S. government has allowed its own citizens to use such encryption schemes, but removed such encryption techniques from its list of controlled export items only in the late 1990s. The United Kingdom and France still forbid the export as well as the use of strong encryption software by their citizens.

The FBI realizes that the Internet has become a means of private communication as popular as the telephone. While a CIA program for monitoring cellular communication (code-named Echelon) has gone almost unnoticed, the FBI's Carnivore project has stirred quite a protest. Apparently, FBI agents, equipped with court warrants, have installed equipment that monitors e-mail at servers operated by commercial ISPs.

Criminals and spies routinely use public communications networks. The FBI, like other law enforcement agencies in the United States and other democratic countries, has asked for and received court warrants that allowed it to tap telephone lines and monitor cellular phones. According to the agency, electronic surveillance has been effective in securing the conviction of more than 25,600 dangerous felons over the years 1987 to 2000. Since the Internet is now a major means of communication, the FBI needs to have similar access to this medium as well. (Chapter 11 delves further into this topic.)

However, if for its surveillance the FBI were to deal with Internet communication the same way it deals with telephone communication, it would have to tap each PC from which a suspect uses the Internet. This is impractical, because people can use the same ISP service from many different locations and PCs. Thus, the agency has to tap the communication at the "gate," which is the suspect's ISP. Since many ISPs lack the facilities to discriminate among communications—that is, identify a particular subject's messages and exclude others—the FBI developed its Carnivore device. The agency argues that this device provides the FBI with a unique ability to distinguish between communications that may be lawfully intercepted and those that may not.

The device is attached to an ISP's servers with the assistance of the ISP's technical staff. The agency says Carnivore can be configured to intercept only those messages transmitted either to or from a particular suspect's e-mail address. The device records messages that can then serve as evidence in court.

Despite FBI claims, many civil advocates say that Carnivore monitors e-mail of law-abiding citizens. It is not what the FBI argues it does with Carnivore that worries these advocates, but what the device *can* do. It can read all incoming and outgoing e-mail messages, including sender and recipient names, the subject, and the content of the message. It can monitor the Web-surfing and downloading habits of the ISP's subscribers; and it can monitor all person-to-person file transfers, online purchases, and chat content. Since the FBI may receive one warrant for each ISP located in the United States, it can potentially monitor all traffic on the Internet by U.S. citizens and by individuals and business partners who interact with individuals and businesses in the United States.

BUSINESS SNOOPING ONLINE

Businesses have always been interested in information about their customers. The most voracious consumers of such information are retailers. For years, information from our credit cards along with information about our purchases has been recorded at the cash register. Often, retail clerks ask us for additional information "so we can send you our flyer." When we shop online, our information is available to online retailers as soon as we make the purchase. In fact, online retailers can now collect information not only about what we have purchased, but also about our entire visit to their site: how long we spend there every time we visit, how long we view each page, and which tabs and banners we click. If retailers need more information, such as per-month number of visits to competitors, they can purchase it from companies that specialize in online collection of consumer data. (See Chapter 9.) Businesses claim that they need such information to compete in the market. In fact, the flow of information really helps our entire economy, because it helps businesses to work efficiently. However, consumers are growing fearful of businesses snooping into their lives and feel that their privacy is under siege. How do legitimate business needs stack up against allegations of "snooping?"

INTERESTING . . .

A MILLION PER HOUR

The FBI has reasoned before the United States Congress why it must have permission to use devices such as Carnivore. The North American Securities Administrators Association has estimated that Internet-related stock fraud results in a loss to investors of approximately $10 billion per year (or nearly $1 million per hour).

Business Needs Businesses need consumer information mainly to provide better service and target their marketing more efficiently and effectively. If a company can identify those people who might want to purchase what it offers, it can target its promotion only to those and leave others alone. This ideally works for the benefit of all parties. If a business knows how its potential customers prefer to browse its site or sites, it can use this information to ensure that the pages are organized to suit the customers' preferences, and that the banners promoting attractive items appear on customer monitors. A business can easily do all that by using cookies, those small files that its site can store automatically on customers' hard disks. (Cookies were discussed in Chapter 4.)

The Internet provides great opportunities for collection of consumer data. Furthermore, the data are readily in electronic form; they do not have to be re-entered into information systems for processing, and this saves the companies much time and money. In Chapter 9, we discussed consumer profiling. Consumer profiling is a legitimate business activity.

Individuals' Fear Consumer profiling may practically result in a detailed electronic dossier on each and every person who shops and purchases online. Much collection of personal data on the Internet is carried out without the knowledge of consumers. You involuntarily provide businesses with information you might never release otherwise.

Consider what personal data Amazon.com collects about anyone who visits its site, in the company's own words posted on the site:

> You provide most such information when you search, buy, bid, post, participate in a contest or questionnaire, or communicate with customer service. For example, you provide information when you search for a product; make an order or an Auction bid; provide information in Your Account (and you might have more than one if you have used more than one e-mail address when shopping with us) or All About You; communicate with us by phone, e-mail, or otherwise; complete a questionnaire or a contest entry form; compile Wish Lists; enter a shopping Community by providing employer, school, or other such information; participate in Discussion Boards, pursuant to our Web-Based Discussion Service Terms of Agreement; provide and rate Reviews; specify a Special Occasion Reminder or a favorite charity in Charity Links; share information with Trusted Friends; and employ other Personal Notification Services, such as "Amazon.com Delivers," "Amazon.com Alerts," and "Oprah®". As a result of those actions, you might supply us with such information as your name, address, and phone number; credit card information; people to whom purchases have been shipped, including address and phone number; people (with addresses and phone numbers) listed in Gift-Click and 1-Click settings; e-mail addresses of Trusted Friends and other people; content of reviews and e-mails to us; personal description and photograph in About You; and financial information, including Social Security and driver's license numbers.

As we discussed in Chapter 9, several companies specialize in collecting personal data for online businesses, such as DoubleClick, Inc. These companies and many online retailers have detailed privacy policies that include pledges to protect individual privacy. Many homepages display links to their policies (see Figure 10.8, page 232). However, despite the attempts of businesses to calm fears, people are afraid that businesses collectively gather too much data. Worse, many people simply do not believe these companies when they promise not to exchange or sell personal data.

The fearful have good reason to fear. ToySmart.com was an online toy retailer. In its published privacy policy, it promised consumers never to share their data with other businesses. In summer of 2000, when the company declared bankruptcy, it tried to pay off debt by selling its customer data to the highest bidder. Despite public protest, a judge refused to block the sale. As it turned out, the company had collected data from children without their consent, an act forbidden by the Children's Online Privacy Protection Act of 1998 (COPPA). After the FTC intervened, the company agreed to sell the data only to another business that had the same privacy policy as ToySmart's.

In September 2000, Amazon.com revised its privacy policy. While it explained its policy in clear, nonlegalistic language, it also included the following point: "We might sell or buy stores or assets. In such transactions, customer information generally is one of the transferred business assets." In other words: The company views customer data as a sellable asset. Amazon.com also deleted the promise not to share consumer data with other businesses. Such cases leave all privacy policies hollow, at least in perception.

In July 2000, the U.S. Federal Trade Commission (FTC) submitted to Congress a list of recommendations on consumer profiling ("Online Profiling: A Report to Congress, Part 2, Recommendations"):

1. *Notice.* Data collectors must disclose their information practices before collecting personal information from consumers.
2. *Choice.* Consumers must be given options with respect to whether and how personal information collected from them may be used for purposes beyond those for which the information was provided.
3. *Access.* Consumers should be able to view and contest the accuracy and completeness of data collected about them.
4. *Security.* Data collectors must take reasonable steps to assure that information collected from consumers is accurate and secure from unauthorized use.

F I G U R E

10.8 "PRIVACY POLICY" AND "CHILDREN'S PRIVACY POLICY" LINKS ON THE SEARS.COM HOMEPAGE

Unless businesses fall into certain categories (such as medical or financial institutions), U.S. law does not require that they abide by any of these. Note that the fourth recommendation is actually two recommendations: ensuring accuracy, and ensuring that only authorized people have access to the data.

U.S. companies are notorious for not following the first recommendation. Some do have policies in place to ensure access only on a "need to know" basis. "Need to know" depends on the business's own definitions, however, and often does not satisfy civil advocates. To enforce privacy rules, some companies have established the position of chief privacy officer (CPO). The appointment of such an officer may calm fears of privacy abuse.

As opposed to the United States, all European Union nations have laws that ensure all the above rules. Violators of the law are prosecuted by a data commissioner and a government agency on behalf of the complainant. U.S. businesses have vigorously objected to the establishment of a similar agency in the United States.

Currently, the only way consumers can stop the collection of their personal data is to opt out—namely, find the Web page where they can ask the data collector to stop the collection. However, many sites do not do the data collection themselves; they hire companies such as DoubleClick to do that for them. Consumers then have to find that third party's site and opt out. To do so, they have to know that the site they visit contracted with the third party, and many consumers are not aware of the third party's role. No one is eager to inform the public about this, either.

As we mentioned in Chapter 4, you can configure your browser to reject cookies. While this sounds like a good option, it often is impractical. Most cookie-hungry sites are designed to disallow you from browsing further if your computer does not accept cookies. It's a conundrum.

To Self-Regulate or Not to Self-Regulate? In the United States, there are three not-for-profit organizations whose purpose is to guarantee that Web sites maintain adequate privacy standards: TRUSTe, BBBOnLine (Better-Business-Bureau Online), and WebTrust. The organizations respond to voluntary invitations of commercial Web sites to examine their standards. If a Web site passes the test, they allow the site to use their seal of approval. While such organizations provide e-commerce firms with a mechanism of self-regulation, most of them have not sought such seals of approval.

By 2001, fewer than 3,000 e-commerce sites had the seal of approval of any of these organizations. TRUSTe has awarded some 2,000 licenses since its 1997 inception, while BBBOnLine has passed out 727 seals since launching last year. WebTrust is considered the most stringent of the three programs. However, due to its costly fees and strict standards, WebTrust had awarded only two seals by 2001.

Several surveys revealed that the public is unimpressed with these seals of approval. Consumer advocate organizations that examined the privacy standards of firms that were awarded the TRUSTe seal found that many of them did not comply with TRUSTe's requirements.

MONITORING AT THE WORKPLACE

The Internet provides workers in today's economy with access to an abundance of information. Numerous organizations have linked their employees' workstations to the Internet. Employees use the resource mostly for two purposes: e-mail and

Web browsing. However, we often hear complaints or uneasy comments that employers monitor both e-mail and employees' navigation on the Web. Employers argue that it is their legitimate right to engage in monitoring so they can ensure productivity and adherence to security policy. Employees claim that their privacy is violated. Since employees started to use the Internet, privacy issues have cropped up concerning e-mail and Web browsing.

E-MAIL PRIVACY

In most countries, e-mail has not yet achieved the same status as traditional mail. There are privacy protections in place for letters and packages sent through the U.S Postal Service. In the case of e-mail, however, U.S. courts usually maintain that since the facilities belong to the company, employees cannot claim violation of privacy when supervisors view incoming and outgoing messages, with or without suspicion. Employees are advised to assume that every e-mail message they send or receive may be intercepted and viewed by a supervisor. In many cases, organizations have fired employees who sent offensive e-mail. In some cases, companies have fired employees who sent e-mail that did not relate to company operations.

Surveys have shown that about 60 percent of U.S. businesses have an e-mail policy. Such policies provide employees with guidelines on what is acceptable or unacceptable when using e-mail. It is important to understand that since many employees enjoy their employers e-mail service outside their offices and during off-work hours, the policies cover communication that take place from employees' homes as well.

The fact that many companies still do not have clear policies is disturbing. However, the lack of a clear policy does not absolve employees from using e-mail improperly, nor does it protect their privacy. Employers are entitled to monitor all e-mail sent and received through the hardware and software that they have made available to their employees.

Employees must also realize that when they "delete" messages, the messages may not actually be deleted from corporate systems. Many companies keep a record of every e-mail message that passes through their facilities. When employers discover private, offensive, or other messages that violate their policies or expectations, they can use the records as reason for dismissal.

A key reason companies monitor employee e-mail is to protect against lawsuits over sexually explicit, racist, or libelous material generated on the job. Monitoring e-mail may deter potential offenders, and dismissal due to offences may save the company from lawsuits. In 2000, the American Management Association reported that nearly 80 percent of companies in the United States were electronically monitoring their employees. Electronic monitoring includes use of e-mail. A 2000 study by the Pew Internet Project found that 10 percent of computer users know someone who was fired for browsing the Web or was dismissed over an e-mail message.

Civil advocates and union operatives have argued that e-mail is a common substitute for traditional mail, and since the law forbids the opening of private mail, it should also forbid the monitoring of private e-mail. In 2000, the European Union started exploring the idea of legislating against employer monitoring of employee e-mail.

Article 8(1) of the European Convention provides that everyone has the right to respect for his private and family life, his home, *and his correspondence*. Yet the United Kingdom, a member of the European Union, passed a law that gives employers and government sweeping power to monitor private electronic communications. The law, the Investigatory Powers Act of 2000, lets the government force an ISP to provide access to a client's communications in secret; allows the government to perform mass surveillance of communications in transit; allows the government to force ISPs to fit their equipment to facilitate surveillance; enables the government to demand that someone surrender keys to protected information; allows the government to monitor people's Internet activities; and prevents the existence of interception warrants and any data collected under them from being revealed in court. The act's "interception warrants" can be served for purposes of "national security," "preventing or detecting serious crime," or "safeguarding the economic well-being of the UK." These terms are not defined and are so vague as to be applicable to just about anyone under any circumstance.

The flip side of the coin often works against employers. Although this is not a matter of individual privacy, it is important that you realize that the company for which you may work as a manager does not enjoy much "privacy" either. Employees have used e-mail records to successfully sue their employers. In one case, a female worker complained that she was fired because of her gender. Her lawyer summoned the company's e-mail records. Apparently, one executive had sent a message to a subordinate in which he called the worker a "bitch." The court interpreted this as sexual discrimination and awarded the worker over two hundred thousand dollars in punitive damages.

The major concern for monitoring employees is productivity. Employers want to ensure that company resources, including paid time, are not wasted. E-mail and chat software may distract employees from productive work. Thus, employers feel it is their right to monitor the use of such resources to minimize unproductive use of computer resources in general, and e-mail in particular.

WEB-BROWSING PRIVACY

Much like e-mail monitoring, supervisors can monitor navigation on the Web unbeknownst to employees. Many companies have strict policies about surfing the Internet for nonbusiness purposes. Many employees have lost their jobs for violating such policies. In 2000, Vault.com, an online recruiting firm, conducted a survey whose results revealed how ignorant employees may be regarding what employers can monitor.

According to the survey, approximately 53 percent of employees believe that their personal use of the Internet goes unnoticed at work, while in reality 42 percent of managers observe employees' Web browsing by using monitoring software or other means. Employers have good reasons for such monitoring. The survey found that 40 percent of the responding workers made online purchases on company time, 37 percent searched for another job, 13 percent downloaded music, and 4 percent visited pornographic Web sites. Only 10 percent of the workers said they never used the Internet at work for personal reasons, while 25 percent said they spent up to an hour a day at non-work-related sites.

SUMMARY

- Security is the most important factor in people's decisions to make purchases online. Threats to the security of online information systems include hacking, Web site defacement, computer viruses, denial of service, and spoofing.

- Hacking is the unauthorized access to an information system. In the Internet age, businesses are highly vulnerable to hacking. Hackers often do not stop at peeking into the files of a site; they often deface Web pages, causing damage to the firm in terms of time and the real risk that potential clients may not visit again.

- Computer viruses spread from computer to computer and destroy data files and software, much as biological viruses spread among living organisms and destroy cells. The Internet, like other networks, is a conduit for spreading viruses. Viruses slow down communication and cause millions of dollars in damages to organizations and individuals. Viruses that spread through computer networks are often called worms. Viruses that are transmitted when camouflaged with benign programs are called Trojan horses.

- Denial of service occurs when perpetrators bombard a site with log-on requests, making it impossible for legitimate users to obtain service. Distributed denial of service occurs when perpetrators use multiple computers to request simultaneous log-on to a site; the owners of the computers do not know their computers were involved.

- Spoofing is the hijacking of a domain name to divert traffic from the intended site to another site, often one that maligns the legitimate site. Telecommunications companies must take the lead in developing antispoofing measures and standardizing them for use. Individual sites can do nothing against spoofing, because spoofing depends on the robustness of DNS servers, which are controlled by these companies.

- To prevent security violations, companies must establish access codes. Usually access codes combine a user ID (also called a username) and a secret password. Biometrics, which are physical characteristics such as fingerprints, voice, or retinas, can be used in lieu of a password system, because a biometric identification is unique to an individual. Use of biometrics requires installation of special readers.

- It is important to make security measures transparent. Noticeable measures that slow down access may irritate clients, business partners, and employees.

- Firewalls are special hardware and software that block outside users' access to designated parts of a networked resource and disable employee access to certain parts of the Internet.

- Businesses must expect to be attacked by hackers and viruses and subject to natural disasters. To avoid loss of data, they must back up all data and software. The backed-up files must be stored off-site.

- Encryption is the ciphering of plain messages into unreadable messages. Encryption enables authentication and confidentiality in communication over computer networks.

- Electronic signatures can replace traditional, physical signatures for validation of commercial agreements. When using the public key method, a digital signature is the digest of a message after it has been encrypted with a user's public key.

- A digital certificate is a computer file that serves as the equivalent of an ID card. Trusted parties called certificate authorities issue digital certificates.

- To minimize the damages of security breaches, companies establish business continuity plans.

- The proliferation of the Internet as an educational and business medium has exacerbated violation of individual privacy. Three parties may violate the privacy of individuals: government, businesses, and employers. All three parties have a legitimate need to collect data on individuals and to monitor people, but their practices often threaten privacy.

- Although encryption software can protect privacy, many governments forbid the sale or export of strong encryption applications. Law enforcement agencies have tapped the Internet to monitor communication among criminals, terrorists, and spies.
- Businesses accumulate personal data mainly through online consumer profiling. While many companies have privacy policies, some have not kept their word, and others clearly see personal data as a sellable asset.
- Businesses monitor their employees' e-mail and Web use to ensure that they do not offend fellow employees and to monitor productivity. Supervisors also monitor employee navigation on the Web to prevent access to controversial sites.

KEY TERMS

online security	DMZ
hacker	encryption
Web page defacement	decryption
computer virus	symmetric key
worm	asymmetric key
Trojan horse	public key
denial of service	electronic signature
distributed denial of service	digital signature
spoofing	hashing algorithm
authentication	message digest
username	digital certificate
biometrics	certificate authority
confidentiality	secure sockets layer
transparency	business continuity plan
firewall	privacy

REVIEW QUESTIONS

1. In what sense are computer viruses similar to biological ones?
2. What is denial of service on the Internet? Is there a remedy to distributed denial of service?
3. Why can individual Web sites do nothing against spoofing?
4. What are biometrics? How are they better as access codes than assigned passwords?
5. What does transparency mean in the context of information system security measures? Why is it important?
6. Why is on-site backup not as good as off-site backup of computer files?
7. What is an electronic signature in the broadest sense of the term? What is a digital signature when the public key method is used to encrypt messages?
8. On the Internet and other computer networks, what is the equivalent of tamper-proof photo identification cards?
9. Do business continuity plans prevent downtime of information systems? What exactly is their purpose?
10. What legitimate reasons do governments, businesses, and employers have for monitoring and collecting personal data?

DISCUSSION QUESTIONS

1. Imagine you visit your favorite site, and the homepage is filled with obscenity. Would you shun the site from now on? What could be the reason for the new appearance?
2. Go to the FBI Web site (*www.fbi.gov*), read the agency's statement on Carnivore, and formulate your own opinion. Is the use of Carnivore or a similar device in violation of civil rights? Even if it might be, should we still accept its use so the agency can protect society better?
3. Visit *www.gator.com*. Read what service the site offers, and watch the online demonstration. Would you install the software on your computer? Why or why not?
4. Civil advocates argue that, at the least, businesses should practice "informed consent" before they collect and sell personal data. What is informed consent?
5. Would you favor a law against monitoring employees' e-mail? Explain your position.

ASSIGNMENTS

1. Research the literature on the economics of information systems security. Suppose you are the chief information officer of your company. Companies have limited resources for IS security. Consider the value of these systems and evaluate the availability of information to your company. How would you estimate the amount of money the company should allocate, annually, to reduce the risk of system downtime and other mishaps (such as data destruction and information theft)? Prepare a report explaining how you would calculate the right amount for your company's IS security budget.

2. Read the privacy statements of DoubleClick, iVillage, Microsoft, and Barnesandnoble.com (*www.doubleclick.com/privacy_policy, www.microsoft.com/info/privacy.htm, www.ivillage.com/help/tos.html,* and *www.barnesandnoble.com/help/nc_privacy_policy.asp,* respectively). Write a two-to-three-page report summarizing the principles of these companies' privacy policies. Give your opinion about the degree to which each of these sites guard individual privacy, and rank the sites in ascending order (from worst to best) in terms of privacy protection.

E-COMMERCE TODAY

Too Much Love

Sometimes, love can suffocate you. Just ask Fran Wood. Wood is the chief operations officer (COO) of the New Mexico State Highway Department. On May 4, 2000, he was sitting in a meeting in Albuquerque when he received an urgent telephone call from his Santa Fe office. He couldn't believe his ears. All the computers of his department had been flooded by e-mail messages, all of which bore the subject "I Love You." The Love Bug worm, a virus multiplying and spreading in networks, had destroyed text files and JPEG files all over his systems. And it was still attacking.

The highway department uses many JPEG files. JPEG is a standard for graphics files commonly used in Web pages. The unit hit hardest was the Engineering Department. Wood estimated the number of files affected to be 50,000 to 60,000. In its engineering design process, the department uses many JPEG files, including those taken with digital cameras and scanned into digital documents. The destruction came at the worst time possible. Wood's organization was in the midst of integrating Microsoft Exchange and Microsoft Outlook into a single e-mail program. It did not have an emergency plan to deal with virus attacks and other security threats.

Wood's first instruction was to shut down every computer and piece of peripheral equipment. The equipment was unplugged for two days. Everything on computers, from design processes to communications, was shut down. During these two days, all employees went back to using paper and pencils.

The next step Wood took was the establishment of an IT crisis management team. The team included employees from his own organization as well as members of several consulting firms and equipment vendors. To check if the virus was still spreading, the team turned on several computers less than 24 hours after the attack, only to shut them down immediately; the virus *was* still spreading. The source, it was determined, was outside computers linked to those of Wood's organization.

An application called Microsoft Information Scan was used to remove the worm from the Exchange e-mail application. Then, an antivirus program called Trend Micro ScanMail was deployed to stop the virus from entering any computers linked to an outside network. Wood scanned all his 100 servers and 1,750 desktop computers in 128 locations throughout New Mexico to locate infected systems and clean them. Next, new software was installed to ensure that no unknown machine could log on to his organization's network until its "identity" was established. Finally, another antivirus application called Sophos was distributed and installed on each of the organization's computers from a single central computer.

In addition to the software solution, a new policy was established. The policy required that employees take precautions with suspected types of files such as Script files, ZIP files, and .exe (executable) files when receiving e-mail.

It took one week to bring 90 to 99 percent of the computers and peripheral equipment back online, in good condition and clean of any virus. Fortunately, not a single project was jeopardized and no federal appropriation was denied as a result of this terrible experience. Wood admitted he was totally surprised by the sophistication of the virus and the speed at which it spread and destroyed files.

Now, security technology is playing a more important role at the New Mexico State Highway Department. Both new software and policies minimize the chances of another such attack.

Source: Fonseca, B., "Security means never having to say 'I Love You'," *Infoworld,* July 10, 2000

Thinking About E-Commerce Today

1. What caused the paralyzing of Wood's organization?
2. Why are the types of files mentioned in this case more dangerous than some others?
3. If you were in charge of the information systems of an organization, what would you do to minimize the chances of a virus attack?

LEGAL ISSUES

■ Explain the current legal challenges facing parties engaged in e-commerce

■ Contrast the two approaches to adjudicating e-commerce lawsuits

■ Discuss the challenges of protecting intellectual property on the Internet

■ Form an opinion about legal restrictions on online commerce and expression

■ Compare the legal approaches of different countries to privacy on the Web

■ Explain how the Web may facilitate unfair trade practices

Using the Internet as a medium for doing business has created an international environment in which multiple laws may govern the same transaction. How does a business prepare for and solve problems in this environment? Consider what the management of the giant extranet firm Bolero.com did before implementing its online commerce hub. To develop its system, Bolero conducted studies of e-commerce laws and legal systems in 18 different jurisdictions, relying on the skills and knowledge of its broad group of backers on several continents. Based on the information gathered, managers were able to set up a system that allowed electronic documents to function, legally, in place of their paper equivalents. To ensure that Bolero deals carry the same legal standing as traditional paper transactions, members of this online trading community must agree to a multipart contract that binds every user of the system.

In Chapter 5 we mentioned that online businesses must be aware of legal obstacles. We specifically discussed how difficult it might be to open auction Web sites in some European countries because of antiquated laws or laws that were recently passed to protect auctioneer guilds. In the realm of legal challenges that relate to the Internet, this is only the tip of the iceberg. There are 191 countries in the world. Some countries, such as the United States, Brazil, and Germany, are federations of states that have their own legislatures as well. Thus, the world has several hundreds, if not thousands, of political units with their own laws, and these laws can be quite different from each other.

As long as commercial activities and information exchanges take place within a political unit, a single law governs the exchange. However, when the parties involved operate from different political units with different laws, the legal environment becomes unclear at best and messy at worst. Questions such as the following arise:

- *Does an electronic transaction have to be signed on paper?* The answer is no for the United States, Ireland, Mexico, and Bermuda, and yes for almost every other country.
- *May Internet auction participants place any item they wish for auction?* The answer is no in most countries, but there are fewer restrictions on auctioned items in the United States than in most European and Asian countries.
- *Are pornographic sites legal?* The answer is yes in the United States and Western Europe and no in almost all the rest of the world.

Remember that a Web site can be technically accessed from virtually anywhere in the world. A site or the activities taking place through the site very well may be legal in some parts of the world and illegal in other parts.

The combination of the proliferation of digital technology and the spread of the Internet and other public networks has created great challenges in several legal areas—primarily contracts, protection of intellectual property, and free speech. Legislatures the world over have tried to sort out which legal doctrines should be applied to the Internet, and which cannot, or should not, govern the Internet. In this chapter we discuss the dilemmas and some legal responses to the dilemmas.

WHERE CAN I SUE YOU?

Suppose you purchased an item from a site located in another country, and the item arrived defective or long after the time it was promised, rendering it nearly useless for your purposes. Imagine also that your request for compensation or another remedy was not addressed satisfactorily after much effort on your part. You decide to sue the e-retailer. Where do you file the lawsuit? Do you file in your own country or in the e-retailer's country? The venue of e-commerce lawsuits is still undecided in many parts of the world.

For centuries, legal maps followed political maps of the world. Laws were passed for defined territories: countries, states, counties, and towns. Territorial law is impractical in e-commerce, because it is often meaningless. The "territory" in question is cyberspace, and cyberspace is everywhere. Therefore, there is currently much uncertainty about jurisdiction for the enforcement of laws as they relate to e-commerce.

In November 2000, the European Union passed a law that lets a consumer file a lawsuit against an online business in any of the 15 member countries comprising the Union. Before the amendment to the 1968 Brussels Convention (an agreement that regulates commercial-legal issues in the Union), consumers could sue an online business only in the courts of the country of the online business. Now, if an online business is operating with consumers in a certain country, the consumers can sue the business in their own national courts. Businesses vehemently opposed this move, but consumer advocates asserted that people would be more confident about buying from international Web sites if they knew they could get redress in their own country's courts.

As we have seen, the issue of e-commerce jurisdiction is a broad one. The U.S. Federal Trade Commission and European government organizations have examined the issue in an attempt to reach an international agreement such as the one reached within the European Union.

There are two approaches to such agreement. One approach is the **country of origin** principle, whereby all legal matters are confined to the jurisdiction of the country from which the site operates. Under this principle, the laws of that country apply to the operations of the site and whoever interacts with the site, regardless of the location of those who interact. A lawsuit can be brought only in the country of the Web site's owner, and it would be adjudicated according to that country's laws. With this approach, it is likely that many firms would opt to establish Web sites in countries with lax consumer protection laws.

The other approach is the **country of destination**, a system in which the laws of the country to which the site caters apply to any dealings with the site, regardless of the site owner's country. This is the approach that the European Union adopted within its territory. It may take several years until we see an international agreement on Web site jurisdiction.

DO I HAVE TO SIGN IT ON PAPER?

Under the laws of many countries, many types of contracts bind the parties only if they are made on paper and signed, in ink, by both parties. Until 2000, the laws of 49 of the 50 U.S. states (the Uniform Commercial Code) required that any contract for the sale of physical goods of $500 or more must be signed on paper. Americans, however, decided to change this requirement.

As we mentioned in Chapter 10, the Electronic Signatures in Global and National Commerce Act became a U.S. law in 2000. The law has the potential to reduce the costs of e-business, as well as to simplify business processes and make them more efficient. The act states that the two parties wanting to use an electronic signature define the signature themselves. An electronic signature could be "an electronic sound, symbol, or process, attached to or logically associated with a contract or other record and executed or adopted by a person with the intent to sign the record."

The act provides that no contract, signature, or record shall be denied legal effect solely because it is in electronic form. However, it does not require anyone to agree to use or accept electronic records, signatures, or contracts. The act also precludes, in most cases, any requirement that one type of technology be used instead of another. In most cases, electronic contracts and records are legally enforceable only if they are in a form that can be retained and accurately reproduced for later reference by relevant parties. As is the case with traditional paper documents, the electronic signature is invalid if the document is changed after the signing.

The United States was not the first country to enact an important law regarding electronic commerce. Bermuda passed one of the world's first e-commerce laws of any country. In the summer of 1999, the government of Bermuda passed the Electronic Transactions Act, which, among other provisions, makes electronic signatures binding in commercial contracts.

In 2000, two other countries made electronic signatures legal: Mexico and Ireland. In April 2000, the government of Mexico passed a law that recognizes Internet purchase orders as binding contracts. The new reforms to Mexico's civil and commercial codes validate electronic signatures used for Internet orders. The new law requires that all electronic transactions comply with existing commerce and advertising standards. The law also says that companies should keep copies of documents related to online transactions for at least 10 years, and that all consumer data submitted electronically must be kept confidential. Ireland passed a similar law in July 2000.

Note that electronic signatures can take many forms and use several techniques. Some of the techniques are the same ones used instead of passwords, such as biometrics. We discussed biometrics in Chapter 10.

ELECTRONIC SIGNATURES: THE PROS

Laws recognizing electronic signatures as legal signatures have some clear benefits. Electronic signatures reduce paperwork costs, save trees, and increase the convenience of processes such as receiving loans and purchasing real estate, automobiles, and insurance policies. In the words of President Clinton's administration, "Consumers will have the option of buying insurance, getting a mortgage, or opening a brokerage account on-line, without waiting days for the paperwork to be mailed back and forth." Proponents of such laws argue that electronic signatures are needed to continue the growth of online commerce.

To the critics who say it is easy to forge electronic signatures, supporters of the measure say that to forge an electronic signature one must know much about the victim, a fact that sets a fairly high threshold for forgery. Fraud, they argue, exists and will continue to exist, offline as well as online. Obviously, the new law does not relieve anyone from criminal prosecution for fraud, regardless how the fraud is carried out.

ELECTRONIC SIGNATURES: THE CONS

Anything contraindicating electronic signatures has much to do with the concerns of consumer advocates. The law may encourage unscrupulous characters to usurp or forge electronic signatures and purchase high-price items while pretending that they are someone else. Advocates have other concerns as well. The law, they say, increases consumers' burden of proof that they did not purchase, for instance, a new house or a Mercedes online. As stated earlier, electronic signatures by definition are not confined to a specific technology—they can be enacted by sounds, symbols, or voice. This leaves the door open, consumer advocates argue, for an unscrupulous telemarketer to tell consumers that they ordered merchandise by pressing a button on a telephone dial pad or by hitting the Enter key on a computer keyboard. Also, critics say, while it is relatively difficult to forge a physical signature, it is not as difficult to forge an electronic one.

When you write, paint, compose music, develop a new technology or software, or create anything else that has value in terms of art or ingenuity, the result may be of commercial value. New machines, new methods, and artistic works have the potential to benefit millions of people in the form of greater productivity, improved well-being, and more enjoyable lives. Some people create for the love of art or the sheer enjoyment of it, but many individuals and organizations would not embark on such efforts without assurances that they can benefit monetarily from the fruits of their efforts. Therefore, nations have laws that regard these fruits as **intellectual property**.

The purpose of intellectual property laws is to provide protections that may encourage people and organizations to spend resources in the development of new technological ideas and artistic works, so that all of us can enjoy and benefit from them. The sole right to sell copies of a work or use new technologies and methods is the incentive that spurs some of us to write books, compose music, invent machines, and develop software. This is why it is so important to have laws that protect the rights one has over one's creative work.

In most countries, the law addresses several types of intellectual property: trademarks, copyrights, patents, and trade secrets. The applicability of laws affecting trade secrets has not been affected much by the information age, and therefore we will not discuss them here. Trademarks and copyrights, however, have been at the center of much legal debate and new legislation because of the Internet. Trademarks are now highly associated with Internet domain names. Copyrights have been challenged by the ease and low cost of duplicating and disseminating artistic work. In addition, software patents have been a sore issue for many years, and issues regarding Internet patents have been even more troubling. What are the laws addressing these types of intellectual property? What is the controversy over the new laws, and how are the old laws applied to this new e-commerce world?

WHAT'S IN A NAME?

When new parents wish to name their baby, they can use any name they wish (unless state law restricts this right). There are millions of Michaels and Jennifers, and no parent of a Michael or Jennifer would try to prevent another newborn from being named the same. This is because people's names are not owned by anyone. Even within the business community, owners of businesses operating in very different markets can, by law, use the same name for their business—they do not compete. One example of such a case is Apple, a name used both by the well-known computer maker and the record company that holds the rights to the Beatles' music.

The legal picture is different on the Internet. Recall that virtually all businesses apply for a domain name that is associated with their assigned IP number; Internet surfers can then use words, which are easier to remember than numbers. Once a domain name is assigned to an IP number, it cannot be assigned to any other IP number. That means that once an individual or business is granted that name, no one else can use it, as long as the name owner continues to promptly pay its fees to the domain-name registrar. As the number of Web sites has increased to many millions, domain names are less and less available. Numerous contentions have caused the courts to deal with domain names in practically the same manner that they deal with trademarks. The phenomenon of cybersquatting has evolved from the opportunity to register a name that may at some point in the future become sought after by someone.

URLs as Trademarks As soon as business started to flourish on the Internet, managers realized that "cybernames" are assets as important to Internet business as they are to traditional business. The *mywonderfulbrandname* in the *www.mywonderfulbrandname.com* Web address identifies the firm and effectively functions as a trademark. A trademark is any text, picture, color, sound, or scent that associates a product with its producer. (A mark associated with a service is a service mark.) Under U.S. law, a business does not have to *register* a trademark, only *use* it, to establish it as a legal trademark. (Note that use of the symbol ™ does not require registration, although many companies do register their trademarks, in which case they are allowed to use the symbol ®.)

Due to the immense potential for legal contentions between parties that may have the same or very similar domain names, courts have adopted the approach of treating domain names as trademarks. However, the potential for conflict is much greater with domain names, because by the nature of the beast the same domain name can be used by only one party. This is very different from what happens offline, where two companies may legally use the same name as long as they do not compete in the same market. Since a trademark communicates the reputation of a certain company and its products, consumers are expected not to confuse fragrance with hardware, or music with computers. If courts could, they would allow a fragrance maker and a doorknob manufacturer to use the domain name *www.rose.com*, and, in addition, they would allow a person named Rose Smith to use the same name for her private Web site. However, this is impossible.

As it stands, then, the current legal approach is to allow only a company that has used a word as a trademark to use it as part of a domain name as well. If more than one company has used a word or phrase as a trademark, the first to register it as a domain name may keep it. Mere ownership of a domain name does not automatically guarantee that the owner can keep the name; the courts have forced owners to give the name to another party in cases where that party passed the above criteria. Owners of generic domain names such as business.com, drugs.com, and flowers.com may keep or sell the names.

How much a domain name may be worth to a new online venture is illustrated by the sums of money that have been paid for some domain names. The owners of drugs.com bought it for $1 million from a person who registered it but had not used it by the time the sale took place. ECompanies, an incubator for start-up Internet businesses, paid $7.5 million for the domain name business.com. The name is now used by one of the companies that ECompanies "incubates."

Both individuals and organizations continue to register domain names in large and increasing numbers. It took three years for the total number of registered names to reach one million, but in 1999 alone over five million names were registered. By 2001, 29 million names were registered, 18 million of them as .com. This glut of domain names prompted ICANN (Internet Corporation for Assigned Names and Numbers) to add top-level domains to the existing .com, .net, and .org (domains such as .edu, .mil, and .gov are reserved for higher education institutions, the military, and government agencies, respectively, and cannot be registered by individuals and commercial organizations). More than 400 additional top domains were suggested, including .biz, .inc, and .corp. ICANN approved .aero for air transportation, .biz for businesses, .coop for cooperative businesses, .info for general use, .museum for museums, .name for individuals and families, and .pro for professionals such as physicians.

Holders of famous trademarks (mainly large corporations) resisted the addition of new domains. Imagine the difficulties that a company such as Coca-Cola might encounter. Instead of defending its trademark against usurpers within three general top-level domains and 243 country top-level domains, the company would have to fight those who register its name with another few hundred suffixes. Smaller companies, to protect themselves completely, would have to spend thousands of dollars registering their names and trademarks with every possible top-level domain name, which might be a financial burden.

Cybersquatting   Registering domain names has always been inexpensive and quick. The ease and economics of domain-name registration has encouraged many individuals and organizations to register domain names in order to sell them later at a much higher price. The phenomenon, mentioned earlier, is known as **cybersquatting**. Many companies have had to wrest domain names from cybersquatters. Among them are Christian Dior, Nike, Deutsche Bank AG, and Microsoft Corporation. The practice is legal as long as another party does not own the domain name as a business name or trademark. To address the problem, the United States adopted the Anticybersquatting Consumer Protection Act of 1999. The rule that the act defines reflects the legal approach of most Western nations: If the domain name registered was in use as a business name or trademark before the registration and the business demands the domain name, the registrar must transfer the domain name to the business; the business pays the owner the registration fee.

In recent years, several global organizations have assumed arbitration roles in disputes over domain names. One is ICANN, and another is the World Intellectual Property Organization (WIPO). WIPO is a United Nations organization with offices in Geneva, Switzerland. ICANN has a set of rules called Uniform Dispute Resolution Policy (UDRP). Both organizations have been criticized for giving preference to large, established companies and for being unfair to individuals and small businesses. WIPO has been accused more strongly, especially because large companies fund the organization.

Observers say that the U.S. act and the UDRP can restrict free speech and suppress smaller companies with legitimate claims to a domain name that do not have the funds to take a dispute to court. In particular, the act's "bad faith intent" may curb what seems to be a legitimate business: Registering domain names currently not in use by anyone in order to sell them later for a higher price. Several firms have engaged in this activity; among them are BuyDomains.com and Domain Collection, Inc. These firms purchase random words that may become popular with the intent of making a profit. They usually pay $15 to $60 per name and resell a name for several thousand dollars. This brings up an interesting question: Who has the right to a word?

The problem becomes more complicated when individuals register private names. In June 2000, Julia Roberts, Hollywood's highest paid actress, won back her own name from a cybersquatter after taking her case to WIPO. It was determined that the man who had registered the domain name clearly did so in bad faith. However, what should WIPO, or any other arbitrating organization or court, decide if a real woman legally named Julia Roberts had registered her own name as a domain name? The actress argued that she had "trademark rights" to her name, which is true, because her name is commercially valuable; but does that mean that another Julia Roberts could not hold on to her own domain name had she registered it?

M. P. III

MP3 is a standard (that is, a format) for digitizing music files. When entrepreneur Michael Robertson wanted to use MP3 as part of his new Web site, he discovered that the name had already been registered to someone else. A quick inquiry revealed that a young man whose initials were M. P. III (son of M. P. Jr.) had registered the domain name. Mr. M. P. had no idea what MP3 was. He sold the domain name to Robertson for $1,000. MP3.com became one of the world's most visited Web sites—and the source of a major legal battle over the distribution of copyrighted music.

The Weak Link   Linking pages on the Web may sometimes blur the lines between the creative work of one party and another. It is perfectly legal to create a link to anyone's site, and you do not need the permission of the site's owner to do so. The owner of the other site may actually welcome such a link. However, you must make sure that you do not misrepresent the work of another site as if it were yours.

For example, you will violate copyright laws if you link other sites in frames at your own site. This is akin to copying the other site's page and pasting it at your site. Similarly, you should never allow users to execute applications directly from other people's sites. If you want to let your visitors know about an application that can be downloaded or run from another site, create a link at your site to the page from which the application can be downloaded. The principle is simple: You must make certain that your visitors know that the link takes them to the other site, and that the art they see, be it illustration or writing or another creative element, belongs to the other site. Otherwise, you will be violating the law.

Copying text, pictures, sound, and animation from any site is very easy on the Web. Doing so without permission breaks the law. Never display other people's materials without permission. Be aware that there are several ways to get caught, and some of them are very trustworthy. Many companies and individuals use a technique called *watermarking*. A watermark is an invisible digital mark embedded in pictures. When you copy the picture, you copy the mark as well. Organizations use special software that scours the Web. When the software detects such a mark, you are "busted"—the organization knows that you illegally used its copyrighted materials. These marks are admissible in court as a clear indication that you violated the organization's copyright.

COPYRIGHT AND COPYWRONG

The purpose of copyright laws is to grant a person or organization the sole right of copying, using, and selling a work, thereby ensuring that the creators of the work can gain financially from it. In the United States, the entire Title 17 of the United States Code is devoted to copyrights. The U.S. Copyright Act of 1976 provides protection for "original works of authorship fixed in any tangible medium of expression, now known or later developed, from which they can be perceived, reproduced or otherwise communicated, either directly or with the aid of a machine or device."

To have a copyright, creators must only fix their creation in a "tangible medium," such as paper or magnetic disk. Authors do not have to add their names, dates, or copyright sign (©) on the medium to have a copyright, but usually they do, as a warning against illegal copying. In the United States, creators can also register the work. Registration makes it easier to file a lawsuit against violators of copyrights.

In this information age, almost every artistic work can be digitized and transformed into electronic form: books, music, pictures, motion pictures, and more. Unlike other methods of copying, digital copying often results in a duplicate that is of quality equal to that of the original. Digital copying is cheap and fast. Dissemination of copied work is cheap and fast. These features of digital copying and dissemination have changed the landscape of copyright protection. It makes such protection very fragile and difficult to enforce.

The United States Congress has amended the law several times to keep pace with technological advancement. In 1998, Congress passed the Digital Millennium Copyright Act (DMCA) to clarify certain issues of the digital copying of artistic works. For example, the act clarifies that protection of copyrights applies to streaming audio over the Internet.

Music and motion pictures are recorded digitally on CDs and DVDs (digital video discs). The recording and motion picture industries have developed methods to ensure that music and motion pictures cannot be copied. However, many talented people (typically teenagers, who have enormous amounts of free time) have developed applications that can overcome such methods. Using such software, millions of people can make illegal copies of music and films, a practice commonly called **piracy**. DMCA prohibits the circumvention of antipiracy mechanisms of digital devices and the use of code-breaking devices to illegally copy software. (However, digital copying is legal when used for encryption research or for testing the security of systems.)

In 2000, the Motion Picture Association of America successfully sued several organizations and individuals who had posted on the Web computer code that helps circumvent DVD encryption. The circumvention allowed users to copy DVD movies onto personal computers. Similarly, the world's largest recording firms successfully shut down some operations of MP3.com, a site that posted thousands of musical pieces the public could download and replay. MP3 is a digital format for storing compressed music files while maintaining high-quality sound. Another site, Napster, provided tools that let subscribers swap unauthorized MP3 music files with each other, bypassing the traditional industry distribution methods. The industry's lawsuit against the hugely popular Napster was successful.

DMCA protects ISPs against lawsuits. ISPs are not responsible if subscribers use their servers to post illegally copied files. ISPs must remove Web sites that violate the law only when the copyright holder notifies them.

"Victims" of the DMCA—operators of sites such as MP3.com and Napster and thousands of their supporters—have used an interesting argument against outlawing their software and services: By doing so, the government violates their right to free speech. In their minds, free speech includes the freedom to post on the Web whatever one likes, including music, sound, and code-cracking software. While this argument may go overboard, it is likely that Congress will take another look at DMCA.

Regardless of what governments do, some critics of the film and recording industries argue that the "big business" industries should adopt the new software themselves and develop an alternative distribution method, collaborating with the Napsters of the world. Such collaboration, they argue, may eventually benefit all parties involved—the artists, the industries, and the public—by providing convenient online techniques to sample and purchase music and films.

One can see early signs of a move in this direction in the settlement that MP3.com reached with Universal Music Group, as well as in the settlement that Napster signed with Bertelsmann AG, a large German media company that owns BMG (Bertelsmann Music Group), one of the world's largest record companies. Before MP3 and Napster were sued, both online companies allowed free downloads and sharing of music that had been recorded by artists for the record companies. Part of the first settlement gave MP3.com permission to include Universal's entire music catalog and recordings for download at its site. In the Napster settlement, the two companies agreed to try a new business model for the service: a monthly subscription fee to compensate artists, record labels (as these companies are known in the business world), and publishers each time a song is shared.

PATENTLY WRONG?

In December 1999, a U.S. district court issued a preliminary injunction against Barnes & Noble, forbidding the bookseller to continue to offer buyers the "one click" feature when making purchases. Once they have made a decision to purchase an item, repeat buyers can execute the transaction with one click of a button on the Web page. This saves them the time of reentering credit information or even the time to review any personal or credit information before they execute the purchase.

Barnes & Noble's formidable competitor, Amazon.com, holds a patent for the one click feature. U.S. Patent No. 5,960,411, titled "Method and System for Placing a Purchase Order Via a Communications Network," gave Amazon.com the exclusive right to what Barnes & Noble called "Express Lane."

A patent gives the inventor of a device or method the exclusive right to make, use, or sell the device or method for 20 years. The invention must be innovative, unobvious, and useful. Until the early 1990s, business methods could not be patented in the United States. Only tangible devices, production processes, and some types of software applications could be patented. For example, patents were granted for the automatic transmission mechanism in motor vehicles and for chemical processes for the production of medications. The first patent awarded for a business method opened the floodgates, and hundreds of such patents have since been awarded. The fact that a single company seizes the right to use a business method, along with the fact that many such methods have been in use for some time and are only reapplied on the Internet, vexes many people.

Again, patents give inventors a monopoly for a limited number of years (20 years for patents, 50 years for individual copyrights, and 75 years for corporate copyrights). The idea is to encourage innovation so that society as a whole can benefit from innovative technologies and methods. The underlying assumption is that while the patent holder reaps economic rewards for 20 years, the rest of us can use the invention free of charge after this period. However, the reality of information technology in general, and of the Internet in particular, is one of fast changes. If we award a patent for a business method on the Web, we will probably never get to the point where we can use the invention free of charge because well before the patent's expiration a better method for the same process may be in place—and that method may be patented as well. In other words, the patent holder is given exclusivity while society does not get its full share of the deal.

The U.S. Patent and Trademark Office (PTO) has been roundly criticized for awarding the one click patent, many other software patents, and **business method patents**. Critics say that the one-click application would be implemented by many organizations whether Amazon.com "invented" it or not. They feel that such patents actually delay the development of productivity on the Web instead of promoting it. They call on the PTO to grant such patents more judiciously. Some argue that the entire idea of granting business method patents is foolish, and that, at the least, such patents should not be granted when the application takes place on the Web.

In 2000, Japan's patent office set higher standards for business method patents. Under the new guidelines, a business method or its associated technology must be considered a major advancement. Small improvements of standard business practices are no longer eligible for patents. The European Patent Office (EPO), which is the equivalent of the PTO for nations of the European Union, is not as generous as the PTO. Current EPO policy does not allow patents for software except when the software is an extricable part of a larger program, such as an operating system. This eliminates any patents for business methods in general and for e-commerce in particular.

In the United States, several members of the House of Representatives introduced H.R. 5364, the Business Method Patent Improvement Act of 2000. If the bill is made a law, it will limit the PTO in granting business method patents. The bill mandates that all business method patent applications be automatically published, and that the public can protest and oppose the sought patent. Applicants will have to reveal if and how a patentability search was conducted. (A patentability search is a search for previous inventions that essentially include the invention claimed in the application.) Currently, the content of a patent application is not subject to public scrutiny.

FREE SPEECH

Free speech has been one of the most important pillars of democratic societies. It is protected by the constitutions of the United States and many other countries. As the Internet has become a highly available and inexpensive means of communication, individuals and organizations use it to transmit potentially objectionable materials in the form of text, pictures, sounds, and movies. However, what is objectionable to one person is acceptable to another. In addition to the classic issue of freedom of expression, the Internet also poses the issue of spamming— that is, bombarding Internet users with unwanted commercial messages.

YOU CAN'T SAY THAT ON THE WEB!

Even in democratic and politically liberal countries, free speech laws are not limitless. In Canada and most European countries, free speech does not include expressions of ethnic, religious, and racist defamation. For example, European countries forbid the dissemination of Nazi writings and images, offline and online. U.S. law does not forbid such communication, but there have been attempts to curb communication of sexual and violent materials.

In the United States, Congress tried twice to restrict Web sites' publication of materials deemed "indecent for minors." The Telecommunications Act of 1996 included prohibiting the inclusion of certain types of information on Web pages. The statute, referred to as the Communications Decency Act, made it a crime to use an interactive computer service to "send" or "display in a manner available" to a person under age 18 "any comment, request, suggestion, proposal, image, or other communication that, in context, depicts or describes, in terms patently offensive as measured by contemporary community standards, sexual or excretory activities or organs, regardless of whether the user of such service placed the call or initiated the communication." The American Civil Liberties Union challenged this part of the act, and the United States Supreme Court agreed and struck it from the law. The Court cited not only the principle of free speech, but also the impracticality of enforcing the provision. The law still prohibits using the Internet for child pornography. This part of the statute has not been challenged.

In 1998, Congress passed a similar law, the Children's Online Privacy Protection Act. This law made a criminal of anyone who "knowingly and with knowledge of the character of the material, in interstate or foreign commerce by means of the World Wide Web, makes any communication for commercial purposes that is available to any minor and that includes any material that is harmful to minors." The ACLU and other organizations went to court again. A federal judge struck down the law as unconstitutional. A federal appeals court upheld the decision.

The court recognized the technological difficulties involved in selective censorship: "We are forced to recognize that, at present, due to technological limitations, there may be no other means by which harmful material on the Web may be constitutionally restricted, although, in light of rapidly developing technological advances, what may now be impossible to regulate constitutionally may, in the not-too-distant future, become feasible."

Some countries have implemented technical measures to curb what their governments deem inappropriate materials. The government of the People's Republic of China closely monitors information posted on servers located inside the country, and it blocks the transmission of such materials from links to external sites. Using information technology to establish a Web site requires a government license, and operators must keep logs of users and their logon and logoff times. Police are allowed to access these records at any time. The Chinese government has ordered the shutdown of several Web sites. The government is especially sensitive to the communication of political and sexual content. Governments of other countries, such as Singapore, Myanmar, and Saudi Arabia, have adopted similar practices (whether anchored in laws or not).

INTERESTING . . .

GARBAGE IN THEIR OWN HOMES

Myanmar, formerly known as Burma, has been under a military dictatorship for over a decade. This country of 48 million inhabitants is among the world's poorest nations. The Myanmar Computer Federation estimates the number of computers there at 50,000, few of which link to the Internet. Unauthorized ownership of modems may result in 7 to 15 years in prison. E-mail is restricted to several hundred government officials and foreign citizens. Technically, it would be easy to connect the country to the rest of the world, but a government official said: "Why would we want to collect garbage in our own homes?"

Source: Communications of the ACM, July 2000, Vol. 43, No. 7, p. 9

In spring of 2000, the International League Against Racism and Anti-Semitism (LICRA), the Movement Against Racism (MRAP), and the Union of French Law Students (UEFJ) filed a lawsuit against the U.S. Internet company Yahoo! in a French court. In the lawsuit, LICRA and UEFJ complained that Yahoo's auctioning of over 1,200 Nazi-related items amounted to "banalization of Nazism." The Nazi items offered for sale on the site included everything from Nazi flags and uniforms to belt buckles and medals. Both groups sought to ban the English-language auction sales from appearing in France.

The sale of Nazi items is legal in the United States because it is considered a practice of freedom of expression under the First Amendment to the Constitution. French law, however, prohibits the sale or exhibition of objects with racist overtones. The judge ruled earlier that Yahoo!'s display of Nazi artifacts in France violated the law and was "an offense against the collective memory of a country profoundly wounded by the atrocities committed by and in the name of the Nazi criminal enterprise."

Yahoo! ensured that the Nazi items did not appear on the French Yahoo! site. However, visitors to the French site could click into the English-language Yahoo! site where the Nazi objects were available. The company argued that it was not technically able to filter out French Web surfers from its auction site. Independent Internet security experts concurred that such filtering is almost impossible. Ostensibly, it is possible to identify where users are located by the telephone number they dial to log on. However, the numbers can be disguised or even misread. Yahoo! agreed to exclude Nazi memorabilia from all its sites, but it also asked a California court to declare that the French court has no jurisdiction over the company's operations outside France. The court made the declaration.

Earlier that year, the giant online retailer Amazon.com stopped selling Adolf Hitler's book *Mein Kamf* (*My Campaign*) in response to complaints made by the German federal government. In Germany, too, Nazi propaganda and the sale of Nazi objects are forbidden by law. Also, in July of that year, Saudi Arabia's only ISP decided to block access to the site clubs.yahoo.com because it deemed it in violation of Saudi values, although not specifically in violation of any law. More than 250 Saudi clubs were part of the site, serving some 60,000 Saudis. (Interestingly, the Saudi clubs were still listed there after the ISP's action.) Practically, it was the government's decision; the Saudi government owns the ISP.

The issue of free speech becomes even more involved when one government tries to encroach on another government's jurisdiction. Consider the situation in which the government of Germany found itself. German laws prohibit denying that the Holocaust happened, the furthering of Nazi ideals, and the display of Nazi paraphernalia. To circumvent the law, German neo-Nazis posted Nazi propaganda on servers located in the United States. The German government could not close down these sites because they were protected by the First Amendment to the United States Constitution. In its frustration, the German government announced that its laws were valid outside of German borders, which in practical terms meant it could prosecute a citizen of any country who posts Nazi propaganda that is accessible by German citizens. All of a sudden, U.S. citizens were exposed to prosecution by another government for acts that they committed in their own country and which were perfectly legal in their own country.

The first important question that these and similar cases raise is one of freedom of speech and trade. The Internet was created without any restriction on what one could post at one's site. In the United States, one may say whatever one wants—anywhere, anytime. This includes the presentation of any items for sale (unless the sale is expressly forbidden, as in the case of illegal drugs). Federal law in the United States does not address so-called hate crimes, although some state and municipal laws do. Most other countries, including Canada and most European countries, have specific laws against offensive expressions.

Some laws are starkly different in philosophy and application. For example, U.S. law regards ISPs only as vehicles for communication, not the parties responsible for the content of the material communicated. French law, on the other hand, specifically holds ISPs responsible for the information posted by parties that use the ISPs' services.

The laws of nations are influenced by different histories and cultures. No one argues with a nation's right to craft its own laws. However, the Internet is shared by all nations. How can you, then, obey different laws that are trying to govern the same space, albeit cyberspace? Whose laws should be obeyed on the Internet? As we have seen, laws across national borders are far from harmonious. If an Internet company abides by the laws of one country, it might violate the rights of people in another country. Even if ISPs are ordered to block access to certain sites, users can still access sites forbidden by their government. In the case of Saudi Arabia, users can do what they did before the Saudi ISP started operations: They can make a long distance call to another country, access another ISP, and have access to *any* site through that service. Thus, laws restricting access on the Internet are rarely effective. Since no single country has jurisdiction on the Internet, these issues are unlikely to be resolved soon.

ANTISPAM LEGISLATION

As soon as prices of fax machines dropped and households started to purchase them, commercial organizations grabbed the opportunity to broadcast thousands of messages to those machines, promoting everything and anything they could sell. However, this commercial "boon" was nipped in the bud by state governments in the United States and by almost every other country. The laws of most countries forbid the transmission of unsolicited advertisement via fax. Yet similar sweeping legislation has not been passed so eagerly for spamming.

Spam, as first defined in Chapter 9, is unsolicited e-mail, usually of commercial nature and broadcast to multiple recipients. It is the electronic equivalent of junk mail. A growing number of e-mail messages that we receive are spam. Recipients complain that spam violates their privacy, wastes their resources, and is just plain annoying, while businesses argue that spamming is a legitimate practice. They also claim that curbing the practice would amount to no less than censorship and violation of free speech.

INTERESTING...

POLITICALLY INCORRECT

A French Web-hosting service that served 40,000 sites went out of business in July 2000. The company was home to many political activists. What was the reason for its going out of business? A new French law that held Web hosting services liable for the content of the sites they host.

Source: "Alternative death," *The Industry Standard,* July 31, 2000, p. 113

Attempts to pass antispamming laws at the federal and state levels in the United States have failed, but the initiative continues. California adopted a law that (1) lets an ISP sue those who send unsolicited commercial messages in violation of its policy if the sender has actual notice of the policy and (2) that imposes criminal penalties upon those who cause computer system disruptions by using a false domain name to send messages. (Spammers often use false domain names to disguise their identities.) The state of Washington also passed an antispam law. Federal courts have since declared both laws unconstitutional. On the other hand, the courts have deemed the sending of e-mail with a false sender address illegal. In one case, a judge ruled that a spammer violated AOL's trademark when he used the company's name in the header of his mass e-mail. He sent the message to seven million addresses, promoting his adult sites.

In the United States there have been several attempts at the federal level to curb the phenomenon. One antispam bill was the Unsolicited Commercial Electronic Mail Act of 2001, which would "protect individuals, families, and Internet service providers from unsolicited and unwanted electronic mail." It passed in the House of Representatives at 427 to 1. The bill would allow recipients of unsolicited commercial e-mail to sue spammers in court for $500 per message and $50,000 per day. The bill would also allow the Federal Trade Commission to sue spammers and would require spammers to honor the opt-out requests of Internet users. Another bill related to spam, the Controlling the Assault of Non-Solicited Pornography and Marketing Act of 2000, would allow states and Internet service providers to sue spammers.

Canadian courts ruled in favor of ISPs that stopped serving subscribers who had violated their "netiquette" (network etiquette) rules. These rules often forbid spam. In Europe, Germany, the Netherlands, Italy, and Austria have also enacted antispam legislation.

Despite the failure to pass effective antispam laws in the United States, intense pressure from antispam activists has forced several major ISPs to pass up signing contracts with companies that spam. Among these ISPs are AT&T and PSINet, Inc. Several organizations are dedicated to the eradication of spam. Notable among them is CAUCE (Coalition Against Unsolicited Commercial E-mail).

LEGAL RESTRICTIONS ON ONLINE COMMERCE

Consumers often misperceive the Web as a virtual place where one can buy everything and anything without legal limits. Reality is quite different. Some types of goods and services are downright illegal in some countries, states, or counties, whether one tries to acquire them on the Web or elsewhere. Here we discuss restrictions on gambling and controlled substances.

ONLINE GAMBLING

We have already mentioned the social reservations and legal restrictions of online gambling. Some governments have extended the legal restriction of traditional gambling to the Internet. In the United States, such extension was not required; although each state can allow gambling within its borders, online gambling is prohibited in the entire country under the Wire Wager Act of 1960.

The Internet hosts more than 700 online gaming sites, potentially generating billions of dollars in revenue. Attempts to further limit online gambling have been made more for economic reasons than for moral ones. Cities that count on revenue from the gaming industry and the tourism that accompanies it find that the Internet poses a viable threat to their bottom line.

According to the nonprofit Pew Internet & American Life Project, by mid-2000 about five million Americans had tried online gambling or played an online lottery. A recent report from the online gaming industry estimates that there are one million Americans who gamble online each day and 4.5 million who have used the Internet to gamble at least once. According to the River City Group, revenues from online gambling blossomed to $1.1 billion in 1999, a sum that is expected to increase to $3 billion by 2002. Bear, Stearns & Company estimated 1999 online gambling revenues at $1.2 billion and agreed with the increase to $3 billion by 2002.

In several legal areas, prosecutors have attempted to apply existing law to emerging legal issues involving the Internet. Congress passed the Wire Wager Act in 1960 to prohibit the use of "wire communication facilit[ies] for the transmission in interstate or foreign commerce of bets or wagers or information assisting in the placing of bets or wagers on any sporting event or contest." In July 2000, an operator of an Internet gambling facility was convicted under this law (see "Interesting . . ."). According to the prosecutor in that case, "an Internet communication is no different than a telephone call for the purpose of liability under the Wire Wager Act."

Whether the attempts to stop online gambling come from moral or economic concerns is unimportant to civil rights advocates. They claim that this type of consensual gambling is yet another victimless "crime" that should not be considered a crime in the first place. If this argument does not impress restriction advocates, then the impracticality of enforcing such restrictions on gambling should. The American Civil Liberties Union and other civil rights groups regard such restrictions as unenforceable. It is doubtful than any government will try to hunt down private citizens who gamble from their home computers.

Nevertheless, bills have been introduced in Congress to address Internet gambling. Although in 2000 the Internet Gambling Prohibition Act did not pass in

INTERESTING . . .

SOUR GAMBLE

In July 2000, a federal court in New York sentenced the first person to stand trial for operating an offshore gambling business that encouraged and accepted bets from Americans over the Internet. Jay Cohen, co-owner of World Sports Exchange, located in Antigua, was sentenced to 21 months in prison followed by two years of supervised release, in addition to a $5,000 fine and an $800 special assessment. Interestingly, Cohen was sentenced under a law that does not specify the Internet as a means of communication. He was sentenced under the Wire Wager Act, which prohibits the use of telephone lines in interstate or foreign commerce to place bets on sports events and also prohibits the transmission of information that assists in betting. Cohen could have stayed in Antigua and never faced a U.S. prosecutor. He returned to the United States only to make his trial a test case for the legality of online gambling.

Source: Macaluso, N., "Bookie sentenced in net gambling case," *E-Commerce Times,* August 11, 2000

the House of Representatives, it seems that similar legislative attempts will continue to surface.

SALES OF CONTROLLED SUBSTANCES

Another area still restricted by law is online sales of alcoholic beverages. Wine e-retailers such as Wine.com, WineBins.com, WineShoppers.com, AmbrosiaWine.com, and eVineyard.com are allowed to ship cases of wine in bottles to 45 states in the United States, but they are totally barred in three states (Utah, Georgia, and Kentucky). Some states leave it to local governments to decide on the legality of such purchases. In Texas, for instance, it is illegal to sell alcohol via the Internet in some counties, but legal in others. Sometimes selling liquor is prohibited because a territory is "dry" (that is, it does not allow the selling of alcoholic beverages in any form). In other cases, old, convoluted regulations are simply retained to support local distributors by minimizing competition. In the latter areas, sellers must obtain local licenses, and in some cases licenses are not granted at all in order to protect local distributors.

Since it is easy to sell almost anything online, people who are unauthorized to sell certain products are tempted to do so. One type of product the government does not want you to be able to buy without regulation is drugs—not the illegal ones, which are "regulated" simply by the fact that they are illegal, but the legal ones, which still must be prescribed by health-care providers. Some reports estimate that there are 400 sites that sell drugs online to U.S. citizens. In the United States, the Food and Drug Administration is responsible for regulating the industry, but the government agency does not have adequate resources to do so on the Web. Apparently, many of the online "pharmacies" are not even in the agency's jurisdiction. In 1998, the U.S. Customs Service intercepted 2,145 unauthorized prescriptions sent into the United States from other countries. In 1999, the number jumped to 9,725 shipments. Obviously, no one knows how many illegal shipments have not been intercepted.

Countries have different restrictions on what can and cannot be traded through public channels. These differences have serious impacts on e-commerce. It is legal to sell some narcotic drugs in the Netherlands, and that country's laws do not bar anyone from offering such drugs on the Web. However, practically every other country forbids the sale and purchase of such drugs. Countries have different laws even concerning much "milder" drugs, such as melatonin, which some people find helps them fall asleep. The drug is freely sold in the United States, but barred in the United Kingdom. How practical is it to stop online purchases of such drugs internationally when they can be legally offered on U.S. Web sites? Only full harmonization of laws among nations can solve the problem. This is unlikely to happen in the foreseeable future.

WHOSE AUCTION IS IT, ANYWAY?

When you go to a public auction such as the ones conducted by Sotheby's and Christie's, there are clear laws that govern the procedure. For example, laws forbid auctioneers to sell stolen items. As we mentioned in Chapter 8, some countries require that a licensed auctioneer be present, and many countries bar the sale of certain offensive or dangerous items, such as Nazi memorabilia or guns. As laws are different across countries, some cannot be enforced.

As mentioned earlier in the chapter, in 2000 a French court ordered Yahoo! to block Internet users in France from accessing its auctions of Nazi items. After the firm claimed it could not comply with the order for technical reasons, the court asked a panel of three experts to determine if blocking was feasible. Vinton Cerf, known as "the father of the Internet," led the panel. Cerf is a scientist credited with a major contribution to the establishment of the world network. The experts said that 70 to 80 percent of French Web users could be identified by their IP numbers. Auction sites, they said, could use a filtering system that would prevent users with French IP addresses from accessing auctions whose descriptions contain Nazi-related topics. The largest consumer-to-consumer Web auction site, eBay, announced that it could comply with the French order.

In the United States, the First Amendment to the Constitution, which protects free speech, protects the right of any person to offer for sale any item. When Web users have complained about auctions of guns and other controversial items, such sites may have tried to respond with some action, but not because U.S. law requires it.

The more interesting question is probably whose responsibility it is to ascertain that items offered for sale at an online auction site are not stolen or bootlegged. A fan of the Grateful Dead rock band in San Francisco asked the court to order eBay to stop the sale of illegal concert recordings. A superior court judge in San Francisco County ruled that the site could not be held responsible for such sales.

Interestingly, the judge cited the Communication Decency Act. Under this law, no one can hold a computer service provider responsible for the speech of those who utilize the provider's service. In his ruling, the judge said: "Plaintiff's attempt to impose responsibility on eBay as the seller of items auctioned over its service is no different from the unsuccessful attempts that have been made to hold computer service providers liable as distributors rather than publishers of defamatory or pornographic materials." Suppose the fan complained about a national retail chain that sold stolen CDs in its stores. Would the judge reach the same decision?

WELCOME TO . . . WHOSE SITE?

Sometimes, linking your site to other sites is not necessarily a matter of violating copyrights. A business may not be in violation of any copyright, and yet it may cause damage to a linked business. Unless you carefully follow the change from one IP number to another as you click on links on a Web page, you may not know whose site you are using at any given time. This "transparency" aspect of the Internet allows site operators to offer information that is not theirs.

Suppose you operate an auction site. Someone is looking to purchase an item that your site does not offer. However, the visitor can use a search engine provided at your site to search for the item at other auction sites. In a way, you have expanded the selection your site offers. The practice has been addressed by a U.S. court.

Bidder's Edge is a site that provides a search engine for auctioned items. If the Bidder's Edge search engine does not find a desired item at the site, it searches competitors' sites and creates a link to the item. However, eBay complained that Bidder's Edge illegally trespassed on its site, violated its copyright and trademarks, and slowed its service for eBay users. In May 2000, a U.S. federal judge issued a preliminary injunction against Bidder's Edge, barring the auction portal from searching the eBay site for auction information. In his decision, the judge said: "Even if its searches use only a small amount of eBay's computer system capacity, Bidder's Edge has nonetheless deprived eBay of the ability to use that portion of its personal property for its own purposes. The law recognizes no such right to use another's personal property."

E-PRIVACY LEGISLATION

We have discussed consumer profiling in Chapter 8 and Chapter 9. As we mentioned, many people feel that consumer profiling violates their privacy. Legislatures the world over have taken notice and tried to minimize invasion of privacy. The European Union adopted the Directive on Data Protection (Directive 95) in October 1998, which limits any collection and dissemination of personal data. In the European Union, a directive is framework law; each member nation may legislate a more restrictive law, but not a more relaxed one. The directive imposes the same rules in all 15 countries of the European Union. These countries have passed laws that reflect Directive 95; some are even more restrictive. The directive provides that no one collect data about individuals ("subjects") without their permission; that the collecting party notify the subject of the purpose of the collection; that the maintainers of the data ask for the subject's permission to transfer the subject's data to another party; and that upon a proper request from the subject, data about the subject be corrected or deleted.

The directive prohibits the transfer of personal data from EU countries to any country that does not impose rules at least as restrictive as those of the directive. U.S. companies that wish to do business in the European Union must comply with this law. To avoid disruption of business and prosecution, U.S. companies can sign up for what is known as the "safe harbor" arrangement. By signing up to the **safe harbor**, an organization declares that it complies with the directive's rules. However, months after the safe harbor was established very few U.S. companies had signed up. (By October 2001, the total was only 102 organizations.)

In 2000, Canada passed the Personal Information Protection and Electronic Documents Act. The act provides that Canadians have the right to know why a business or organization is collecting, using, or disclosing their personal information, such as name, age, medical records, income, spending habits, DNA code, marital status, etc. They also have the right to check their personal information and correct any inaccuracies. According to the act, businesses must obtain the individual's consent when they collect, use, or disclose personal information, except in some circumstances, such as information needed for an investigation or an emergency where lives or safety are at risk.

Like members of the European Union, Canada established a privacy commissioner. The privacy commissioner is an officer of Parliament, reporting directly to Parliament. Under the act, individuals may complain to the privacy commissioner about how organizations handle their personal information. The commissioner functions as an ombudsman; initiates, receives, investigates, and resolves complaints; conducts audits; and educates the public about privacy issues. He or she has two sets of powers: the power of disclosure, which is the right to make information public; and the power to take matters to the Federal Court of Canada, which can in turn order organizations to stop a particular practice and award substantial damages for contravention of the law.

The act contains a set of fair information principles. These principles are based on the Canadian Standards Association's Model Privacy Code for the Protection of Personal Information. The code was developed with input from businesses, governments, consumer associations, and other privacy stakeholders.

The act applies to the collection, use, and disclosure of personal information by organizations during commercial activities both with brick-and-mortar and online businesses. Personal information is any information about an identifiable individual whether recorded or not. Organizations include associations, partnerships, persons, and trade unions. The term "commercial activity" includes the selling, bartering, or leasing of donor, membership, or other fundraising lists.

It is expected that a growing number of countries will adopt privacy laws to foster e-commerce. Privacy laws in the United States are significantly more lax, especially with regard to nongovernment organizations. In the United States, governments are significantly more limited in the collection and dissemination of private data than are private businesses. Businesses that are not financial institutions or medical organizations are not limited by law. The U.S. approach has been to expect businesses to impose self-regulation on data collection through the Internet. Whether or not this has happened to any significant degree is questionable. The U.S. government, however, has stepped in despite limitations, and Congress has adopted some laws to curb violation of privacy.

CHILDREN'S ONLINE PRIVACY PROTECTION ACT OF 1998

The Children's Online Privacy Protection Act of 1998 (COPPA), which took effect in April 2000, requires online businesses to secure parental consent before collecting personal information from preteen Web surfers. The law makes it a federal offense for commercial Web sites to collect personal information from children under 13 without parental permission. It also forbids the release of such information if it has already been collected.

To collect information from children, site operators must obtain "verifiable parental consent." This is a problematic point for businesses. The law defines such consent as "any reasonable effort (taking into consideration available technology), including a request for authorization for future collection, use, and disclosure described in the notice, to ensure that a parent of a child receives notice of the operator's personal information collection, use, and disclosure practices, and authorizes the collection, use, and disclosure, as applicable, of personal information and the subsequent use of that information before that information is collected from that child." How can the consent be verified online? Some jurists suggested that the presentation of a credit card account satisfies the law, because only adults can receive credit cards. Children, however, can use credit cards without their parents' permission.

PRIVACY OF CONSUMER FINANCIAL INFORMATION ACT

The Privacy of Consumer Financial Information Act (also called the GLB Act, after the initials of the U.S. senators who authored it) states that a U.S. financial institution must provide its customers with a notice of its privacy policies and practices. It prohibits a financial institution from disclosing nonpublic personal information about a consumer to a nonaffiliated third party unless the institution satisfies various disclosures and opt-out requirements and the consumer has not elected to opt-out of the disclosure. Financial institutions include banks, brokerages, and insurance companies. A "nonaffiliated third party" is any organization that is not owned by the financial institution and any organization that does not have a business relationship with the consumer.

Note that the organization must provide an opt-out option (first discussed in Chapter 10), which means if the consumer does not elect to be excluded, the organization is allowed to transfer his or her personal data to another organization. U.S. privacy advocates have long required opt-in options. With opt-in, as long as the consumer has not opted to allow the transfer of his or her data, the organization is barred from doing so. Countries that are members of the European Union enforce opt-in online and offline, because the EU Directive on Data Protection mandates that organizations must receive people's permission to transfer their data to another party.

INTERESTING . . .

WELCOME TO SAFE HARBOR

Companies operating from European Union countries are barred by law from trading with U.S. companies that do not abide by European privacy laws. To overcome the problem, the U.S. government offered to create a list of U.S. companies that voluntarily agree to obey these laws. This list is referred to as a safe harbor. A safe harbor is a legal provision that provides protection against prosecution. Now, European businesses have a protection against prosecution if they deal with U.S. businesses that signed up as members of the arrangement. This arrangement is an official agreement between the United States and the European Union. A European company can look up a U.S. business on the list, which is published online, to see if that business participates. U.S. organizations must comply with the seven safe harbor principles, as spelled out by the U.S. Department of Commerce:

Notice: Organizations must notify individuals about the purposes for which they collect and use information about them. They must provide information about how individuals can contact the organization with any inquiries or complaints, the types of third parties to which it discloses the information, and the choices and means the organization offers for limiting its use and disclosure.

Choice: Organizations must give individuals the opportunity to choose (opt out) whether their personal information will be disclosed to a third party or used for a purpose other than the purpose for which it was originally collected or subsequently authorized by the individual. For sensitive information, affirmative or explicit (opt in) choice must be given if the information is to be disclosed to a third party or used for a purpose other than its original purpose or the purpose authorized subsequently by the individual.

Onward transfer (transfers to third parties): To disclose information to a third party, organizations must apply the notice and choice principles. When an organization wishes to transfer information to a third party that is acting as an agent, it may do so if it makes sure that the third party subscribes to the safe harbor principles or is subject to the EU Directive on Data Protection or an acceptable similar law. As an alternative, the organization can enter into a written agreement with such a third party requiring that the third party provide at least the same level of privacy protection as is required by the relevant principles.

Access: Individuals must have access to the personal information about them that an organization holds and be able to correct, amend, or delete that information where it is inaccurate, except when the burden or expense of providing access would be disproportionate to the risks of the individual's privacy, or where the rights of others would be violated.

Data integrity: Personal information must be relevant to the purposes for which it is to be used. An organization should take reasonable steps to ensure that data are reliable for their intended use, as well as accurate, complete, and current.

Enforcement: In order to ensure compliance with the safe harbor principles, there must be (1) readily available and affordable independent recourse mechanisms; (2) procedures for verifying that the commitments companies make to safe harbor principles have been implemented; and (3) obligations to remedy problems arising out of a failure to comply with the principles. Sanctions must be sufficiently rigorous to ensure compliance by the organization. Organizations that fail to provide annual self-certification letters can lose safe harbor benefits.

Source: Department of Commerce Website, *www.export.gov/safeharbor/sh_overview.html*

ANTITRUST LAWS AND THE INTERNET

One of the greatest advantages of the Internet is the ability to turn a single Web site into a world market for products. Exchanges in specialized industries have attracted thousands of sellers and buyers alike. However, the same tool that makes markets so efficient can also be used to violate **antitrust laws** relatively easily. In the United States and most other countries, there are laws that forbid two or more organizations to coordinate prices. Organizations may cooperate in using the same technology and, in the Internet age, the same "platform" for auctioning, selling, and buying products. However, they must stop short of actually communicating with each other about the prices that they set or the bids that they intend to offer to sellers.

An exchange site can become a competitive market or an arena for price-fixing. The latter may occur when buyers or sellers that represent large portions of the market participate in the trade. If such sellers or buyers offer the same price, suspicion of collusion will arise, and regulatory agencies are likely to investigate. Sites engaged in these practices may be shut down as a result.

If a group of competitors representing a significant proportion of a market does decide to jointly sell their products, the government will be wary that they may fix prices, as it creates the potential of a cartel with monopolistic power, mentioned earlier. The same fear applies to large purchasers in a market who join forces for joint buying. This creates an effect called *monopsony.*

So far, the U.S. government has investigated only a few exchange sites, and all are ones that involve the largest players in their industry. The Federal Trade Commission opened an investigation into Covisint, the auto-part purchasing site established by the three large U.S. automakers, General Motors, Ford, and DaimlerChrysler. The Department of Justice also scrutinized an exchange set up by the six largest U.S. meat and poultry processors as well as Orbitz, a site established by some of the largest airline carriers for ticket sales.

Companies have methods to signal each other without explicit communication or even when the communication between them is in the public eye. One example was the bidding in a wireless-telephone license auction, in which telecommunications firms competed for regional licenses. Some companies added coded digits to their bids. For example, instead of bidding $3.99 million, one telephone carrier offered $3,990,204. The odd 204 was the area code in which this company was eagerly interested, signaling to two other companies not to compete with it in that area. The other two collaborators yielded, signaling their own strong interests in other regions using the same technique. The carriers were prosecuted and fined.

There are ways to minimize collusion on the Web. For example, at close of bidding, instead of showing all bidders the bids of their competitors, each bidder is notified only of his rank (first, second, third, and so on). Only the winning bidder knows the final price paid.

No country has passed special laws to address antitrust principles relating specifically to the Internet. The reason is simple: The Internet and Web technologies are only one more means that can facilitate collusion. The laws are adequate, but now they must be applied to online activities in addition to traditional practices.

SUMMARY

- Laws have always governed well-defined geographical territories. In e-commerce, though, parties conduct business in cyberspace. This poses legal challenges. Two opposing principles have been suggested for jurisdiction: country of origin and country of destination.
- Electronic signatures are now legal and binding in the United States and several other countries. Electronic signatures facilitate e-commerce but are prone to error and forgery.
- Unlike other names for individuals and businesses, Internet domain names are unique. There has been much contention over possession of domain names. Courts have applied trademark laws to domain names. To avoid long legal procedures, parties can take their cases to arbitrators such as ICANN and WIPO. Both organizations have been accused of favoring businesses over individuals.
- It is easy to copy artistic work on the Web, but to do so legally, one must receive permission from the copyright holder. Companies have embedded invisible marks that identify their intellectual property in works, and special software is available that can scour the Web and catch copyright-violating culprits.
- The ease of digitizing artistic work has tempted several entrepreneurs to offer artistic work such as music for online enjoyment and for downloading without permission from the copyright holder. The movie and recording industries have sued sites that engaged in these practices. However, there are signs that the creative industries and the entrepreneurs will eventually collaborate to distribute artistic work over the Internet.
- Critics have opposed software patents for a long time. Calls against patents for Web software and Internet business methods are even stronger. Patents grant long-term monopolies and, therefore, may restrict development of e-commerce. The one click shopping and other Web-based business methods are perceived as features that should not be patented.
- Cultural and historical factors play an important role in what we know as free speech. What is considered legitimate expression in one country may be considered offensive in another. Free speech, it turns out, does not refer

only to expressing opinions on the Web, but also to selling certain items. Since any Web site is international, the question of which countries' laws a site must obey raises an important legal issue. A French court's attempt to stop Yahoo! from auctioning Nazi items emphasized the importance of this issue.

■ Some people consider spam a form of free speech. Several European countries, though, have enacted laws against spam. Attempts to legislate against spamming have failed in the United States. Advocacy groups have been more effective than the legal system in curbing the phenomenon.

■ Several laws restrict gambling and the sales of certain substances. It is difficult to enforce these laws when gambling or the sales practices meet up with Web technology.

■ When a site offers its services to sell or otherwise transfer questionable information or merchandise, U.S. law usually gives the site immunity against lawsuits. It regards the site only as a conduit for the sale. This is an important legal shield for auction sites.

■ By linking to other sites, an online business can offer services that are not actually its own. This may deteriorate the services that the other sites provide, especially in terms of response time to consumer queries. In one U.S. case, it was ruled that such linking is illegal unless permission is given.

■ As companies collect huge amounts of personal data on the Internet, privacy is the subject of legal contention. The European Union has adopted strict laws to protect its citizens' privacy. The United States does not restrict commercial businesses but does restrict financial and medical institutions. To avoid disruption of business with Western Europe and possible litigation, U.S. businesses can sign on to the safe harbor arrangement between the European Union and United States. By signing on, U.S. businesses agree to abide by the EU Directive on Data Protection.

KEY TERMS

country of origin	piracy
country of destination	business method patent
intellectual property	safe harbor
cybersquatting	antitrust laws

REVIEW QUESTIONS

1. How are domain names linked with the concept of intellectual property in the eyes of the law? How are they similar to, and how are they different from, this type of intellectual property?
2. What is cybersquatting?
3. What is the difference between opt-in and opt-out in the context of privacy and personal information?
4. What is spam? Why have attempts to pass antispam laws failed so far?
5. Why is it so easy to implement online gambling?
6. On the Web, you may actually create the impression that your site offers a much greater service than it really does. How? Why are such practices outlawed?
7. Are privacy laws bad for business? Why or why not?

DISCUSSION QUESTIONS

1. Do you think that the use of electronic signatures will encourage fraud? What new types of fraud might electronic signatures facilitate?
2. Of the two approaches to international e-commerce laws, country of origin and country of destination, which approach do you favor? Why?
3. Which approach to protection of privacy do you prefer, that of the European Union or the United States? Why?
4. Do you agree with the judge who said it was impossible to screen harmful materials for minors on the Web? Why or why not? Even if you disagree with censorship, what do you think can be done to protect minors against harmful communication on the Web?
5. Should the practice of granting patents for Web-based business methods stop? Why or why not?
6. Is there anything that you would forbid, by law, to be published on the Web? If you would, explain what and why.
7. Why do online business find the Children's Online Privacy Protection Act difficult to implement?
8. What is the safe harbor arrangement between the European Union and United States?
9. The U.S. Federal Trade Commission has conducted an investigation of almost every industry's online hub. What is the FTC's fear concerning these hubs?

ASSIGNMENTS

1. Assume you are the president of an exchange Web site that accepts bidding for buying and selling a certain type of product. Prepare a list of measures that you would put in place to reduce the possibility of collusion and price-fixing in violation of antitrust laws.

2. Assume you are a federal legislator. Form an opinion on the morality of spam. Prepare arguments to support your opinion. Use examples.

E-COMMERCE TODAY

Steel-Clad Antitrust Measures

The steel industry in the United States has been under government investigation for violating antitrust laws several times in the past. The giant steel corporations founded by industrialists Andrew Carnegie and J. P. Morgan were early targets of U.S. antitrust laws starting in the late nineteenth century. The industry also felt the government's scrutiny several times in the 1960s. Given this historical environment, the executives who established MetalSite.com were extra cautious in attempting to eliminate any possibility of collusion among the parties trading metals at the site.

MetalSite.com was established in 1998 as a Web site at which steel mills could auction off low-grade and scrap steel. Former executives of three of the largest steel manufacturers in the United States established this independent organization. It was designed to be a Web-based market center that the $50 billion (annual sales) U.S. steel industry could use to trade excess and nonprime steel. From the three original sellers that subscribed to the service, the number grew to 7,000 users. Patrick Stewart, MetalSite's president, said the site handled more than 5,200 transactions totaling 150,000 tons per month, with the average transaction in the $10,000 to $30,000 range. Thus, the monthly worth of transactions exceeded $40 million, from which MetalSite charged fees of .25 percent to 2 percent.

An auction site that serves competitors in an industry may be tricky to manage, because, after all, competitors are supposed to *compete*; they are not supposed to collaborate in their effort to sell at the highest price. MetalSite managers had to ascertain that the sellers did not collude and violate antitrust laws. Patrick Stewart and his executive team took "excruciating efforts" to make sure that the sellers do not collaborate via the site. Maintaining secrecy between the sellers was a prime concern.

In 1998, the entire organization of 25 employees included only two members who came from the same organization. All others came from different organizations to eliminate any influence of past allegiance, and therefore favoritism, to former employers. Every employee was educated on antitrust law and had to sign a long document outlining what is permitted and what is forbidden. In addition, representatives of the audit firm Arthur Andersen visited the organization's office semiannually to audit antitrust compliance.

Subscribers paid nothing to join the exchange. All they needed was a connection to the Internet and a Web browser so they could log on. Before they could bid, however, they had to fill out a form to apply for credit from the sellers. Sellers used their own criteria for deciding to whom they should grant credit. MetalSite established this measure not only to allow them to share their criteria, but to avoid collusion as well.

The MetalSite exchange brought together some of the biggest producers of steel, aluminum, and other metals that served thousands of customers. It had strong safeguards against collusion. The company religiously followed antitrust policies and rules for information exchange. In June 2001, MetalSite stopped operations due to severe negative cash flow.

Source: Pressman, A., "Antitrust gauntlet thrown, exchanges examine options," *The Industry Standard*, July 24, 2000, pp. 110–118; Rafter, M. V., "Steely-eyed auctioneers," *The Industry Standard*, December 7, 1998, pp. 14–21, 31.

Thinking About E-Commerce Today

1. Of all exchange Web sites, MetalSite was especially sensitive to and cautious about antitrust laws. Why?
2. Sellers have previously colluded in electronic bidding without any obvious communication. How can that happen? Give at least one example. How could it happen on MetalSite?
3. One measure that MetalSite took was the recruitment of employees from different organizations. Is this really necessary as a measure to reduce the possibility of violating antitrust laws? Explain.

- Explain how a digital cash system is set up and used
- List and compare online alternatives to traditional payment methods
- Discuss the challenges of online micropayments
- Explain how online person-to-person payments are executed
- Appreciate the economic value of points programs on the Web

I n 2000, payment by credit card accounted for 98.5 percent of all payments in online transactions. The research firm ActivMedia predicted that this rate would decline to 90 percent by the end of 2001 as new payment technologies were developed. The firm also predicted that smart card and e-wallet transaction volumes would grow from $500 million in 2000 to $5.7 billion in 2001 and to $20 billion in 2002. For the study, ActivMedia surveyed over 1,000 small, medium, and large online businesses, including those operating B2B and B2C sites as well as online content providers and ISPs. Source: Saliba, C., "Credit cards losing grip on e-commerce," *E-Commerce Times*, September 28, 2000

MONEY: IT'S WHAT WE TRUST IT IS

Money fulfills two main purposes. It is a medium for storing value, and it is a medium of payment. Without money, we would have to barter. That is, we would exchange whatever we produce—goods or hours of work—for whatever we need. Instead, by receiving the value of what we sell in the form of money, we can easily purchase whatever we need. Unlike in bartering, money enables us to purchase items whose worth does not exactly equal the worth of a good or service we have just sold. Small denominations help us purchase items of small value, and large denominations help us purchase items of high value.

Money allows us to accumulate and store value in a convenient manner. By storing the value of our work and other things that we sell in money, we can delay the use of the value we accumulate; we can earn the money now and spend it later.

In the past, the value of money was in the metal coins used by people. The value of a silver coin, for example, was determined by the value of the silver from which the coin was made. With the Chinese invention of paper money, the value of paper bills was, practically speaking, determined by the trust that the holder put in the institution that issued it: a government or a bank. The paper itself was worthless; it was the promise to pay something of value, usually so many ounces of gold, that lent value to the bill. Nowadays, the value of money is simply the value of the things we can purchase with it. In modern times, money can be in any form: paper, such as banknotes and IOUs, or an electronic record.

The fact that money does not need to be represented by tangible objects makes any form of electronic money a viable means for storing value and making payments. As long as we trust that our electronic money will be accepted by others as payment and is secure, it can fulfill all the purposes of traditional money.

E-MONEY? WHAT E-MONEY?

While we still keep cash in our pockets, most money has no physical form. Rather, it is literally digitized in some form of computer-readable information, such as magnetic fields or marks on compact discs. In other words, much of the world's money is in *electronic form*. Does this fact, which has been true for at least three decades, mean that all cash, checks, and other physical means of payment in Web-based, online commerce will soon be eliminated?

Not necessarily. As in many cases, first appearances do not tell the whole story. A study released in July 2000 by the Gartner Group showed that more than 80 percent of payments for online B2B transactions were made with paper checks sent through the mail. The last step in most B2B transactions is still made in a very traditional fashion. Much of the other 20 percent of payments in B2B transactions were executed using credit and charge cards.

Monetary transactions in B2B commerce are of much greater value than those in B2C. In business deals involving large amounts of money, the seller must have assurances of payment before it commits shipments to buyers. To facilitate transactions through their exchange sites, online B2B firms often find themselves acting as banks or insurance companies. They check the creditworthiness of buyers and guarantee payment to the sellers. Web exchanges (Internet business ventures that bring together sellers and buyers) are particularly interested in assuring payment security. If a buyer reneges on payment, the exchange owes the seller the money, and damage amounts can be quite large. Gofish.com, for example, is an exchange for sellers and buyers of raw seafood; it could not be successful without providing such security to fishermen. To minimize its liability, Gofish screens buyers and sellers. (Review Chapter 7 for information on business models.)

The primary method of payment in B2C e-commerce transactions is through credit cards. Most online retailers do not even allow any other method. Where does this leave the status of other—paperless and cardless—methods? Evidence shows that these payment methods are slowly taking hold. The new U.S. federal law that recognizes electronic signatures as valid for all commercial transactions may already be boosting purely electronic methods of payment. In this chapter, we discuss the most important forms of electronic money, popularly called **e-money**. We start with an example of one model that actually creates electronic "coins." From there we move on to cover more common models for the electronic transfer of money for Web-based e-commerce.

DIGITAL COINS

One of the boldest attempts to create e-money is DigiCash. David Chaum, an expert in cryptography, founded DigiCash, Inc. in 1990. Chaum's purpose went beyond providing a means to transfer money electronically; he actually wanted to create the electronic version of cash, *electronic cash*, or, as it is popularly known, **e-cash** or **digital coins**. He focused on the concept of anonymity in spending. Anonymity is one of the main reasons for cash payments; the payer does not care to be identified by anyone except the payee. It is impossible to be anonymous when paying by check or credit card. Chaum suggested a system whereby payments are unconditionally untraceable. The use of complex cryptographic algorithms made this possible. (The technology is now offered by eCash Technologies, Inc., which purchased DigiCash in 1999.)

To participate in the DigiCash system, both the merchant and the customer must open accounts with a bank that issues e-cash. Participants first must fund their accounts before executing any transactions. Both parties also must register with DigiCash to obtain the *cyberwallet* software. **Cyberwallet** is a program that generates digital coins. The process of creating these coins begins when a customer receives a random number from the bank for his or her *coin*, or unit of money in his or her account. That number is multiplied by a number known only to the payer. This process "blinds" the coin; the payer who uses it can remain anonymous, because the bank cannot know the identity of the party making the request.

The payer transmits the blinded numbers to the bank. The next step occurs when the bank validates the coin by adding its own numbers to it. Finally, an electronic coin is created; the coin is essentially a string of numbers provided by both the payer and the bank. The bank subtracts the amount of the coin from the payer's account. Since the coin is blinded, the bank does not know the payer's identity, only the amount validated and the payee. The payee receives the coin and unblinds it.

To make a purchase, the customer contacts the merchant, and the cyberwallets of both the customer and merchant connect for the transfer of coins. When the customer confirms the transfer, the bank executes it.

The merchant sends the coin to the bank that validated the coin. The bank makes sure the coin had not been spent previously by checking the number that it had added to the blinded coin. The bank's software compares this number to all the numbers of spent coins. The numbers reside in a database of spent coins. If the coin is found unspent, the bank transfers the money to the merchant's account. If the coin has been spent, the bank does not transfer the money. All the communication is encrypted using the public key method, as is the case with any other type of money transfer on the Internet. You may think of this method as a blind debit card: The bank reduces your balance by the amount you pay the merchant, but the bank does not know your identity. Figure 12.1 illustrates the process from beginning to end.

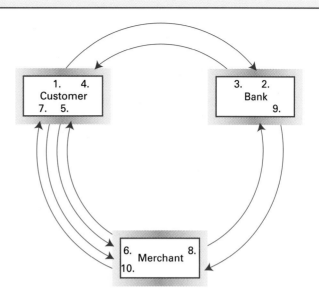

Creating E-Cash

1. The customer's cyberwallet software generates random serial numbers for the e-cash coins and blinds those serial numbers. The blinded coins are sent to the bank.
2. The bank checks the signature and debits the signature owner's account.
3. The bank validates the coins and returns them to the customer.
4. The customer unblinds the coins.

Spending E-Cash

5. The customer sends a buying request to the merchant.
6. The merchant sends a request to the cyberwallet software to send the money.
7. The customer confirms the transaction; the software transfers the exact number of coins.

Redeeming E-Cash

8. To check the validity of the coins, the merchant sends them to the bank that issued the coins.
9. The banks check the serial number for double spending. If the coins are valid, the bank destroys the coins, adds the serial numbers to the database of spent coins, and transfers the amount to the merchant's account.

Concluding the Transaction

10. The merchant sends a receipt to the customer.

ADVANTAGES OF E-CASH

The main advantage of e-cash is that it is simultaneously a payment mechanism and a system that protects personal information. Buyers can purchase and pay without leaving any traces of their payments with any financial institution. If a coin has not been spent, the merchant only knows that the coin is valid, and the bank only knows that it issued the coins and that they have not been spent, but not to whom the coin was issued.

Another advantage is the security inherent in the difficulty of forging this kind of money. It is easier to counterfeit physical bills than to forge e-cash. This system can also be applied to smart cards, a topic we discuss later in this chapter.

DISADVANTAGES OF E-CASH

The major disadvantage of e-cash is the need to maintain huge databases of spent coins. The larger the number of people who use the method, the larger the databases. Note that every coin that has ever been spent must be kept in such a database to enable the bank to ascertain that this particular coin had not been previously used for payment. The databases could become unmanageable.

Another disadvantage is the inflexibility of the system. Digital coins are of preset amounts. Because the system has no mechanism for giving change, for each transaction the buyer must ask the issuing bank for a certain number of coins of specific values. The system may be suitable for situations in which people pay a specific amount every time, such as in collection of highway tolls, but perhaps not in many situations that require flexibility.

Government agencies and many financial institutions have refused to adopt e-cash because they are not willing to deal with untraceable payments. DigiCash and other companies that have developed similar methods have not been able to create large enough alliances to create what economists call the **networking effect,** a situation in which so many people are using a certain technology that others must adopt it in order to communicate or exchange goods and services with a large group of people. Without the cooperation of banks that would be willing to issue digital coins, e-cash cannot succeed. Therefore, other methods of online payment have been more popular, even though they do not guarantee untraceable anonymity.

A SPIN ON TRADITIONAL CREDIT CARDS

Until 2001, the most popular way to pay for online purchases was by plastic—either the good old credit card or the equally good charge card or debit card. This is resoundingly true in the United States, where these cards, especially credit cards, are in use by about two thirds of the adult population, and still true in Europe and Japan, where these cards are significantly less popular. In most of the world, credit, charge, and debit-card processing software is regarded as a necessary module of any transaction processing application set for a Web-based business. These cards will probably continue to be highly popular in online transactions.

Yet, the growth of online purchases, especially the growth of B2C transactions, has encouraged card issuers to develop technologies that add convenience to payments. Three new payment technologies, e-wallet, virtual credit cards, and one-time credit cards, are discussed here. Note that any discussion of credit cards in this chapter holds for charge cards and debit cards as well.

E-WALLET

The term **e-wallet** refers to a variety of electronic information that aids in delivering personal and financial information for online purchases. The purpose of e-wallets is to provide convenience in online purchases, mainly to consumers. Instead of retyping the credit card type, account number, expiration date, and personal details, a PC user can store the information once in a file that resides on the

A PICTURE IS WORTH . . .

In November 1999, MasterCard announced that it would offer its cardholders the option to have images of their existing credit cards placed on their computer desktops for online shopping and one-click access to account and purchasing information. In February 2000, Discover Financial Services announced it would implement identical technology. Both companies released the technology to their member banks (MasterCard has 23,000 member banks). It is the banks' responsibility to make the technology available to cardholders. By downloading and installing the free software from these companies' sites, you can create an electronic wallet, or e-wallet, on your PC. Similar software is also available for handheld computers.

hard disk. Whenever the user makes an online purchase, the file can be accessed, and the fields of any form the online business brings up can be "instantly" completed with the relevant information.

Several companies, including Microsoft and the major credit card issuers, provide e-wallet software free of charge. Some of the applications can store information about all the cards a user holds, regardless of issuer. Some credit card issuers, such as MasterCard, encourage cardholders to download the software and use it by guaranteeing zero risk; the companies promise to bear the full cost of unauthorized purchases. E-wallets provide convenience in two ways:

1. The user fills out billing and shipping information only once and can update the file whenever needed. From that point on, the user fills out forms with a single click. Users can also drag and drop selected information from the file.
2. The file "remembers" passwords, account numbers, and login names of the various sites to which the users have subscribed.

Some of these applications provide security measures, but none is fully protected from hackers, who may invade a personal computer in search of credit card information.

VIRTUAL CREDIT CARD

A **virtual credit card** is linked to the digital information of a real credit card, but has no physical link to any plastic card. Instead, it takes the form of an "alias" or "shortcut"—an image of a credit card that sits on your computer's desktop. Several credit card issuers offer this "way to pay" technology to consumers. For example, the Desk$hop virtual credit card is a graphic image of a Discover credit card that sits on a desktop and accesses Discover's central server to authorize and track transactions. The card is an online version of the cardholder's physical card, but the card numbers are not displayed, and a PIN must be entered every time the card is used. All that the user has to do to get started is click on the card's image.

Virtual credit cards use digital certificates, which we discussed in Chapter 10. Digital certificates are electronic credentials used to verify the identities of business partners on the Internet and enable secure, verifiable online transactions and communication. For online payments, a digital certificate service can associate a customer's identity with a digital representation of a payment account (as represented by a physical payment card), thereby enabling secure and authenticated online payments.

ONE-TIME CREDIT CARDS

Consumers have two main fears when making payments online: either that someone will steal their account number and make unauthorized purchases or that they may lose some of their privacy by releasing credit card information (because much information can be accumulated about customers through their purchases).

To cope with both problems, American Express and other credit issuers have devised the **one-time credit card**, also called one-use credit card. The card is virtual, not physical. Every time the holder uses it to pay, a new number is generated for that particular purchase. A number becomes invalid immediately after it is used. Since credit card issuers use 16-digit account numbers, they have a potential inventory of over 10 quadrillion (10^{16}) account numbers for assignment. With this system, no imposter can use the account of a cardholder, and no business can track the purchases of the cardholder.

Any type of a virtual credit card—a one-time card or a card with a permanent account—carries the risk of fraud: An unauthorized person who has access to the computer on which the software is stored can make purchases. In such a case, the convenience of the virtual card is its worst security vulnerability; the unauthorized party does not have to know the password or any other information of the lawful holder. With one click, the form required by the merchant is filled out. Therefore, virtual credit cards should be used only on personal computers at homes and other places where only the lawful holder has physical access to the computer.

METERED PAYMENTS

Another method designed to minimize theft of credit card information and disclosure of personal information is the use of metered payments. **Metered payments** are so called because they are charged to an existing account that the consumer has set

INTERESTING . . .

CREDIT CARD FRAUD

The Gartner Group tracked credit card fraud at 165 conventional, online, and hybrid (click-and-mortar) retailers. The firm found that 1.15 percent of all online purchases were fraudulent. This rate is 18 times higher than the rate of fraud offline. Worldwide business and personal losses due to credit card fraud were about $2 billion in 1999. Interestingly, most fraudulent transactions do not involve credit cards. The National Consumer League reported that in 1999, 85 percent of fraudulent transactions were paid by money order or check; credit card payments constituted only 5 percent of fraudulent transactions.

Sources: Fishman, T. C., "The check is in the mail," *The Industry Standard Grok*, February-March 2001, pp. 92–96; Apicella, M., "Worry-free payment processing keeps the customer satisfied," *Infoworld*, November 13, 2000, p. 63.

up with a provider of regular, metered services. Such a provider may be a utility company, a telephone company, or the consumer's ISP. Since the account already exists, the consumer can ask the online merchant to charge that account as a convenience.

When you buy something, you instruct the merchant to bill a preexisting account, such as your phone bill or your ISP bill. The telephone company or ISP will pay the merchant. Provided the utility company or ISP agrees to this arrangement, this method is useful because it is confidential to the buyer. No one can steal your credit information or access your personal information. Both stay confidential with the provider of the metered service.

This method, and all virtual card methods, makes consumers happy, but it makes banks unhappy. Why? With these methods, banks can no longer charge their customers credit card transaction fees.

SMART CARDS

The technology of smart cards has been around for about 25 years, long before the advent of the Web. **Smart card** is the name for a variety of payment cards that use some form of computer technology to store information or process it. The simplest ones store information on an embedded magnetic strip; the more sophisticated ones contain an entire circuitry that makes up a tiny processor. Smart cards have been used to store values, usually in the form of a balance that diminishes as the owner makes purchases. This payment system has been significantly more popular in Europe than in the United States and other parts of the world.

Historically, smart cards were developed to solve a predominantly European problem. Because European phone charges are high, callers have had to feed piles of coins into pay phones, a situation that attracted thieves. Prepaid calling cards with an embedded chip were the answer. High phone rates also hindered retail credit card usage in Europe, because merchants have not wanted to dial into a remote computer to authorize each sale. Again, cards with chips were the solution. Figure 12.2 shows a typical smart card.

Smart cards are the major vehicle of the **stored value** model. In this model, the holder pays to store value either on a physical smart card or in an electronic account that is kept by a firm that offers the service. The latter works like a bank. When value is stored on a card, each payment is deducted from the card rather than from a bank account.

Until 2000, the smart card industry remained mainly a European phenomenon. Americans and consumers in other non-European nations were extremely slow to adopt the technology, but this is changing. Within a year after American Express launched a major U.S. smart card, its Blue Card, two million Americans had signed up for it.

TWO SMART CARD TECHNOLOGIES

There are two types of smart cards, *contact cards* and *noncontact cards*. Figure 12.3 shows the differences. Contact smart cards must be inserted into a smart card reader.

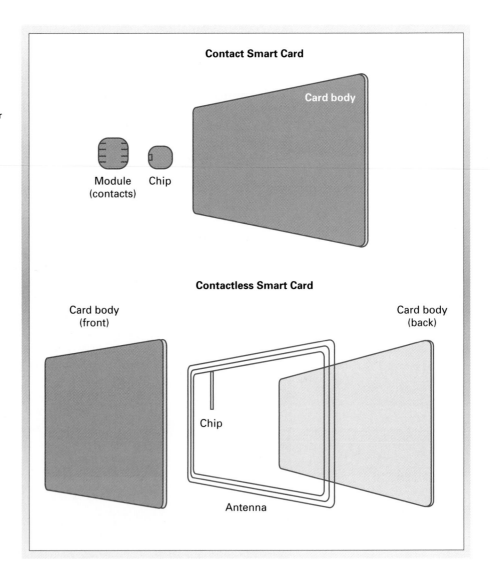

Contact Smart Card

Card body

Module (contacts)   Chip

Contactless Smart Card

Card body (front)   Card body (back)

Chip

Antenna

Instead of a magnetic strip on the back, contact smart cards have a small gold plate about one-half inch in diameter on the front. When the card is inserted into a reader, it makes contact with electrical connectors that transfer data to and from the chip. Noncontact smart cards are passed near a reader's antenna to carry out a transaction. Unlike contact cards, these cards have an antenna embedded inside. The card's antenna enables the electronic chip to communicate with the reader without physical contact. Noncontact cards are often used when transactions must be processed quickly, such as in mass-transit fare systems or highway toll collection booths. You may have seen special lanes with names such as EZ-Pass or I-Pass at U.S. toll plazas for smart card holders. Drivers use their noncontact smart cards to avoid long lines. The booth's reader reduces the toll from the balance stored on the card.

SPECIAL READERS

To make smart cards a useful method of online payment, special readers must be attached to any computer from which one makes purchases. Systems with this technology have been in use for a long time. For example, students in many universities are issued smart cards to pay for anything from phone calls to books and entry to on-campus clubs. However, to make the purchase the cardholder must physically come to the store or business and have the merchant swipe the card at the establishment's computer.

Smart cards can be used for e-commerce only if individuals and organizations are interested in a cooperative effort that would have each party hooking up card readers to their computers. Individuals have been very slow to adopt card readers. Even in Europe, where the cards are popular, few people have installed readers.

CONFIDENTIALITY

Smart cards that are designed for payment are usually constructed so that the merchant cannot see the cardholder's account number. We are all wary of having our credit cards or credit card account numbers stolen. If that happened to you, the thief could use your account number to make multiple purchases. However, if the thief stole your smart card, he would not be able to make a single purchase without your password. When you use a smart card and password, the merchant does not see your account number, only an authorization that there are sufficient funds to allow the purchase. Thus, smart cards provide security that is not provided by credit cards.

In 1999, a hacker stole 300,000 credit card numbers from the online music retailer CDUniverse. The hacker could have used all of them to make purchases or could have sold the information to other criminals. If the customers of CDUniverse had used smart cards, no card numbers could have been stored, because customers would have been making purchases without disclosing their numbers. All they would need to do is swipe the smart card into a reader attached to their personal computer and type in their password. The merchant would receive only a code authorizing the sale. American Express's Blue Card utilizes such a card reader. Both individuals and businesses are invited by the company to purchase the readers.

MICROPAYMENTS

You may have noticed that it is extremely difficult to shop online for any item whose cost is less than five dollars. The reason is simple: Almost all transactions on the Internet are carried out using credit cards. Because merchants pay credit card companies several dollars to process each payment, it does not pay to sell items whose price, let alone profit, is smaller than the payment processing cost. The Internet is not yet ready for transactions worth "small money," or, as they are known in professional circles, **micropayments**. Sometimes small amounts of money, especially when used online, are called *microcash*.

Micropayments usually are defined as payments of less than five dollars. Many people would be willing to make such payments for digital products that can be sold online: articles, newsletters, real-time data feeds, streaming audio, MP3 music, electronic postage, video streams, maps, financial data, multimedia objects, interactive games, and small software applications. Figure 12.4 lists typical items for which we would pay such small amounts. Although the amount charged per unit is small, the revenue and profit from sales of inexpensive items could be huge. For example, it would be technically easy to sell a music single online for 50 cents; the buyer could simply download it. It is processing the payment that is problematic. Similarly, people could purchase content, such as newspaper articles, digitized pictures, and financial news. However, because of the cost and complexities of credit card payment processing, businesses judiciously give up such sales.

Some companies, such as eCharge, Qpass, and Trivnet, have devised innovative micropayment schemes. A unit of Compaq (Compaq Digital Products and Services) offers its Millicent service for payments as small as one-tenth of a cent. These companies work hard to convince merchants to join their networks so the merchants can sell products for cents, nickels, and dimes.

In one method, consumers can purchase low-cost items and be charged the small amount directly through a metered bill, such as their phone or ISP bill, as we discussed before. Another method, used by Qpass, does not involve a third party. Assuming a consumer makes multiple purchases, each person's microcharges are accumulated in an individual's online account, administered through Qpass. At the end of the month, customers pay by any means they wish—credit, charge, or debit card. Usually, the monthly charge is large enough to justify the processing cost.

Some critics say that the fact that so few businesses accept micropayments has indirectly caused massive violation of intellectual property laws, especially in the music market. If people could buy music for several dollars, critics argue, they would pay for it. Since they cannot, many download music illegally. Indeed, one survey (by the Pew Institute) revealed that of the 13 million Americans who had downloaded music from Web sites, only 2 percent paid for it.

FIGURE

12.4 ITEMS THAT COULD BE PURCHASED WITH MICROPAYMENTS

Music	Purchase a single track instead of an entire CD
Games	Play a single electronic game online
Greeting cards	Purchase a greeting card
Pictures	Purchase images
Research articles	Purchase a single article instead of a subscription
Literature	Read a story of your choice
Movies	Watch a video on demand

One company that has taken a realistic approach to this phenomenon is Corbis. The company sells digital photographs and screen savers. Realizing that people would pay only a few dollars for its products, Corbis subscribed with Qpass. Visitors to Corbis's site can buy a picture with 640 by 480 pixel resolution for three dollars, or a screen saver featuring a slide show of 12 to 15 images for $3.95. Qpass processes the payments. Sales have exceeded the company's expectations.

Interestingly, Corbis did not contract with Qpass for the lower cost of payment processing, but for other reasons. In fact, Qpass may be charging more than a bank would. A bank typically charges a merchant 1.75 to 4 percent per transaction, depending on the merchant's expected sales volume, the type of product sold, and the average item price. The lower the price, the higher the percentage the bank charges for every transaction. In addition, the merchant pays a flat fee, usually 20 cents, per transaction for use of the bank's telephone line network for verification of cards and sufficient balances. This does not leave much profit, if any at all, on a sale of one dollar.

Micropayment processing companies charge hefty fees as well. For example, eCharge receives a fee of 2 to 8 percent on volume, depending on the sales volume size, in addition to a per-transaction fee of 10 to 25 cents. Qpass charges 25 to 40 percent of sales volume, depending on how large the volume is. What other reasons, then, do companies have for contracting with processing firms such as eCharge and Qpass? Customers are more likely to purchase a low-cost item when it is made easy for them. Merchants that offer micropayments hope to make money from sheer volume of items sold. Micropayment purchases are usually impulse purchases, which people tend to avoid if they must use a credit card. A Corbis executive likened the phenomenon to the unlikely situation of a passenger who wants to purchase chewing gum at a train station and is requested to pay for it with a credit card. Also, micropayment processing firms claim that the comparison with credit card processing is inappropriate because credit card processing requires businesses to install special processing software and security measures, which costs money. The software, security measures, and cost are included in the services of the micropayment processors.

To further accommodate impulse buying, eCharge and Trivnet do not ask the buyer to fill out any forms. There is no need for that. The companies can identify the customer immediately through his or her telephone company or ISP and add the charges to the customer's bill.

It may take a long time for micropayment systems to become a common form of online payment. According to a 2000 survey by the Gartner Group, less than one percent of online merchants used the services of micropayment processing firms in that year. The reason may be that businesses are waiting for a single processing company to emerge as a leader before they subscribe, rather than make a long-term commitment to a company that will become a minor player in the market. Also, some companies claim that there is little demand for micropayments because most shoppers like to purchase several items at once, which adds up to a large-enough sum, rather than to buy one item at a time.

PERSON-TO-PERSON PAYMENTS

Suppose you owe a friend a few dollars, but you are away and will not be able to see the person for several months. One way to handle payment is to send a check, but nowadays you can also e-mail the money. Apparently, an increasing number of people are interested in e-mailing money to buy an auction item, settle a restaurant bill with friends, pay a portion of rent to roommates, and many other purposes. Paying this way is often called online *person-to-person payment*, or **P2P payment**.

To send money, you begin by visiting one of the sites that support P2P. You fill out a form detailing how much money you want to send and to whom. The site then sends an e-mail message to the receiving party to let that person know that the money is waiting. The message says something such as "You've got cash!" and includes a clickable link. Clicking on the link, the payee connects to the payment service site, registers (if he or she does not have an account yet), and collects the money electronically. Where does the money come from? Subscribers to such services can replenish their online account from their checking or credit card accounts. Money they receive can be deposited in such accounts, or transferred into regular bank accounts.

Several companies provide this service, among which are PayPal (at *www.x.com*), eCount, ProPay, and eMoneyMail. The veteran money transfer company Western Union also offers the service, as does the traditional bank Bank One. However, some companies whose core business is not necessarily money transfer provide this service, too. For example, eBay, the huge auction site, owns Billpoint, Inc. Wells Fargo, a traditional bank, supports Billpoint's service. Figure 12.5 describes the steps in a typical P2P payment process.

The cost for P2P payments varies. Western Union's eMoneyMail charges $1.00 to $1.50 per transfer; eBay's Billpoint service charges 35 cents plus 3.5 percent of the value of the money sent; and eCount and PayPal do not charge fees for the service. The latter generate revenue from interest on the money that they transfer. The interest is accrued on the period between the sender's launch of the request and the payee's transfer of the money into his or her account. PayPal actually pays people five dollars to register for the service or for a successful referral. (Customers must, however, deposit at least $50 in the new PayPal account to receive the five dollars.)

Some observers are not enthusiastic about the business models of these services, to say the least. They cite early entrants into this industry in the mid-1990s, such as DigiCash, First Virtual, and CyberCash. All these companies either went bankrupt or changed their business focuses completely.

F I G U R E

12.5 STEPS OF P2P PAYMENT
Source: PayPal, 2001

Step 1: The sender designates the payment recipient.

Add Credit Card

Credit card number

Type
Visa ▼

Expiration date
9 ▼ 2000 ▼

Card Type
◉ Credit Card ○ Debit Card

First name

Last name

◉ **Use existing address as the billing address**
asdfasdf, asdfasf, palo alto, CA 94303 (Home) ▼

○ **Enter a new billing address**

Street

City

State
▼

Zip

Country
USA

For your protection, we confirm credit card billing addresses.
The process normally takes about 30 seconds, but it may take longer during certain times of the day. Please **DO NOT** cancel your submit request until you have received a final response from the server.

[Add Credit Card]

Step 2: The sender provides his or her credit card information or specifies a bank account from which the funds will be withdrawn.

Send Money - Check the details of your payment

Recipient
chad@hotmail.com

LEARN MORE ABOUT A RECIPIENT BEFORE CONFIRMING PAYMENT

Recipient Status
Verified Premier Account   Member Info

Amount
$25.00

☐ Click here if you would like a receipt of this transaction sent via email

[Send Money] [Edit] [Cancel]

Step 3: The sender verifies the details of the payment.

THIS IS WHAT THE RECIPIENT GETS IN THEIR EMAIL INBOX

| ...se | Addresses | Folders | Options |

Inbox 0 new   **(Bulk Mail** 0 new)

[Delete] [Block Sender(s)]   Move to

☐ ▷	**From**	**Subject**
☐	ryan@hotmail.com	ryan donahue has sent you $25

Step 4: The payee receives an e-mail message.

Step 5: The recipient registers for the service, unless the recipient has already registered.

Account Overview

Name: Chad Hurlington
Email: chad@hotmail.com
Balance: $25.00

Inbox

File	Date	Name/Email	Type	Status	Amount
☐	9-5-00	ryan donahue	payment recieved	completed	$25.00

Step 6: The sender receives a payment confirmation.

SECURITY CHALLENGES

Security challenges, too, may make people think twice before they transfer money with P2P companies. In January 2000, a security expert discovered that anyone could open an account with PayPal and perform unauthorized fund transfers from any other account in the banking system. All that the perpetrator would need was a bank routing number and account number—both are visible on checks—and use them to transfer money from the victims' bank accounts into the PayPal account. Immediately thereafter, the perpetrators could transfer all the money into their own bank accounts and cash out. Executives for the company said they fixed the problem by requiring new-account openers to fax or mail a copy of a canceled check.

Security challenges and brand-name recognition may drive potential P2P users to the "tried and true"—companies that are perceived as more experienced and reliable. These companies include Western Union and Bank One. The growing volume of trade on online sites and other popular activities on the Web that require payment may encourage people to try P2P services. Also, micropayments are easily handled by P2P services; the minimum payment value that the services process is one cent.

If past performance is any indication, then it is reasonable to assume that the popularity of P2P services will continue to grow. For example, by July 2001 more than 9 million people had used PayPal's service. About 150,000 payments, worth $1 million, pass through its system daily, and about 20,000 new customers and 3,000 businesses sign up every day. About half of all eBay customers accept PayPal payments. PayPal's site is one of the Web's most visited; two million people visit it weekly. It seems that the number of companies entering the P2P market is growing. Some companies specialize in developing software that specifically supports P2P processing by Web sites. These companies include eCommony, Inc. Yet, despite the rush to this market, Jupiter Research predicted that by 2002 only 1 percent of all payments on the Web would be in the form of P2P transfers.

ONLINE STORED VALUE SERVICES

Recall our discussion of smart cards. You can replenish the card with more "money." Similarly, several firms offer online accounts in which you can store value. You replenish your account by deducting the sum from either your credit card or your checking account, or, in some cases, even in exchange for cash. Cybermoola, eCharge, Flooz, and InternetCash are among the companies that offer this method of payment online. Since the money can come from sources other than your credit card, such a service lets people who do not carry credit cards make online purchases. Some companies, such as eCharge, require a credit card for replenishing accounts, but many others offer replenishment by credit card, checking account, and cash.

For example, despite the "cyber" in its name, Cybermoola allows you to purchase credit at your local supermarket, another chain with which the company has a contract, or via snail mail in $20 to $100 amounts, just as you would with a prepaid phone card. You receive a receipt with an access code that enables you to visit the company's site and upload the "money." From now on, you can charge this account with purchases. (If you lose the Cybermoola receipt and do not remember the access code, you cannot get a refund.) Interestingly, merchants do not pay "chargebacks" to the company. They pay referral fees to Cybermoola for every customer who pays with Cybermoola currency. Recall from Chapter 9 that the referral fees of affiliate programs are set by merchants. These fees are usually 3 to 12 percent of each purchase, and this is how Cybermoola makes money. While retailers may like the approach for attracting first-time shoppers, the referral fees for repeat shoppers may deter some of them.

The advantage to merchants is that many such services charge merchants fees that are lower than those banks charge for credit card processing. To accept such payments, merchants must subscribe to the service. The downside of these services is their limited acceptance by merchants. However, a growing number of online retailers are subscribing to some or all of these services.

The online stored value model is convenient for parents. Parents can store value in their children's accounts and thereby limit what their children can spend online. For this reason, some companies, such as Doughnet and Rocketcash, target their marketing specifically to teenagers and their parents.

POINTS

The Web offers the opportunity for businesses to offer "electronic coupons" in the form of what are called **points**. A system of points on the Web is similar to the credit card system in which a customer accumulates frequent flier miles for airline tickets through use of the card. However, points can be gained on the Web by purchasing from many sources.

Beenz.com, Inc. is a business that serves as a point bank. It promotes the use of points, which it calls beenz, through alliances with companies that are willing to give rewards of beenz for purchases. Usually, the larger the amount one spends, the greater the number of beenz awarded. These points can be redeemed as if they were money; many online merchants are willing to accept them instead of real money. This gives the points purchasing power equal to that of money. We provide a detailed account of the model in the case study at the end of this chapter.

Another company, MyPoints.com, runs what is known as a diversified loyalty program, which offers points to consumers who are willing to release their shopping demographics. Program members can earn points by reading targeted e-mail, filling out surveys, accepting trial offers, checking out Web sites, and referring friends to the program. MyPoints partner businesses target these consumers with specific deals, the acceptance of which adds more points to the consumers' bank account of points. The points can then be redeemed for goods and services at many businesses; Sprint and Red Lobster are two examples. While no money actually changes hands, the points practically serve as money: like beenz, they maintain value and can be exchanged for goods and services at any time. Web points may turn into a medium closer to real money once all Web businesses (and, better yet, non-Web businesses as well) accept them.

Unlike MyPoints, CyberGold actually calls its "cybermoney" *cash* instead of *points*. The company operates similarly to MyPoints, offering consumers dollars for demographic information. It collaborates with other businesses in direct marketing campaigns. However, owners of its dollars are not limited to using the e-money for purchases. They can spend CyberGold dollars online, automatically transfer CyberGold dollars into a bank account, or credit their value to a credit card account.

UPSIDE, DOWNSIDE

Shoppers are looking for payment methods that are easy and provide a decent measure of security against fraud and violation of privacy. While credit, debit, and charge cards are still the leading methods of making payments online, there are many alternatives, which we have discussed in this chapter. Some methods and programs fulfill purposes different from those of other methods or programs. For example, points do not replace payment by credit cards or P2P payments. Each method has advantages and disadvantages, which are summarized in Figure 12.6.

12.6 ADVANTAGES AND DISADVANTAGES OF ONLINE PAYMENT METHODS

Payment Method	Merchant subscription required with a firm or bank?	Pros	Cons
Credit, debit, or charge card	Bank	Almost universally accepted.	Only two thirds of U.S. adults have one. Not popular among shoppers outside North America and Europe. High fraud rate.
Digital coins (e-cash)	Bank with e-cash system	Payer's anonymity and untraceability. Not susceptible to fraud.	Requires huge databases. Unpopular with governments.
Virtual credit card: permanent account	Bank	Convenience.	Susceptible to fraud; may be misused by anyone with access to the PC.
Virtual credit card: one-time account	Bank	Convenience. Low probability of fraud and violation of privacy.	Exists only in electronic form.
Metered payments	No; payer must have an arrangement with a utility firm or an ISP.	Convenient charging of micropayments. Good level of privacy.	
Stored value: smart cards	No	Convenience, especially for people who do not carry credit cards.	Payer must install a card reader for online purchases.
Stored value: electronic account	Issuing firm	Convenience, especially for people who do not carry credit cards.	Low subscription among merchants.
Micropayment processing (nonmetered payments)	Processing firm	Convenience in purchases of one tenth of a cent to $5.	Processing fees charged to merchants may be greater than with credit cards.
Person-to-person (P2P) payments	Intermediary firm	Convenience, especially at online auction sites. Fast-growing subscription of individuals and businesses.	Susceptible to fraud.
Points	Issuing firm	Most programs allow purchase of a wide variety of items online. Some programs allow conversion of points to real money.	Limited number of subscribed merchants. High cost for merchants.

- The widespread use of the Internet for commercial transactions has encouraged the development of electronic money systems and of methods to enhance the use of payment cards, including credit cards, debit cards, and smart cards.

- Electronic cash, also known as e-cash, consists of digital coins that can be validated by an issuing bank while ensuring the anonymity of the payer. Both payer and payee must subscribe to the bank's services. E-cash has not gained popularity because of the system's requirement that large databases of spent coins be maintained and the reluctance of government agencies and financial institutions to process untraceable payments.

- Computer users can keep their personal and credit details in a file on their PC with an e-wallet. With one click they can transmit all the information that is required for payment.

- A virtual credit card establishes on a user's computer desktop an image of a credit card that the user holds. To pay, the user clicks on the image.

- Onetime credit cards are a digital credit mechanism that consumers may prefer for two reasons: They reduce the chance that someone will seize the credit account number and use it, and they reduce the ability of data collection companies to create a buying-habit profile of a shopper. A new account number is generated for every purchase.

- Another method that protects private information is the use of a metered payment account, such as a telephone or ISP account, to charge online purchases. This method is also suitable for small payments, which merchants usually do not charge to credit cards because of the high per-transaction fee associated with charges.

- Smart card technology predates the Internet. It has been highly popular in Europe for some time and is now becoming increasingly popular in the United States. Smart cards are the size of credit cards but contain a microprocessor and memory circuitry. Smart cards follow the stored value model. They maintain values that can be replenished. Special readers must be installed in computers used to charge smart cards.

- Another approach to storing value is online accounts. The accounts are maintained by a firm whose subscribers charge credit cards or pay cash to replenish their accounts.

- Micropayments are payments of less than five U.S. dollars. Many merchants refuse to accept credit cards for such payments. Several companies offer micropayment processing services; they accumulate consumers' purchase amounts and charge their credit account at the end of a given period, usually the end of each calendar month. Micropayments enable customers to purchase low price items or services online, such as online newspapers and articles, movies, or a few tracks of music.

- Person-to-person (P2P) payments online are becoming increasingly popular. One Internet user can send money to another Internet user via the service of a third party. Several companies serve as intermediaries. Some charge a fee, and others generate income from the interest they collect while holding the money.

- Since any vehicle that is used to transfer and hold value can serve as money, points on the Web can be considered money, especially if many parties accept them. Several companies offer points programs through which shoppers can receive promotional points and redeem them to purchase items.

KEY TERMS

e-money
e-cash
digital coins
cyberwallet
networking effect
e-wallet
virtual credit card

one-time credit card
metered payment
smart card
stored value
micropayment
P2P payment
points

REVIEW QUESTIONS

1. What is the main advantage of using e-cash? What is the main impediment?
2. What is an e-wallet? What technology would allow you to carry one in your pocket?
3. What is a virtual credit card? Why is it virtual?
4. What is the one feature that differentiates a traditional credit card from a virtual credit card? What is the most important thing that a virtual credit card gives its holder?
5. What is a micropayment? Why do micropayments require special treatment?
6. If smart cards are such a great technology, why have we not used them for online shopping?

DISCUSSION QUESTIONS

1. E-cash hides the identity of the payer. Do you consider this an important feature in online payment? Why or why not?
2. Can points totally replace money as we know it? What conditions might allow that?
3. If a great number of businesses and individuals used points on the Internet for payment, would this have an adverse impact on our monetary system? Should a nation's central bank (in the United States, the Federal Reserve) intervene? Explain.
4. What is the difference between points and digital coins (e-cash)? Can points accomplish the same goal as digital coins—untraceability?
5. Do you foresee a day when all forms of money and money equivalents on the Internet will be accepted as interchangeable? What conditions are necessary for this to happen?

ASSIGNMENTS

1. Visit *www.transaction.net/payment/atm.html*. Read about the various online payment methods and how they operate. Choose one in particular that you like and might use, and prepare a PowerPoint presentation explaining why it would be useful to you.

2. Devise a new method of online payment that is not mentioned in this chapter. It does not have to ensure anonymity, nor does it have to generate income for any company. What will attract an individual to using your e-money? What will entice businesses to accept it and use it to pay other businesses? Does it involve a "central bank"? Prepare a two- to five-page report outlining the principles of your e-money program.

E-COMMERCE TODAY

Beenz Everywhere!

Many of us are members of points programs. We collect gas-station points, grocery-store points, movie-rental points, and many other types of points. Some wallets almost literally burst with magnetic cards that record accumulated points. Every so often, we cash in these points for gas, groceries, and other items. Point systems are popular and motivating. The genius of points is that often your purchases are something you would buy anyway, so it becomes only a question of *from whom* to make a purchase. The merchant offering the most points wins.

Until several years ago, Charles Cohen was just one of several million people who collected points. Then one bright day it dawned on him: Why not establish a system that would consolidate all these points programs? The system would serve two audiences: shoppers, who would conveniently collect points that they could use to buy goods or services, and merchants, who would be able to lure consumers and receive information on their buying habits. The points would take one step closer to becoming money.

In 1998, Cohen founded Beenz.com, a New York company that issues such points. The points are called "beenz." Beenz collectors can redeem them for any item or service of a participating merchant; they are not limited to one particular item or merchant. Online businesses use beenz to pay customers for completing tasks online, such as visiting Web sites, shopping, and filling out customer satisfaction surveys.

By July 2000, approximately two million consumers were collecting beenz, and over one million beenz were in circulation worldwide. The company augmented its Web site to accommodate residents of 15 nations in their own local languages.

Beenz.com charges one U.S. cent for every beenz that it "mints." It pays a half a cent for every beenz that a customer spends. Companies purchase beenz to lure customers. Customers use the beenz to purchase goods and services from the same vendors or other online businesses. The businesses can then sell the beenz to Beenz.com. Some sites only give beenz to attract customers, some only accept them as payment, and some do both. Beenz.com makes money either way: It sells for a cent and redeems for a half a cent.

While the business model seems simple, implementing it was not. Cohen had to develop a globally acceptable currency that accounts for international exchange rates. He had to implement it on a real-time, online system. Cohen made good use of his work experience at Band & Brown, Ltd. in London, England, a public relations and brand development company. As an account executive for the company, he managed the execution of online business strategies for many large companies and developed a specialty in Web marketing and e-business.

In March 1999, he and two friends launched operations in the United Kingdom and United States. Since then, the company has grown to 250 employees with offices in North America, Europe, and the Asian Pacific region. Cohen developed a product that lets consumers use beenz anywhere they see the MasterCard logo. They can download their points onto a physical debit card and spend them in the physical world. For instance, if consumers accumulated 2,000 beenz, they could spend them as $20 at any store that accepts MasterCard.

Cohen is a rare case: He is both the CEO of his company and its chief technology officer. His technical involvement was significant when only he and his two friends were the company. Now, his technical input is more strategic than practical. He no longer writes code. What does Cohen see as his mission? Beenz everywhere!

Source: "A hill of online 'beenz' translates into cash," D. Ryan, *Infoworld,* July 3, 2000. Copyright © 2000 InfoWorld Media Group, Inc. Reprinted by permission via the Copyright Clearance Center.

Thinking About E-Commerce

1. Is beenz practically money? Start your answer with your own definition of money.
2. What are the technical and non-technical challenges of establishing a system like the one Cohen and his colleagues implemented?
3. Few CEOs are also the CTOs of their companies. Do you think it is important for Cohen to continue to be the CTO now that the company has grown so much?
4. If you owned an online business, would you purchase beenz? Explain.

13

- Discuss how e-commerce will cease to be separate from *all* commerce
- Explain how the Internet will enhance customer service by offering customized products and quick delivery
- Describe how new technologies will add the senses of smell, touch, and even taste to the Internet experience
- Give examples of Internet-connected appliances and Internet appliances

In December 2000, General Motors promised to deliver the Chevrolet Celta, a subeconomy car that would be configured at a South American factory to the specifications of online buyers who live throughout Brazil. A similar effort was planned for the Minneapolis-St. Paul area. Visitors to www.celta.com.bt have 20 different "build configuration" plans from which to choose when ordering customized cars. In the future, you will be able to log on and customize almost any imaginable product you wish to purchase on the Internet. *Source:* "e-GM expands its online sales model," *Infoworld,* December 6, 2000, p. 29

E-COMMERCE IS EVERY COMMERCE

The *e* in e-commerce will probably disappear in the future. The Wharton School of Business has estimated that the total volume of B2B commerce in 2004 will be $133 billion, just 10 years after it was but a few million dollars per year. Some observers predict that eventually about 80 percent of all B2C commerce will take place online. People will shop at bricks-and-mortar stores only for those items that they actually want to touch and feel before buying, experts predict. The term *e-commerce* is on its way to simply becoming *commerce*. Does anyone call an Excel spreadsheet an electronic spreadsheet? Not anymore—it is just called a spreadsheet, because the application has become much more commonplace than its paper predecessor. Similarly, the novelty of e-commerce (and it is still a novelty for billions of people) will gradually wear off as it becomes commonplace. However, you will continue to see significant changes in both B2C and B2B commerce.

This chapter outlines some of the major changes in e-commerce business strategy and technology that you very likely will see in the future. You may see more of one technology or practice and less of another, and there may be some entirely new business models or technologies that at the moment cannot even be imagined. Have fun as you make your own evaluations and predictions.

CONSUMER-CENTRIC MARKETS

Sophisticated software enables merchants to create dynamic profiles of their customers. The word *dynamic* is key to the description because the software is designed to fine-tune consumer profiles as an increasing amount of data is collected about each person. Products will become more and more personalized, based on much information about consumer tastes and needs. On the executive side, instead of seeing their corporations as the center of economic activity, executives will gradually regard customers as the center of the activities. They will be able to do so with good results thanks to the wealth of information their corporations will have about individual consumers. The result will be products that are designed and delivered with the individual consumer at the center of commercial activity. They will address the needs of **consumer-centric markets**.

CUSTOM MANUFACTURING

Increasingly, the Internet is forging direct links between customers and factories, so that buyers—now mainly corporate customers—can tailor products to their own needs. Individual online consumers can wield similar pressure. Dell Computer Corporation and other computer makers have encouraged shoppers for years to customize products to their liking at suppliers' Web sites.

The next step will be more complex. Mark Hogan, the executive appointed to head a new General Motors division, announced that customers would be able to configure their new cars via the Internet. Not surprisingly, the new division is called e-GM. GM is joining Ford and Toyota in this effort. In 2000, it took several weeks to deliver a customized car. New, flexible assembly lines, connected to information systems linked to the Internet, will help shorten this time to a few

INTERESTING . . .

GROWING, GROWING . . .

The worldwide B2B market was worth US$433 billion in 2000. The Gartner Group expects B2B sales to reach US$3.6 trillion in 2003 and US$6 trillion by the end of 2004.

Source: NUA, February 12, 2001

days. After a century of mass production, you may witness a move to "one each" production, but, significantly, through systems that are as efficient as mass production. Experts expect that other industries will follow suit; consumers will be able to order customized items from ovens to cellular phones.

Custom manufacturing does not have to be more expensive than mass production, because the seller does not necessarily spend more labor hours on customized products. Consider Cisco Systems, Inc., the world's largest vendor of telecommunications equipment. When ordering equipment, customers' computers talk to Cisco's computer. Cisco outsources most of the production process to contract manufacturers that operate 37 factories. All of them and Cisco are linked through an extranet. The contractors' suppliers manufacture all the components, perform 90 percent of the subassemblies, and also do 55 percent of the final assembly. In other words, much of what Cisco sells it does not really make; many contractors ship equipment directly to Cisco's customers, equipment that no Cisco employee has ever touched. However, Cisco takes the orders and helps its customers communicate configurations. If Cisco had to do the work done by its suppliers, it would have to spend another $500 to $800 million per year.

And how does the company take orders? Very little paperwork is involved in the process. Over 80 percent of Cisco's sales are generated on its Web site. Customers use a program that walks them through the configuration of a system that fits their specific needs. The software communicates the order to Cisco's contractors, who actually fulfill the order. The company uses monitoring software on the Internet to maintain contact with its contractors. Cisco managers know exactly what each contractor is doing with its orders at any given time.

THE FIVE-DAY MADE-TO-ORDER CAR

Other companies use methods similar to Cisco's. Hewlett-Packard, IBM, and SGI (formerly Silicon Graphics) have sold manufacturing facilities to other companies and immediately signed contracts with the buyers; the buyers now serve as the manufacturing facilities of HP, IBM, and SGI. These computer companies find that their core expertise is in product design, engineering, and marketing, not manufacturing. However, they can use the Internet to channel orders to their manufacturers and monitor the status of each order.

Experts say that similar methods in the auto industry may enable consumers to receive their customized cars five days after ordering them. While increased outsourcing in the U.S. car industry is impeded by labor unions, there is still much that the automakers can do to further efficiency. Web-based ordering and manufacturing systems can eliminate the ubiquitous site of dealership lots loaded with hundreds of cars waiting for customers. Eliminating these large inventories can cut up to 30 percent of a car's price; money would not be tied up and cost interest, and labor and materials involved in maintaining the cars could be trimmed to zero.

The task is not trivial, though. Automakers typically hold a two-month supply of cars, because they do not want dealers to miss sales when cars with certain colors or equipment options are not available. This inventory translates into $60 billion in finished products at any given moment.

Ordering a new car will be simple. Customers will come to a showroom and use a touch screen to customize a car. The touch screen is connected to an order center that is connected to a manufacturing facility. Toyota has had showrooms equipped with Internet terminals for custom orders since 1995. While dealing directly with customers sounds easy, it is not. GM often struggles to satisfy the needs of its 6,000 dealers. Imagine how difficult it will be to deal with millions of customers. In late 2000, GM's goal for 2001 was to deliver 85 percent of dealer orders on the date promised or within the week before.

Those who suspect that automakers will never be able to deliver cars to order as fast as computer makers deliver custom-made computers cite the difference in logistics: While Dell has 25 suppliers, DaimlerChrysler has 900 suppliers. The complex challenges have reduced hopes of delivering cars in three days to hopes of 10 days. In 2000, GM, Ford, and DaimlerChrysler shared the 10-day goal. In fact, 98 percent of the vehicles that customers want in the United States at any given moment are somewhere in the country. So, the challenge currently is not to *make* the car to order but to *locate* it to order.

Overall, however, the combination of networking corporate systems via the Internet, providing customer access to the systems, and improving assembly robots may result in tremendous cuts in cycle time and cost. At Lexmark, IBM's printer subsidiary, cycle time has been reduced by 90 percent. A printer that once took four hours to assemble now takes only 24 minutes. Its consumer price has been reduced from about $200 to about $50.

CONSUMER-CENTRIC SERVICE ON THE INTERNET

Many online businesses have made great strides in personalizing shoppers' experiences. This trend will continue both for individual (B2C) and corporate (B2B) buyers. Personalized Web pages and dynamic pricing are two major services that have resulted from this effort. You will also witness a solution to the major challenge in e-commerce: fulfillment.

OUR SITE IS YOUR SITE

Capturing data on click streams, frequency of page views, and duration of page views will continue to help companies tailor their Web pages to individual visitors. The pages will display pictures and lists of items that the visitor is likely to purchase and provide information that intelligent software determined would be of the highest interest to the visitor. In the future, you may be sitting next to another person who is simultaneously logging on to the same URL as you, and each of you may be seeing completely different elements on the page.

As an individual Web user, your click stream will be captured and analyzed. The links on the page will be changed to better fit your preferences and tastes, as will the graphics and accompanying sounds. Special software will not wait to

INTERESTING...

CUSTOMIZED CAR EXPERIENCE

On average, an owner spends $68,000 on his or her car during its lifetime. Only $24,000 is spent on the car purchase. Ford Motor and other automakers intend to use the Internet to create a "total consumer experience" so that they can be the ones to earn all or some of the other $44,000.

make the changes after you leave the site; it will implement the changes "on the fly" as you browse the site.

Such extreme personalization will exacerbate violation of privacy, unless tighter government or self-regulations are implemented. Tighter regulations do not mean less personalization; they only mean explicit opt-in features at Web sites. Many people will be willing to give up some privacy for convenience.

DYNAMIC PRICING

If you have taken a basic course in economics, you are probably familiar with the term *consumer surplus*. Price in a competitive market is determined by the aggregate supply on the one hand and the aggregate demand on the other. The price at which different people are willing to purchase a certain quantity of a good varies; many would be willing to purchase a given quantity of an item at a higher price than the one eventually set in the market, which economists call the *price of equilibrium*. For those people, the difference between the highest price they would be willing to pay for the item and the actual price they pay is called *consumer surplus*; they can keep all this money in their pocket rather than pay it to the sellers.

In some industries, sellers have taken advantage of consumer surplus and have created different prices for different groups. Economists call this practice *price discrimination*. Merchants prefer the more subtle term **dynamic pricing**. You may have experienced price discrimination when you used the service of an airline. While your airfare was $560, the person sitting next to you paid only $220. You paid more because of one factor or a combination of several. For example, you made the reservation only days before the flight, you belong to a demographic group (age or income bracket) that is typically willing to pay more, or you will not stay at your destination over Saturday night. Airlines use special yield management software that considers many such factors and determines how to price flights on certain routes on certain dates.

Similarly, online merchants will price items individually for every person who shops at their site. The pricing will be based on the degree of interest in a certain item or group of items, on demographic data, and on other data that have been collected (both at the site and other sites that sell the data they collect). The success of dynamic pricing will largely depend on how conscientious the shopper is regarding other prices for the same item. In the airline industry, passengers often discover the discriminatory price only after they settle into their seat. This may or may not be the experience on the Web. In 2000, for a brief time Amazon implemented dynamic pricing for consumer electronics. Soon, angry buyers reported the practice at group news sites on the Web, and some complained to Amazon. Although Amazon executives said this was only a limited experiment, the buyers' uproar caused the company to halt the practice. However, early failures of business policies may not mean that the policies will not work in the future.

INSTANT FULFILLMENT

The major hurdle in e-commerce concerning physical goods has been *fulfillment*, a nice word for packing, shipping, and prompt delivery. On the one hand, a consumer can order from a site that is thousands of miles away, which is the bright side of e-commerce. On the other, the item still needs to be shipped over this distance. Consumers often receive their ordered items days or weeks after they made the purchase. Regional warehouses have alleviated the problem to some extent but have not resolved it fully. Delays hamper the shopping experience because many consumers seek immediate gratification; they want to see, touch, and use the product shortly after they buy it.

In the future, customers will be able to receive the product on the same day—there will be **instant fulfillment**. The large e-commerce firms will solve the fulfillment problem by hiring the services of local affiliates. After a shopper selects a product, the site will direct the buyer to the store closest to the customer's home or office, so that the product can be picked up in minutes. For a small fee, the affiliate business will deliver the product the same day.

M-COMMERCE

As we mentioned in Chapter 8, much of the relationship between retailers and consumers in the future may be conducted via handheld mobile devices. These devices will be a combination of a palm computer and cellular phone. Special promotions will grab people's attention when they travel within a certain radius from the store.

Figure 13.1 shows how Ovum, an information-technology consulting firm, foresees the growth of mobile commerce, or, as it is popularly called, m-commerce. The chart shows businesses' cumulative revenue from commerce conducted via mobile devices. Apparently, m-commerce is already more popular in Europe than in North America, and the disparity is expected to grow.

INTELLIGENT AGENTS

Much of what you do on the Web can be done by software: searching for information, comparison shopping, payments, and other activities. In the future, special programs called **intelligent agents** will do these tasks for you. For example, if you want to look for articles on a certain topic, you will ask an intelligent agent to find and retrieve these articles. Instead of spending time surfing from one retail site to another looking for a particular item, you will provide the intelligent agent with the specifics of the item and ask it to look for a site that

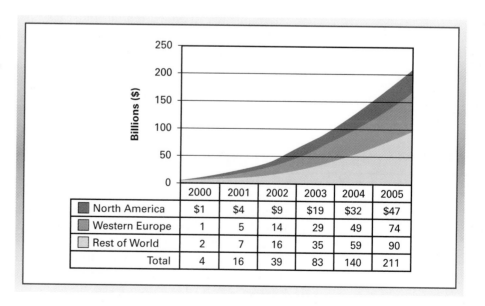

F I G U R E

13.1 THE FORECASTED GROWTH OF M-COMMERCE
Source: Graph "Forecasted growth of m-commerce" Copyright © Ovum. Reprinted by permission.

	2000	2001	2002	2003	2004	2005
North America	$1	$4	$9	$19	$32	$47
Western Europe	1	5	14	29	49	74
Rest of World	2	7	16	35	59	90
Total	4	16	39	83	140	211

sells the item. The agent will be able to look for the best combination of quality, price, and convenience of the product or service, based on your preferences. The lion's share of transactions on the Internet will not be executed by people but by their intelligent agents.

Intelligent agents will represent both buyers and sellers. The agents will negotiate a price and then execute the transaction for their respective owners. The buyer's agent will use a credit card account number or another type of online payment to pay for the service or good. The seller's agent will accept the payment and transmit the proper instructions to deliver the item under the terms agreed upon by the agents.

Intelligent agents are so called because they use artificial intelligence software. Often, they are called **bots** (short for *robots*) because they automate manual and mental work. While scientists are working to improve the performance of artificial agents, some of the scientists' work is already embedded in search engines. Some engines are programmed to accept not a single word but a whole question. They use artificial intelligence to interpret the question in a context that can narrow the search to only the most relevant Web pages.

One such attempt is the Ask Jeeves search engine, although critics cite its many flaws. In response to user questions, the site often produces Web addresses that have little to do with the subject matter of the question. In the comparative shopping arena, Lycoshop.com, DealTime.com, MySimon.com, and RUSure.com are all sites that let visitors use shopping bots, agents that help consumers find the best deals. Currently, most shopping bots list sites with the lowest prices for a given product. In the future, they will be able to compare several variables, such as quality, quantity discount, delivery time, and others. All shopping bots are now offered at commercial sites. Future bots, like all intelligent agents, will reside on individuals' computers, learn about their owners' shopping preferences, and calibrate themselves to perform more efficient inquiries and purchases in subsequent requests.

Intelligent agents will serve both consumers and businesses. In businesses, their uses will range from assessment of the need for a raw material or office supply to payment for the purchase made. For example, here is how a company might order paper supplies: It uses an intelligent agent to monitor the quantity and usage patterns of paper within the company, dynamically determines the minimum quantity at which reorder must take place, and launches itself on the Internet when that low level has been reached. Then, the intelligent agent automatically collects information on vendors and products that fit the needs of the company in terms of paper quality, quantity, and price. It evaluates different options, makes a decision on which suppliers and products to pursue, negotiates the terms of transactions with these suppliers, and finally places an order and executes the payment.

POTENTIAL INTERNET TECHNOLOGIES

In the next five to ten years, several new technologies will take hold. One will be the integration of a third sense to online experiences: smell (you already use vision and hearing). New technologies will enable you to verify the color and ensure the fit of items you purchase online. The very experience of browsing the Internet may become more efficient, thanks to three-dimensional browsing. In addition, you may see a slew of appliances that are linked through the Internet.

ONLINE VOTING? DON'T HOLD YOUR BREATH

In the wake of the 2000 U.S. presidential elections, many people expected that the government would adopt the idea of voting on the Internet. However, a report released by the National Science Foundation recommended against it. The agency sponsored a study that concluded that allowing Internet users to vote from home or work would compromise the integrity of the electoral process. It said that Internet voting could not be used in public elections until "substantial technical and social issues are addressed." Potential problems with remote Internet voting include the creation of spoof sites that mimic official voting sites and the spread of viruses that could undermine election integrity. Thus, online voting is one idea that you should not expect to see implemented in the near, or even remote, future.

Source: NUA, March 8, 2001

THE SMELL OF FRESH WEB PAGES

You have just logged on to a Web site that arranges flower deliveries. You are in the process of picking a bouquet for your mother. A nice one shows up on your PC monitor. You click the Smell button. Ah, what a wonderful smell these exotic flowers give off. You purchase the bouquet.

Wild imagination? Not necessarily. Dexter Smith, a software engineer, and Joel Belenson, a biochemist, incorporated DigiScents, Inc. in February 1999 to make this technology a reality. They developed software that encodes smells and hardware that they call iSmell, which is a box that can be connected to a computer consisting of a scent cartridge and a scent "player." The cartridge is similar to an ink-jet printer's cartridge and contains several substances, the combinations of which can produce thousands of different scents. The substances are the same ones used in the cosmetic and food industries. Upon a proper cue (which may be the clicking on a fruit basket picture), iSmell whiffs the scent through a plastic tube.

B2C Web sites that sell food, cosmetic products, and flowers will probably use this technology. Candy makers may use it to fine-tune the smell of their products. They can ask a sample of shoppers to smell a new product online, then change smells according to the input received.

DigiScents also plans to incorporate its technology into other products, such as electronic greeting cards, computer games, and the broadcast of sports events. The firm received requests for its programming kit from more than 3,900 software and Web developers. It says its hardware and software may help incorporate scent into many things, including Web sites, e-mail, e-commerce, interactive games, streaming media, and online advertising. The company's ScentWare Web Development Kit, a set of tools "to provide unforgettable scented online experiences," is available. Detractors say the firm's site is a "snortal."

Another company, TriSenx, Inc., is developing both smell and taste technologies for the Web. Much like the way you now print images, the company's technology will allow you to "print" the smell of the objects we see on the monitor. When we see a chocolate cookie on the screen, we will be able not only to smell it, but also use the printerlike device to create a small wafer that tastes like the cookie. We can use it to taste a sample before we click to purchase ten pounds of the cookies.

FIT TO WEAR

Imagine you purchase a denim shirt online. You like the blue hue. You wait a day or two, the shirt arrives at your door, you open the box, and, alas, the color is not the one you saw on your monitor. New software will ensure that what you see is what you get. Companies such as Datacolor have developed databases of colors especially for use by textile manufacturers. You will be able to click a button to see a true representation of the object's color on your screen.

GRAB, UNZIP, AND TURN INSIDE OUT

When you shop in the physical world, you like to grab items and look at them from different angles. In the future, you will be able to do so with every item you view online. Companies such as Viewpoint and Geometrix have developed software that let you use a mouse to grab an object, turn it, and observe it from every imaginable angle. Furthermore, when you examine a clothing item you can unzip or unbutton it, and even turn it inside out. If you want to read the label to see if it really is made of 100 percent cotton or what the washing instructions are, just use the zooming button to get a closer, clearer look.

The technology is not limited to serving consumers. Viewpoint is actually focused on the engineering and manufacturing sectors. It lets industrial model designers of anything from a vase to an automobile view a model from all angles. In the future, designers will be able to take apart an item as large as an automobile or even an aircraft and examine each part from all angles. They will also be able to "reassemble" the items back into a "finished product." Such technologies may save millions of dollars in materials and time in the model design process because modelers do not have to build a physical model.

YOU AND YOUR VIRTUAL MODEL

You like the jacket that you have selected online, but you want to be sure that it will look good on you. In the future, you will supply the e-retailer your measurements and other body characteristics, perhaps transfering the data from a file that resides on your hard disk. A three-dimensional image of a mannequin whose body looks similar to yours will appear on the screen. This is your **virtual model**. With a click or two the mannequin will don the jacket. You can have the mannequin turn around. Now you have a much better idea of how you will look in the jacket. If this sounds too futuristic to you, it should not; the Web sites of both Lands' End and J.C. Penney began offering simple versions of online mannequins as early as 2000. Both use technology called My Virtual Model, developed by MyVirtualModel, Inc. Figure 13.2 shows the form one fills out to build one's virtual model and the resulting virtual model of a specific profile.

TOUCH IT, FEEL IT

In the future, you will be able to experience tactile shopping, which is so important when you purchase items such as clothes. Immersion Corporation, a company that developed software called TouchSense, promises that you will soon not only be able to see, hear, and smell on the Web, but also feel. "Visit an e-commerce Web site where you could experience the texture of fabrics, finishes, and lotion; enter a Web site by reaching in and feeling the contours of its environmental

Create My Virtual Model ™ - Quick Questionnaire

The following **Quick questionnaire** will be used to determine the way your
Virtual Model looks and is based on general body shapes.

To obtain a more accurate model, fill in your precise measurements on the
⏩ **Exact questionnaire**

1 My Model's name

2 My hair style

○   ○   ○   ○

3 My hair color

○   ○   ○   ○   ○   ○

4 My face shape

○   ○   ○

5 My eyes are shaped most like

○   ○

6 My skin tone

○   ○   ○   ○   ○

7 My weight is approximately   pounds.

8 My height is   -choose- ▾

My Virtual Model™ at

Hello I'm Effy, your Virtual Model.
I am meet to be your reflection.

I'll accompany you on your shopping trips and help
you decide what clothes suit you best.

Remember, I will look like you as much as you
want. So, if you lie to me, then I'll lie to you too.
If I don't quite look like you, then feel free to
modify me.

[☆ Modify]   [≫ Continue]

Working with me is absolutely free, so come back
as often as you like, and have fun

[◁][☆ Modify][▷]

design, from a desert landscape to a topographic map of Mars; go to the family
Web site and while you're chatting with your sister, reach out and tickle her too,"
the company's Web site says.

To be able to feel objects presented on Web pages, you will need to purchase a
special input and touch device, which will create force-feed and vibrations. Force-
feed is a simulation of the pressure that you feel in your hands when you, for
example, push an object, drive a nail into wood, or use a knife to cut something.
Vibrations simulate the special feeling you have when passing your fingers over
different types of fabrics and other materials.

In the future you may also expect a new input and touch device to take the
place of the traditional mouse or trackball. The new device will probably be an
electronic glove similar to the one used for virtual reality applications. You will
wear the glove to point, click, drag, pinch, cut, rotate, and do many other things
that you now do with your hands. Mice and trackballs have been used only for
input; the new glove will serve users both for input and for feeling. Your feeling
sense will be used for shopping and design.

THREE-DIMENSIONAL BROWSING

Most people open one window of a Web browser and surf the Internet. Some people open more than one window and surf in each of them, one at a time. However,
even when several Web browser windows are open, the information in one window is usually not related to information displayed in another window. Now, a
new type of browser is emerging: the **three-dimensional browser**.

13.3 A THREE-DIMENSIONAL WEB BROWSER

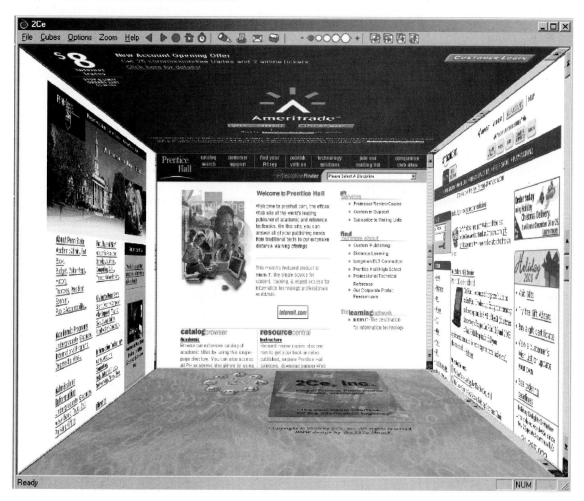

2Ce, Inc., a start-up company, offers the browser shown in Figure 13.3. The user does not view a page, but rather a "cube" in which each panel hosts a Web page. Web pages can be either from the same site or from different sites. The user views the pages and interacts with them as if he or she were standing inside a room, where the pages are on the walls, the floor, and the ceiling. Users can rotate the cube in any direction, zooming in on and out of specific pages. At full zoom in, the user can fill the window with a single page but still rotate the walls, which results in fast switching from one browsed page to another. While two-dimensional browsers allow you to designate favorite pages, this browser allows you to designate favorite cubes.

Web site designers can use special tools to organize their favorite Web pages of a site so that the information in all the pages is related. For instance, one can view the month, week, and daily calendar on three different, but related walls. When an entry is made into one of the pages, it is also reflected in the other two. Three-dimensional browsers will eventually also let users manipulate three-dimensional objects and view them in full motion, from all angles, inside the "room" created by the displayed Web pages.

For the time being, the predominant device you use to log on to the Internet is the personal computer. However, for some time experts have been predicting an increasing role for non-PC electronic devices in Internet activity. Furthermore, many existing household appliances are expected to be connected to the Internet for ease of control both from inside the home and remotely. The first type of appliances are Internet appliances; the second type we will term Internet-connected appliances.

INTERNET APPLIANCES

Mobile commerce uses hardware in a category called *Internet appliances*. **Internet appliances** are either mobile or stationary devices that enable you to connect or stay connected to the Internet in much the same way you do now with computers. The mobile devices include cellular phones and handheld PDAs (personal digital assistants). The stationary devices are now mainly television sets.

Many people will find it easy to use their television set to connect to the Internet. Some of the time they may surf on one part of the screen and watch a television broadcast on another part. Broadcast and Internet technologies will be intertwined. When people view a commercial, they will be able to move the cursor to the promoted item, click it, view it from all angles on the screen (as the commercial goes on!), bring up the vendor's Web site, and purchase the item.

PDAs already are combined with mobile phones from which users can log on to the Internet. In the future, you will be able to surf the net from a PDA with the same picture and sound quality of PCs. Product promoters may take the opportunity and bombard you not only with text spam, but also with fragrance samples. The unit's GPS (global positioning system) capability will not only help you find your way around but also enable local merchants to invite you into their stores for special sales.

The devices allow a telecommunications service provider to locate the user within a 50 yard radius. This poses a serious privacy threat. You will probably be uncomfortable knowing that the service provider (and therefore anyone who can tap into that firm's computers) can track you down as long as the device is on.

INTERNET-CONNECTED APPLIANCES

Some of the appliances you use daily will be connected to the Internet and possibly to each other. With this added technology, many if not all of your home appliances will become **Internet-connected appliances.**

Consider this scenario: Your refrigerator is linked to your shopping application. A sensor detects that you are low on milk. The sensor orders so many gallons of milk from your favorite supermarket, or—if you prefer to shop for the best deal—will turn on your intelligent agent to shop for milk and purchase it for you. Many of the items you will purchase in the future will have a tiny electronic chip in their package or casing, be it a carton, box, or bottle. The sensors in your refrigerator, pantry, and medicine cabinets will be able to detect when you are down to a reorder level. Since the sensors will be connected to the Internet, you will be able to program them to shop and reorder these items from grocers and pharmacies. If the pharmacy's online system asks for information such as the name and license number of the prescribing doctor, the sensor will furnish the preloaded information. In a way, online product replenishment for consumers will be implemented in a manner similar to how it is already implemented between supplier and buyer in B2B relationships.

Now imagine that you are in the office. You remember that there was a television show you wanted to record, but you forgot to set up your DVD recorder. You use your personal computer to connect with your home appliance panel. You bring up an image of your VCR, set it up to record the proper channel with start and end times, and launch the signal via the Net. When you are back home, the DVD is ready for your viewing.

Here is another scenario: You have just received a call from a friend whom you have not seen in years. She is in town and would like to come visit you at your home. You are in the office, and you remember the carpets have not been vacuumed in several months. "Of course," you tell your friend. "Why don't we meet at my home after I leave the office?" Now you use your PC or handheld device to tell your vacuum cleaner to vacuum the carpets.

Finally, say your microwave oven stopped functioning properly. You press a few buttons that connect the appliance to the manufacturer's site. The microwave downloads the software needed to fix it. It is fixed within seconds.

It is difficult to say how Internet-connected appliances will change e-commerce. Vendors of both goods and services will have their systems connected to your appliances. They will know much more about how you live your life—how much you eat per week of what foods; how much of a medication you take each day; which vitamins you take; how often you use your refrigerator, microwave oven, and vacuum cleaner. All this will enable vendors to create very accurate consumer profiles, which creates a frightening threat to your privacy. More than ever, you will have to balance convenience and a desire for a high standard of living with your need for privacy.

SUMMARY

- In just a few years, the distinction between e-commerce and commerce will disappear because almost all B2B commerce will be online and a large proportion of B2C commerce will be executed through the Internet.
- Information technology will enable markets to become increasingly consumer-centric. Using the Web, consumers will more often be invited to customize the new products they purchase online.
- The cycle time of producing any product will be reduced significantly.
- Web sites will be dynamically altered to reflect individual visitor preferences and interests.
- Sellers will use dynamic pricing to take advantage of the economics behind discriminatory prices and maximize their revenues.
- Using local affiliates, merchants will cut the fulfillment cycle to several hours.
- The increase in use of cellular phones and handheld computers will support the growth of mobile commerce, or m-commerce.
- Intelligent agents will be employed to monitor the need for reordering goods, for finding the best sources, for negotiating prices, and for payment.
- New technologies will enable consumers to experience the smell and feel of the items they consider purchasing online.

- New Web browsers will be three dimensional, enabling you to browse as if you were standing in a room whose walls are covered by Web pages.
- Handheld devices will enable people to interact with the Internet just as they do from personal computers. Some home appliances will be connected to the Internet. Some, such as refrigerators and electronic pantries, will be programmed to order groceries when quantities are low; others, such as vacuum cleaners, will be operated from remote computers.
- Increased consumercentric products and services and the linking of home appliances to the Internet will exacerbate violation of privacy.

KEY TERMS

consumer-centric market
dynamic pricing
instant fulfillment
intelligent agents
bots

virtual model
three-dimensional browser
Internet appliances
Internet-connected appliances

REVIEW QUESTIONS

1. What is a consumer-centric market?
2. How can use of the Internet help customize consumer goods?
3. What is dynamic pricing? Why do merchants believe that they can implement the practice more effectively online than in physical stores?
4. What are bots, and how are they used on the Web?
5. What is three-dimensional browsing? How can it enhance shoppers' experiences? Can it make our jobs more efficient?

DISCUSSION QUESTIONS

1. Do you believe dynamic pricing on the Web will succeed? Why or why not?
2. In Chapter 4, we spoke of virtual reality and how it is used on the Web. How can virtual reality technologies enhance online shopping experiences?
3. No online retailer is now providing intelligent agents for comparison shopping. Why?

ASSIGNMENTS

1. Search the Web for information on future developments in e-commerce. Pick the three technologies or business practices that you like, and prepare a 10-minute PowerPoint presentation. Explain each development and tell why you find it exciting, novel, or reflective of good business practices.

2. At the end of the chapter there is an allusion to increased violation of privacy. Imagine you work for a privacy advocacy group. Prepare a report (approximately five pages) explaining how certain new technologies and practices may exacerbate invasion of privacy unless proper steps are taken.

3. Search the Web and look for three-dimensional browsers. (Try *www. 2000cities.com* and *www.2Ce.com*, but find another two or three sites that offer such browsers.) Prepare a short report comparing and contrasting the features of each browser. Identify which of them you think may become a standard Web browser, and why.

E-COMMERCE TODAY

The Wired Home

You are driving back from school or work. It is winter. You want to prepare your home to welcome you, nice and cozy. You glance at the control center embedded in the dashboard. You turn up the heat, turn on the lights, light the fireplace, and start preparing dinner. When you are just a quarter mile away from home, you turn off the burglar alarm.

If this sounds like wild imagination, consider how a British company is going to implement this vision. Invensys PLC, a large electronics and software company, which is a world leader in automation and control systems, introduced a device called the Invensys Control Server. It connects lights, heat, air conditioning, entertainment systems (such as sound and television sets), washers, dryers, and kitchen appliances. It lets the user control these devices from a home PC, a TV set equipped with cable and a cable modem, or wireless devices such as Internet-enabled cell phones or PDAs. The price of the control center is a mere $2,500 to $3,500.

Roy Schumacher, Invensys's vice president of business development, said the control system requires no new wiring; it can use existing coaxial cable, AC power lines, and wireless technology designed for the home. The device was introduced and demonstrated at the Comdex exhibition in Las Vegas in November 2001. Invensys aims its marketing at homebuilders.

Large retail chains that sell home appliances and home security firms also may be interested in installing and servicing such systems. Interestingly, Invensys, Sears, Roebuck & Co., and other companies have formed an organization called the Internet Home Alliance to promote smarter uses of the Internet in the home. The Invensys equipment can also monitor the working condition of home appliances, letting service companies more quickly diagnose problems and minimize the number of trips required to repair a malfunctioning device.

At Comdex, Schumacher demonstrated what Invensys called the first "Internet Home." It included a Turkish-made refrigerator and American-made cooking range and microwave, all equipped with embedded Invensys chips. They enabled users to program functions or turn the appliances on and off from a Web-browser interface on a personal computer that is set up on a kitchen counter, a touch-screen controller on the refrigerator, or a television set in the living room.

As part of the demonstration, Schumacher used the system to scan a pizza box equipped with a new device called an RF (radio frequency) tag, which can transmit information on the contents of the box to the Internet Home's central controller. The controller then searches an Internet database for information on how to cook the pizza. Once the pizza is placed in the microwave, the home controller—rather than the controls on the microwave—can be used to start the cooking process. Schumacher said that RF tags on food products could be employed to keep a real-time inventory of items that have been used. This enables the homeowner to create a computerized shopping list that can be sent to a grocery store automatically over the Internet. Currently, RF tags are too costly for wide use on grocery products, but their price is dropping quickly enough to allow wide use within a year or two.

Schumacher also said that the success of the control server depended on how quickly heating, air conditioning, appliance, and entertainment product manufacturers adopted Invensys's smart chips, which enable the control center to monitor and control the devices in the home. Being a large electronics manufacturer, Invensys has an advantage over competitors because it already makes electronic components used by many of the world's manufacturers of home appliances and consumer electronics. Schumacher predicted that once the company has established widespread demand for the central control units, it will be able to offer the RF chips at a very low cost—perhaps pennies per chip—to manufacturers who are already Invensys customers.

Source: "Comdex: Internet home of the future is now," S. Konicki, *InformationWeek Online*, November 14, 2000

Thinking About E-Commerce Today

1. Who are the people most likely to purchase the system discussed in this case?
2. In addition to Invensys, what other companies must be involved to make this idea successful?
3. Do you have any reservations about such systems? If you do, what are your reservations? If you do not, why do you think people should embrace the technology without fear?
4. Invensys intends to generate revenue not only by selling the technology, but also by providing services. What kind of services associated with this technology do you think it can sell?

CREDITS/REFERENCES

Chapter 1

Page 3/Figure 1.1: Timeline, *Infoworld*, October 4, 1999, pp. 34–36. Copyright © 1999 InfoWorld Media Group, Inc. Reprinted by permission via Copyright Clearance Center. Page 5/Figure 1.2: Figure from "How the Net Works," S. Finnie, Cnet. Taken from http://www.cnet.com/?networks/ss01.html. Reprinted with permission from CNET, Inc. © Copyright 1995–2001 www.cnet.com. Page 9/Figure 1.3: Graph "The Number of Internet Domain Servers Continue to Grow." From Internet Software Consortium (http://www.isc.org. Page 11/Figure 1.6: Pie chart "Non-English languages spoken by Web users." Global Reach, 2000. http://glreach.com. Reprinted by permission. Figure 1.7: "Web Surfer Profile." *The Industry Standard*, March 8, 2000. Copyright © 2000 Mediamark Research, Inc. Reprinted by permission. Page 12/Figure 1.8: Table "Demographics of U.S. Web Users." Mediamark Research, from *The Industry Standard*, March 8, 2000. Copyright © 2000 Mediamark Research, Inc. Reprinted by permission. Page 14/Figure 1.9: Bar graph "U.S. Businesses on the Web." *The Industry Standard*, February 21, 2000, p. 203. Copyright © 2000 Mediamark Research, Inc. Reprinted by permission. Page 20: "Oracle Corp. Takes Its Own Advice." C. Kang, Knight Ridder News Service, May 21, 2000, Q7.

Chapter 2

Page 26/Figure 2.3: Table "Top Ten Domain Suffixes." *Network Wizards*, January 2000. Copyright © 2000. Reprinted by permission. Page 35: "A Wireless LAN Unfettered by Pigeons." L. Stone-Collonge, *Internet Week*, October 26, 1998.

Chapter 3

Page 42/Figure 3.2: Table "The Most Trafficked Web Sites." *PC Data Online*, March 2000. Page 45/Figure 3.3: © Dell Computer Corporation. All rights reserved.

Chapter 4

Page 57/Figure 4.2a: © Texas A&M/Rajesh Kaiml. Used with permission. Page 71/Figure 4.9: TerraExplorer software used by permission from Skyline Software Systems, Inc. Image produced by National Capital Planning Commission for the Washington Geographic Information System. Distributed by VARGIS LLC of Herndon, VA. Page 72/Figure 4.10: © 2001

Viewpoint Corporation, Inc. Page 75: "Getting the Dirt." M. Dahir, *The Industry Standard*, June 26, 2000.

Chapter 5

Page 81: "Seven New Domain Suffixes Approved." Ariana Cha, *Washington Post*, 11/17/00, E1. © 2000, The Washington Post. Reprinted with permission. Page 83/Figure 5.3: Reprinted with permission from http://www.internet.com. Copyright © 2001 INT Media Group, Incorporated. All rights reserved. search engine watch and internet.com are the exclusive trademarks of INT Media Group, Incorporated. Page 88/Figure 5.4a: Homestead and the Homestead Logos are the registered trademarks of Homestead Technologies Inc., Menlo Park, California, U.S.A. Figure 5.4b: Used with permission from Bigstep.com. Page 105: "Say It with Blenders." D. Helft, *The Industry Standard*, June 19, 2000, p. 157.

Chapter 6

Page 117: "The Paper Chaser." J.A. Nickell, *Business 2.0*, June 13, 2000. Copyright © 2000. Reprinted by permission.

Chapter 7

Page 135/Figure 7.6: © 1999 EzGov, Inc. All rights reserved.

Chapter 8

Page 159/Figure 8.6: Reprinted by permission of *The Wall Street Journal*. © 2001 Dow Jones & Company, Inc. All Rights Reserved Worldwide. Page 163/Figure 8.8: Chart "Growth of Online Bill Presentment." Copyright © Ovum. Reprinted by permission.

Chapter 9

Page 181/Figure 9.1: Copyright © 2000 Jupiter Media Metrix. Reprinted by permission. Page 183/Figure 9.2: Adobe and Acrobat Reader are either registered trademarks or trademarks of Adobe Systems Incorporated in the United States and/or other countries. Reproduced by permission. All rights reserved. Page 185/Figure 9.3: Courtesy of Wal-Mart. All rights reserved. Page 186/Figure 9.4a: © Cyberian Outpost, Inc. All rights reserved. Figure 9.4b: © 2001 Amazon.com, Inc. All Rights Reserved. Page 188/Figure 9.5b: © First National Bank of Chester County. Reprinted by permission. Page 193/Figure 9.9: © 2001 Amazon.com, Inc. All Rights Reserved. Page 195/Figure 9.10: Table by Anderson Consulting in *Business Week*, Feb. 7, 2000. Page 199/Figure 9.11: Table by Forrester Research, *Business Week*, Feb. 7, 2000, p. 114. Page 208: "The Paper Chase." P.S. Cohen, *The Industry Standard*, October 2, 2000, pp. 186–188. Copyright © 2000.

Chapter 10

Page 210/Figure 10.1: Copyright © 2000 Jupiter Media Metrix. Reprinted by permission. Page 223/Figure 10.4: Flow chart from Digital Signature Trust Company, *Infoworld*, June 19, 2000, p. 8. Copyright © 2000 InfoWorld Media Group, Inc. Reprinted by permission via the Copyright Clearance Center. Page 231: Quote, © 2001 Amazon.com, Inc. All Rights Reserved. Page 238: "Security Means Never Having to Say 'I Love You.'" B. Foneeca, *Infoworld*, July 10, 2000. Copyright © 2000 InfoWorld Media Group, Inc. Reprinted by permission via the Copyright Clearance Center.

Chapter 12

Page 273/Figure 12.2: Smart card image. Page 278/Figure 12.3: Reproduced with permission from Gemplus Corp., www.gemplus.com. Copyright © 2001 Gemplus SA. All trademarks herein are the property of their respective owners. All rights reserved. Page 286: "A Hill of Online 'Beenz' Translates into Cash." D. Ryan, *Infoworld*, July 3, 2000. Copyright © 2000. InfoWorld Media Group, Inc. Reprinted by permission via the Copyright Clearance Center.

Chapter 13

Page 293/Figure 13.1: Graph "Forecasted Growth of M-Commerce." Copyright © Ovum. Reprinted by permission. Page 298/Figure 13.2: © My Virtual Model, Inc. Reprinted by permission. Page 303: "Comdex: Internet Home of the Future Is Now." S. Konicki, *Information Week Online*, November 14, 2000.

GLOSSARY

A

Active server pages: Dynamically created Web pages. A method that works similarly to CGI (common gateway interface) and enables Web site visitors to search and retrieve information from databases connected to the site's Web server.

Affiliate program: A program that encourages organizations and individuals to lure visitors to click through to the sites of businesses in return for fees from those businesses.

Antitrust laws: Laws that forbid collusion between businesses to fix prices in activities that prevent free competition.

Applet: A small program usually coded in the Java or Jscript programming languages and embedded in a Web page.

Application server: A server computer, usually linked to the Internet, that processes an application invoked by online users. Often, the application server is linked to a database server that is dedicated to maintaining databases but not the applications that manipulate them.

Application service provider (ASP): A business that generates revenue by selling the use of applications online to other organizations.

Asymmetric key: In encryption, a method of using two different keys to encrypt and decrypt messages. The public-key/private-key encryption method makes use of an asymmetric key.

ATM: Asynchronous transfer mode; a telecommunications standard for high-speed digital transmission of voice and data.

Auction site: A Web site that supports online auctions and payment for auction transactions.

Authentication: In confidential communication, verifying the party that sent a message.

B

Backbone: The physical guided (physical lines) and unguided (radio) communication lines that make up the Internet.

Bandwidth: Telecommunications speed; the bit rate of a telecommunications line.

Biometrics: Methods that use body characteristics for identification of computer users seeking access to information systems. Commonly used body characteristics are fingerprints and retina maps.

Bitnet: The academic part of the Internet that preceded the commercial use of the network.

Bots: Short for robots; software applications with various degrees of artificial intelligence that are used in search engines and other tasks on the Web.

Brick-and-mortar: A popular term for traditional businesses, those which conduct business from a building, rather than through the Internet exclusively.

Browser: An application that enables Internet users to retrieve information in the form of text, images, animations, and sound.

Bus topology: An arrangement through which computers are connected to an open-ended communication line.

Business method patent: A patent protecting a business method (rather than a device or processing of materials). Business methods could not be patented in the United States until the early 1990s. A patent granted for an original idea of conducting business. Several such patents have been granted for business methods that utilize the Internet.

Business continuity plan: An emergency program invoked in cases of natural and other disasters to enable an organization to continue its business, albeit to a limited degree. Often, such a plan lays out the responsibilities of employees regarding information systems, some or all of which may be offsite.

Business model: A method of doing business and generating revenue. At the least, a business model details what products or services the business will deliver, the target audience, who is expected to pay for the products or services, and how payment will be made.

Business recovery plan: A program to guide an organization in recovering from a natural or other disaster that cripples its major facilities, such as information systems. Often, the term is synonymous with *business continuity plan*.

C

Cable modem: A modem used for communication of digital data through television cable. Cable modems are used by millions of households connected to the Internet.

Caching: Temporary storage of data either in RAM or on a hard disk for immediate use. Caching saves the time of data retrieval. Caching is often used when using the Web.

Certificate authority: A firm that issues digital certificates (digital IDs) and makes the public key of the certificate available to anyone who wishes to communicate with the certificate's holder.

CGI (common gateway interface): Software that facilitates inquiries from Web site visitors to organizational databases.

Channel conflict: A situation in which a manufacturer competes with its own retailers for the same customers. Channel conflicts can occur when manufacturers begin selling their products online in competition with retailers that offer the very same products for sale. One channel is the Web and the other channel is retail.

Chief privacy officer: An executive in charge of creating privacy policies and enforcement of the policies in an organization. The number of chief privacy officers has increased, especially in organizations that sell to consumers online.

Click stream: The series of mouse-clicks generated by a person who visits Web sites. Many organizations capture the click streams to generate information about online shopping and buying habits. Also called *click-throughs*.

Click-and-mortar: A popular term for organizations that conduct business both from store buildings (*mortar*) and online (*click*), as opposed to *brick-and-mortar* organizations, which do business only from buildings.

Client-server network: A computer network consisting of a server, which is a computer that maintains databases and/or applications, and other computers connected to the server through communication lines, which use the server's databases or applications.

Co-location: Placing equipment of several clients (who are often competitors) in the same facility. Internet service providers (ISPs) often provide such service. In addition to maintaining the equipment, they test it periodically for the client.

Communication path: Communication line; communication channel.

Computer virus: A destructive computer program that spreads through networks or through exchange of disks.

Confidentiality: In telecommunications, using encryption and other means to maintain secrecy about the content of messages.

Consumer profiling: Collection and analysis of personal data to generate digital dossiers on the shopping and buying habits of consumers. Consumer profiling has increased since the emergence of the Web as a means for business-to-consumer activity.

Consumer-centric market: A market in which businesses focus on consumer needs rather than on what and how the businesses would like to produce and sell. In consumer-centric markets, businesses customize many of their products and services to the needs of individual consumers.

Content: On the Web, articles and artistic works offered for sale online. Consumers have been generally reluctant to pay for content on the Web.

Content delivery network: A system of replicated and cached content of Web sites or portions of them. When the content is replicated on several servers throughout the Internet, visitors have faster access to it.

Cookie: A small file containing information that uniquely identifies the computer from which a Web user visits a site. The site's server can then automatically retrieve information tailored for that visitor. Cookies ease browsing, but also create security concerns.

Copyright: The exclusive right of an individual or organization to reproduce, use, and sell artistic works and their derivatives. Copyright holders face serious challenges because of the ease of digitizing many forms of art, replicating them, and disseminating them through the Internet.

Country of destination: The country from which a visit to a Web site is made. In legal terms, the country-of-destination approach maintains that the laws of the country to which the site caters apply regarding dealings with the site, regardless of from which country the site originated (as opposed to the *country-of-origin* approach).

Country of origin: The country in which a Web server resides. In legal terms, all legal matters regarding the site are confined to the country from which the site operates (as opposed to the *country-of-destination* approach).

Cross-linking: The arrangement between two online businesses in which each business places a link to the other site on its own site. Cross-linking often takes place between two businesses that sell related products or items.

Cross-luring: Using a search engine to produce information about a commercial site when the user searches for information about a competitor. Usually, both entries show up, but the entry of the site the user did not mean to search for appears first to draw the user's attention.

Cultural imperialism: The perceived invasion of a foreign culture into a region of the world whose own culture is affected or somehow threatened by the invading culture. Mass media and the Internet have imported foreign cultures to many countries.

Culture: A set of behaviors and preferences that characterizes the people of a certain country, region, ethnic group, or organization.

Customer relationship management (CRM): Managing all aspects of the relationship with a customer. Usually, the term refers to the software that an organization employs to this end. CRM applications help collect and analyze information to aid customers, especially customers who make purchases online. CRM software helps customers find the products and services they need, and it can help them find answers to questions about use and maintenance of purchased items.

Cybermall (storefront): A Web site that is maintained by a single organization and provides links to the Web pages of multiple businesses that subscribe to the service. Usually, the clients of such services are small businesses that find such an arrangement more economical than maintaining their own Web servers.

Cybersquatting: Registering a domain name of value to another party in the hope that that party will later offer a price for the domain name that is significantly higher than the registration fee. Cybersquatting is illegal in the United States and most other countries.

Cyberwallet: Software on one's personal computer that holds information that enables online payment.

Usually, this is the same information found on physical credit cards or charge cards.

D

Database server: A server linked to the Internet and to another server. The other server contains the organization's Web pages through which visitors to its site can access information retrieved from the database server.

Day trading: The attempt to make a profit by placing multiple orders to buy and sell stocks through an online broker. Day traders expect to make a profit by buying and selling stock for very short periods, often on the same day, rather than by investing for the long haul.

Denial of service: Attacking a Web site with multiple logons or inquiries to the extent that the site cannot respond to legitimate requests. Denial of service is difficult to stop.

Digital coins: See E-cash.

Digital certificate: The digital equivalent of an ID card. Digital certificates are issued by certification authorities and are used along with a public key that is used for encryption.

Digital signature: Digital data that guarantees that a communicated message has not been altered after it has been sent. A digital signature is the product of encrypting a message digest (a hashed message) with the recipient's public key, or by decrypting the message digest with the recipient's private key. Decrypting the digital signature with the recipient's private key reproduces the digest. If the digest that was sent only after hashing the original message is identical to the decrypted digest, the message was not changed.

Distributed denial of service: Denial of service (see above) by attack from multiple computers. Distributed denial of service is impossible to prevent.

Domain name: The address of an Internet site. Also called URL (universal resource locator). It is associated with an Internet protocol (IP) number.

Domain name recognition: Consumers' association of a domain name with the quality of service and/or products that the site provides. Domain name recognition is perceived to be an important factor in the site's ability to attract visitors.

Domain name registrar: An organization certified by ICANN (Internet Corporation for Assigned Names and Numbers) to register domain names. The service involves a fee.

DSL: Digital service line, a high-speed (broadband) communications line using a regular telephone line that connects a subscriber to the Internet. DSL provides an "always on" connection, unlike a dial-up modem.

Dynamic pricing: A euphemism for price discrimination in electronic commerce.

E

E-cash (digital coins): Digital signals that have online the same characteristics that cash has offline: They come in predetermined denominations and leave the payer untraceable.

EDI: Electronic data interchange; the exchange of electronic documents between businesses. Much EDI is still carried out through VANs (value added networks), but it can also be executed through the Internet.

Electronic marketplace: A Web site where sellers can offer goods or services, and buyers can electronically examine the goods or services, purchase them, and pay for them. The site owner usually collects a fee for the service.

Electronic signature: Any electronic encoding of a person's signature, such as a digitized fingerprint or a digitized written signature. Electronic signatures are valid signatures for doing business in several countries.

E-money: A general term for any method of making payments through computer networks.

Encryption: Enciphering; encoding a message so that one cannot convert it back to the original message without a proper key.

E-wallet: Cyber-wallet; software that holds digital cash to make online purchases convenient. The e-wallet can be a smart card or a tag (such as EZPass) or simply contain credit-card information.

Extranet: An Intranet that is also accessible to selected business partners such as suppliers and clients.

F

File transfer protocol: Also known as FTP (and as a verb: to FTP), an application that supports the transfer of files through the Internet. FTP software is now embedded in Web browsers and is transparent to users. Whenever you download a file from a site you use FTP software.

Find mechanism: A search mechanism of a Web site. A local search engine.

Firewall: Hardware and software, or only software, that controls access to networked resources. Firewalls are employed to prevent unauthorized online access to organizational information systems and, sometimes, to prevent employees from accessing certain resources on the Internet.

Frame: In a Web page, an independent scrollable window.

G

Glocalization: A contraction of *globalization* and *localization*; recognizing the need of business to design their sites for global use while paying attention to local cultures and needs.

H

Hacker: In the negative sense of the term, one who accesses an information system without authorization, usually through a public communication network such as the Internet. Process sometimes called *cracking*.

Hashing algorithm: A mathematical formula that converts a plain message into a digital digest.

Hits: Visits to a Web site. In the early days of the Web, the number of hits per set period (such as day or month) indicated how popular a site was. Since a number of hits can come from several people or the same person, hits are not a reliable indicator for the effectiveness of advertising at a site.

Homepage: The first page that a visitor to a site sees.

Horizontal market: A market composed of organizations that sell the same products or services. Despite the competition, such organizations often collaborate, especially through the Web. Horizontal markets often use Web sites as hubs for auctions and exchange of information.

Host: A server, a computer linked to several other computers; the other computers can use applications and/or data off the server. To connect to the Internet, a host is linked to the backbone, and many other computers are connected to it.

HTML: Hypertext Markup Language, the original programming language that enabled the Web. Browsers are designed to interpret HTML tags so they can display content properly in retrieved Web pages. When XML was merged into HTML, the language became known as XHTML.

HTTP: Hypertext Transport Protocol. A telecommunications protocol that supports communication of Web pages among Web servers.

I

IAB (Internet Architecture Board): An organization of volunteers that provides guidance on Internet architecture.

ICANN: Internet Corporation of Assigned Names and Numbers. A not-for-profit organization that licenses and oversees domain name registrars, approves new top-level domains, and arbitrates conflicts of domain name ownership.

IETF (Internet Engineering Task Force): An organization of volunteers, consisting of several working groups that identify problems and propose technical solutions for the Internet.

Instant fulfillment: The notion of fulfilling online orders immediately. While it is easy to do with software and any other digital products, instant fulfillment is a great challenge in the delivery of physical goods.

Intellectual property: Any invention, method, or work of art that belongs to a person or an organization.

Intelligent agents: Software programs that incorporate artificial intelligence to fulfill tasks on the Internet. Sometimes called *bots*.

Internet: A worldwide network of communications networks connecting millions of computers and other pieces of equipment. The Internet is the infrastructure for the Web.

Internet2: A high-speed network developed by over 100 universities with aid from private companies and the U.S. government. The network serves academic and research purposes.

Internet appliances: Electronic devices that use the Internet, including devices that merge cellular phones with hand-held computers.

Internet-connected appliances: Home appliances connected to the Internet for remote programming and operation, including microwave ovens and vacuum cleaners.

Intranet: A LAN or several linked LANs incorporating Web technologies for internal use by the organization's employees.

IP address: A unique four-block number that is assigned to a server or any other device connected to the Internet. Also called *IP number*.

IRC: Internet Relay Chat. A network of Internet servers that enables individual users to hold real-time online conversations.

ISDN: Integrated services data networks; a standard for 64-128 bps communication lines.

J

Java: An object-oriented programming language used for Web-based applications. Java's greatest asset is its developed code, which has the ability to run on a variety of operating systems.

Java Virtual Machine: Java interpreter that converts the intermediate code (called *bytecode*) into machine language and executes it. Java Virtual Machine is incorporated into Web browsers so they can run Java applets.

JavaScript: Programming language, with a syntax similar to Java's, whose purpose is to enable Web page authors to design interactive sites.

L

LAN: Local area network; a computer network that serves employees in a building or on a campus of several adjacent buildings.

Load balancing: The act of diverting Web traffic from a highly busy server to a less busy server. Load balancing is carried out by special software that controls a set of servers, all used by the same Web site.

M

M-commerce: Mobile commerce; online commerce performed from mobile devices, such as cellular phones or hand-held computers.

Message digest: A hashed digital message. Also called *hash*. Obtained by processing a plain message through a special algorithm called a *hashing algorithm*. Message digests are used in public key encryption.

Metatag: An HTML tag that identifies the contents of a Web page, such as the title of the site, a description of the site, and key words for search engines.

Metered payment: Any payment that is determined by amount of use. Utilities, telephone service, and Internet service are typically metered.

Micropayment: Payments of a fraction of one cent to five U.S. dollars. Due to the fixed cost portion of credit-card processing, processing micropayments for online purchases has been a challenge.

Mirroring: The replication of a server's content on several servers. Mirroring is done mainly for two reasons: speeding access to Web sites and security.

N

Network protocol: The set of rules that govern communication in a network.

GLOSSARY

Next Generation Internet: Also known by its acronym NGI, an initiative by the U.S. federal government to research high-speed network technologies. Some NGI funds have supported Internet2 projects.

Non-repudiation: In electronic commerce, the inability of the sender of a message to deny the message was sent. Non-repudiation is an important element in EDI, and difficult to implement on the Internet when no intermediary manages the communication.

O

One-time credit card: A digital credit card that is assigned a new account number for each transaction. The method minimizes the chances of illegal capture of credit-card numbers for fraud.

Online bill payment: Payment of bills through the Internet. Usually after online bill presentment.

Online bill presentment: Sending consumers' bills by e-mail. Consumers can authorize drawing payments from their credit-card accounts or pay in person.

Opt-in e-mail: E-mail that is sent after the recipient actively accepted an invitation to accept e-mail messages from a Web site.

P

PTP (person-to-person) payment: Any method for making payment online from one individual to another. PTP payment methods also enable individuals to make payments to businesses. PayPal is an example of a PTP payment method.

Packet switching: In digital telecommunications, a method of breaking a message into groups of bits that travel to the destination computer independently and are assembled in the proper order before the message is read. Each packet may be routed through a different path in the network.

Patent: A legal vehicle by which to protect intellectual property. Patents are granted for 20 years from the date of application for the patent. They are granted for innovative, useful, and unobvious machines, processes, and methods, and guarantee the sole right of the holder to make, use, or sell the subject of the patent.

Pay per click: A method for determining the fee paid to the owner of a site who maintains a link to another site. The site's owner receives a fixed dollar fee for each time a visitor clicks through to the other site.

Pay per lead: A method for determining the fee paid to the owner of a site who maintains a link to another site. The site's owner receives a fee for each visitor who may become a customer of the linked site. Usually a lead qualifies only if the visitor filled out a registration form.

Pay per sale: A method for determining the fee paid to the owner of a site who maintains a link to another site. The site's owner receives a percentage fee whenever a visitor clicks through to the other site and purchases something there. The fee is calculated as a certain percentage of the sale's value.

Peer-to-peer networks: A network that enables each computer to communicate with another computer directly, without the need to route the signal to another computer first.

Perfect market: A market where all buyers and sellers have access to the same information at the same time and anyone who wants to enter or leave the market can do so at any time.

Piracy: In the field of information technology, software piracy is illegally copying software.

Plug-in: An application that works in conjunction with a Web browser for enhanced features and processes.

Points: On the Web, a method of holding value, either as a substitute for money, in which case the points owner can use the points for purchasing anything online; or as an equivalent of coupons, in which case the owner can purchase only specific items from specific vendors. Points are often granted as rewards for online purchases.

Portal: A Web site that visitors use as the first site whenever they access the Web. Portals provide a large array of general information or information that is important to a certain interest group, such as a profession. Yahoo! is an example of a portal.

Post-office protocol (POP) account: An e-mail account managed under a POP standard. In particular, POP 3 is a standard for handling e-mail.

Privacy: In the context of information, the ability of individuals to control information about themselves.

Pure play: A jargon term for organizations that engage in business purely on the Internet, not having physical stores. Usually mentioned as opposed to "brick-and-mortar."

Public key: One of the two keys that must be used in encryption when using the public-key/private-key method. The public key is not secret; the private key is. The method relies on the mathematical relationship between the two keys.

R

Redundancy: The existence of the same hardware or software in more than one place, usually for backup purposes. On the Internet, organizations often maintain more than one server; if one goes down, another can be used for the same purpose.

Referral fee: The fee paid by a site owner to the site of another party whenever a visitor to the other party's site clicks through to the owner's site (and, usually, purchases something there).

Resolver: Software that translates a logical address into a physical address in a computer system or network. On DNS (domain name server), the software that converts a domain name (Web address) to an IP address (IP number).

Reverse auction: An online auction whereby sellers, rather than buyers, name their prices. The buyer places the description of the product or service sought, and bidders offer to sell it for competing prices.

Ring topology: A computer network in which each computer is connected to another two computers.

Router: A computer or other piece of hardware that routes digital messages in a telecommunications network.

S

Safe harbor: In the context of privacy, the arrangement between the United States and the European Union whereby U.S. companies that agree to uphold European privacy laws are allowed to exchange data with European companies. The arrangement was agreed upon between the E.U. and the U.S. government to overcome the gap between the European privacy laws and the less stringent U.S. law.

Scalability: The ability to increase the capacity of a system relatively easily. A Web site enjoys good scalability if it can, without much effort, augment its set of servers to accommodate greater traffic of Web visitors.

Search engine: A software application that helps find information based on keywords entered by the user.

Secret key: A code, such as a number, known only to the parties participating in communication. Without the key, a third party needs the key to decipher encrypted messages.

Secure sockets layer: SSL, a security protocol for communication through the Internet, using the public-key method.

Security: The state of secure systems, including information systems. Security measures include access codes and encryption methods.

Server: Host; a computer linked to several other computers; the other computers can use applications and/or data off the server. To connect to the Internet, a host is linked to the backbone, and many other computers are connected to it.

Server management: Management of a set of servers. Special software can be employed to control the load of visitor traffic among several servers.

Servlets: Software application that communicates an information request from a Web server to a database or an application server,

retrieves the information, and sends it to the visitor.

SGML: See Standard Generalized Markup Language.

Smart cards: Plastic cards the size of credit cards, embedded with computer chips that can be loaded with information and the digital equivalent of cash.

Spam: Unsolicited commercial e-mail.

Spoofing: On the Web, employing software that deceives visitors and directs their requests to a site that pretends to be the one they wanted to visit.

Standard Generalized Markup Language (SGML): An International Standards Organization (ISO) standard for defining documents with marked elements. A standard for development of markup languages, including HTML and XML.

Star topology: A communications network in which all the computers communicate through a central computer or communications device.

Stored value: The equivalent of cash, usually stored on a smart card.

Subdomain: The domain name of an internal communications network within an organization. For instance, *www.gv.psu.edu* and *www.hbg.psu.edu* are subdomain names of *www.psu.edu*. Subdomain names are assigned by the operators of the organizational network with the higher level domain name.

Symmetric key: Secret key; symmetric because both parties to the encrypted communication use the same, secret key for decryption.

T

T1 line: A telecommunication line that accommodates bit rates of up to 1.544 Mbps (64 channels of 64 Kbps each).

T3 line: A telecommunication line that accommodates bit rates of up to 44.736 Mbps (672 channels of 64 Kbps each).

TCP/IP: Transmission Control Protocol/Internet Protocol. A set of standards for communication on the Internet.

Three-dimensional browser: A Web browser that presents five pages at a time in a "room" arrangement.

3-D viewer: A software application that enables the user to view three-dimensional objects in Web pages. Often, such applications also allow the user to use the mouse to grab and move the object in any angle.

Top-level domain: Any of the suffixes of Web addresses (URLs). In 2002, in addition to country domains, top-level domains included .com, .net, .org, .edu, .gov, .mil, .int, .biz, .aero, .pro, .museum, .info, .name.

Topology: The physical layout of a network, including a telecommunications network.

Trading partners: Organizations conducting business with each other, online or offline.

Traffic: On the Internet, a term indicating the frequency of visits to a Web site.

Transaction integrity: A state of an online transaction kept and executed fully. Transaction integrity can be supported when executed in VAN EDI, but faces challenges in Internet-based EDI.

Transparency: In information technology, the apparent absence of intermediary hardware or software when communicating with an information system. If users are not aware of other hardware or software that facilitate communications (especially data retrieval) between them and a destination system, the hardware or software are said to be transparent.

Trojan horse: A malicious program hidden in a benign software application.

U

URL: Universal Resource Locator; an Internet address. In a browser, the URL follows *http://*.

Usability engineering: Designing software and Web sites, in particular, to optimize ease of use. When designing a Web site, the purpose of usability engineering is to provide menus, icons, search engines, and other features that not only make it easy to use but also "sticky"—one that tempts the user to spend much time at the site.

Usability testing: Testing targeted to see how useful and "sticky" a Web site is. Usually, such testing involves focus groups.

V

VAN: Value-added network; an organization that generates revenue by operating and managing a private telecommunications network, especially for digital communication. Many companies use EDI through VANs.

Vertical market: A market of buyers and sellers in which the seller sells raw materials to the buyer. The buyer uses the purchased products or services to produce its own products or services.

Virtual credit card: Software residing on a computer to be the equivalent of a physical credit card. Usually, the owners can view an image of a credit card on the monitor, which they can click to provide all the information needed to make a payment.

Virtual model: An image of a person created by software. Virtual models can be designed by visitors to a retail Web site to reflect their own physical appearance and "dress" them with clothes offered by the site.

Virtual Web server: A URL (Web address) that is seemingly owned and registered by an organization but is actually a sub-address of an ISP.

VPN: Virtual private network; a combination of private local area networks and Internet communications lines for use only by an organization's employees (intranet) or employees and business partners (extranet). Although messages pass also through the Internet, users may mistake the network as private thanks to the security measures taken to ensure that only authorized people can access the organization's LANs.

VRML: Virtual reality modeling language; a programming language for producing three-dimensional images that can be remotely manipulated through the Internet. Web browsers work together with special plug-in applications to retrieve and manipulate the 3D objects.

W

W3C (World Wide Web Consortium): An international not-for-profit organization that was established in 1994 to suggest and promote standards for Web technologies.

WAN: Wide area network. The telephone network and Internet are WANs.

Web crawler: A program that searches information on the Web. Crawlers are used to find and index new Web pages. They follow links from server to server.

Web hosting service: An ISP that sells server and disk space to businesses that wish to establish a Web site.

Web master: The person or business responsible for maintaining an organization's Web site.

Web page defacement: The act of maliciously changing the content of a site's Web pages to make the site, or its owner, look bad. Usually, the victims are commercial organizations.

WML (Wireless Markup Language): A software standard for displaying Web pages or parts of Web pages on wireless handheld computers.

XML (Extensible Markup Language): A convention of special tags in an HTML source code to characterize elements used in business transactions, such as company name and telephone number. The elements are surrounded by less than and greater than (< >) tags.

Worm: A computer virus that spreads through networks.

APPENDIX

MEASUREMENT UNITS

Click-through rate: In e-mail advertising campaigns, the percentage of people who clicked a link embedded in an e-mail message out of the total number of people to whom the message was sent. On the Web, the rate of clicks on a certain link out of the number of people who view the page; usually an inaccurate measurement.

Conversion rate: In Web marketing, the number of people who visited a retail site and purchased something divided by the total number of visitors, calculated for a certain period of time.

Gbps: Billion bits per second.

Impressions: In online advertising, the number of times a Web ad reaches users' displays. Also called *views*. Most advertising on the Web is priced according to so many dollars per one thousand impressions.

Kbps: Thousand bits per second.

Mbps: Million bits per second.

Open rate: In e-mail advertising campaigns, the number of people who have received and opened a promotional e-mail as a proportion of the total number of people to whom the message was sent.

Reach percentage: The percentage of Web users who have visited the site in the past month. An estimated measurement used to indicate the effectiveness of Web-based advertising.

Unique visitors per week: In online advertising, the number of people who have visited a Web site once or more during a week. Often, the standard of measurement is per day or per month. Each visitor is counted only once, regardless of how many times that person visited the site.

AUTHOR/NAME INDEX

A
Andreessen, Marc, 7

B
Beckman, Jeff, 143
Belenson, Joel, 295
Berners-Lee, Tim, 3, 7, 15, 58
Bezos, Jeff, 171, 181
Borders, Louis, 176
Bruce, Donald, 130

C
Cargile, Andy, 75–77
Carnegie, Andrew, 264
Carr, Nicholas, 148
Cerf, Vinton, 257
Chaum, David, 268
Choruby, Bonnie, 53
Clinton, William Jefferson (Bill), 16, 110, 243
Cohen, Charles, 286–287
Cohen, Jay, 255

D
Davidson, Alan, 81
Delhagen, Kate, 53–54
Doherty, Greg, 96
Duncan, Andrew, 118–119
Dyson, Esther, 81

E
Ellison, Lawrence, 160
Evans, Philip, 184, 187

F
Fader, Peter, 149, 204
Fox, William, 130
Fuld, Leonard, 77

G
Gaither, Jim, Sr., 52
Garcia, Juan Carlos, 105
Gates, Bill, 213

H
Haas, Robert, 141–142
Hamm, Mia, 52
Hilfiger, Tommy, 141
Hochman, Steve, 52–54
Hogan, Mark, 289

J
Johnson, Bill, 53
Jones, Kevin, 121
Joyner-Kersee, Jackie, 54

K
Kibur, Joseph, 81
Kline, Charlie, 1

L
Lauren, Ralph, 141
Lech, Gary, 35–37
Levin, Sue, 52–54
Licklider, John, 3
Lohse, Gerry, 171, 196

M
Marineau, Philip, 142
McSpadden, Kevin, 142
Mitnick, Kevin, 212
Mockapetris, Paul, 80
Moe, Wendy, 204
Morgan, J.P., 264
Moritz, Rob, 182

N
Nader, Ralph, 182
Nelson, Ted, 58
Nielsen, Jakob, 94
'N Sync, 203

O
Odysseus (fictional character), 213
Orwell, George, 229

P
Polly, Jean Armour, 3

R
Raskind, Cliff, 172
Reed, Vicky, 53
Relan, Peter, 177
Roberts, Julia, 246
Robertson, Michael, 247

S
Sawhney, Mohanbir, 151–152
Schumacher, Roy, 303–304
Shaheen, George, 176
Solter, Michael, 129–130

Spears
Spears, Britney, 203
Stengl, Brian, 120
Stewart, Patrick, 265
Strauss, Levi, 140
Street, Picabo, 52
Swoopes, Sheryl, 52

T
Thomas, Jay, 142
Thompson, Norm, 53
Tisch, Katy, 53
Tomlison, Ray, 1
Tynen, Daniel, 180

W
Walker, Jay, 156
Williams, Troy, 208
Wood, Fran, 238–239
Wu, Artie, 76
Wurster, Thomas, 184, 187
Wyden, Ron, 138

Y
Younger, Bill, 52–53

Z
Zimmerman, Phillip, 226

COMPANY INDEX

Webvan.com, 152–153, 161, 169, 176–177
WebVision, 64
Weebok, 150
Wells Fargo, 278
Western Union, 212, 281
WhatsHotNow.com, 97
WineBins.com, 256
Wine.com, 256
WineShoppers.com, 256
WinWin.com, 199
Works.com, 127
WorldCom, 4, 5, 16

WorldRes, 126
World Sports Exchange, 255

X

XOSoft, 92
Xros, Inc., 31

Y

Yahoo!, 7, 40, 42, 48–49, 82, 83, 86–87,
    180, 214, 252, 256, 263
Yankelovich Partners, 164
Yourownworld.com, 93

Z

ZD Net, 214
Zona Research, 82
ZoneTrader.com, 126, 127, 133

SUBJECT INDEX

A

Accessibility for disabled users, Web sites, 100

Accounts payable, online bill payment, 161–163

Accounts receivable, online bill present-ment, 161–163

Active Server Pages (ASPs), 66–67

Addresses. *See also* Domain names; URLs

  IP (Internet Protocol) numbers, 13–14, 25–27

Advertising. *See also* Marketing, Web-based

  targeted, 199–202

  Web sites, 40–41

Affiliate marketing, 130–134, 190–195

Agriculture, B2B (business-to-business), 126

Airline industry, 132, 154–155

Antispam legislation, 253

Antispoofing measures, 219

Antitrust laws, 261–262

Applets, defined, 64

Application servers, 97

Application Service Providers (ASPs), 47–49, 128–130

ARPANET, 2–3

ASPs (Active Server Pages), 66–67

ASPs (Application Service Providers), 47–49, 128–130

Asymmetric key method, decryption, 220. *See also* Public key method

Asynchronous Transmission Mode (ATM), 30–31

ATM (Asynchronous Transmission Mode), 30–31

Auction and matchmaking businesses, 125–127

Auctions, B2C and C2C, 155–157, 256–257

Audience, Web sites, 94–95

Audiovisual applications, Internet, 7–8

Authentication, 216

Automotive industry

  business alliances in, 131–132

  custom manufacturing, 289–291

B

B2B (business-to-business) e-commerce, 120–143. *See also* EDI; Marketing

  agriculture and, 126

auction and matchmaking businesses, 125–127

business alliances, 130–134, 190–195

excess products and equipment, 133

government and lost tax revenue, 130

growth in, 289

history of, 125

marketplaces, 123–124

revenue models at B2B sites, 127

Web sites, 126

B2C (business-to-consumer) e-com-merce, 144–177. *See also* Click-and-mortar businesses; e-money

  auctions, 155–157

  bill presentment and payment, 161–163

  brand names, 147–148

  buildover strategy, 152–153

  business models, 171–172

  caching strategy, 153

  channel conflict, 149–151

  charities, 163–164

  consumer auctions, 155

  content providers, 158–160

  customer service, 164–165

  delivery challenges, 149, 150, 151–152

  dynamic pricing, 292

  elements of, 147

  failures, 165–167

  gambling, 158

  growth in, 145–146

  information providers, 158–160

  interaction with consumers, 169–170

  "last mile" problem, 151–152

  m-commerce (mobile commerce), 172, 293

  mergers, 171

  needs of consumers, 168–169

  niche strategy, 153–154

  perishables, 160–161. *See also* Grocery industry

  personalization of Web sites, 169–170

  portal strategy, 152

  repeat business challenge, 148–149

  reservation systems, 154–155

  reverse auctions, 155–157

  service, 169

  software sales, 160

  speed strategy, 153

  stock trading, 157–158

  strategies, 152–154

  success, 154–165, 167–170

transition of businesses, warehouse-to-retail, 151–154

travel industry, 154–155

trends, 171–172

updating technology, 170–171

waves in retailing, 146–147

Backbone, defined, 4

Backup, 219

Bandwidth, 4–5, 27–31, 92

Banking, 115, 197. *See also* e-money

  credit cards, 188, 271–272

  EFT (electronic funds transfer), 2, 108

Bill presentment and payment, B2C e-commerce, 161–163

Biometrics, 216

BITNET, 3–4

Bots, 293–294

Brand names, 147–148. *See also* Trademarks

Browser-server intermediaries, 65–67

Browser software. *See* Web browsers

Budgeting, Web site creation, 95

Buildover strategy, B2C, 152–153

Business alliances, 130–134, 190–195

Business considerations in telecommuni-cations, 32–33

Business continuity plans, 226–227

Businesses, established. *See* Click-and-mortar businesses

Business method patents, 250

Business models, 123, 124–125, 171–172

Business snooping, 230–233. *See also* Cookies

Business-to-business. *See* B2B e-commerce

Business-to-consumer. *See* B2C e-commerce

Bus topology, 22

C

C2C (consumer-to-consumer) e-commerce, 155, 156, 277–281

Cable modems, 28–29

Cable television companies, 28–29

Caching, 93–94

Caching strategy, B2C, 153

Cash. *See* e-money

Cell-switching, 30–31

Certificate authorities, 221–222

CGI (Common Gateway Interface), 65–67

Channel conflict in B2C, 149–151

Links. *See* Hyperlinks
Litigation. *See* Jurisdiction
Load balancing, 92–93
Local area networks. *See* LANs
Localization of Web sites, 190
Local search mechanisms, 99, 186

M

Manufacturing, custom, 289–291
Marketing, Web-based, 178–208. *See also*
  Demographics
  affiliate marketing, 190–195
  complaints by consumers, 195–197
  consumer profiling, 197–199
  cultural differences, 187–190, 191
  domain-name recognition, 179–182
  e-mail marketing, 202–203
  measuring success, 204–205
  targeted advertising, 199–202
  Web site design, 182–190
Marketplace, electronic, 123–124
Market research, measuring success,
  204–205
Markup languages, 56. *See also* HTML;
  SGML
  WML (Wireless Markup Language), 67
  XML (Extensible Markup Language),
    59–64
Matchmaking businesses, 125–127
M-commerce (mobile commerce), 172,
  293
Menus, use on Web sites, 187, 188
Mergers, B2C firms, 171
Message digests, 221, 224
Metatags, 84–85
Metered payments, 272–273
Micropayments, 275–277
Military communications, ARPANET, 2–3
Mirroring, 93
Mistakes, Web site development, 94–96,
  184–190
Mobile commerce, 172, 293
Modems, cable, 28–29
Money. *See* Banking; e-money
MP3 name, 247
Multinational Web site design, 187–190,
  191
Multiplexing, 23
Multitiered affiliate marketing programs,
  194
Myanmar, 251

N

Names, 244–247. *See also* Domain name
  suffixes; URLs
  IP numbers, 13–14, 25–27
  MP3 name, 247
  usernames or user IDs, 216
National Science Foundation (NSF), 8
Navigation ease, 98
Networking effect, e-money, 270

Network protocols, 3, 23–24. *See also*
  Protocols
Networks. *See also* Internet; LANs;
  Network protocols; Scalability;
  Security and privacy issues; VANs
  ATM (Asynchronous Transmission
    Mode), 30–31
  cable modems, 28–29
  content delivery network, 92
  DSL (Digital Subscriber Line), 29–30
  Ethernet, 28–29
  extranets, 24, 109–110, 111–112
  intranets, 24, 109–110
  ISDN (Integrated Services Digital
    Network), 27–28
  switching techniques, 23, 30–31
  topologies, 21–22
  VPN (virtual private networks), 24–25,
    110
  WANs (wide area networks), 24, 30–31
Next Generation Internet (NGI), 16
Niche strategy, B2C, 153–154
Noncontact smart card technology,
  274–275
Nonrepudiation, EDI, 113
NSF (National Science Foundation), 8

O

One-time credit cards, 272
Online bill presentment and payment,
  161–163. *See also* e-money
Online content, defined, 49
Online gambling, 158, 254–256
Online payment methods. *See* e-money
Online security. *See* Security and privacy
  issues
Opt-in e-mail, 202

P

P2P (person-to-person) payments,
  277–281
Packet switching, 23
Partner Interface Processes (PIPs),
  114–116
Passive Web sites, 39–43
Patents, 247–250. *See also* Intellectual
  property
Payment. *See* e-money
Pay-per-click affiliate marketing model,
  193–194
Pay-per-lead affiliate marketing model,
  194
Pay-per-sale affiliate marketing model,
  192–193
Peer-to-peer networks, 22
Perfect market, defined, 123
Perishables, B2C e-commerce, 160–161.
  See also Grocery industry
Personal information, 229–230. *See also*
  Security and privacy issues
Personalization of Web sites, B2C,
  169–170

Personal names in domain names, 182
Person-to-person (P2P) payments,
  277–281
PGP (Pretty Good Privacy), 226
Pictures, Web site design imperatives, 99
PIPs (Partner Interface Processes),
  114–116
Plug-ins, 68–73, 296
Points ("electronic coupons"), 282
POP (Post Office Protocol), 90
Portals, 81, 82
  defined, 41
  U.S. government e-business, 136, 138
Portal strategy, B2C, 152
Post Office Protocol (POP), 90
Potential Internet technology, 294–299
Pretty Good Privacy (PGP), 226
Pricing, dynamic, 292
Privacy, 227–235. *See also* Security and
  privacy issues
  EDI, 113
  e-mail, 234–235
  legislation, 258–260
Privacy of Consumer Financial
  Information Act, 259–260
Profiling, 230–233. *See also* Consumer
  profiling; Demographics
Programming languages, 56–65. *See also*
  HTML; SGML
  COBOL, 64
  Java, 64–65
  VRML (Virtual Reality Modeling
    Language), 70
  XML (Extensible Markup Language),
    59–64
Protocols
  FTP (file transfer protocol), 6
  HTTP (HyperText Transport Protocol),
    6–7, 225
  IP (Internet Protocol), 3, 13–14, 23–27
  SHTTP (Secure HyperText Transport
    Protocol), 225
  TCP/IP (transmission control protocol),
    3, 23–24
  WAP (Wireless Application Protocol),
    67
Public key method, decryption, 220, 222,
  224–226
Pure play companies, 46–49

Q

Questionable practices
  cross-luring, 194–195
  hacking, 211–212, 213
  spam, 202, 203, 253
  spoofing, 215

R

Reach percentage, 42
Readers for smart cards, 275
Redundancy, defined, 4

Referral fees, affiliate marketing, 190–191
Registrar, domain names, 78–79
Registration. *See also* Domain names
  with search engines, 83–84
Remedies for security and privacy issues,
  215–219
Repeat business, B2C, 148–149
Reservation systems, B2C, 154–155
Resolvers, 98
Retailers. *See also* B2C e-commerce
  business alliances in, 131
  waves in, 146–147
  Web sites used for improvement and
    enhancement of existing businesses,
    43–46
Revenue models at B2B sites, 127
Reverse auctions, B2C, 155–157
Ring topology, 22
Routers, defined, 4

S

Safe harbor list, 260–261
Scalability
  defined, 32
  Web hosting service selection, 90
Scripts, CGI (Common Gateway
  Interface), 65–67
Search engines, 48, 82–85
  checklist, 85
  local search mechanisms, 99, 186
  metatags, 84–85
  registering with, 83–84
  Web crawlers, 85
Searching. *See also* Search engines
  local find mechanisms, 99, 186
  Web crawlers, 85
Secure HyperText Transport Protocol
  (SHTTP), 225
Secure Sockets Layer (SSL), 224–226
Security and privacy issues, 33, 210
  business continuity plans, 226–227
  credit card fraud, 272
  EDI, 113
  e-mail, 234–235
  encryption and decryption, 220–226
  firewalls, 110, 218–219
  insurance, 217
  legislation, 258–260
  P2P payments, 280
  remedies, 215–219
  threats, 211–215
  Web-browsing privacy, 235
  workplace monitoring, 233–235
Server management, 91
Servers, 4, 8. *See also* Domain servers;
  Web hosting services
  application servers, 97
  ASPs (Active Server Pages), 66–67
  browser-server intermediaries, 65–67
  caching, 93–94
  connection with, 86–90

cybermalls, 86–87
database servers, 97
defined, 4
DMZ (DeMilitarized Zones) security
  approach, 218–219
IIS (Internet Information Server), 67
JSPs (JavaServer Pages), 67
load balancing, 92–93
management of, 90–91
mirroring, 93
servlets, 64
storefronts, 86–90
virtual Web servers, 87
Service providers. *See also* Telephone
  companies; Web hosting services
  ASPs (Application Service Providers),
    47–49, 128–130
  cable television companies, 28–29
  ISPs (Internet Service Providers) as Web
    site hosts, 92–94
Servlets, defined, 64
SGML (Standard Generalized Markup
  Language), 56. *See also* HTML; XML
SHTTP (Secure HyperText Transport
  Protocol), 225
Signatures. *See also* Electronic signatures
  digital signatures, 221, 223
  electronic signatures, 220–221, 242–243
Singapore, government e-business,
  137–138
Sizing flexibility in Web site design, 100
Smart cards, 273–275
Smell technologies, 295
Software. *See also* Web software
  application servers, 97
  ASPs (Application Service Providers),
    47–49, 128–130
  firewalls, 110, 218–219
  intelligent agents, 293–294
  sales, B2C e-commerce, 160
Spam, 202, 203, 253
Speed, 155
  bandwidth, 4–5, 27–31, 92
  caching, 93–94
  strategies, B2C, 153
  Web site design imperatives, 98
Spoofing, 215, 219
SSL (Secure Sockets Layer), 224–226
Stand-alone transaction sites, 46–49
Standard Generalized Markup Language.
  See SGML
Standards
  SHTTP (Secure HyperText Transport
    Protocol), 225
  W3C (World Wide Web Consortium), 15
Standards, Web. *See also* SGML
  3-D viewers, 70, 73
  EDI and Internet standardization,
    112–113
  online retail standards, 186
  XML tags, 63
Star topology, 22

Statistics. *See also* Demographics
  market research, measuring success,
    204–205
  traffic on Web sites, 40–42
Stock trading online, 157–158
Stored value payment, 274, 281–282
Storefronts, 86–90
Subdomains, 89
Success
  B2C e-commerce, 154–165, 167–170
  Web-based marketing, measuring
    success, 204–205
Switching techniques, 23, 30–31
Symmetric key method, decryption,
  220

T

T1 and T3 lines, 30
Tactile technologies, 296, 298
Tags, 84–85. *See also* Markup languages
Targeted advertising, 199–202
Target markets, 121, 122
Taste technologies, 295
Tax revenue lost in B2B commerce, 130
TCP/IP (transmission control protocol),
  3, 23–24
Technology, potential, 294–299
Telecommunications. *See also*
  Telephone companies; Wireless com-
    munications
  business considerations in, 32–33
  essentials, 21–37
  services offered by telecommunications
    companies, 28
Telephone companies
  DSL (Digital Subscriber Line), 29–30
  ISDN (Integrated Services Digital
    Network), 27–28
  T1 and T3 lines, 30
3-D digital scanners, 148
3-D viewers, 68–73, 296
Three-dimensional browsers, 298–299
TLD (top-level domain), 79
Topologies, network, 21–22
Trademarks. *See also* Intellectual
  property
  URLs as, 245–246
Trading partners, 106–107. *See also*
  EDI
Traffic on Web sites, 40–42
  load balancing, 92–93
Transaction sets, 107
Transmission control protocol (TCP/IP),
  3, 23–24
Transparency, 216–218
Travel industry, B2C, 154–155
Trojan horse (computer virus), 213

U

"Under construction" Web sites, 100
United Kingdom, computer fraud, 211

Universal resource locators. *See* URLs
URLs (universal resource locators), 8, 14.
    See also Domain names
    as trademarks, 245–246
U.S. government
    ARPANET, 2–3
    e-business, 136–138
    FBI (Federal Bureau of Investigation),
        227, 229–230
    free speech rights, 250–254
    military communications, 2–3
    privacy legislation, 258–260
    safe harbor list, 260–261
    voting, online, 295
    Web site security gaps, 217
Usability
    engineering for Web sites, 95–96
    testing of Web sites, 96
Username or user ID, 216

V

VANs (value-added networks), 107, 108.
    See also EDI
Vertical markets, 121, 122
Viewers, 3-D, 68–73, 296
Virtual credit cards, 271–272
Virtual models, 296, 297–298
Virtual private networks (VPN), 24–25,
    110
Virtual Reality Modeling Language
    (VRML), 70
Virtual Web servers, 87
Viruses, computer, 212–213
Visual HTML editors, 58–59
Voting, online, 295
VPN (virtual private networks), 24–25,
    110
VRML (Virtual Reality Modeling
    Language), 70

W

W3C (World Wide Web Consortium), 15
WANs (wide area networks), 24, 30–31
WAP (Wireless Application Protocol), 67
Watermarking, 247
Web. *See* World Wide Web
Web browsers. *See also* Three-dimen-
    sional browsers
    beginnings, 7
    cookies, 67–70
    privacy at work, 235
    SSL (Secure Sockets Layer), 224–226
    3-D viewers, 68–73, 296
    three-dimensional browsers, 298–299
    Web site design imperatives, 98

Web crawlers, 85
Web hosting services, 87, 88
    e-mail, 90
    France, 253
    POP (Post Office Protocol), 90
    selection of, 89–90, 92–94
Webmaster, 91
Web pages. *See* Web sites
Web sites, 38–54. *See also* B2B; B2C;
    Domain names; EDI; HTML;
    Hyperlinks; Search engines; Security
    and privacy issues
    accessibility for disabled users, 100
    advertising, 40–41
    audience for, 94–95
    B2B (business-to-business), 126
    budgeting for, 95
    choice and control, 185, 187
    color, 183, 184, 187–190, 296
    connection with server, 86–90
    consistency in design, 99–100
    creation, 78–105
    cultural differences, 187–190, 191
    defacement, 211–212
    design, 91, 97–100, 182–190
    detail, attention to, 189
    development considerations, 94–100
    existing businesses, sites used to
        improve and enhance, 43–46
    find mechanisms, 99, 186
    foreign legal challenges, 101
    frames, 99
    globalization, 189
    growth, 96–97
    homepages, defined, 39–40
    interactivity, 185, 187
    levels of, 38–54
    localization, 190
    menus, 187, 188
    mistakes in development, 94–96,
        184–190
    multinational Web site design, 187–190,
        191
    navigation ease, 98
    page organization, 182–183
    passive Web sites, 39–43
    personalization of, 169–170
    pictures, use of, 98
    pizzazz, 184
    simple frameworks, 39
    sizing, flexibility in, 100
    stand-alone transaction sites, 46–49
    traffic on, 40
    "under construction," 100
    usability engineering, 95–96

usability testing, 96
    Webmaster, 91
Web software, 55–77. *See also* HTML;
    Search engines; SGML; Web browsers
    browser-server intermediaries, 65–67
    CGI (Common Gateway Interface),
        65–67
    cookies, 67–70
    crawlers, 85
    encryption and decryption, 220–226
    intermediaries, 65–67
    Java, 64–65
    JavaScript, 65
    load balancing software, 93
    PIPs (Partner Interface Processes),
        114–116
    plug-ins, 68–73, 296
    programming languages, 56–65
    resolvers, 98
    server management, 91
    VRML (Virtual Reality Modeling
        Language), 70
    WML (Wireless Markup Language), 67
    XML (Extensible Markup Language),
        59–64
Wide area networks (WANs), 24, 30–31
Wireless Application Protocol (WAP), 67
Wireless communications, 31–32
    m-commerce, 172, 293
    WAP (Wireless Application Protocol), 67
    Wireless Markup Language (WML), 67
WML (Wireless Markup Language), 67
Workplace monitoring, 233–235
World Wide Web (WWW), 6–7. *See also*
    HTML; Marketing; Web browsers; Web
    sites; Web software
    ASPs (Application Service Providers),
        47–49, 128–130
    demographics, 11–13
    gender and Web usage, 199, 201
    HTTP (HyperText Transport Protocol),
        6–7, 225
    languages used on, 11, 41
    SHTTP (Secure HyperText Transport
        Protocol), 225
    standards, 67
    user profiles, U.S., 11, 12
    W3C (World Wide Web Consortium), 67
World Wide Web Consortium, 67
Worms, 213
WWW. *See* World Wide Web

X

XML (Extensible Markup Language),
    59–64